Portrait of Carl Peters, *c.*1890 (Peters Papers, Altena).

Carl Peters and German Imperialism 1856–1918

A Political Biography

ARNE PERRAS

CLARENDON PRESS · OXFORD

*This book has been printed digitally and produced in a standard specification
in order to ensure its continuing availability*

OXFORD
UNIVERSITY PRESS

Great Clarendon Street, Oxford OX2 6DP

Oxford University Press is a department of the University of Oxford.
It furthers the University's objective of excellence in research, scholarship,
and education by publishing worldwide in

Oxford New York

Auckland   Cape Town   Dar es Salaam   Hong Kong   Karachi
Kuala Lumpur   Madrid   Melbourne   Mexico City   Nairobi
New Delhi   Shanghai   Taipei   Toronto
With offices in
Argentina   Austria   Brazil   Chile   Czech Republic   France   Greece
Guatemala   Hungary   Italy   Japan   South Korea   Poland   Portugal
Singapore   Switzerland   Thailand   Turkey   Ukraine   Vietnam

Oxford is a registered trade mark of Oxford University Press
in the UK and in certain other countries

Published in the United States
by Oxford University Press Inc., New York

ISBN 0-19-926510-0

To my parents

BARBARA AND HUBERT

ACKNOWLEDGEMENTS

Numerous individuals and institutions have supported me in writing this study. I am greatly indebted to my academic supervisor, Hartmut Pogge von Strandmann. His encouragement, guidance and critical advice were of particular value at all stages of research. His insight and interest have been most inspiring. Tony King and Geoff Mortimer have read the manuscript and made helpful suggestions. The map is by Daniel Braun. Moreover, I have benefited from discussions with many people, including J. W. Burrow, John Darwin, J. Gardner, J. Glassman, G. Deutsch, M. Epkenhans, C. Jessen-Klingenberg, F. Müller, I. Kimambo, T. O. Ranger, A. Sheriff, H. Sippel, P. Weindling, and J. C. Winter.

I am grateful to the staff of the libraries and archives for their assistance. The research for this book has involved a great deal of travelling, and it would not have been possible without the hospitality and help of the following individuals: Franziska Allweyer, Marie Chêne, Klaus Enderle, Geoff Mortimer, and Arnulf Jäger-Waldau in Berlin; Damir Fras and Karin Maler in Cologne; Margareta Schaffitzel in Eichstätt; the King family in Birmingham; Pablo Astorga, Harald Braun, Cathy Kohler, Ingrid Scheiblauer, and Soren Schonberg in Oxford; Gloria Mengual in Madrid; I also owe a great deal to Deograsias Mushi, his family, and friends who have helped me in so many ways in Tanzania.

I am much indebted to the *Süddeutsche Zeitung* in Munich, which has supported this project and funded me for two years, to the British Foreign Office, from which I received a Chevening Scholarship, and to St Edmund Hall and the Beit Fund, who provided further financial assistance.

Finally, special thanks go to my family. My grandmother Elisabeth Perras (†) taught me to read the old German script. Boris, Christine, Anna, and Clara shared their home with me in Lübeck. Jan, Gitti, Jonas, and Jana always cheered me up during my visits to the Alps. Without the loving support and understanding of my wife Susanna, this study would never have been completed. My parents Barbara and Hubert have encouraged me more than I can say. My debts to them are immeasurable.

CONTENTS

Contents

ABBREVIATIONS

AA	Auswärtiges Amt
ABM	Archiv der Bethel-Mission, Wuppertal
ADV	Allgemeiner Deutscher Verband
AMZ	*Allgemeine Missions-Zeitschrift*
BAB	Bundesarchiv Berlin
BAF	Archiv der Otto-von-Bismarck-Stiftung, Friedrichsruh
BA-FA	Bundesarchiv-Filmarchiv
BAK	Bundesarchiv Koblenz
CEH	*Central European History*
CMS	Church Missionary Society
DKG	Deutsche Kolonialgesellschaft
DKZ	*Deutsche Kolonialzeitung*
DKV	Deutscher Kolonialverein
DOAG	Deutsch-Ostafrikanische Gesellschaft
EHR	*English Historical Review*
EMDOA	Evangelische Missionsgesellschaft für Deutsch-Ostafrika
FP	Frank Papers
FO	Foreign Office
GfdK	Gesellschaft für deutsche Kolonisation
GG	*Geschichte und Gesellschaft*
GP	*Die Große Politik der Europäischen Kabinette, 1871–1914*
GS	Gesammelte Schriften
GStA-PK	Geheimes Staatsarchiv Preußischer Kulturbesitz
GW	Gesammelte Werke
GWU	*Geschichte in Wissenschaft und Unterricht*
HJ	*Historical Journal*
HStA	Hauptstaatsarchiv
HZ	*Historische Zeitschrift*
IISH	International Institute for Social History, Amsterdam
IJAHS	*International Journal of African Historical Studies*
JAH	*Journal of African History*
JHI	*Journal of the History of Ideas*
JMH	*Journal of Modern History*
KA	Kreisarchiv Altena
KPB	Kayser Papers, Berlin
KPH	Kayser Papers, Hamburg
KPK	*Kolonial-Politische Korrespondenz*
LAS	Landesarchiv Schleswig-Holstein
MGM	*Militärgeschichtliche Mitteilungen*

NAZ	*Norddeutsche Allgemeine Zeitung*
NM	Neukirchner Mission
NPL	*Neue Politische Literatur*
NSG	Niedersächsische Staats- und Universitätsbibliothek Göttingen
PA-AA	Politisches Archiv Auswärtiges Amt
PJ	*Preussische Jahrbücher*
PP	Peters Papers, Berlin
PPA	Peters Papers, Kreisarchiv Altena
PRO	Public Record Office
RKolA	Reichskolonialamt
RT	Reichstag
SB-PK	Staatsbibliothek zu Berlin Preußischer Kulturbesitz
SP	Schnee Papers
Sten.Ber.	Stenographische Berichte
TNA	Tanzania National Archives
TNR	*Tanganyika Notes and Records*
UJ	*Uganda Journal*
UMCA	Universities' Mission to Central Africa
ZfG	*Zeitschrift für Geschichtswissenschaft*
ZNA	Zanzibar National Archives

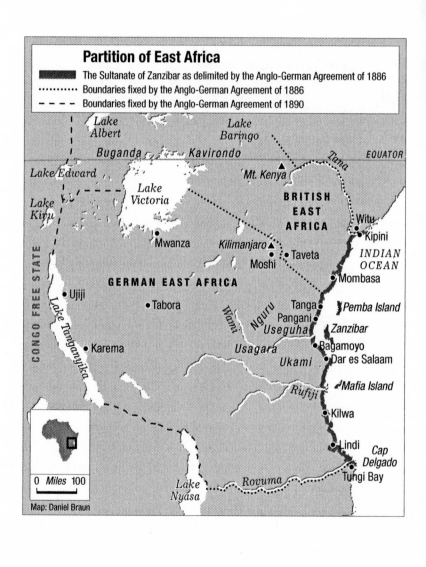

Partition of East Africa

▬▬▬ The Sultanate of Zanzibar as delimited by the Anglo-German Agreement of 1886
·········· Boundaries fixed by the Anglo-German Agreement of 1886
– – – Boundaries fixed by the Anglo-German Agreement of 1890

Lake Albert

Lake Baringo

Buganda

Kavirondo

Tana

EQUATOR

Lake Edward

Mt. Kenya ▲

Lake Victoria

Lake Kivu

BRITISH EAST AFRICA

Witu

Kipini

Mwanza

Kilimanjaro ▲

Taveta

INDIAN OCEAN

Moshi

GERMAN EAST AFRICA

Mombasa

CONGO FREE STATE

Ujiji

Tabora

Tanga

Pemba Island

Wami

Nguru

Pangani

Useguha

Zanzibar

Karema

Lake Tanganyika

Usagara

Bagamoyo

Dar es Salaam

Ukami

Rufiji

Mafia Island

Kilwa

0 Miles 100

Lindi

Cap Delgado

Lake Nyasa

Rovuma

Tungi Bay

Map: Daniel Braun

Introduction

On 17 December 1884 a strange caravan approached the Swahili coastal town of Bagamoyo. A fever-ridden young German, a historian by profession and a scholar of Schopenhauer, was returning from a brief visit to the hinterland. The man had to be carried in a hammock. At times he would wave his revolver about to drive his porters on. In his pocket, he kept twelve pieces of paper with a number of crosses on them. They were to be of crucial importance for the political future of East Africa. Thousands of miles further north, in the German capital of Berlin, the papers were recognized as legitimate treaties. It was claimed that with their signatures African leaders had ceded their territorial rights to the young traveller, Carl Peters. In February 1885 Kaiser Wilhelm I issued an imperial charter placing a territory of an estimated 140,000 square kilometres under German protection. Such was the birth of *Deutsch-Ostafrika*.

Many Germans came to regard East Africa as the pearl of their colonial possessions, their imagination inspired by the thought that it provided the seed for a 'German India in Africa'. Peters was only 28 years old when he returned with his treaties, and he had never been in the tropics before. Nor did he have any experience in overseas trade or any other commercial field. He was an academic who wrote about metaphysics. Now he had won an empire for Germany.

No other figure could have better illustrated the peculiarities of German colonial expansion than Carl Peters. The Reich was totally unprepared when it acquired its overseas possessions. It had no trained personnel to handle colonial affairs, and there were no legal provisions which could be applied to the new territories. Germany, one could say, became a colonial power overnight. Its case thus contrasted sharply with that of Britain or France, which looked back over a long period of imperial activity overseas. In less than a year, between April 1884 and February 1885, Bismarck pegged out an overseas empire in Africa and the Pacific that was many times larger than the mother country itself. The Chancellor placed Angra Pequena, Togoland, and the Cameroons under German protection. He established a protectorate on the East African mainland, and he seized the north-eastern part of New Guinea plus a number of islands in Melanesia and Micronesia.

Germany's sudden appearance on the colonial stage raises important questions about the forces behind that expansion. Carl Peters's coup appears particularly puzzling in this context; how was it possible that Bismarck, the Iron Chancellor, acted upon a few dubious documents which a young Hotspur produced? Where was the link between the colonial pioneer Peters and Bismarck's overseas policy? How did this young man fit into the wider picture of German imperialism? These are some of the major questions which will be addressed in this biography, which is a study of the rise, fall, and resurrection of one of Germany's most popular, but also most controversial, colonial figures.[1]

I

Bismarck's decision to establish a colonial empire has long been debated among historians. In the 1970s the dispute was revived through Hans-Ulrich Wehler's work *Bismarck und der Imperialismus*,[2] the first in-depth study of Bismarck's colonial policy since Hagen's monograph of 1923.[3] Although Wehler's interpretation came to influence a number of subsequent studies in the field of German imperial expansion,[4] there were also critical voices which doubted its overall validity.[5]

What was the core of Wehler's thesis? Essentially, he argued that the major cause of German colonial expansion was a domestic economic crisis. Bismarck, he held, pursued a counter-cyclical economic strategy which was to offset the effects of depression. This policy is described as manipulative

---

[1] This book is a partly revised version of my doctoral thesis: A. Perras, 'Carl Peters and German Imperialism 1856 to 1918. A Political Biography' (University of Oxford, D.Phil. thesis, 1999).

[2] For a list of reviews see P. Hampe, *Die ökonomische Imperialismustheorie. Kritische Untersuchungen* (Munich, 1976), 276.

[3] M. von Hagen, *Bismarcks Kolonialpolitik* (Stuttgart, 1923).

[4] See, for example, E. Bendikat, *Organisierte Kolonialbewegung in der Bismarck-Ära* (Heidelberg, 1984); H. P. Meritt, 'Bismarck and the German Interest in East Africa, 1884–1885', *HJ*, 21 (1978), 97–116; B. Wedi-Pascha, *Die deutsche Mittelafrika-Politik 1871–1914* (Pfaffenweiler, 1992).

[5] The range of Wehler's critics include H. Böhme, 'Thesen zur Beurteilung der gesellschaftlichen, wirtschaftlichen u. politischen Ursachen des deutschen Imperialismus', in W. J. Mommsen (ed.), *Der Moderne Imperialismus* (Stuttgart 1971), 31–59; H. Henning, 'Bismarck's Kolonialpolitik—Export einer Krise?' in K. E. Born (ed.), *Gegenwartsprobleme der Wirtschaft und der Wirtschaftswissenschaft* (Tübingen, 1978), 53–83; H. Pogge von Strandmann, 'Consequences of the Foundation of the German Empire: Colonial Expansion and the Process of Political-Economic Rationalization', in S. Förster, W. J. Mommsen, and R. Robinson (eds.), *Bismarck, Europe and Africa. The Berlin Africa Conference and the Onset of Partition* (Oxford, 1988), 105–20; Hampe, *Ökonomische Imperialismustheorie*; I. L. D. Forbes, 'Social Imperialism and Wilhelmine Germany', *HJ* 22 (1979), 331–49.

social imperialism. It allegedly functioned as an instrument to divert internal tension and thus to maintain the political status quo. For this purpose Bismarck adopted a technique of pragmatic expansion, leading to a series of colonial acquisitions in 1884–5.

As far as the economic aspect of the model is concerned, we are faced with a number of problems. First, politicians in the late nineteenth century did not have the instruments and the knowledge to pursue a sophisticated counter-cyclical policy.[6] This economic theory was a product of the twentieth century, and it could not possibly have formed the basis of Bismarck's policy. Secondly, Africa was by no means able to absorb a great quantity of exported products. Figures for the early 1890s show that the exchange of goods with *all* German protectorates amounted to less than 0.2 per cent.[7] Nor is there sufficient evidence to suggest that German industrialists had great expectations of an African market.[8] Indeed, they seemed fairly sceptical as far as quick profits were concerned.[9]

It should also be noted that the tariff policy in the German colonies did not favour the import of German goods as opposed to those from other countries.[10] The levying of customs was a major source of revenue for the colonies, and its purpose was to reduce German state subsidies and to make the colonies self-sufficient. In fact, the customs policy contradicted the idea of promoting German exports to the colonial periphery. It is thus unlikely that German policy-makers regarded the acquisition of colonies as a short-term economic strategy to offset the effects of an economic crisis.

The other major component of Wehler's thesis is Bismarck's alleged manipulative social imperialism. It is held that the Chancellor's imperial policy served to divert internal tensions to the periphery. Allegedly, Bismarck counted upon the integrative function of colonial policy in his attempts to hinder the rise of social democracy. However, as we will see in the course of this study, there were plenty of occasions in the 1880s and 1890s when colonial issues *divided* the nation rather than having an integrative effect. In fact, colonies provided a welcome weapon for Social Democrats, Left Liberals, and at times the Centre Party, to use to attack the government. Moreover, they even began to cause friction within the right-wing political spectrum.

---

[6] See Pogge, 'Consequences', 107.

[7] See Hampe, *Ökonomische Imperialismustheorie*, 277.

[8] See Böhme, 'Thesen', 41. [9] Pogge, 'Consequences', 107.

[10] See F. Schinzinger, 'Die Rolle der Zölle in den Beziehungen zwischen dem Deutschen Reich und seinen Kolonien', in M. Feldsieper and R. Groß (eds.), *Wirtschaftspolitik in weltoffener Wirtschaft* (Berlin, 1983), 125–42.

Therefore, it is not very convincing to argue that colonial policy was an instrument to reduce internal tension. Moreover, there is insufficient evidence to suggest that such a belief influenced Bismarck's decision at all.

More recently, another idea has been revived and elaborated for explaining Bismarck's colonial expansion.[11] This is the so-called 'Crown Prince thesis', which originally goes back to the historian Erich Eyck. It may be summarized as follows: Bismarck was haunted by the fear that Crown Prince Friedrich Wilhelm, who was to succeed the ailing Kaiser Wilhelm I on the throne, might establish a liberal German cabinet on the Gladstonian model. This prospect was seen by the Chancellor not only as a threat to his life work but also to his own future position. Therefore, it is argued, Bismarck 'took refuge'[12] in colonial policy. The decision to acquire an overseas empire is interpreted as part of a preventative strategy which sought to drive a wedge between the Crown Prince and his wife (Friedrich Wilhelm's wife Victoria was the daughter of the British queen) and the British. It was to create an artificial rivalry[13] which would ensure that the Crown Prince was discouraged from opening 'a new English era'. With particular regard to East Africa, Riehl goes so far as to suggest that only the 'Crown Prince thesis' can provide a convincing explanation for Bismarck's expansionist policy.[14]

Riehl's study, it may be argued, also runs into various problems. First, it is quite clear that colonial claims in Africa could only be realized if they were ultimately sanctioned by the British. Bismarck was well aware of that fact, so it is implausible to assume that he regarded colonial acquisitions as a means to create an Anglo-German quarrel. On the contrary, the realization of colonial claims made it necessary to negotiate with London and to find a modus vivendi. If we look at the first acquisition in South-West Africa, for example, it is clear that the German government counted upon British consent in return for German support of Britain in the Egyptian question.[15] The British relied on Bismarck's support in the international debt commission to settle Egypt's financial crisis. Britain was not in a very strong diplomatic position at that time, because of her quarrels with Russia over Afghanistan[16] and her continued trouble in Egypt. Therefore, the British ultimately accepted German colonial claims.

---

[11] A. T. G. Riehl, *Der 'Tanz um den Äquator'. Bismarck's antienglische Kolonialpolitik und die Erwartung des Thronwechsels in Deutschland 1883 bis 1885* (Berlin, 1993).
[12] Ibid. 778.   [13] Ibid. 443.   [14] Ibid. 674.
[15] See Hatzfeldt to Bismarck, 24 May 1884, GP 4, no. 742, 57; for the use of the Egyptian lever see also AA to Münster (draft corrected by Bismarck), 24 Jan. 1885, R 5665 (England 78), PA-AA, Bonn.
[16] See Herbert von Bismarck's notes, Bismarck Papers, D 46, 137, BAF.

Despite this favourable international situation, however, the Chancellor shied away from risking a serious crisis in Africa by challenging interests which the British regarded as of primary importance. Such an action might have endangered his colonial venture altogether. Ultimately, German colonial territory was only secured in areas which were not seen as primary British interests. As we will see later, the Chancellor had to drop the plan to acquire St Lucia Bay in southern Africa, where the British made clear that they were not prepared to accept any 'nonsense',[17] and arguably British opposition also prevented a German takeover of Zanzibar. Certainly, Germany's entry into the colonial field caused Anglo-German friction,[18] as we will see later. But this was hardly a Bismarckian goal as such. The Chancellor, rather, sought ways to secure international recognition of German claims and to reduce the risk of a serious crisis. The West African conference which Bismarck convened in Berlin between November 1884 and early 1885 illustrates this effort quite clearly. It was intended to sanction Germany's entry into the colonial field on the international stage. Contemporaries were proud that Germany had taken up a leading role in world affairs.[19] Thus Bismarck also strengthened his own charisma by demonstrating that Germany was now a global player. The conference endorsed Germany's advance into the rank of a world (i.e. colonial) power. The East African acquisition in the immediate aftermath of the conference was to crown Germany's new empire.

Thirdly, the general argument that fear of the Crown Prince's prospective regime made Bismarck embark on an anti-British course of colonial expansion is not consistently applied throughout. At one point Riehl holds that the Imperial Charter for East Africa was intended to intimidate and publicly discredit the future Kaiser and his wife;[20] later it is argued that Bismarck sought to achieve Anglo-German cooperation in the colonial field so that the new Kaiser would be more inclined to retain him as Chancellor.[21] Bismarck's concern about the Crown Prince is said to have triggered an anti-British course of action, then the same reason is advanced to explain the opposite. One can't have it both ways.

Fourthly, it is by no means clear that the acquisition of colonies really had a dramatic impact on the Crown Prince's political attitudes. There is evidence to suggest that controversies between Bismarck and Friedrich Wilhelm continued after 1885, while how committed the Crown Prince had

---

[17] See *Pall Mall Gazette*, 3 Jan. 1885, clipping in RKolA 8892, 12, BAB.
[18] See Granville to Bismarck, 20 Aug. 1884, Bismarck Papers, B 48, 254 ff., BAE.
[19] See *PJ* 54 (1884), 478.   [20] Riehl, *Tanz*, 647.
[21] Ibid. 719, 717, 724, 787.

been to the Left Liberal cause before the colonial coup remains obscure. Obviously, Bismarck himself was not sure whether the Crown Prince would adopt a liberal line 'in principle'.[22] Riehl speaks of 'a future liberal era'[23] to which Bismarck was opposed, but it should be recalled that the Chancellor was flexible enough to cooperate with the National Liberals in the Reichstag. Riehl's work has made it clear that the relationship between the Crown Prince and the Chancellor was complex and full of contradictions. Whatever Bismarck's fears and complaints may have been, he had also expressed some positive views about the future successor to the throne. At least once he stated that political reforms might be more easily achieved with Friedrich Wilhelm than with his father.[24]

Finally, a major weakness of the 'Crown Prince thesis' lies in its implicit tendency to reduce Bismarck's colonial policy to a mere episode of the years 1884–5. One scholar has gone so far as to suggest that Bismarck 'stopped' colonial policy in June 1885 when Gladstone was replaced by Salisbury.[25] This view is highly misleading. Until his fall, the colonies kept the Chancellor busy, whatever his complaints and disillusions about them may have been. It will be shown in this study that the Chancellor could not afford to neglect colonial issues. As far as East Africa is concerned it will be demonstrated that he paved the way for a consolidation of company rule and the securing of territorial borders. On the whole, it seems that the 'Crown Prince thesis' and Bismarck's alleged anti-British strategy is too inconsistent and reductionist to provide a satisfactory explanation.

On the other hand, the domestic context is still crucial to understanding Bismarck's move. The timing of Bismarck's colonial coup is quite telling: 1884 was an election year, and it therefore seems possible that the Chancellor hoped to exploit the colonial issue for short-term political ends.[26] More precisely, he sought to regain a working majority in the Reichstag. Above all, he hoped that the colonial cause would improve the standing of the National Liberals in the new Reichstag. In this sense his policy certainly displayed a manipulative tendency, but there is a risk of overemphasizing this point. Obviously Bismarck sought to exploit the enthusiam for colonial policy for his own ends, but there had to be an affinity among potential voters in the

---

[22] Riehl, *Tanz*, 88.   [23] Ibid. 778.

[24] See ibid. 59: Bismarck's conversation with Ritter von Schulte, 12 Jan. 1873, GW 8, 48, on the reform of the *Kreisordnung* and the Prussian Upper Chamber: 'Wäre der Kronprinz am Ruder, so würde es leicht sein, sofort große organische Neuerungen zu machen.'

[25] K. Hildebrand, review of Riehl's study, *HZ* 261 (1995), 601.

[26] H. Pogge von Strandmann, 'Domestic Origins of Germany's Colonial Expansion under Bismarck', *Past and Present*, 42 (1969), 140–59.

first place. It could not simply be generated and imposed from above. It is not enough to emphasize that Bismarck mobilized the press and interest groups for an attack on the political opposition.[27] Rather, the government itself rode a wave of popular feeling which it perceived as being advantageous.

However, this movement was not easily controlled. It will be shown that when conflict arose between colonial interest groups and the government over colonial issues, Bismarck did not fully succeed in unifying these groups behind his own goals. Rather, they continued to turn against him. Therefore the relationship between the colonial movement and the government could not have been a simple pattern of mobilizers at the top and willing followers below. It is important to recognize in this context that colonial demands had been popular in bourgeois circles since before 1848. In their close connection with the national question, they formed an important drive for expansion in their own right.[28]

Historians have also neglected another crucial point about Bismarck's colonial policy: the task of supervising colonization had been written into the Imperial Constitution of 1871.[29] The relevant passage was taken over from the previous constitution of the North German Federation. If the expansion needs of the German Reich had really already been satisfied, as is often emphasized, such a section would hardly have been necessary and Bismarck could have done without it. However, in Article 4 it is stated among other points that the Reich claims the supervision of colonization.[30] In addition to Article 3, which states that all Germans have an equal right to protection throughout the Reich, this provision formed a constitutional basis for future colonial acquisitions. Any German who from then on demanded state support for colonial projects could refer to these articles. Against this background, Bismarck was perhaps not as hostile towards colonial projects as some of his utterances in the 1870s seem to suggest.[31]

[27] K. Bade, *Friedrich Fabri und der Imperialismus im der Bismarckzeit. Revolution—Depression—Expansion* (Freiburg im Breisgau, 1975).

[28] H. Fenske, 'Imperialistische Tendenzen in Deutschland vor 1866. Auswanderung, überseeische Bestrebungen, Weltmachtträume', *Historisches Jahrbuch*, 97/98 (1978), 337–83; F. L. Müller, ' "Der Traum von der Weltmacht." Imperialistische Ziele in der deutschen Nationalbewegung von der Rheinkrise bis zum Ende der Paulskirche', *Jahrbuch der Hambach Gesellschaft*, 6 (1996/7), 99–183.

[29] B. Wedi-Pascha, *Die deutsche Mittelafrika-Politik 1871–1914* (Pfaffenweiler, 1992), 29, seems to be the only scholar who has hitherto recognized this point.

[30] See E. R. Huber, *Dokumente zur deutschen Verfassungsgeschichte*, ii (Stuttgart, 1964), 289 ff.

[31] In 1871, for example, Bismarck is reported to have said that for Germany colonial possessions would be like the sables of a Polish nobleman who had no shirt to wear under them; see A. Zimmermann, *Geschichte der Deutschen Kolonialpolitik* (Berlin, 1914), 10.

He may not have been a colonial enthusiast, but he obviously felt obliged to keep the path open for the future.

After the foundation of the Reich, colonial demands were increasingly expressed in public. The Foreign Office was confronted with an increasing number of colonial plans submitted by private individuals who asked for annexation.[32] When Bismarck decided to go ahead and acquire colonial territories in 1884 and 1885, he could count upon a good deal of public enthusiasm, above all in bourgeois circles. Fulfilling colonial aspirations was likely to revive his own popularity.

On the whole, it is misleading to interpret colonial enthusiasm simply as a product of government propaganda. Bismarck could certainly pour oil on the flames, but there had to be a fire in the first place. It seems that Wehler and his followers have put far too much emphasis on manipulation from above. What Marilyn Coetzee has said about the patriotic societies in the Wilhelmine period is also true for the colonial activists in the Bismarckian period: they were not like 'marionettes on a string that could be forced to perform perfunctory rituals of support'.[33] Above all, the pioneering work by Geoff Eley has demonstrated the dynamics of nation-alist forces in Wilhelmine Germany and the limits of official manipula-tion.[34] The colonial movement of the 1880s may be seen in a similar light. If we accept that Bismarck *reacted* to mounting colonial demands, then his policy appears rather opportunist and tactical, instead of being guided by a grand design. This also means that the colonial movement as such, and the ideas that underpinned it, need to be taken seriously and deserve further scrutiny.

It seems that the premises of Wehler's model have also led to a distorted picture of what he called the 'ideological consensus' in favour of coloniza-tion. Wehler has portrayed the question of export as the overriding element of colonial ideology. Klaus Bade, on the other hand, has demonstrated that this analysis fails to recognize the significance of emigration in the debate about overseas possessions.[35] Woodruff D. Smith has focused on both aspects, trade *and* emigration. His interpretation, however, runs into another problem. According to Smith, colonial ideology since the mid-1870s displayed two major tendencies, 'economic imperialism' and 'migrationist

[32] RKolA 7154–7161, BAB, contains these proposals (1860–1901).

[33] M. S. Coetzee, *The German Army League. Popular Nationalism in Wilhelmine Germany* (Oxford, 1990).

[34] G. Eley, *Reshaping the German Right*, 2nd edn. (New York, 1991).

[35] Bade, *Fabri*.

colonialism'.[36] These are viewed as 'two distinct varieties of thought' or
'idea-sets', which later developed into two different 'ideological aggrega-
tions', *Weltpolitik* and *Lebensraum*. In fact, this separation appears rather
artificial and misleading, as economic aspects and the question of emigration were often closely intertwined in colonial literature. A strict
dichotomy is not reflected in the sources. In general, existing studies of the
colonial movement have one point in common: none of them has sufficiently examined the nationalist dimension of colonial ideology.

A look at recent historiography reveals that nationalism as a force in
history has attracted an enormous amount of scholarly attention.[37] A great
deal of work has focused on the origins of nationalist movements, sentiments, and politics. As a theoretical framework, constructivist approaches
have become increasingly influential.[38] However, despite this general
revival of interest, the relationship between nationalism and Germany's
imperial drive under Bismarck has not yet been examined in great depth.
Certainly, general statements have been made that national motives were of
some relevance in this context.[39] However, for a long time Wehler's work
and its socio-economic emphasis has been influential. Only rarely have
historians focused on the nationalist drive in the context of imperial policy
under Bismarck.[40] Thus it seems worthwhile to explore this aspect in more
detail, and the present study is intended as a contribution to this field of
research. By tracing the career of Carl Peters as a colonial agitator, the study
seeks to throw light on the nature and dynamics of what may be called
'imperial nationalism' in the 1880s and 1890s.

---

[36] W. D. Smith, *The Ideological Origins of Nazi Imperialism* (New York, 1986), 21; see also
idem, 'The Ideology of German Colonialism, 1840–1906', *JMH* 46 (1974), 641–62.

[37] For recent discussions of major works and approaches see A. D. Smith, *Nationalism*
(Oxford, 2001); idem, *Nationalism and Modernism* (London, 1998); J. Breuilly, 'Approaches to
Nationalism', in E. Schmidt-Hartmann (ed.), *Formen des nationalen Bewußtseins im Lichte zeitgenössischer Nationalismustheorien* (Munich, 1994), 15–38; a useful review of recent literature
may also be found in D. Langewiesche, 'Nation, Nationalismus, Nationalstaat: Forschungsstand
und Forschungsperspektiven', *NPL* 40 (1995), 190–236; for a systematic survey of nationalism
as a form of politics see J. Breuilly, *Nationalism and the State*, 2nd edn. (Manchester, 1993).

[38] For a critical discussion of these approaches see A. D. Smith, 'The Nation: Invented,
Imagined, Reconstructed?', in M. Ringrose and A. J. Lerner (eds.), *Reimagining the Nation*
(Buckingham, 1993), 9–28; Breuilly, 'Approaches to Nationalism', 15–18.

[39] See, for example, H. Gründer, *Geschichte der Deutschen Kolonien*, 3rd edn. (Paderborn,
1995), 30.

[40] See, for example, Pogge, 'Domestic Origins', and idem, 'Consequences'; see also the
brief passage on 'Nation and Power' in K. Bade, 'Die "Zweite Reichsgründung" in Übersee:
imperiale Visionen, Kolonialbewegung und Kolonialpolitik in der Bismarckzeit', in A. M.
Birke and G. Heydemann (eds.), *Die Herausforderung des europäischen Staatensystems: Nationale Ideologie und staatliches Interesse zwischen Restauration und Imperialismus* (Göttingen
and Zurich, 1989), 183–215.

II

Carl Peters's colonial ideology was essentially nationalist. On the whole, however, historians have paid little attention to his role as a leading colonial propagandist. In general, Friedrich Fabri, Wilhelm Hübbe-Schleiden, and Ernst von Weber have been presented as the most prominent colonial writers of the Bismarckian period.[41] Peters, on the other hand, is often viewed as a pathological case. Wehler calls him a criminal psychopath,[42] while Chickering suspects that he may have been mentally ill.[43] For a historical analysis, however, these assessements are of limited value, quite apart from the problem that a psychiatric opinion is hard to verify in historical retrospect. It is striking that contemporaries had quite a different perception of the man. Heinrich Schnee, for instance, the last governor of East Africa, was well aware of Peters's brutality, yet he noted: 'Peters was one of the sharpest-minded men and one of the most stimulating companions I ever met in my life. He was brimming with original and sometimes paradoxical ideas and arguments.'[44] Whatever Peters's pathological features may have been, they should not obscure his political role in the colonial movement and his activities as an agitator. After all, pan-German circles were keen to win him as their leader in the 1890s. And the government did not shy away from employing Peters as an imperial officer either.

Given the vast amount that Peters wrote, there is a need to analyse his writings and ideas in greater detail and depth than previous works have done.[45] It should be noted that some more recent works on Wilhelmine

---

[41] See, for example, Gründer, *Geschichte der deutschen Kolonien*; J. Bückendorf, *Schwarz-weiß-rot über Ostafrika. Deutsche Kolonialpläne und afrikanische Realität* (Münster, 1997), 162–4.

[42] See H. U. Wehler, *Bismarck und der Imperialismus* (Frankfurt, 1984), 338; for similar judgements see H. Stoecker, 'The Annexations of 1884–1885', in idem (ed.), *German Imperialism in Africa* (London, 1986), 29; W. Baumgart, *Imperialism. The Idea and Reality of British and French Colonial Expansion, 1880–1914* (Oxford, 1982), 150.

[43] R. Chickering, *We Men Who Feel Most German. A Cultural Study of the Pan-German League, 1886–1914* (Boston, 1984), 125.

[44] Schnee Papers, Rep 92, vol. 22a (manuscript for his memoirs), 73, GStA-PK, Berlin-Dahlem.

[45] H. Krätschell, *Karl Peters 1856–1918. Ein Beitrag zur Publizistik des imperialistischen Nationalismus in Deutschland* (Diss. Berlin, 1959). This short work provides the best of the existing accounts but leaves plenty of room for further analysis. H. M. Bair, 'Carl Peters and German Colonialism: A Study in the Ideas and Actions of Imperialism' (Stanford University Ph.D. thesis, 1968). Unfortunately, Bair has detached his ideological analysis from the context of Peters's activities. Moreover, he does not examine sufficiently the nationalist dimension of Peters's writings. J. A. Winfield, 'Carl Peters and Cecil Rhodes. A Comparative Study of

Germany have not paid much attention to Peters. Roger Chickering's work on the pan-Germans has not focused on his ideology at all,[46] nor does Geoff Eley's study *Reshaping the German Right* devote much attention to him.[47]

Peters's significance was not confined to the field of ideology. In fact, there is no other figure within the German colonial movement who combined at least three important functions to promote the imperial cause: colonial theory, public agitation, and colonial pioneering. Peters's involvement in the acquisition of East Africa may provide interesting insights into the political mechanisms which influenced the conduct of imperial politics. In this sense, the present study is also an inquiry into the link between a young activist and his political patrons. This approach may improve our understanding of how public enthusiasm came to influence governmental action in the colonial field.

Previous works on Peters have not paid sufficient attention to such issues.[48] They assumed that Bismarck enjoyed a degree of autonomy that made it irrelevant whatever happened below the level of the government. Colonial policy was seen as just a part of Bismarck's foreign political alliance strategy,[49] in line with the then dominant thesis of a *Primat der Außenpolitik*.[50] Some historians even went so far as to suggest that the colonial venture was merely an 'accidental by-product of an abortive Franco-German Entente'.[51] However, this is to confuse cause and effect: Franco-German rapprochement was not an end in itself but rather a means to realize the colonial venture.[52] Nevertheless, more recent works on Bismarck have again referred to this argument.[53]

In any case, the orthodox foreign policy approach has nothing to say about the relationship between the colonial movement and imperial politics. In such a framework, people like Peters necessarily lack any impact on the political process, and whatever they do remains without real significance for the decision-makers at the top. But this picture is too simplistic, as I hope to show in this study.

Imperialist Theory and Practice' (University of Connecticut, Ph.D. thesis, 1972). This work suffers from a lack of archival sources. Nevertheless, the study raises some interesting questions about the fundamental difference in the ways in which Rhodes and Peters were perceived in their own countries after their deaths.

[46] Chickering, *We Men*.   [47] Eley, *Reshaping the German Right*.
[48] See n. 45.   [49] Bair, 'Peters', 46; Krätschell, *Peters*, 19.
[50] See, for instance, W. H. Langer, *European Alliances and Alignments 1871–1890* (New York, 1954).
[51] A. J. P. Taylor, *Germany's First Bid for Colonies 1884–85* (London, 1938), 6.
[52] See H. A. Turner, 'Bismarck's Imperialist Venture: Anti-British in Origin?', in P. Gifford and W. R. Louis (eds.), *Britain and Germany in Africa* (London, 1967), 47–83.
[53] L. Gall, *Bismarck: Der weiße Revolutionär* (Frankfurt, 1980).

After Bismarck's dismissal and the establishment of a state-run colony in East Africa, the new German government faced the problem of how it could integrate colonial pioneers such as Peters into their policies. This period has been equally neglected by Peters's previous biographers. However, the years between 1891 and 1896 are crucial if we want to explain Peters's political fall in 1896. Moreover, a closer examination of this period reveals interesting insights into the relationship between the government and a mounting nationalist opposition. Not surprisingly, Peters again featured prominently in these struggles.

Neither Peters's rise nor his fall as a colonial figure can be sufficiently understood without taking into account his actions on the ground, i.e. in East Africa. Between 1884 and 1892 Peters visited the region four times, first to acquire treaties for the envisaged German colony, and then to negotiate a treaty with the Sultan of Zanzibar, Said Bargash. His third trip aimed at the rescue of Emin Pasha from the Equatorial Province. Finally, he was sent as a representative of the imperial government to Kilimanjaro in 1891 and 1892. All four periods need to be examined in some greater detail, as previous biographers have not paid much attention to these ventures. For Peters's trips in the 1880s, however, one work has been of particular value, namely the book written in 1959 by the East German historian Fritz Ferdinand Müller, *Deutschland—Zanzibar—Ostafrika*. He was the first historian to draw upon an enormous body of primary sources that are indispensable for any scholar in this field. Although Müller, in line with Marxist theory, presented a distorted picture of Peters as being merely a puppet of finance capital, his study touched upon a number of important issues which are pursued further in this study.

Finally, two short chapters deal with the period after Peters's political fall. The first sheds light on the course of his political rehabilitation between 1897 and 1918, while the second is a brief look at Peters's *post mortem* glorification by the Nazis. For the wider historical background the latter draws largely on existing work by other historians, above all Klaus Hildebrand's study on Hitler and the colonial question.[54]

Peters's career turns out to be more complex and extensive than one might initially expect, and the limited scope of this work therefore made it necessary to leave out certain aspects of his later life. Above all, it has not been possible to deal with his studies on the biblical El Dorado Ophir and his mining ventures in South Africa. Since these activities fell into the

---

[54] K. Hildebrand, *Vom Reich zum Weltreich. Hitler, NSDAP und koloniale Frage 1919–1945* (Munich, 1969).

period after his political fall, they do not seem to be of primary importance for the political focus of this work.

Finally, a few remarks should be made on the archival sources which were used for this study. The bulk of material is to be found in the files of the Reichskolonialamt and has been used frequently in the past. Nevertheless, the existing literature has by no means exhausted its great wealth. The other major source, the Peters Papers, are in two parts, of which only the Berlin section has been used to a limited extent. The other part, at Altena, seems not to have been considered at all.[55] This section, however, is of enormous value for the Peters scandal. Similarly, the two parts of the Kayser papers have not been exploited to the full. In addition, I have consulted rarely used files of the German consulate in Zanzibar.[56]

Of the other archival sources that are listed in the bibliography, special mention should be made of the Frank collection at Koblenz. These sources were not yet available when Krätschell and Bair wrote their theses on Peters. The Frank Papers contain copies of an enormous range of official files and private papers which the historian had prepared for his planned book on Peters. Comparing some of the copies with surviving originals I have found them to be reliable in general, apart from minor typing errors. However they are not always direct citations. Sometimes, they are only paraphrases. The Frank Papers are of crucial importance for the Kilimanjaro affair and the Peters scandal, since the original files for the incident appear to have been destroyed during the Second World War. Frank also copied large numbers of documents which do still exist, so that a reference to his papers does not necessarily mean that the relevant original has been destroyed. However, I have attempted to use as many originals as possible.

---

55 Bair's thesis lists the material in the bibliography, but it is not examined in the text.
56 H. Schneppen, *Sansibar und die Deutschen* (Münster, 2003) is not being dealt with in this book as it was published after this study had been sent to press.

I

Academic Laurels and Empty Pockets: Peters's Early Years (1856–1883)

We hope that his belief that he is
a genius will be shaken soon!
A teacher on Carl Peters, 1876[1]

SCHOOL AND UNIVERSITY

As a young boy, Carl Peters encountered Africa in shape of a large map which was kept in his parents' living room. His father was fascinated by Livingstone's accounts. He was a friend of the German African traveller Carl Klaus von der Decken, whose relatives lived not far from Peters's home. From time to time von der Decken came to visit the Peters family; Peters's father, who had never travelled very far, was keen to hear the stories of his expeditions. In 1865 the family were shocked when they learned that von der Decken had been killed in Somaliland. If we can believe Carl Peters's memories, it was this incident which first stimulated his imagination about Africa.[2]

Carl Peters grew up in the countryside. His birthplace, the little village of Neuhaus, lies on the eastern bank of the Elbe, south-east of Hamburg. In the mid-nineteenth century some 1,000 people lived there. His father was the local Lutheran pastor, while his mother maintained a little farm to secure their day-to-day needs. The couple raised nine children. Carl, born on 27 September 1856, was the eighth.[3]

In the 1850s Neuhaus still belonged to the kingdom of Hanover, but

---

[1] H. Schnee, 'Peters, Carl', in *Deutsches Biographisches Jahrbuch*, ii (Berlin, 1928), 286.

[2] Interview with Elli Peters, in 'Notes on Carl Peters', Schnee Papers, 1 HA, Rep 92, vol. 24, 49/109, GStA-PK; C. Peters, *Die Gründung von Deutsch Ostafrika. Kolonialpolitische Erinnerungen und Betrachtungen* (Berlin, 1906), repr. in W. Frank (ed.) *Carl Peters. Gesammelte Schriften*, i, (Munich and Berlin 1943), 121 (hereafter cited as GS); C. Peters, *Lebenserinnerungen* (Hamburg, 1918), reprinted in GS i. 20.

[3] Peters, *Lebenserinnerungen*, GS i. 17 ff.; his full name was Karl Friedrich Hubertus Peters. He later changed his first name to Carl; in the literature, both spellings are used.

after the war of 1866 the state was annexed by Prussia. This was welcomed by Peters's father, who also supported the foundation of the German Reich in 1871. As Carl Peters recalled later, 'German unity under Prussian leadership' was the political credo at home. His father had joined Bennigsen's Nationalverein and supported the National Liberals at Neuhaus.[4]

Like his elder brothers, Carl was to receive a classical education. His father taught him Greek and Latin at home. Furthermore, he made him familiar with geography, astronomy, and history.[5] The boy loved books on nature, such as Hermann Masius's *Naturstudien*,[6] and he was curious to learn more about history and natural science. A lot of his time, however, he spent in the villages, fields, and woods around Neuhaus, like most of the other children around him.[7] Since Peters senior wanted his son to go to university, Carl had to leave home at the age of 14. He moved to Lüneburg to attend the local *Gymnasium*, called the Johanneum. A little later, however, his father chose a different school for his son. In spring 1871 he sent him to the prestigious *Klosterschule* at Ilfeld, situated in the Harz mountains east of Göttingen. This school was attended mainly by pupils from wealthy bourgeois and aristocratic families.[8] A relative of the Peters family, Dr Schimmelpfeng, had recently become headmaster of the school there.[9] It seems that this contact was decisive for arranging the transfer.[10]

While Carl spent his first months at the Lüneburg *Gymnasium*, Prussian troops fought their third war within four years. Bismarck's policy of 'blood and iron' succeeded in unifying Germany under Prussian supremacy. The military victory and the establishment of the new Reich were also celebrated at Carl's school.[11] Peters states in his memoirs that the foundation of the Reich transformed him into a 'conscious patriot'.[12] Statements of this kind need to be treated with some caution, as personal recollections often provide a good opportunity for invention. In this case, however, Peters's own judgement seems to have been quite close to the truth. The foundation of the Reich appears as a central reference point in his writings at almost any time in his life, from his earliest essays until his late memoirs. This continuity suggests that the event indeed occupied a central place in his thinking.

Under the impact of nationalist euphoria, Germany's future may have looked splendid to the 14-year-old boy Carl. His own life, however, began

[4] Peters, *Lebenserinnerungen*; GS i. 19.   [5] Ibid. 27.
[6] H. Masius, *Naturstudien*, 3rd edn. (Leipzig, 1857).
[7] Peters, *Gründung*, GS i. 121 ff.   [8] Peters, *Lebenserinnerungen*, GS i. 33.
[9] Ibid. 32.   [10] Schnee, 'Peters', 285.
[11] Peters, *Lebenserinnerungen*, GS i. 31.   [12] Ibid.

to look less fortunate in those days. His father was ill, and he died in July 1872. This confronted his mother and the children with serious financial difficulties. They all had to live off the small widow's pension that was granted to Mrs Peters. From this time onwards Carl's further education was overshadowed by a constant fear of slipping into poverty.

Carl was then 16 years old. He could only continue at the *Klosterschule* at Ilfeld by taking up extra work as a tutor. Letters to his family from those years often deal with his financial difficulties,[13] but he was always keen to continue with his education. In this period Peters's strong will and ambition became apparent. He continued his school education, although his family would have liked to see him embarking on a career in the customs office.[14]

Ilfeld was a boarding school with a Prussian curriculum and attended mainly by pupils from the aristocracy.[15] With his rural background, non-aristocratic origin, and his modest, indeed poor, financial standing, the young Carl did not feel very comfortable there. Many of his classmates maintained a reserved, even hostile, attitude towards him. One of them, with some contempt, described him, as 'being of small stature, with a bony face, a projecting nose, short-sighted eyes surrounded by red, inflamed eyelids and thin, dishevelled hair, wearing sloppy clothes'.[16]

In this rather hostile environment, Peters tried to stand up for himself by improving his physique through sports and exercise. Later he claimed that it was his physical strength which had helped him to gain respect among the others. Furthermore, Peters began to practise his rhetorical skills to achieve a leading position among the rival factions of pupils. According to his recollections, the headmaster once referred to him as a little tribune of the people (*Volkstribun*).[17]

On the other hand, the boy was very anxious that nobody learned about his financial difficulties, of which he felt ashamed. In the course of his life Peters did not easily forget this experience of being an outsider. Some years later, when describing some Prussian officers, he still referred to his time at school: 'This contemptible clan which I got to know at Ilfeld . . . cowardly and vile when they are on their own, rude and overbearing as a clique.'[18]

On the whole, Peters's performance as a pupil was good and he achieved high marks at *Abitur*.[19] From his own account one might gain the impression

---

[13] Peters to his mother, 23 Nov. 1875; Peters to his sister Elli, 16 April 1876; Frank Papers 2 (hereafter cited as FP), Bundesarchiv, Außenstelle Koblenz (hereafter cited as BAK).
[14] Schnee, 'Peters', 286.   [15] Ibid. 285; Peters, *Lebenserinnerungen*, GS i. 33.
[16] Cited in Krätschell, *Peters*, 11.   [17] Peters, *Lebenserinnerungen*, GS i. 39.
[18] Peters to Jühlke, 6 Oct. 1883, Kleine Erwerbungen 141, BAK.
[19] Schnee, 'Peters', 286; Peters, *Lebenserinnerungen*, GS i. 42.

that he often behaved like an *enfant terrible*;[20] he claimed that he had repeatedly been punished with detention for provoking his teachers.[21] It is quite likely that, in retrospect, he exaggerated his rebellious nature. At least some of Peters's teachers later maintained that his school stories were inaccurate.[22] Another myth which Peters created about his youth was that of his outstanding physical strength, references to which are so frequent in his memoirs that they seem to indicate that he suffered from an inferiority complex, perhaps because of his small stature. From letters to his sister we know that he had often been sick as a child.[23] The descriptions given by his classmate which we mentioned above also seem to suggest this. At the age of 20 Peters applied to sign up for his year of military service, but he was turned down. When he went to a check-up on 31 March 1876 the doctors rejected him on the grounds that he had only 'a limited degree of fitness'. According to his own version, the reason was his shortsightedness.[24] Before Peters took his *Abitur* at Ilfeld, his teachers characterized him as follows:

Peters is very talented and this would be even more evident, if he had only been equally diligent throughout, and if he had not rather limited his otherwise truly profound education through his whimsical nature and his inclination to conceit and overestimation of himself. We hope that his belief that he is a genius will be shaken soon![25]

When Peters went to university in the late 1870s, he wanted to be the 'chairman of a society' and therefore founded his own student's club (*Verbindung*) at Göttingen.[26] He spent the first two semesters there reading widely and without any specific direction. He took a course in organic chemistry and practical training in psychophysiology; he was not sure whether to take a seminar in English constitutional history or on the German Empire, but decided eventually to do it on the French Revolution; he thought about attending a course in philosophy and logic, and he read von Hartmann, Kant, and eventually Schopenhauer.[27]

In financial terms, his situation had hardly improved.[28] When he left home he had 489 marks in his pocket, gifts from his godfathers. In addition, he earned some money by giving private lessons in Greek and Latin. He made his first small journalistic steps by writing articles for a local paper in

---

[20] Krätschell, *Peters*, 11.   [21] Peters, *Lebenserinnerungen*, GS i. 40–1.
[22] See Schnee Papers, 1 HA, Rep. 92, vol. 24, 48, GStA-PK.
[23] Peters to Elli, 21 Oct. 1881: 'Die alten Kränkeleien sind dahin!', FP 2, BAK.
[24] Peters, *Lebenserinnerungen*, GS i. 42.   [25] Schnee, 'Peters', 286.
[26] Peters, *Lebenserinnerungen*, GS i. 46.
[27] Peters to Elli, 22 April 1876, FP 2, BAK; Peters, *Lebenserinnerungen*, GS i. 46.
[28] Peters to Elli, 16 April 1876, FP 2, BAK.

Seesen. It was only some months later that his situation improved. He managed to get a scholarship from the Klostermeyer-Foundation, which helped to ease his financial problems.[29]

Disappointed by his rejection for the military, he took up lessons in fencing which became a real passion during his student years. After moving to Tübingen for his third semester, he repeatedly went fencing in the student clubs. Tübingen, he claimed later, was the climax of his time as a student.[30] He was so keen on these ritual fights that he did not care very much about the often bloody and painful results. In a letter to his sister of 19 May 1877 he wrote, full of pride:

Yesterday I left my bed, although my wounds have not yet healed. They still fester; ... I have six wounds on my head, one on my forehead above my left eye and my (beautiful) nose is deformed in a terrible way by another one. ... No contest has been so bloody in the last three or four years. There was plenty of blood flowing, but my opponent was worse off than I ... My wounds required 10 stitches, the wounds of my opponent 26.[31]

His bragging was to increase. There are numerous other occasions and episodes which indicate Peters's strong drive to prove his own superiority, be it physical or intellectual, among his fellow students and friends.[32]

After one semester at Tübingen Peters continued his studies at the University of Berlin. It became apparent that his performance in the academic field was indeed promising. He won a prize from the faculty for a historical essay on the Peace of Venice of 1177. The examiners praised his 'useful method' and his 'vivid and elegant style', which would 'justify good expectations with regard to his future performance'. He received the gold medal from the faculty.[33] The work was eventually published in 1879, as a booklet with the title 'Untersuchungen zur Geschichte des Friedens von Venedig'. Peters submitted parts of this study as his doctoral dissertation, which he finished in the summer of 1879. In November 1880 he completed his teacher's certificate, which entitled him to teach geography and history at the *Gymnasium*. However, he was always horrified by the prospect of working as a teacher,[34] and, as we will see later, he was never to pursue this career.

Peters wrote that in Berlin he had attended the lectures and seminars of various famous academics,[35] including Theodor Mommsen on Roman

---

[29] Peters, *Lebenserinnerungen*, GS i. 45.   [30] Ibid. 47.
[31] Peters to Elli, 19 May 1877, FP 2, BAK.
[32] Peters, *Lebenserinnerungen*, GS i. 46, 48, 51.   [33] Ibid. 51.
[34] Peters to Elli, 24 Nov. 1881, FP 2, BAK; see also Peters, *Gründung*, GS i. 127.
[35] Peters, *Lebenserinnerungen*, GS i. 49.

history, Johann Gustav Droysen on Prussia, Heinrich von Treitschke on politics, Georg Waitz on source criticism, Wilhelm Wattenbach on manuscripts, Rudolf von Gneist on constitutional law, Kiepert on geography, and Nitsch on medieval and constitutional history. Previous historians have taken this version for granted,[36] but it needs to be treated with caution. Of the lecturers mentioned, Mommsen, Treitschke, and Droysen are not listed on his university certificate.[37] Thus, we lack conclusive evidence in this respect.

However, we do know that Peters loved Mommsen's work on the Roman Republic, a copy of which he would later carry with him on his expeditions.[38] Treitschke, being an ardent nationalist and keen supporter of Bismarck's foundation of the Reich, was obviously an idol whom the young Peters wished to copy. In a letter to his brother he explained that he wanted to pursue a university career, to become a professor, and then gain a seat in the Reichstag, in the same way as Treitschke himself had done.[39] He also wanted to join Treitschke's party, the National Liberals, which in his view stood for 'the most noble Prussian policy'.[40] In another letter he again pointed out that he would like to participate in 'parliamentary life'.[41]

Some years later his admiration for the historian was still unshaken. As he wrote to Treitschke himself, he still stood by the professor 'with the utmost and immutable respect'.[42] He corresponded with him to ask for historical advice and material for his later publications.[43] Peters, like many other contemporaries, seems to have been captivated by the 'deaf Demosthenes of Prussia' and his nationalism.[44] In the words of a contemporary observer, Treitschke 'with his strong voice, gave expression and emphasis to the emotions of the national soul and the enthusiasm of our young people. He made the latter fully aware of their own feelings.'[45]

---

[36] See Bair, 'Peters', 11.

[37] University certificate, Peters Papers (hereafter PP), 81, Bundesarchiv, Berlin–Lichterfelde (hereafter BAB).

[38] See Peters to Mommsen, 14 April 1894 and 31 May 1895, Mommsen Papers, Karl Peters, Staatsbibliothek zu Berlin Preußischer Kulturbesitz (hereafter SB-PK).

[39] 8 Feb. 1884, FP 2, BAK.   [40] Peters to Elli, 21 Oct. 1881, FP 2, BAK.

[41] Peters to Elli, 29 July 1881, FP 2, BAK.

[42] Peters to Treitschke, 22 Feb. 1894, Treitschke Papers, SB-PK; see also P. Winzen, 'Treitschke's Influence on the Rise of Imperialist and Anti-British Nationalism in Germany', in A. Nicholls and P. Kennedy (eds.), *Nationalist and Racialist Movements in Britain and Germany before 1914* (London, 1981).

[43] Peters to Treitschke, 22 Feb. 1894, Treitschke Papers, SB-PK.

[44] Winzen, 'Treitschke's Influence', 162.

[45] T. Ziegler, *Die geistigen und sozialen Strömungen des neunzehnten Jahrhunderts* (Berlin, 1899), 546–7.

THE ENGLISH EXPERIENCE

In December 1880, only a few weeks after the completion of his teacher's certificate, Peters accepted an invitation from his wealthy uncle, Carl Engel, to come to London for a visit. Engel, a brother of Peters's mother, had settled in Britain in 1850 and established himself as a musicologist of international reputation.[46] He sought his young nephew's company because his wife had recently died and he felt lonely. Peters's letters from London display what a tremendous impact the English experience had on his own view of life, society, and politics. The young man was deeply impressed by his uncle's lifestyle in the British metropolis. 'Uncle has a very comfortable situation here', he wrote on 22 March 1881 to his sister Elli, explaining that his relatives are all 'enormously rich, much richer than Uncle'.[47] Peters's own life had also changed substantially: 'How pleasant it is here, the warmth and the great food.'[48] He was proud that he could now appear in public like an English gentleman: 'in possession of a solid gold watch, exquisitely groomed, jingling gold in my pocket . . . Money I always have in abundance . . . Uncle has the very reasonable principle that a gentleman must always have at least forty or fifty marks in his pocket.'[49] Carl Engel had acquired his privileged standing in London through his marriage to a daughter of the wealthy Paget family from Leicester. Among his relatives was Sir William Bowman, a doctor to Queen Victoria, and the mother-in-law of Joseph Chamberlain, then Minister of Trade in the Gladstone cabinet. Peters was introduced into these circles by his uncle. He regularly took part in private balls, receptions, and other events, and he also gained an insight into the political discussions of the time, as he recalled later.[50]

While Peters was in London, British involvement in Africa was approaching a new stage. In the southern part of Africa, British claims to paramount authority were rejected by the Boers and led to war in 1880. In Egypt, the Khedive was facing bankruptcy.[51] Control over the region was crucial for safeguarding the Suez route to India. As Charles Dilke pointed

---

[46] Peters, *Gründung*, GS i. 129.
[47] Peters to his sister Elli, 22 March 1881, PP 86, BAB.
[48] Peters to his family, [Easter 1881?], PP 86, BAB.
[49] Peters to Elli, 22 March and 6 May 1881, PP 86, BAB.
[50] Peters, *Lebenserinnerungen*, GS i. 59.
[51] For the Suez Crisis see R. Robinson and J. Gallagher, *Africa and the Victorians*, 2nd edn. (London, 1981), 74 ff.

out, '82 percent of the trade passing through the Canal is British trade'.[52]
As the crisis mounted in 1882, Gladstone eventually ordered the invasion of
Egypt. Although the Egyptian crisis and the conflict with the Boers are not
explicitly mentioned in Peters's extant letters of the time, it is quite clear
that he could not have escaped such fundamental themes of current politics. His London environment did in fact stimulate in him a keen interest in
colonial history and politics. Peters studied the English archives of the
sixteenth and seventeenth centuries at the Record Office in Chancery Lane
in order to make himself familiar with the course of British overseas policies. He also sought to meet people from the colonies in order to gain some
first hand views.[53]

As Peters tells us in his memoirs, he made the acquaintance of an
American named Stacy in the summer of 1883. This man had just returned
from Mashonaland in southern Africa, where he had been digging for
gold.[54] Peters suggested that Stacy should start a colonial project in the
region and acquire the territory for the German Reich. But Stacy, primarily interested in business, shied away from political ambitions and turned
down the suggestion.

Peters's first stay in London lasted some sixteen months. By April 1882
he had decided to return to Germany and, most likely, to continue with his
university career. This had not been an easy decision. On the one hand,
Peters was deeply impressed by the big city of London and its social life. He
enjoyed the balls and parties,[55] and he loved walking through the park at the
side of young ladies from the English upper classes,[56] though confessing to
his sister Elli: 'My heart will not cling to the pale daughters of Albion.'[57] At
times he complained that his uncle was a hypochondriac,[58] but on the whole
he thought that 'London is much more pleasant than Berlin'.[59]

On the other hand, his need to identify with his country made him miss
Germany: 'Only when you are abroad do you learn to love your home!', he
wrote to his sister Elli in November 1881. 'When I walked over the promenade the other day they played the *Wacht am Rhein*. Tears came into my
eyes! Oh, I love Germany more than anything else.'[60] But then his uncle
urged Peters to stay permanently in Britain: 'It is a vicious dilemma. On the

[52] Cited in Ibid. 117.   [53] Peters, *Lebenserinnerungen*, GS i. 60.
[54] Ibid.   [55] Peters to his sister Elli, 6 May 1881, PP 86, BAB.
[56] Peters to Elli, 21 Oct. 1881, PP 86, BAB.
[57] Peters to Elli, 27 Oct. 1881, FP 2, BAK.
[58] Peters to Elli, 2 March 1882, FP 2, BAK.
[59] Peters to Elli, 29 July 1881, PP 86, BAB.
[60] 24 Nov. 1881, PP 86, BAB.

one hand, there is wealth for ever, the opportunity to work as an author; on the other hand, there is the prospect of a good career, possibly privation, but within Germany and with some influence among my own people.'[61] In those days he also contemplated moving to North America, possibly to join his other uncle Anton, who had established a pig-farm near Chicago.[62] He also mentioned a new university in Milwaukee which was to be built on 'a German model' and which might open up opportunities for a young academic like him.[63] In the end, however, he was to pursue neither of these two options. He decided to leave London and return to Berlin.

Peters's decision disappointed his uncle so much that their relationship deteriorated significantly during the last weeks before his departure.[64] Having returned home in April 1882, he was soon to receive a completely unexpected message from London. On a Friday morning in autumn 1882 he found a short telegram: 'Come at once. Carl Engel found dead.'[65] His uncle, it turned out, had committed suicide the night before he was to marry a young woman who had been the servant of his first wife.

The reasons for Carl Engel's suicide are not clear. In a letter to his friend Carl Jühlke, Peters pointed out that there had been three other relatives in his mother's family who had committed suicide.[66] Thus there may have been a predisposition to suicide in the family which could explain such a step to some extent. Peters himself pointed out later that, with the new liaison, his uncle was likely to face difficulties with his other English relatives.[67] They obviously were not in favour of Engel's second marriage because his new wife's social position was thought to be inappropriate.

Almost fifty years later, the German author Balder Olden published a novel on Carl Peters, entitled *Ich bin Ich*. In this story, Peters raped Carl Engel's new fiancée in London and thus drove his uncle to commit suicide.[68] In 1929 Peters's widow strongly protested about the book and accused the author of spreading lies about her dead husband. Olden then brought a libel suit against the journalist who had published Thea Peters's accusations. The author claimed that he had 'studied and recognized' Peters from his works. Being a novelist, he also claimed 'a right to intuition'. Engels' ex-fiancée, who was then in her seventies, never appeared to give

---

[61] Peters to Elli, 21 Oct. 1881, PP 86, BAB.
[62] Peters to his brother Hermann, 24 Nov. 1883, FP 2, BAK; Peters, *Lebenserinnerungen*, GS i. 20. [63] Peters to Hermann, 11 Nov. 1881, 24 Nov. 1883, FP 2, BAK.
[64] Peters to Elli, 2 March 1882, FP 2, BAK. [65] Peters, *Gründung*, GS i. 135.
[66] Peters to Jühlke, 6 Oct. 1883, Kleine Erwerbungen 141, BAB.
[67] Peters, *Gründung*, GS i. 135.
[68] B. Olden, *Ich bin Ich* (Berlin, 1927); *Berliner Stadtblatt*, 8 March 1929; *Berliner Tageblatt*, 27 Jan. 1929; clippings in PP 82, BAB.

evidence, and the matter was eventually settled out of court. The available documents provide no evidence to support Olden's version.

Peters went back to London to settle his uncle's last will. Peters's mother was to recieve 30,000 marks, which meant a significant improvement of their financial standing.[69] 'My dear sister, this is the end of our poverty', Carl wrote to Elli. 'I have not overlooked myself in this matter either.'[70] By this he meant that he had received his uncle's entire literary assets. Peters estimated their value at between 4,000 and 32,000 marks. In addition his uncle had granted him 3,672 marks before his death in order to finance his future university career. This amount alone, Peters estimated, allowed him a comfortable life for two years. He also awaited the return of outstanding debts of some 1,250 marks. On the whole this meant indeed that the 'period of beggary'[71] had ended for the Peters family. Carl, in particular, now had a solid financial base for the near future with which to pursue his university plans. He eventually returned from London to Berlin in October 1883.

Drawing on his London experience, Peters had published an essay in the Berlin newspaper *Die Gegenwart* on 12 May 1883. Not only did this mark the beginning of his journalistic activity in Berlin; apart from his letters, it was also the earliest manifestation of the image of Britain that occupied a central place in Peters's assessment of current politics. Throughout his life, Britain and its empire remained a major reference point for the formulation of his political agenda. It ran like a thread through his writings.

Peters's essay of May 1883 was entitled 'Deutschtum und Engländertum'. In it the young academic tried to identify major differences between the English and the Germans. First, Peters discerned a strongly developed individualism on the side of the English: this, he explained, would be displayed by the Manchester school in the field of economics, 'which significantly had grown on English soil'.[72] The principle of individualism led to a growth of private enterprise and favoured a certain self-confidence which did not require a confirmation from the outside world. Therefore the Englishman did not much care about titles, had only little desire for medals and uniforms, and lacked the feeling of belonging to a certain professional group.[73]

The Germans, on the contrary, had a much less developed awareness of their ego (*Ichbewußtsein*), but a strong awareness of status

---

[69] Peters to his mother, 25 Jan. 1883, FP 2, BAK.

[70] Peters to Elli, 29 Jan. 1883, FP 2, BAK.

[71] Peters's phrase in a letter to his brother Hermann, 27 Oct. 1881, FP 2, BAK.

[72] Peters, 'Deutschtum und Engländertum', GS iii. 267.

[73] Ibid. 268.

(*Standesbewußtsein*). 'The German officer feels in the first instance like an officer.' He saw himself above all as part of a community and only in the second place as 'a single ego'. The same tendency could be discerned in German student life, with its fraternities. In social terms, the difference could be seen in the apartment-house system in Berlin as opposed to the single-house system in London.[74]

Secondly, Peters claimed that the Englishman 'has a practical nature to an outstanding degree'. His intellectual activity was almost exclusively at the disposal of his will to live. 'The satisfaction of his material interests... is the subject of his thinking and planning.' These efforts, he explained, have led to the creation of the world empire with its powerful colonial system and its ruling position at sea. They also created English industry and led to the accumulation of a mass of capital on the island: 'This entire development has led to a national wealth which is at least enviable.'[75]

The Germans, on the other hand, were more inclined to theorizing. This had made Germany 'the great scientific and intellectual centre of the world', but, in Peters's eyes, it also contributed to an 'almost irresponsible neglect of the pursuit of real interests over centuries', just as the tendency towards particularism had done.[76] The German was 'more an idealist', the Englishman, on the other hand, a 'matter-of-fact man'.[77]

To explain the differences between the two peoples, he employed terms from Arthur Schopenhauer's philosophical system. The English, with their practical nature, were stronger on the side of *Wille*, whereas the German idealists tended more towards the side of *Vorstellung*. Both *Wille* and *Vorstellung* were seen as the fundamental forces which, in their respective combination, shaped the nature of each individual.

In the same essay, Peters also pointed to those features which the Germans and English had in common. These were, for instance, 'loyalty, courage, diligence, hospitality'. He suggested that the late nineteenth century marked the beginning of a development through which 'these two major representatives of the Germanic race would come to the fore on the stage of historical life'. If Darwin was right, Peters maintained, then a time may come in which they would perhaps both be the masters of the world and their relationship would then fill the history of mankind.[78] If English individualism and German talent for organization, if English *Unternehmungsgeist* (spirit of enterprise) and German *Geisteskraft* (intellectual power) were united, if the best army

---

[74] Peters, 'Deutschtum und Engländertum', GS iii. 269.
[75] Ibid. 270.   [76] Ibid. 271.
[77] Ibid. 272.   [78] Ibid. 265, 266.

in world history united with the biggest fleet of the present day, 'who could then resist?'[79]

Despite Peters's rather optimistic view that a harmonious future between Germany and England should be 'natural',[80] his essay comes to a somewhat surprising conclusion. At the end Peters paints a different picture, in which the potentially peaceful relationship between the two nations turns into conflict:

If the future leads to a deterioration of the relationship between the two Germanic great powers, then at least we can always take comfort in the fact that it would not be the first time in history that a poorer but militarily strong land power had crushed a wealthy and flourishing sea power. The fights between Sparta and Athens, between Rome and Carthage are not forgotten, and the fiction of the 'unmatchable Albion' is not quite believed here any longer.[81]

Peters gives no indication in this essay as to the circumstances in which such a conflict could arise. However, it is remarkable that he concludes his analysis with this pessimistic view, which contrasts with his earlier emphasis on possible harmony.

SCHOPENHAUER, DARWIN, AND PETERS'S 'RECONCILIATION OF PHILOSOPHY AND SCIENCE'

Beside his growing interest in colonial policy and his reflections on the Germans and the English, Peters continued to study Schopenhauer's philosophy. 'This work', he wrote with great enthusiasm to his sister Elli on 31 May 1881, 'often excites me so much that I can't sleep at night at all.'[82] The result was a massive text of some 400 pages which Brockhaus in Leipzig published in 1883 under the title 'Willenswelt und Weltwille. Studien und Ideen zu einer Weltanschauung'.[83]

In this book, Peters attempted both an extensive critique of Schopenhauer and a continuation of the philosopher's work. As he recalled later, he sought to establish a less pessimistic outlook on the world than the philosopher, whom he admired for his distinctness and clarity of style.[84] 'I seek to prove that no attempt at explaining the world is possible without the assumption of a universal *vorweltlich* [pre-existing] intelligence, which has given birth to the plan of the world and the cosmos out of itself', he wrote

[79] Ibid. 273.   [80] Ibid. 272.   [81] Ibid. 273.   [82] FP 2, BAK.
[83] C. Peters, *Willenswelt und Weltwille. Studien und Ideen zu einer Weltanschauung* (Leipzig, 1883).   [84] See Peters, *Lebenserinnerungen*, GS i. 46, 57; *Gründung*, GS i. 132.

in a letter to his family.[85] This book displays fundamental features of Peters's *Weltanschauung*, which, in one way or another, appear again in his colonial and political writings and remain important throughout his later life. It is all the more surprising that scholars have hardly paid any attention to this work.

The fundamental conclusion of Peters's philosophical discourse can be summarized as follows. Starting from Schopenhauer, he postulates the existence of a universal *Weltwille* as the fundamental creative principle of the world. However, by seeking 'a transcendental solution' which is 'naturally theistic',[86] Peters claims to extend Schopenhauer's ideas and to derive an entirely new world-view on the basis of *Willensphilosophie*.[87] *Weltwille* in Peters's work means the 'eternal deity himself'.[88] He calls his philosophical system pantheistic and locates it 'very close' to the Christian world-view.[89]

At the time of completion Peters was convinced that his work was much better than his previous historical study, for which he had been awarded the gold medal of the faculty.[90] However, the response to the book in the academic world was mixed. Eduard von Hartmann, whose writings Peters had criticized, denounced the work as unscholarly.[91] In a similar way, the *Literarisches Zentralblatt* concluded that his study could only be seen as a start, and that it required a deeper foundation if it was to be called 'scientific'. On the other hand, the newspaper acknowledged Peters's 'stimulating thought' and his profound critique of Schopenhauer and other philosophers.[92] The review in the *Deutsche Literaturzeitung* was more positive.[93] It judged that Peters's work occupied 'a remarkable place' in the literature on Schopenhauer. His consistent reference to Kant's position made the work even more valuable in the eyes of the reviewer. The article also acknowledged Peters's sharp dialectics and his good grasp of the contradictions of the systems he discussed. Nevertheless, the article generally regretted that such 'a sharp mind' indulged in some speculative theism which was not worth very much.

Peters's book was also positively reviewed by Professor Hermann in Leipzig.[94] His teacher, Waitz, congratulated the young academic and

---

[85] Peters to Elli, 31 May 1881, FP 2, BAK.
[86] *Willenswelt*, 351.
[87] Ibid. 344.   [88] Ibid. 353.   [89] Ibid. 359.
[90] Peters to Elli, 29 July 1881, FP 2, BAK.
[91] Peters to Hermann, 21 April 1883, FP 2, BAK.
[92] Review of 7 June 1884, *Literarisches Zentralblatt für Deutschland*, ed. Friedrich Zarncke, no. 24 (Leipzig 1884), 812.
[93] Review by Fr. Jodl, 14 April 1883, *Deutsche Literaturzeitung*, 15 (1883), 516.
[94] Peters to Hermann, 17 Feb. 1884, FP 2, BAK.

encouraged him to carry on.[95] Peters, however, had built up such high expectations that he was very disappointed by the response to his book, later remarking that it had been a flash in the pan.[96] Nevertheless, Peters's philosophical work continued to occupy prominent philosophers, such as Eduard von Hartmann,[97] and it was still reviewed positively in the 1890s.[98]

Whatever the significance of Peters's book for contemporary academic debates, it provides interesting insights into his perception of the world and his intellectual interests. One important aspect is the way in which Peters attempted to combine the two major streams of nineteenth-century thinking: 'There can be no question that the course of our time presses powerfully for a reconciliation of philosophy and science', he explained.[99] Throughout the book we find various references to Darwinism.[100] Peters postulates that his work enables the incorporation of Darwin's theory of descent into philosophy. He employs the Darwinist term 'struggle for existence',[101] to which every individual is exposed, and which, he explains, is the result of two fundamental drives, 'the powerful drive for being and the boundless longing for individual comfort, called happiness'.[102]

Both together are ultimately seen as an expression of wanting (*Wollen*). In this way he constructs a bridge between the Darwinist struggle for existence and his transcendental principle of *Weltwille*, which is part of every individual and determines his acts in one way or another.

We see that Peters's philosophical work, although deeply rooted in idealist and Christian traditions, displays a certain affinity with Darwinist thinking. He argues that there is no contradiction between Darwin's theory and his own theistic view.[103] The positivistic element of Peters's philosophical work, based on Darwinism, is crucial in his later writings, in which he refers to the political situation of Germany and calls for colonial expansion.

The Darwinian theory, as other scholars have demonstrated, had a significant impact in Germany and 'permeated the intellectual community relatively quickly'[104] after the publication of *The Origin of Species* in 1859. Perhaps the most important proponent of Darwinist ideas in Germany was

---

[95] Peters to Elli, 14 Feb. 1884, FP 2, BAK.

[96] Peters, *Lebenserinnerungen*, GS i. 61.

[97] See E. von Hartmann, *Grundproblem der Erkenntnistheorie* (1889), as mentioned in *Leipziger Zeitung*, 128 (25 Oct. 1892).

[98] M. Brasch, 'Carl Peters als Philosoph', in Wissenschaftliche Beilage, *Leipziger Zeitung*, 128 (25 Oct. 1892).   [99] Peters, *Willenswelt*, 260.

[100] Ibid. 245, 257, 262, 320, 321.   [101] Ibid. 315.   [102] Ibid. 313.

[103] Ibid. 321.

[104] R. Weikart, 'The Origins of Social Darwinism in Germany, 1859–1895', *Journal of the History of Ideas*, 54 (1993), 471.

Ernst Haeckel, whose *Natürliche Schöpfungsgeschichte* became very popular.[105] First published in 1868, it went through its first seven editions in only eleven years. In his work, Haeckel applied the concept of the struggle for existence also to human life:

Everywhere you find an unsparing, highly embittered *bellum omnium contra omnes*. Nowhere in nature, wherever you may look, does that idyllic peace exist, about which the poets sing—rather everywhere there is struggle and striving to destroy one's neighbour and opponent. Passion and selfishness, conscious or unconscious, is everywhere the motive force of life . . . Man in this respect is no exception to the rest of the animal world.[106]

Other examples may be advanced, such as the Austrian Ludwig Gumplowicz, professor of sociology in Graz, who published a book entitled *Der Rassenkampf*.[107] He asserted that the subjugation of one ethnic group by another was the foundation of civilization, and that 'we do not hesitate to recognize that the most cruel and barbarous conquerors are the blind instruments of human progress and powerfully promote civilization, even found it'.[108]

Peters repeatedly referred to Darwin in his writings.[109] He also mentioned Wallace, who had reached quite similar conclusions on the process of evolution to Darwin's. A good deal of public attention was given to Darwin's death in April 1882,[110] and Peters may have taken notice of it as well.[111]

There is another revealing passage in *Willenswelt und Weltwille* where Peters, with reference to Julius Bahnsen, speaks about the 'pulse of our time': 'Steam and electricity have built colossal bridges over which men have been moved into immediate proximity to each other. The planet already looks too small against the background of the restless roving spirit which has totally inflamed the Germanic race . . . The struggle for existence is more passionate than ever.'[112] Peters connects rapid industrialization with an intensified human struggle for existence. The idea that the

[105] Weikart, *Journal of the History of Ideas*, 475.
[106] E. Haeckel, *Natürliche Schöpfungsgeschichte*, 5th edn. (Berlin, 1874), 18.
[107] L. Gumplowicz, *Der Rassenkampf: Soziologische Untersuchungen* (Innsbruck, 1883).
[108] L. Gumplowicz, *Outlines of Sociology* (trans. of *Grundriss der Soziologie*, Vienna, 1885), ed. Irving L. Horowitz (New York, 1963), 125–6.
[109] Peters, *Lebenserinnerungen*, GS i. 59; Peters, 'Deutschtum und Engländertum', GS iii. 265, 274.
[110] See A. Desmond and J. M. Moore, *Darwin* (London, 1991), 664–77.
[111] The precise date of Peters's departure from London is unknown. He stated in his recollections that he left in April 1882. Darwin died on 19 April 1882.
[112] Peters, *Willenswelt*, 244.

planet may soon be too small for mankind also influenced scientists at the time. A prominent example is the geography professor Friedrich Ratzel, who developed the concept of a *Kampf um Raum* (struggle for space).[113] Both Ratzel and Haeckel were to become acquainted with Peters later.

After Peters had returned to Germany he soon embarked on his *Habilitation* (a second academic thesis). The study was entitled: 'Inwieweit ist Metaphysik als Wissenschaft möglich?' (To what extent can metaphysics be pursued as science?).[114] He described his work to his brother, with typical self-praise, as being 'dashing, spirited, clear',[115] but despite the great pleasure he felt when working on philosphical questions[116] he felt uneasy at times about his projected academic career. For the moment, his financial situation was secure. However, it would take a long time to become a professor. His professor told him that he would have to endure this insecurity for a couple of years, 'but later you will not lack anything'.[117]

Peters still remembered the miserable days of his youth when he had had to ask his mother for money when he needed new trousers.[118] The last thing he wanted now was 'to fall back to the level of a starving proletarian bothering other people'.[119] So he was only willing to become a private lecturer if, in the longer term, he could secure another source of income.

A few days earlier Peters had even rejected the idea of a *Habilitation*: 'I don't want to be a lecturer . . . Actually, the entire antiquated clan of the German professorate fills me with upright scorn.'[120] He was put off by the the idea of the misery of 'German job-hunting', and he did not want to join those sections of German youth which would swell the 'academic proletariat'.[121] Virchow, among others, had pointed to the problems young academics were facing in finding appropriate work and income. During the early 1880s this situation seems to have grown worse.[122]

Nevertheless, Waitz, director of the *Monumenta Germaniae Historica*, seems to have encouraged the young Peters to carry on with his academic

[113] Weikart, 'Origins', 485–6; W. D. Smith, *Politics and the Sciences of Culture in Germany, 1840–1920* (Oxford, 1991), 221–2.   [114] Peters, *Gründung*, GS i. 149.

[115] Peters to Hermann, 21 May 1884, FP 2, BAK.

[116] See Peters to Elli, 14 Feb. 1884, PP 87, BAB.

[117] Waitz, as cited by Peters, in ibid.

[118] See Peters to his mother, 23 Nov. 1875, PP 85, BAB.

[119] Peters to Elli, 14 Feb. 1884, PP 87, BAB.

[120] Peters to Hermann, 8 Feb. 1884, FP 2, BAK.

[121] Peters to his sisters, 11 Feb. 1884, FP 2, BAK.

[122] See C. Essner, *Deutsche Afrikareisende im 19. Jahrhundert. Zur Soziologie des Reisens* (Wiesbaden, 1985), 90 ff., 139, 163; K. H. Jarausch, 'Frequenz und Struktur. Zur Sozialgeschichte der Studenten im Kaiserreich', in P. Baumgart (ed.), *Bildungspolitik in Preußen zur Zeit des Kaiserreiches* (Stuttgart, 1980), 119–49.

career. As Peters wrote to his sister, Waitz had recommended that he look to a big university for his further career, such as Leipzig, Göttingen, or Halle. He could then later be appointed to Berlin. 'In the field of philosophy, in particular, the chances would nowadays be very favourable for a productive lecturer', Peters quoted his professor as saying.[123] Eventually, Peters decided to apply to Leipzig University. In June 1884, he handed in his *Habilitation* thesis and awaited his probationary lecture.[124] However, for reasons which are explained in the following chapter, he did not pursue his academic career any further.

[123] Peters to Elli, 14 Feb. 1884, PP 87, BAB.

[124] Peters to Faculty of Philosophy, University of Leipzig, 25 June 1884, PA 6053, Universitätsarchiv Leipzig; Peters to his brother, 21 May 1884, PP 87, BAB. Neither the Peters Papers nor the University Archives in Leipzig hold a copy of Peters's *Habilitation* thesis.

2

The Quest for East Africa
(1884–1885)

They have always appeared
to me like faithful dogs.

Peters on Coastal Africans,
1885[1]

THE BEGINNING OF PETERS'S COLONIAL AGITATION

In October 1883 Peters returned to Berlin to prepare for his *Habilitation*.
Walking down Friedrichstraße one morning, he met an old friend, the
Protestant pastor Diestelkamp from the Nazareth Church. The clergyman
introduced Peters to the newly founded Konservativer Klub, located at
Behrensstraße 29.[2] There the young academic became acquainted with
Count Felix Behr-Bandelin, a Pomeranian landowner and the Kaiser's
chamberlain (*Kammerherr*), who was to become one of Peters's major
mentors in the following months. He was hated by left-wing circles, and
those who associated with him were usually labelled reactionary.[3] As Peters
wrote to his family, he was 'swimming hellishly in the conservatives' political wake'.[4] In part, he sought the company of well-connected figures like
Behr because he hoped that they could be of advantage for his future
career.[5] In this environment he no longer cultivated the image of an English
gentleman. Now he was anxious that his image in the club reflected a good
deal of chauvinism. He always showed up 'with hunting-whip and
breeches'.[6]

[1] C. Peters, 'Die Usagara-Expedition', GS i. 301.
[2] Peters [to his brother Hermann], 24 Nov. 1883, PP 92, BAB; Peters, *Gründung*, GS i.
149.   [3] Peters, *Gründung*, GS i. 150.
  [4] Peters to his family, 24 Nov. 1883, FP 2, BAK.
  [5] Peters to his sister Elli, 1884, FP 2, BAK: 'Um meinen Unterhalt während meines
Docententhums ist mir gar nicht mehr bange, habe diesen Winter eine Menge guter Freunde
gemacht'; see also Peters to his sisters, 11 Feb. 1884, FP 2, BAK.
  [6] Peters to his family, 24 Nov. 1883, FP 2, BAK.

In those days, Peters was on intimate terms with pastor Hapke, a well-known Jew-hater who presided over a conservative association in Berlin.[7] He also took part in the assemblies organized by pastor Adolf Stöcker, who was a leading anti-Semite in the German capital. Peters got the chance to speak about *Deutschtum* in London. Furthermore, he prepared a leader for the *Deutsches Tageblatt* on Stöcker's activities. Peters was obviously swimming with the anti-Semitic tide in Berlin, but this never became a lasting or primary interest for him. Rather, his thinking circled around projects concerning his own future career. For a short time he attempted to establish his own journal, which was intended to secure for him a regular income for his time as a private lecturer. It would have competed with the Berlin daily, *Die Gegenwart*, and, in political terms, reflect the position of the Free Conservatives.[8] However, this plan collapsed because Peters could not obtain the necessary capital.

At the same time, colonial matters began to occupy Peters more and more. This interest also reflected the current political climate. Since the late 1870s demands for a colonial empire had been revived, and these began to influence political discussions more and more. Authors such as Fabri, Hübbe-Schleiden, and von Weber discussed the necessities of a more active overseas policy. These names are often mentioned, but the nationalist dimension of their aspirations has often been neglected by historians. Friedrich Fabri, for example, who became well known as the 'father of the colonial movement', focused largely on the question of emigration. However, he did not see the issue in purely economic terms. 'Important national aspects' also necessitated the organization and direction of emigrants. The loss of language and nationality which resulted from emigration into non-German territories, such as the United States, was not acceptable in his eyes. 'Is this not a question of life and death for the German Reich in national terms?', he asked in his widely read pamphlet *Bedarf Deutschland der Colonien?*[9] Fabri wrote that the Germans 'had been granted a powerful world position by divine prophecy'. Therefore Germany could not make the execution of a national task dependent on the dislike of other peoples or states.[10]

Ernst von Weber, another colonial author, wondered whether the German Reich could maintain its power and status in the world if the Anglo-Saxons and Russians continued to double their populations while Germany could not do the same because of a lack of space: 'Shouldn't

[7] Peters to his family, 24 Nov. 1883, FP 2 BAK; M. Schön, *Die Geschichte der Berliner Bewegung* (Leipzig, 1889), 138.   [8] Peters to Hermann, 8 Feb. 1884, FP 2, BAK.
[9] F. Fabri, *Bedarf Deutschland der Colonien?* (Gotha, 1879), 26.   [10] Ibid. 56.

Germany also be a queen among the nations, ruling widely over endless territories, like the English, the Americans, the Russians?' He maintained that opponents of German colonies 'only had the prosperity of individuals in mind, but never the position of the German nation as an equal sister among the other nations'.[11] He compared the German people to a young ostrich being kept in a chicken-shed providing too little space for the bird to grow.[12] He pleaded for the establishment of 'the basis of a German master nation overseas', which would 'free itself from a miserable and disgraceful erosion of nationality'.[13]

Most interesting in this context is the work of Wilhelm Hübbe-Schleiden, a lawyer from Hamburg who had spent some time in London and in western Africa. In his book *Deutsche Colonisation* (1881), he stated that 'the results of our external policy in the years 1866–71' had created a 'national political self-assurance' essential for 'the viability of our nationality'. 'National pride, or better, national self-confidence, is the seed of national vitality', which can only be active in competition with other states, by the development of its own nationality.[14]

The acquisition of colonies was seen as a task for the younger generation, which had grown up under the influence of three wars and the founding of the German Reich.[15] A future empire overseas was a political project which was to consolidate and expand German nationality. Hitherto, Germans abroad had only been recognized as diligent human beings, but not as Germans. Their nationality had been pushed into the background by other nations. Therefore, the Anglo-Saxon would regard the German as being the weaker of the two rivals.[16] The phrasing here is telling. The assertion of nationality is part of a wider power struggle in which stronger and weaker nationalities compete with each other. In broader terms, Hübbe's ideas can be interpreted as a social Darwinist conception. Hübbe's diaries, which are full of philosophical considerations, also reveal his interest in and admiration for Darwin's evolutionary theory. Although he stated that only a few experts could ultimately check whether Darwin's theory of the origin of species was correct or probable, he nevertheless regarded it to be 'a genius hypothesis'.[17] Given this affinity, it is possible, and perhaps even

---

[11] E. von Weber, *Die Erweiterung des deutschen Wirtschaftsgebietes und die Grundlegung zu überseeischen deutschen Staaten* (Leipzig, 1879), 63.   [12] Ibid. 64.

[13] Ibid. 69.

[14] W. Hübbe-Schleiden, *Deutsche Colonisation* (Hamburg, 1881), 3–4.

[15] Ibid. 3.   [16] Ibid. 16.

[17] See notes of 20 May 1879, Tagebuch 1878–1883, W. Hübbe-Schleiden 1011, NSG; further references to Darwin, evolutionary theory, and the *Kampf ums Dasein* ('struggle for existence') in notes of 16 Nov. 1878 and [24 Sept. 1878], ibid.

likely, that the Darwinian concept of a struggle for survival influenced Hübbe's imperial conceptions as well. It is also interesting that his remarks on Darwin are entered in his diary at a time when he was busy with the preparation of his colonial publications.

Hübbe saw cosmopolitanism as a betrayal of one's own nationality to the English tribe.[18] The English brother was rapidly growing, as Dilke described it, and there was a tendency in various countries to resist a final anglicization of the European race.[19] The German people had to regenerate itself if the foundation of the German Reich were not to be a last flare-up in the life of an ageing people. Only then could it secure its survival in the struggle between rival cultures.[20]

The pro-colonial movement became increasingly organized. Different associations were founded which focused on the promotion of the colonial cause.[21] In 1878 the Centralverein für Handelsgeographie und Förderung deutscher Interessen im Auslande, under the presidency of Robert Jannasch, was formed in Berlin. It gradually expanded by establishing local branches in other German cities. A large chapter emerged in Leipzig, under the leadership of Ernst Hasse, the later president of the Pan-German League. Jannasch's organization was in contact with the Munich Verein zum Schutz deutscher Interessen im Auslande, led by the prominent geographer and National Liberal, Friedrich Ratzel.

In 1880 Bismarck made a first attempt to embark on a more active policy overseas. With the so-called Samoa Bill the Hamburg merchant house Godeffroy was to be granted a state subsidy. This enterprise operated in the Pacific islands and had got itself in financial trouble through speculation. This provided Bismarck with an opportunity to take a first step towards a colonial policy. However, it seems that the Chancellor miscalculated the strength of the free-traders in the Reichstag, who were opposed to his initiative. In the end, a large proportion of the Reichstag members remained undecided and abstained from voting, so that Bismarck failed to gain the necessary majority. The bill was defeated by 128 votes from the Left Liberals and the Centre against 112 from the Bismarck camp.[22]

The Chancellor had burnt his fingers with his first colonial initiative. The Samoa debacle made it clear that the Reichstag, too, was a factor that had to be taken into account if Germany was to embark on colonial expansion. But

---

[18] Hübbe-Schleiden, *Deutsche Colonisation*, 32.   [19] Ibid. 37.
[20] Ibid. 48.
[21] The best account of the colonial movement is still to be found in Bade, *Fabri*, 136 ff.; see also Pogge, *Consequences*, 112 ff.
[22] For the Samoa Bill see Wehler, *Bismarck*, 215 ff., and Bade, *Fabri*, 112 ff.

there was also another side to the failure of the Samoa Bill. It revived the political discussion over the need for a colonial policy and thus gave a new boost to the colonial movement. In early 1881 Friedrich Fabri founded the Westdeutscher Verein für Kolonisation und Export in Düsseldorf. Wilhelm Hübbe-Schleiden was appointed managing director. A year later the Deutscher Kolonialverein (DKV) was established as a colonial organization, and Prince Hermann zu Hohenlohe-Langenburg, a prominent Free Conservative, became its president. It is likely that Hohenlohe also had the Chancellor's ear on colonial matters. The minutes of the DKV's General Assembly in early 1884 make it clear that Hohenlohe had approached the government at various times with the colonial ideas of the association.[23] Hitherto it has not been clear who actually talked to Bismarck about colonial issues.[24] The evidence from the Deutsche Kolonialgesellschaft (DKG) files indicates that Hohenlohe may have played a key role in this respect, but whether he did so through Foreign Office channels or in direct contact with the Chancellor remains uncertain.

Interestingly, Hohenlohe also emphasized in his speech to the Kolonialverein that besides wondering what the government was doing one should also focus on one's own interests.[25] This is a remarkable statement, given that the Free Conservatives were usually known for their loyalty to Bismarck. Hohenlohe obviously believed that the Chancellor had to be pushed if he was to take another step forward in colonial matters and seemed dissatisfied with the lack of further colonial initiatives

By the time of Peters's return to Berlin, the colonial cause had thus become a matter which was widely discussed and found an increasing number of supporters. By early 1884 the Kolonialverein had attracted 3,500 members.[26] Clearly, colonial associations can hardly be described as a political mass movement. But given that they attracted numerous prominent figures of the political establishment, they were a force which could not easily be ignored.

In spring 1884 Peters discussed his own imperialist ideas with his friends in the club. One evening, when he and Behr were playing snooker, the young scholar told his mentor about his plans to establish a colony on the Zambezi. We do not know for sure whether Peters formally submitted his plan to the Foreign Office, as he later wrote.[27] No reference to the

---

[23] Minutes of the executive board meeting, 5 Jan. 1884, DKG 899, 81–7.
[24] See Pogge, *Consequences*, 113.
[25] Minutes of the General Assembly, 5 Jan. 1884, DKG 899, 81–7.
[26] See *Kassen und Geschäftsbericht des Deutschen Kolonialvereins* (1887), DKG 928, 69–75, BAB; by the end of 1885 its membership had risen to 11,900 (see ibid.).
[27] See Peters, *Gründung*, GS i. 146.

project can be found in the official files. If Peters's version is correct, it was Paul Kayser, the later Colonial Director, who told him in July 1884 that the German government could not support his plan because it regarded the Zambezi as a British sphere of interest.[28]

On 1 March Peters published his first essay on German colonial politics in *Die Gegenwart*. As in his earlier publications, he chose an 'English perspective' from which to put forward his arguments. The text displayed a clear linkage between his individual experiences in London and Berlin, and his more general view of society and politics in the two countries. He argued that the young Englishman at the age of 19 or 20 had no problem in finding an adequate occupation. 'In short, English society, with its amazing colonial possessions, is capable of using those forces which it has produced, or to be more precise, of caring for its members in an adequate way.'[29] The young German, on the other hand, faced hopeless competition in his country. If he could only enjoy a greater social independence, then 'the beautiful aspects of his character would surface in an even purer form'. He employed a metaphor from nature to illustrate his point: 'The English state is like a tree which gets light and air in order to develop its branches freely and luxuriantly in all directions; the German state is like an even more noble trunk which is confined in a gorge among rugged mountains, and is thus hindered on all sides from developing its boundless vitality.'[30] In other words, Germany needed space to develop properly and to undertake the struggle between the states; otherwise it would not be able to survive.

Colonial territory, in Peters's eyes, could help to resolve the academic crisis and give the younger educated generation a new field of activity and source of wealth. Again he advanced historical examples, or more precisely, the historical interpretations of his professors, in order to support his argument:

The Hohenzollerns . . . have a broad class of ambitious young men, for whom the homeland is in reality becoming too small. Why not lead them out under the eagle banner, into a field of peaceful and useful endeavour abroad? Theodor Mommsen sees as the greatest achievement of the Greeks and the Caesars that, with an eye of genius, they opened up places around the Mediterranean to millennia of socially useful work for their races. The laurel wreath also awaits a German statesman for the solution to such an important economic question![31]

[28] Peters, *Gründung*, GS i 146.
[29] C. Peters, 'Deutsche Kolonialpolitik aus englischer Perspektive', GS i. 329.
[30] Ibid.   [31] Ibid.

This demand was part of a larger agenda. Germany should obtain 'her own tracts of land' in which the German emigrant would be the master and the national customs and language would be preserved. In Peters's eyes, colonization was not only a question of the state. Rather, 'the entire nationality is at stake'.[32]

With regard to the future he warned that, at least outside Europe, the Anglo-Saxons would soon have absorbed the other Indo-European nationalities with regard to language and culture. Not only would this have fatal consequences for the German nation. It would also mean a danger for world culture at large: 'For it is precisely the balance between the pragmatic English nature and the idealist approach of *Deutschtum* which provides the civilization of our race with this harmonious internal equilibrium, through which alone the peak of human development may be reached.'[33] Preserving and expanding German culture and language in the world was at the core of Peters's vision. Against the background of this global task German colonization was a vital step. These territories may well separate later from their homeland, as the Hellenic colonies did in the past, and as the English ones would do increasingly in the future. The important thing was that they would preserve their German nationality.

Ultimately, Peters saw colonization as a 'moral national task which, from a higher perspective, may perhaps be greater than all the small tasks of its continental European politics, as far as the latter were not concerned with self-preservation'.[34] What he postulated was a primacy of overseas politics to secure the expansion of *Deutschtum*. This was not a defensive strategy of social imperialism in the Wehlerian sense, nor a safety valve in Fabri's sense, to prevent social revolution. Peters's agenda was primarily focused on the expansion of German nationality in the world and its importance for the development of *Weltkultur*. Peters demanded a new German role in the world *not* to preserve any status quo at home, but precisely because he was discontented with the situation at home. From Peters's perspective, colonization would give the young generation a new field of activity and secure their income. He called for the increase of German influence and power worldwide in order to develop the kind of national pride and wealth that he attributed to the British. Again, the British model was a central reference point for his thinking.

Four weeks later, Peters's growing enthusiasm for the colonial cause entered a further stage. He agreed with Count Behr to call for a meeting in the club, at which a new society should be founded to promote practical

[32] Ibid. 330, 331.   [33] Ibid.   [34] Ibid. 332.

colonization. On 28 March 1884 thirty people came to listen to what Peters had to say. It was his first speech on colonial policy. In contrast to the existing Kolonialverein, the new group called for the acquisition of a colony through private activities if the Reich was not willing to promote German colonization. The society was called the Gesellschaft für deutsche Kolonisation (GfdK), and Behr was appointed chairman, with Peters as deputy.

The group formulated a manifesto[35] to be circulated to all major newspapers.[36] 'The German nation has come away empty-handed from the partition of the earth as it has proceeded from the fifteenth century until now', the pamphlet complained. 'The German Empire, great and strong through unification achieved by blood, stands as the leading power on the continent of Europe', but 'the great stream of German emigration flows into foreign races and disappears within them.' '*Deutschtum* abroad', Peters maintained, 'is doomed to constant national ruin.'

This would mean 'an enormous economic disadvantage for the German people', he suggested in the following paragraph. Every year 200,000 Germans were lost to the fatherland, because they moved 'into the camp of our economic competitors and increased the strength of our enemies'. Further economic points are added in this context. German imports from tropical areas would come from foreign trading posts, through which many millions of marks of capital would be lost every year. German exports, on the other hand, would be exposed to the arbitrary imposition of foreign tariffs. Finally, 'a completely secure market for our industry does not exist, because we have no colonies'.

These economic points were incorporated in order to make the central aim of the new society more acceptable: 'The Society for German Colonization wants to implement carefully thought-out colonization projects in a decisive and ruthless manner.' Its main tasks were formulated as follows: (1) the acquisition of colonization capital; (2) the discovery of areas suitable for colonization; (3) the directing of German emigration to these areas. In the final paragraph the society presented its aim as a great national and historic task. Its completion required some sacrifices by the people. Every German was asked to support the society's activities in order to compensate for the 'failures of centuries'.

Peters played the economic card in his manifesto in order to give his demands greater urgency and to enhance their credibility. Economic catchwords were to give greater weight to his political demands, but it is unlikely

---

[35] For a copy see DKG 263, 22, BAB.
[36] See circular letter in DKG 263, 8/9, BAB.

that his own colonial agenda was really rooted in economic considerations. In his early life he never displayed a great interest in economic questions. Nor did he think about any business or trade strategies. He thought more in political and philosophical terms.

According to Peters, economic wealth would result from political action. The British were wealthy because they had acquired a colonial empire. But he ignored the fact that, in the process of colonization, trade very often preceded political control. He obviously believed that it could also work the other way around. The expansion of the nation was of primary importance and economic benefits would follow somehow.

The contradictions of his agenda did not seem to bother him; he admitted, for instance, that most parts of the world were already under the control of other powers. This had obviously not prevented economic growth in Germany. Those parts of the world which were left, mainly on the African continent, were of minor economic importance for Germany. Their future economic potential was difficult to judge, and only of long-term, if any, significance. By no means was there an option in the mid-1880s to acquire a colonial empire in any sense comparable to that of the British. But all this did not matter to Peters. He firmly maintained that Germany must have colonies, otherwise she would collapse. Once colonial expansion was achieved, the Reich would be glorious, wealthy, and powerful, like the British Empire. This was the quintessence of his colonial programme.

In a newspaper article for the *Tägliche Rundschau*,[37] he renewed his colonial propaganda by attacking what he saw as popular twaddle (*Stammtischgewäsch*) opposing German overseas expansion. He argued first against the view that through colonial acquisitions Germany would lose British friendship. He held that the British looked down upon the Germans anyway, and that therefore British friendship did not exist. Furthermore, since the days of the battles of Königgrätz and Sedan, the British felt an instinctive fear of Germany's military power. A mixture of those two feelings allegedly resulted in a 'barely hidden aversion' to all things German.[38] All this led Peters to maintain: 'One has never commanded the English cousin's respect by weakly showing consideration for his wishes; but he has always understood the fist under his nose.'[39]

He implied that a hard line had to be adopted towards Britain in order to

<hr>

[37] 'Alltagspolemik und Kolonialpolitik', *Tägliche Rundschau*, no. 90, 17 April 1884 (reprinted from the manuscript in Peters, *Deutsch-National. Kolonialpolitische Aufsätze* (Berlin, 1887), 48–58). The date of 9 May 1884, as given in *Deutsch-National*, is not correct; see Frank's note in GS i. 145, fn. 1.   [38] Peters, *Deutsch-National* 49.
[39] Ibid. 50.

realize colonial expansion. This meant the primacy of power politics through which expansionist goals were to be achieved. 'The German Empire is the recognized leading power in the European order', he held. 'England will take good care not to intervene in any German colonial plans.'[40] Peters then referred to the British fleet, which had grown step by step on the basis of 'practical needs'. The German fleet might not yet look 'very frightening', but for colonial purposes it would develop 'systematically and organically'.[41] This was Peters's first explicit commitment to an enlargement of German maritime power, closely linked to the process of colonial expansion.

Secondly, Peters turned on the contemporary argument that colonial acquisition would be too expensive for Germany. He referred to Hannibal, who had 'secured the means for war through war'. Equally, Germany would see after a while that it is 'colonial policy which supplies the means for colonial policy'. To substantiate this he pointed again to Britain. Everybody who knew the English only a little, he argued, could see that they would not be involved in 'such massive expenses' for their overseas policy if they did not know that it would eventually pay. 'The fact that England still pursues a colonial policy, despite all costs and inconveniences, proves that a colonial policy would also be profitable for us.'[42]

Thirdly, Peters elaborated on the view that German colonization would actually increase emigration and therefore damage the Reich. Here he pointed out that the drive behind emigration was purely economic, and that it could not be effectively influenced through political means. The only way to reduce emigration would be from within the Reich, by improving the domestic economic situation. But as long as there was a massive stream of emigration one could at least guide it into German colonies: 'As long as we have no colonies this natural drain is like the bleeding to death of a tapped birch tree.' This was a popular image within the emigration debate. To solve the problem, national colonization would be necessary, as it had been pursued by the Phoenicians and the Greeks long ago, and as it was still practised by the Dutch and the British in present times. The German, on the other hand, with his 'national indifference', had for centuries been watching the loss of the 'blood of his heart'. And he did nothing, Peters lamented, to hold back this drain on the 'power of our nationality'.[43]

Fourthly, Peters dealt briefly with the argument that the Reich should focus on domestic economic reform which was badly needed, rather than

[40] Peters, *Deutsch-National*, 50.   [41] Ibid. 51.
[42] Ibid. 52.   [43] Ibid. 53, 54.

embark on a colonial policy. Remaining extremely vague, Peters confirmed that domestic reforms were important, but claimed that colonial policy would be complementary, or, rather, that it could help to cure various economic grievances at home if it was only carried out 'in a vigorous way'.[44]

He concluded his essay with three points which in his view were vital for the establishment of German colonies: (1) that a potential colonization area should not be in the sphere of interest of any other major colonial power; (2) that it should not be situated in the linguistic area of another *Kulturvolk* because the Germans would tend to lose their separate identity in such an environment; (3) that such regions should be suitable for establishing settlement colonies (*Ackerbaukolonien*), because only this would make it possible 'to built up our nation systematically on foreign soil'. Trading colonies could not perform this task since they were 'by nature international'. Therefore, Peters saw the latter only as an addition to settlement colonies.[45] This point again casts interesting light on the economic dimension in Peters's programme. The trade argument played a minor role whereas the expansion of German nationality formed the vital component of his colonial agenda. 'Enough words have been exchanged—now let us see deeds.' With this motto he pointed in conclusion to the need for private as well as state colonization. Both could go hand in hand, he maintained, but it would be important to suggest to the government that it should take a relevant initiative—in other words lay its hand on unclaimed territories.[46]

'AT LAST, AT LAST!':[47] BISMARCK'S BID FOR COLONIES

On 24 April 1884, Bismarck made a first bid for Angra Pequena in southern Africa. The Chancellor cabled the German consul in Cape Town and the ambassador in London that the merchant Adolf Lüderitz had 'a claim on the protection of the German Reich for his holdings'.[48] In May rumours spread in the German press, and the government publicly confirmed its commitment.[49] Colonial enthusiasts eventually saw their efforts rewarded, and soon Bismarck would take more action to secure further claims overseas. He dispatched Gustav Nachtigal, German consul in Tunis, as an Imperial Commissioner to the West African coast, to conclude treaties with

[44] Ibid. 56.   [45] Ibid. 57.   [46] Ibid. 58.
[47] H. von Treitschke, 'Die ersten Versuche deutscher Kolonialpolitik', *PJ*, 54 (1884), 561.
[48] Bismarck to London Embassy, 24 April 1884, printed in 'Angra Pequena' [Weißbuch], Sten. Ber. 1884/5, VI. Leg. Per, 1. Sess., Anlagen, vol. 5, no. 13, 173.
[49] See *Kölnische Zeitung*, 27 May 1884 and 21 June 1884.

local chiefs there. By the beginning of August the German flag had been hoisted in Togoland, the Cameroons, and Angra Pequena. In Treitschke's words, this news went 'like an electric shock through German youth'.[50] And it certainly lent wings to Peters's plans as well.

The West African acquisitions cannot be treated here in any greater detail. However, a few remarks should be made to place them in the general context of Bismarck's colonial policy. At first sight, is tempting to interpret Bismarck's actions in West Africa as a response to the pressure from Hamburg mercantile circles, who demanded government protection against European rivals. It is true that a memorandum of the Hamburg Chamber of Commerce of 6 July 1883 asked for the acquisition of a coastal strip in West Africa.[51] Commercial rivalries on the periphery may thus be seen as an additional factor which came to support the domestic drive for expansion. On the whole, however, the Hanseatic merchants were not a significant political force in Germany, nor were their businesses very important in economic terms. Most overseas traders did not engage in colonial agitation. The merchant Adolph Woermann, a driving force behind the colonial petition of 1883,[52] appears to be an exception in this context. But it should be noted that he had political aspirations and ran for a seat in the Reichstag in 1884. So he may well have hoped to exploit the general favourable climate for colonial policy for his own political goals.

Traders in Hamburg or Bremen were generally keen to maintain good relations with Britain, given their close commercial ties with British partners. Thus, one may argue in line with Stoecker that merchant interests were hardly sufficient to build up enough pressure on the government to embark on a colonial course.[53] Washausen seems to exaggerate the importance of the petition when he calls it 'the decisive impulse' for Germany's colonial policy.[54] Rather, it provided a welcome opportunity for Bismarck to realize a colonial course which fundamentally had roots other than commercial pressures.

The timing of the colonial coup indeed suggests that Bismarck sought

[50] Treitschke, 'Die ersten Versuche deutscher Kolonialpolitik', *PJ*, 54, (1884), 555.
[51] H. Washausen, *Hamburg und die Kolonialpolitik des Deutschen Reiches, 1880 bis 1890* (Hamburg, 1968), 142; for German merchant interests in West Africa see also H. P. Jaeck, 'Die deutsche Annexion', in H. Stoecker (ed.), *Kamerun unter deutscher Kolonialherrschaft. Studien*, i (Berlin, 1960), 29–96; K. Bade, 'Imperial Germany and West Africa: Colonial Movement, Business Interests, and Bismarck's "Colonial Policies" ', in S. Förster, W. J. Mommsen, and R. Robinson (eds.), *Bismarck, Europe and Africa: The Berlin Africa Conference and the Onset of Partition* (Oxford, 1988), 121–47.   [52] See Jaeck, 'Annexion', 56.
[53] See H. Stoecker, 'The Annexations of 1884–1885', in idem (ed.), *German Imperialism in Africa* (London, 1986), 24.   [54] Washausen, *Hamburg*, 142.

to exploit it for the Reichstag elections in October 1884.[55] In particular, it was to strengthen the National Liberals who had witnessed heavy losses in the last election. As has been convincingly argued, Bismarck hoped that a national cause such as colonial policy would help them to consolidate their parliamentary position. In July, he invited them 'to jump back into the arena',[56] in other words to join the Bismarckian camp in the new parliament again. The international situation at the time was favourable for Bismarck. Britain, the country most affected by Germany's new initiative, was still dependent on German support in the Egyptian question. Therefore it had only limited room for diplomatic manoeuvre. The Berlin government, on the other hand, could negotiate from a position of strength. In the eyes of Herbert von Bismarck the Egyptian 'apple of discord' was 'a present from heaven' for German policy.[57]

In Germany, the conservative parties and the National Liberals made colonial policy a major theme of their election campaign.[58] In this situation, Peters was a welcome drummer. It provided him with a good opportunity to prove his agitational skills. Observers of the scene in Berlin noted that he was quite successful in this respect.[59] He also sought to rally support among the conservative electorate. Their support was not straightforward. As far as agrarian interests were concerned, they had in fact good reason to be sceptical about colonial schemes. Agricultural colonies could cause further competition for grain producers east of the Elbe.[60] Peters encountered reluctance when he approached conservative politicians in Berlin. One evening, he went to see Count Mirbach, a leading conservative, in a Berlin hotel to discuss colonial matters. Mirbach, who had just got dressed, told Peters: 'You see, my shirt is close, but my skin is closer.'[61]

Nevertheless the conservative parties eventually came to support the colonial cause. To some extent, this may be interpreted as a political trade-off: a Reichstag majority for Bismarck was hardly feasible without the

---

55 See H. Pogge von Strandmann, 'Domestic Origins of Germany's Colonial Expansion under Bismarck', *Past and Present*, 42 (1969), 140–59.

56 Ibid. 145.

57 H. von Bismarck to W. von Bismarck (copy), 1 Sept. 1884, Bismarck Papers, D 22, 230–1, BAF.

58 See, for example, *Die Post*, nos. 173 and 261, 27 June and 23 Sept. 1884, 1; *Neue Preussische Zeitung*, nos. 141, 142, 210, 19 and 20 June, 7 Sept. 1884, 1; *Kölnische Zeitung*, 21 June and 21 Aug. 1884; see also E. Bendikat, *Wahlkämpfe in Europa 1884 bis 1889: Parteisysteme und Politikstile in Deutschland, Frankreich und Großbritannien* (Wiesbaden, 1988), 86 ff.

59 Schön, *Geschichte*, 447.

60 Bismarck's marginal comment on Berchem's note 18 July 1886, RKolA 360, 5, BAB.

61 'Episoden aus dem Leben von Carl Peters auf Grund mündlicher Berichte', PPA 60.

National Liberals. They had to be integrated if Bismarck was to be kept in the saddle. Thus the conservatives had to compromise, too. On the other hand, a significant part of the conservative spectrum, above all the Free Conservatives, seems to have had a more genuine interest in overseas policy. Otherwise, the firm commitment by people like Behr, von Arnim, or Kardorff cannot be fully understood. A look at the conservative press at the time might help to shed some more light on the issue. The Free Conservatives praised Bismarck for adopting the principle of *civis romanus sum* all over the world. Thus they expressed their commitment to a German worldwide empire. The 'Reich's protective hand' should be promised to 'all colonization projects that are worthy of the Fatherland'.[62]

The *Neue Preussische Zeitung* (called *Kreuz-Zeitung*), mouthpiece of the German Conservative Party, also dealt with the issue of colonization. An extensive leader in two parts approached colonization from a historical perspective. It concluded that in retrospect the Germanic race, and above all the Germans, had displayed a superior ability to colonize. They were portrayed as the 'genuine state-builders of Europe'. A striking feature of this article is its explicit reference to the state as the leader of colonization. 'All great colonization has occurred under a state guarantee. . . . The first and most decisive question for founding colonies was, is and will always be the flag under which it has occurred.' The article claimed that 'a state, not people, colonizes'.[63]

In another issue of the *Kreuz-Zeitung* it was held that 'as a large nation we will need a lot of space'. World history would not simply stop with the status quo of British world rule. Rather, it would ruthlessly pass over everything hollow and decayed. Presently, the 'unhappy Gladstone' would be facing signs of decay all over the British Empire, above all in India and South Africa.[64] Thus it was hinted that British supremacy might soon come to an end.

It seems that if there was anything that appealed to conservatives in the colonial question then it was the expression of state power. Colonial policy overseas demonstrated that Germany claimed a place among the leading states in the world. In this sense, it had more the character of a status symbol than corresponding to specific economic pressures.

In the run-up to the elections, the National Liberals, too, increased their campaigning for colonial policy. The *Kölnische Zeitung*, for instance, stated

[62] 'Civis Romanus', *Die Post*, no. 173, 27 June 1884, 1.
[63] 'Colonisation und Colonisations-Theorien', Parts I and II, *Neue Preussische Zeitung*, nos. 141 and 142, 19 and 20 June 1884, 1.
[64] 'Zur Colonialfrage', *Neue Preussische Zeitung*, no. 210, 7 Sept. 1884, 1.

that Germany must not come away empty-handed in the recently opened partition of the world. Germany needed a place for her emigrants where they could live together as Germans and maintain ties to their fatherland.[65] 'Where the German banner flies there are our hearts', the paper commented on the flag-hoisting in West and South-west Africa. It built a bridge between Germany's wars of the past and its current overseas policy; just as German hearts had followed their flag to foreign battlefields, so they would now follow it to the coasts of Africa as well.[66]

In the election campaign in Munich, the prominent geographer Friedrich Ratzel declared that colonial policy established an important link to the national aspirations of the past and would certainly help the National Liberal Party very much in gaining new strength.[67] 'Great power policy has become world policy.'[68] In Ratzel's eyes the world belonged to only a few civilized peoples. The other backward peoples would have to retreat. A powerful *Volk* was like a strong tree whose thirsty roots grew exuberantly. Ratzel's tree metaphor was similar to the images used by Peters. It served to illustrate the national vigour of the Germans who needed space to develop properly. These ideas of cultural superiority and national greatness had little to do with cool economic reasoning; rather, they appealed to national-ist sentiment.

The elections of 28 October 1884 resulted in a slight increase in seats for the National Liberals, who won 51, as opposed to 47 in 1881. The Conserv-atives won 28 seats more than in the last elections. The new Bismarckian Block (National Liberals, Free Conservatives, and Conservatives) now consisted of 157 Reichstag members, out of 397 seats in total. This meant that Bismarck, to secure a majority, still depended on the Centre Party.

On the other hand, the Left Liberals had suffered a severe defeat. As they themselves conceded, they had 'lost a big battle'.[69] They gained no more than 67 seats, losing 41,[70] which was more than a third of their origi-nal strength. This is not the place to discuss the complex reasons for this defeat.[71] However, colonial policy was arguably one factor which contributed to the election disaster of the party, and it was also preceived as

---

[65] 'Deutschland', *Kölnische Zeitung*, 21 June 1884.
[66] 'Deutschlands erste Kolonien', *Kölnische Zeitung*, 21 Aug. 1884.
[67] F. Ratzel, *Wider die Reichsnörgler. Ein Wort zur Kolonialfrage aus Wählerkreisen* (Munich, 1884).   [68] Ibid. 8.
[69] Cited in Bendikat, *Wahlkämpfe*, 70.
[70] For election figures see G. A. Ritter, *Wahlgeschichtliches Arbeitsbuch. Materialien zur Statistik des Kaiserreichs, 1871–1918* (Munich, 1980), 39.
[71] For a concise analysis see Bendikat, *Wahlkämpfe*, 65 ff.

such within Left Liberal circles.[72] In the opinion of the *Norddeutsche Allgemeine Zeitung*, mouthpiece of the government, the cause of defeat was obvious: by opposing Bismarck's colonial policy, the Left Liberals had sinned against the national consciousness of the German people.[73]

THREE MEN AND A MAP: PEGGING OUT A 'GERMAN INDIA'

In April 1884, Peters moved to Hanover to complete his *Habilitation* thesis. At the same time he wanted to gain support for the foundation of a branch of the Gesellschaft für deutsche Kolonisation at Hanover. Initially he was very optimistic. Bennigsen, a leading National Liberal, had signalled his interest and Peters was invited to a party meeting. But then his hopes were completely dashed; instead of following Peters's scheme they founded a local chapter of the Kolonialverein (DKV). The DKV was suspicious of the new group around Behr and Peters. Its president, Prince Hohenlohe-Langenburg, claimed that they wanted to prevent further fragmentation of the colonial movement,[74] but they also dismissed the 'thoughtlessness' of the new society's agitation and their methods of raising money.

Peters, on the other hand, sought to recruit new members for his society inside the Kolonialverein.[75] Thus, from the very beginning, friction and competition among the colonial activists absorbed a good deal of their energy and prevented the movement from gaining its full strength as a united pressure group. For three years they failed to unify their efforts and to channel their demands through a common organization. It took until 1887 to bring about a merger of the two rival organizations to form the Deutsche Kolonialgesellschaft.

In 1884 major friction emerged even within the small Gesellschaft für deutsche Kolonisation. This was because its leaders could not agree on a common project for colonization. Peters and his friends had an African project in mind, while the other faction within the executive committee favoured colonization in South America. They held that the Argentinian government was willing to supply land if the society would in turn organize the transfer of a certain number of German emigrants.[76] The precise

[72] See Bendikat, *Wahlkämpfe*, 70.   [73] Ibid. 75.
[74] Hohenlohe to Bennigsen, 9 July 1884, FP 13, BAK; see also DKV to GfdK, [Summer 1884], DKG 263, 20, BAB.   [75] Peters to Lange, 2 May 1884, FP 15, BAK.
[76] F. Lange, 'Kolonialpolitische Erinnerungen', 14 Sept. 1889, as printed in idem, *Reines Deutschtum. Grundzüge einer nationalen Weltanschauung*, 5th edn. (Berlin, 1904), 263; J. Wagner, *Deutsch-Ostafrika* (Berlin, 1988), 5.

location is not mentioned in the sources. Nevertheless, it is reasonable to assume that, in terms of climate and fertility, the projected area was more suitable for European settlement than tropical Africa.

Why then were Peters and his faction so heavily opposed to this scheme? In the first place it was unacceptable because it would have meant the conversion of the colonial society into an emigration association (*Auswanderungsverein*). Since the proposed region was subject to Argentinian sovereignty there was no chance of acquiring territory to be placed under the German flag. It would have meant giving up the plan of a 'German national colony',[77] which was a *sine qua non* to Peters and his group. The realization of a South American emigration colony would have meant sacrificing the 'German national character' of the enterprise.

The Peters group remained firmly committed to a project in Africa. This sheds some light on their concept of emigration overall. For Peters and his associates, emigration was the vehicle to expand German nationality overseas. The entire project eventually required protection through the Reich, in order to avoid control by any other state. Considering this priority, it is comprehensible why Peters rejected South America as a field of action. This aspect has been largely ignored by previous scholars, but it has important implications; it shows that Peters had no real preoccupation with the social question and its alleged solution through guided emigration on a large scale.

In this respect he differed from Friedrich Fabri, and it is no coincidence that Peters's territorial choice looks almost like a reversal of Fabri's priorities; the missionary favoured 'southern Brasil, Uruguay, Argentina and Chile with northern Patagonia' for the settlement of 'millions' of Germans. However, large-scale emigration to Central Africa was absurd in his eyes. He was realistic enough to see that in climatic terms the region was simply not suitable for large-scale European settlement.[78] Fabri, to summarize his view, saw guided emigration as the instrument for a massive scheme of social policy. Peters, on the other hand, supported emigration because he saw it as a vehicle to achieve his expansionist national agenda.

For some time it looked as if the South American faction would gain control over the society. After Peters had moved to Hanover, their leader, Baron Molitor von Mühlfeld, replaced Count Behr as chairman.[79] The pro-African case was then mainly defended by Peters's associate Friedrich Lange, the 32-year-old editor of the newspaper *Tägliche Rundschau*. Lange

77 Lange, *Deutschtum*, 263.   78 Bade, *Fabri*, 86.
79 Wagner, *Deutsch-Ostafrika*, 5–6.

managed to keep the society 'mentally alive' while Peters was in Hanover. For some time the journalist was 'our real spiritual leader', Pfeil recalled. Moreover, Lange was the only person who had 'a general overview of the current political situation' and who 'had a good feeling for public opinion and how to influence it'.[80]

After Peters returned to Berlin in the summer he succeeded in regaining control over the society. One evening, when only a few members of the rival faction were present, he managed to have further members who supported the African plan co-opted onto the committee.[81] This provoked a strong protest among the supporters of the South American plan, but the Peters group did not give in. Eventually most of their opponents dropped out.[82] Peters was elected the new chairman, and the way was free for tackling an African project.

Having defeated their internal rivals the group now pressed for quick action.[83] In Lange's words, 'the immediate realization of any acceptable project was a thousand times more important' than 'any substantive dispute over the map of Africa'.[84] Obviously the young men expected that they could ride the tide of public sentiment and mounting colonial euphoria in the summer of 1884. As Pfeil recalled later: 'Everywhere there was support for the colonial idea, so that I soon became convinced, inexperienced as I was, that the will to acquire colonies had already been so firmly established that it only required a decision as to where to do it.'[85] For a long time Peters had favoured a venture near the Zambezi, but while he was away in Hanover the other leading members agreed on a different region which had been proposed by the missionary Merensky. They decided to send an expedition to the southern part of Angola (Mossamedes), which was to make treaties with the natives and to reserve the territory for Germany.[86] According to Lange, some 'African experts' had characterized the territory favoured by Peters as 'the most unhealthy region in the whole of Africa'.[87]

The major obstacle to further action was now the lack of resources. The group started a fund-raising campaign, offering 500- and 5,000-mark shares in an 'independent German agricultural and trading colony' to be founded in Mossamedes. In addition they also sold small shares of 50 marks

---

[80] J. Pfeil, *Zur Erwerbung von Deutsch-Ostafrika* (Berlin, 1907), 48.

[81] Wagner, *Deutsch-Ostafrika*, 16; Peters, 'Persönliche Rückblicke', in *Deutsch-National*, 137–8.

[82] Kurella, Hentig, and Wittig to GfdK, 14 Nov. 1884, note in FP 24; see also Wagner, *Deutsch-Ostafrika*, 22.   [83] Lange, *Deutschtum*, 263.

[84] Ibid.   [85] Pfeil, *Erwerbung*, 37.

[86] See Wagner, *Deutsch-Ostafrika*, 22, 23.   [87] Lange, *Deutschtum*, 262.

to most of their members, so that they would have a chance to participate in this major national event. Pfeil pointed out that many of their followers were highly enthusiastic about the idea of colonization, but lacked the means to invest larger sums.[88]

By September 1884 the GfdK had recruited between 300 and 400 members.[89] Big capital was not represented at all in the early days of the society, nor did the group attract any entrepreneurs who were active in overseas trade. Apart from a few aristocrats, the members seem to have come largely from a bourgeois background; there were merchants, civil servants, lawyers, artists, scientists, pastors, and military officers.[90] The fact that there were no established overseas interests involved at all reveals a lot about the nature of the Peters venture, which was mainly supported by emigration enthusiasts and ardent nationalists.

Within a few weeks the group had collected 45,000 marks from the big shares and an additional 20,000 marks from the small ones.[91] This was completely inadequate for such an ambitious project as founding a colony. But given that the proposed venture must have looked extremly risky and dubious to any investor—there being no detailed information, no economic calculations, nor any guarantee of the expedition's success—it is surprising that anybody was willing to finance it. What were the reasons?

One may attribute this phenomenon partly to the colony fever (*Kolonialfieber*) of the time, which had reached a climax in the run-up to the October elections in 1884, but it is also important to note Peters's personal effort in the campaign. During the early days of the society Peters demonstrated a special talent for agitation, and his rhetorical skills were such that they could mobilize his audience even for dubious projects like the Mossamedes venture. Count Pfeil still admitted this at a time when he had turned into an opponent of Peters:

I saw in him a man of unusual talent, a skilful man . . . , with the power to move people, a thinker, but also a man of action. I also believed that I had recognized an organizer, a man of creative talent, the man who without regard for his personal interests would engage the power of his character and his intellectual skills for the task he had undertaken.[92]

When the group invited people to a fund-raising meeting on 19 August 1884 they were facing the 'terrifying task' (Pfeil) of convincing their guests,

---

[88] Pfeil, *Erwerbung*, 47–8.   [89] See Wagner, *Deutsch-Ostafrika*, 19.
[90] See Pfeil, *Erwerbung*, 47–8; Wagner, *Deutsch-Ostafrika*, 8.
[91] See Wagner, *Deutsch-Ostafrika*, 19–21.   [92] Pfeil, *Erwerbung*, 43–4.

who had become suspicious because of hostile press attacks.[93] But this was precisely the sort of situation that Peters was capable of mastering. He was able 'to impress his will . . . on our audience', so that they would give their money 'to a group of young people who had not yet excelled in any outstanding way'.[94] Peters had an extraordinary talent for persuasion, for which people like Pfeil admired him.[95] The latter saw him as a 'master' of agitation,[96] and thus as the 'guiding spirit of the enterprise'.[97]

According to Pfeil, 'he had the gift of unifying people behind a viewpoint, to promote those elements which were supportive, and defeat the hostile ones.'[98] There were other people, too, who referred to Peters's charisma. Friedrich Fabri, for instance, discerned a similar appeal in his public appearances:

All the lines of the movement always eventually came together in the person of the young *Führer*. Lucid and quick of perception, he was always determined and often dictatorial in his manner. Towards those who opposed his goals, he was sometimes selfconsciously provocative and ruthless. He dominated his milieu, which was excited by the liveliest of stimuli.[99]

This did not mean that Fabri had great sympathy for Peters. On the contrary, he later saw in him 'a degree of conceit which comes close to megalomania'. In his eyes, this was rooted in 'the devotion of the crowd' that followed Peters in those years.[100]

According to Friedrich Lange, Peters was a 'good judge of human nature' in the sense that he was quick to see the 'weaknesses and imperfections' of people and to exploit this understanding for his own ends.[101] Moreover, Lange was convinced that one could hardly expect 'more energy' from anyone than Peters had developed for their plans.[102]

On 13 August 1884 Peters sent a letter to the Imperial Chancellery, outlining their project. Their plan was to travel to Mossamedes and to move inland into the Humpata mountains, disguising themselves as an English hunting party. Then they would buy land from the natives and hoist the

---

[93] Pfeil, *Erwerbung*, 52.   [94] Ibid. 53.   [95] Ibid. 52.
[96] Ibid. 61.   [97] Pfeil to Beck, 24 Sept. 1888, FP 17, BAK.
[98] Pfeil, *Erwerbung*, 50.
[99] 'Deutsch-Ostafrika. I', *Kölnische Zeitung*, 16 July 1886, RKolA 360, 6. The articles had been published without the name of the author. They were then reprinted as a little pamphlet under Fabri's name: *Deutsch-Ostafrika. Eine colonialpolitische Skizze* (Cologne, 1886). Initially the Foreign Office obviously suspected that Peters himself stood behind the articles (see Krauel's marginal note, RKolA 360, 4).
[100] Fabri's Promemoria to Bismarck, 5 July 1889, RKolA 6925, 45, BAB.
[101] Lange, *Deutschtum*, 264.   [102] Ibid. 268.

German flag. Finally Peters enquired whether the government would grant protection if the plan succeeded.[103] Paul Kayser, the later Colonial Director, who at the time acted as Rottenburg's deputy in the Imperial Chancellery, forwarded the request to the State Secretary for Foreign Affairs, Count von Hatzfeldt.[104] Kayser was then instructed by the Foreign Office to tell Peters that the Reich could not put 'such an adventureous project under its protection'.[105] The files contain no formal reply to the GfdK, but there is some evidence to suggest that Kayser met with the Peters group in August to inform them about the government's position.[106] If Peters's version is correct, they were told that Berlin regarded the relevant region as a Portuguese sphere of interest and would not be prepared to grant protection for any possible acquisition there.[107] This put a rapid end to the Mossamedes scheme.

Immediately Peters called together his associates for a meeting. Now they had to conjure up a new project if the collected money were not to be lost. They studied Pfeil's large map of Africa to see what was left.[108] Pfeil happened to have read Stanley's *How I found Livingstone*, and he remembered that in the book the area of Usagara in East Africa was described as a suitable spot for European settlement. Initially, however, Peters hesitated to accept the plan.[109] He was only pursuaded by the opinion of the African traveller Ernst von Weber.[110] Count Behr was later to confirm that it had been Stanley's description of the 'paradise in East Africa'[111] which gave birth to the project.

All this did not keep Peters from claiming in retrospect that the East African project had been his idea alone. Lange and Pfeil, on the other hand, complained about Peters's self-praise and his attempt to present himself as the sole founder of German East Africa. Like many of Peters's early associates, they turned away from him in later years because of his dictatorial behaviour and uncompromising will to dominate.

At the end of September 1884 the little expedition consisting of Jühlke, Pfeil, and Peters eventually set out from Germany. On 1 October they left Trieste on the steamer *Titania*, accompanied by a fourth man. August Otto,

---

[103] Peters to Rottenburg, 13 Aug. 1884 (copy), RKolA 390, 6–7, BAB.
[104] Kayser to Hatzfeldt, 14 Aug. 1884, RKolA 390, 5, BAB.
[105] See marginal note, ibid.
[106] This is implied by a letter of W. von Bismarck to Kayser, 23 Aug. [1884], Kayser Papers, vol. 3, 127–8, BAB.
[107] See Peters to Foreign Office (copy), 20 Sept 1884, RKolA 390, 9; Peters, *Gründung*, GS i. 159; Pfeil, *Erwerbung*, 55.   [108] Pfeil, *Erwerbung*, 49.
[109] Lange, *Deutschtum*, 267.   [110] Pfeil, *Erwerbung*, 57.
[111] Behr to Bismarck, 30 Jan. 1885, RKolA 390, 39, BAB.

a young merchant, hoped to establish a profitable business in East Africa. In Aden they boarded the *Baghdad* taking passage to Zanzibar. To obscure the real purpose of their journey, Peters and his friends travelled as deck passengers and sought to disguise themselves as Englishmen.[112]

A few days after the group had departed from Italy the paper *Die Gegenwart* published two articles by Peters, dealing with *Deutschtum* in London.[113] In these essays he complained that no other *Kulturvolk* had so little 'instinctive national pride' as the Germans. He claimed that his fellow-countrymen suffered from an 'incomprehensible drive for assimilation'.[114] As a consequence of this 'weak national humility' other nations looked on his people with contempt. A dog displaying fear was kicked with pleasure.[115] In London, he claimed, a large proportion of Germans were 'nationally indifferent', in particular the 'cosmopolitan Jews' and the 'aristocracy of beggars', by which he meant German people of the lower classes who sought work in the city.[116]

Overall he discerned a 'process of national decay' which proceeded in stages, from an original German identity (*Urdeutschtum*), through 'stages of cosmopolitan colourlessness', to a 'grotesque caricature of adopted Englishness'.[117] The stream of German emigration disappeared into the body of other nations. 'If German politics proudly and decisively employs its means of power in the world in the interests of our nation, then we will have found the safest way to maintain all our limbs which are spread across foreign lands.'[118] With this appeal in the final section of the article he emphasized again the need for state intervention to protect and promote *Deutschtum* abroad. It was precisely this which he expected from Bismarck should his East African venture be successful.

PETER'S USAGARA EXPEDITION AND THE IMPERIAL CHARTER

During the journey from Trieste to Zanzibar, Peters had plenty of time to contemplate his fancy ideas. He planned to march straight to Usagara and to 'buy land everywhere'. Then he would try 'to sail along the coast and acquire the coastal strip down to Mozambique', and 'possessions in Swaziland and Santa Lucia'. From the Cape, he wrote to Lange, he could

---

[112] See Peters to his mother, 9 Oct. 1884, PP 85, 14–15; Peters, 'Usagara-Expedition', 288.
[113] Peters, 'Deutschtum in London', *Die Gegenwart*, 6 and 13 Oct. 1884, printed in Peters, *Deutsch-National*, 20–38.　　　　[114] Ibid. 20, 21.　　　　[115] Ibid. 23.
[116] Ibid. 27, 28.　　　　[117] Ibid.　　　　[118] Ibid. 37–8.

eventually return to Europe.[119] On the ship he behaved like a little despot, being proud of 'disciplining his expedition'.[120]

Four weeks after Peters's departure from Berlin, another German set out for Zanzibar too, Gerhard Rohlfs, the newly appointed consul-general.[121] He was to take over the post from the merchant house O'Swald, which had hitherto administered the consulate in the name of the Germans. It is difficult to trace the precise purpose of Rohlfs's assignment as the documentary evidence on the topic is sparse. In particular, we lack information about Bismarck's own intentions in this respect. Rohlfs was an explorer and a colonial enthusiast. He wished to see the Sultan of Zanzibar brought into a relationship with Germany which was similar to that between the Bey of Tunis and France.[122] However the instructions for the consul-general did not indicate any colonial plans in the region. Rohlfs's task was to pave the way for negotiating a new treaty of friendship, commerce, and navigation with the Sultan.[123] It was to replace the old Hanseatic treaty of 1859.[124] The Foreign Office suspected that Consul O'Swald possibly supplied insufficient and inaccurate information on the trade conditions in Zanzibar. Furthermore, there were legal concerns about the old trade agreement, as it appeared doubtful whether it applied to the entire Reich. Hence it was believed that a professional German consul was needed to match the other powers on the ground, such as France, Britain, and the United States.[125]

But was the Rohlfs mission also intended to pave the way for a takeover of Zanzibar? Clearly, the dispatch of the new consul was more than routine diplomatic business. Otherwise, it is not clear why his mission should have been kept secret.[126] Bismarck seems to have wanted a mobile official in Africa who could act whenever a new opportunity arose. A case in point was Bismarck's attempt to secure St Lucia Bay in southern Africa. An

---

[119] Peters to Lange, 16 Oct. 1884, 29 Oct. 1884, FP 15, BAK.

[120] Peters to Lange, 29 Sept. 1884, 21 Oct. 1884, FP 15; Peters to his mother, 9 Oct. 1884, FP 2, BAK.

[121] On Rohlfs see K. Guenther, *Gerhard Rohlfs: Lebensbild eines Afrikaforschers* (Freiburg, 1912).

[122] See Rohlfs's memo 'Die Ostküste von Afrika', [August 1884], RKolA 950, 2–9, BAB.

[123] Chancellor's instructions to Rohlfs, 3 Oct. 1884 (copy), RKolA 8895, 151–8; AA to Rohlfs, 30 Oct. 1884, RKolA 8892, 1, BAB.

[124] For a copy of that treaty see RKolA 8891, 109–13, BAB.

[125] Zimmermann's memo, 'Deutschlands Handel mit Zanzibar nach deutschen, amerikanischen und englischen Konsularberichten', RKolA 8891, 89–94; further AA memo, ibid. 95–104; Chancellor's instructions to Rohlfs, 3 Oct. 1884, RKolA 8895, 151–8, BAB.

[126] See AA note to Admiralty, 5 Jan. 1885, RKolA 8892, 14, BAB.

acquisition had been considered as early as the summer of 1884, and Rohlfs had been informed about such plans.[127]

Having arrived at Cape Town, Rohlfs was ordered to board the cruiser *Gneisenau* and to set course for the coast of Zululand, where Lüderitz had allegedly secured a claim.[128] However, the landing was called off[129] as the German consul at Cape Town cabled that the report by Lüderitz's agent was false.[130] Furthermore, Bismarck may have got cold feet as the British public was outraged about German activities there. The *Pall Mall Gazette* wrote on 3 January 1885 that 'there is reason to believe that there will be serious trouble about St. Lucia . . . unless our Government stands firm as a rock, and let it be clearly understood that on that point they will stand no nonsense.'[131] Only two days later Rohlfs was ordered not to stop at Zululand, but to continue his journey directly to Zanzibar.[132]

If the Chancellor had designs on Zanzibar as such, then he must have learned quickly that the sultanate was an important British interest, too, which London would not readily sacrifice. As Salisbury remarked a few years later, it was not possible for Britain to leave Bismarck a free hand in Zanzibar. He felt that 'the English and Indian interests are both too strong.'[133]

When rumours about Rohlfs emerged in public in late 1884, and there was speculation that he was to place Zanzibar under German protection, Bismarck quickly denied such intentions in a note to the British ambassador.[134] It seems that Bismarck had by then dropped any possible designs on Zanzibar, otherwise he would have chosen a more evasive answer which left more room for manoeuvre. Nevertheless, from Bismarck's perspective it was still desirable to assure the Germans at home that he would not silently watch other powers partition the African cake. The German public

[127] AA to Rohlfs, 2 Dec. 1884, RKolA 8892, 9.   [128] Ibid.

[129] AA note to Admiralty, 5 Jan. 1885, RKolA 8892, 14.

[130] Wehler, *Bismarck*, 294.

[131] Enclosed in RKolA 8892, 12, BAB; for British concerns about a potential German interference in Zululand see also Krauel to Herbert von Bismarck, 11 April 1885, Bismarck Papers, B 64, 253–4, BAF.

[132] AA to Admiralty, 5 Jan. 1885, RKolA 8892, 14, BAB.

[133] See G. Cecil, *Life of Robert, Marquis of Salisbury*, iv (London, 1932), 234–5; Salisbury's East African policy, and the factors that influenced it, are still a subject of debate. Above all, the primacy of strategic motives has been questioned; see for a recent discussion J. Darwin, 'Imperialism and the Victorians: The Dynamics of Territorial Expansion', *English Historical Review* (1997), 614–42.

[134] Malet to H. von Bismarck, 16 Jan. 1885, RKolA 8892, refers to this assurance of 28 Nov. 1884; see also R. Coupland, *The Exploitation of East Africa 1856–1890: The Slave Trade and the Scramble*, 2nd edn. (London, 1968), 398.

did not hold back with their complaints about British expansion in the south and the north of the continent. If Rohlfs managed to place German relations with the Sultan on a new national basis, then this was a signal that the Reich was active in overseas affairs. It would then be more difficult for the British to put in an exclusive claim to the area. The real or envisaged economic advantages to be gained in the region were less important in this context. What counted was that Germany would not silently watch and leave the field to other nations.

On 4 November 1884, shortly after Rohlfs's departure from Germany, the Peters group disembarked from the steamer *Baghdad* at Zanzibar. They encountered a world which they knew only from hearsay. They had arrived at the commercial centre of the East African coast. Zanzibar was then ruled by the Arab Sultan Said Bargash whose dynasty had turned the region into a prosperous commercial empire trading slaves and ivory.[135] European entrepreneurs had established businesses there for some decades, but the bulk of trade lay in the hands of local Arabs and the Indian community, who maintained close commercial links with their home country across the ocean. Of the European powers, British interests were the most prominent in the region, both in economic and strategic terms. Not only did British and Indian merchants increase their share in Zanzibari trade;[136] the island also provided a naval base for protecting the Cape route to India. It thus formed an important part of Britain's wider defence strategy in the Indian Ocean.[137]

By the 1880s the British exerted paramount influence in the region. The Sultan's collaboration was secured by leaving the customs revenue in his hands. Increasing income from trade compensated for the partial loss of political independence. In the absence of any serious European competitor, this pattern of control proved both fairly stable and beneficial for Europeans, Arabs, and Indians alike.

Not surprisingly, the newcomers around Peters were not taken very seriously by the other Europeans on the ground. The German ivory merchant Kurt Toeppen recalled that the four young men alternately disguised themselves as hunters, scientists, or travellers—without success. 'After a few days it was an open secret that these gentlemen wanted to annex territory',[138] he

[135] For Zanzibar see C. S. Nicholls, *The Swahili Coast. Politics, Diplomacy and Trade on the East African Littoral, 1798–1856* (London, 1971); A. M. H. Sheriff, *Slaves, Spices and Ivory in Zanzibar* (London 1987); N. R. Bennett, *Arab versus European. Diplomacy and War in Nineteenth-Century East-Central Africa* (New York, 1986).

[136] See D. K. Fieldhouse, *Economics and Empire* (London, 1973), 362–83.

[137] R. Robinson and J. Gallagher, *Africa and the Victorians* (London, 1st edn. 1961), 41–2.

[138] Kurt Toeppen [to Consul General?], 1885, FP 24, BAK.

wrote. They prepared their journey with 'mad haste', a rather amusing scene for more experienced travellers.[139] The British consul Kirk, however, became suspicious, reporting home that 'there are mysterious Germans travelling inland'.[140]

Justus Strandes, local agent of the Hamburg merchant house Hansing, told Peters that an expedition to the interior would require at least three to four months' preparation.[141] However, the German party did not follow his advice. With Strandes's assistance, the newcomers purchased some equipment and hired a number of *pagasis* (porters). Eventually, Peters ordered them to leave behind two-thirds of the food they had bought. He wanted to reduce weight in order to gain more room for presents: talars, pearls, cotton fabric, cloth, and twenty-five dolmans. They hired six servants whom they armed with muzzle-loaders. In addition, they contracted thirty-six porters equipped with spears. Each of them had to carry a load of sixty to seventy pounds. Peters bought a Martini-Henry rifle for himself; Otto, Jühlke, and Pfeil each got a double-barrelled shotgun.[142]

Only nine days after their arrival the group departed for the mainland. According to Toeppen, their equipment was 'entirely inadequate',[143] measured against contemporary European standards. Stanley, for instance, had hired 300 askaris for his expedition in 1874.[144] In the early morning of 10 November Peters and his men sailed in a hired dhow from Zanzibar to the coast. They put ashore at Saadani, where they met the 'Sultan's governor'. This could have been none other than Bwana Heri, a key figure in organizing caravan trade on the Saadani route. He was in contact with hinterland chiefs along the route and seems to have exerted quite far-reaching influence there.[145] His origins are obscure, but he was obviously born near Saadani, and he is said to have had an Uzigua mother. Heri generally became regarded as the Sultan's representative, as Peters indicated as well. Recent research, however, has suggested that Heri in fact commanded a largely autonomous position at Saadani.[146] Peters had allegedly received 'a sort of letter of recommendation' from the Sultan before their departure.[147] If this was true, Said Bargash was certainly not aware of the group's real intentions.

[139] Toeppen [to Consul General?], 1885, FP 24, BAK; Peters, 'Usagara-Expedition', GS i. 291.
[140] Bennett, *Arab versus European*, 129.
[141] Peters, 'Usagara-Expedition', GS i. 290.   [142] Ibid. 291.
[143] Toeppen to Consul General, 1885, FP 24, BAK.
[144] F. McLynn, *Stanley* (Oxford, 1991), 246.
[145] See Bennett, *Arab versus European*, 65.
[146] See J. Glassman, *Feasts and Riot. Revelry, Rebellion, and Popular Consciousness on the Swahili Coast, 1856–1888* (Portsmouth, NH, 1995), 150.
[147] Peters, 'Usagara-Expedition', GS i. 293.

On 12 November 1884 the caravan set out for the interior. Peters was deeply impressed by the alien tropical environment which he encountered on the mainland. He was excited by the 'strangely intoxicating smell' which surrounded them. He observed butterflies and beetles of 'glowing gorgeous colours', and encountered 'bizarre, often grotesque forms of trees' along the way.[148] 'I felt as though I had been thrown onto another planet where life pulses through nature even more passionately.' His image of the African population, however, did not match his high appreciation of tropical nature. 'To me they have always appeared like faithful dogs', he noted.[149]

They moved along the caravan track into Uzigua and the Nguru mountains. Then they continued to Usagara, where they turned towards the coast again. Passing Ukami they eventually reached the coastal town of Bagamoyo, opposite the island of Zanzibar. Between 19 November and 14 December 1884 Peters claimed to have concluded treaties with ten so-called 'sultans'.[150] He described these encounters as follows. Every time they approached a settlement, 'I gathered my interpreter and those of my people around me who could tell me something about the ruler of the area.' Peters had shaved his head and grown a beard, as he believed this would make him look like an old and respected man. First they would ask the Sultan for permission to camp on his territory. At the same time they circulated rumours about Peters's power and position. Then they offered the man some rum and handed over their presents. Such were the preparations for what Peters called his 'diplomatic negotiations', which resulted in the 'conclusion of treaties'. The Sultan placed his sign in the form of a cross on a piece of paper which the visitors had prepared. The Germans raised their flags and Jühlke began to read out the contract loudly in German, followed

---

[148] Ibid. 295.   [149] Ibid. 301.

[150] Copies of these documents may be found in RKolA 390, 42 ff. It should be noted that no. 5 is a declaration stating that the Sultan of Zanzibar had no sovereignty on the East African mainland. The names of the African signatories are as follows: no. 1: 'Mbuela ruler of Mbusine etc. sultan in Useguha', 19 Nov. 1884; no. 2: 'Mafungubiani, ruler of Quatunge, Quaniani, etc., Sultan of Nguru', 23 Nov. 1884; no. 3: 'Sultan Mafungo of Nguru', 'owner of Kwamkungu, Kwindokaniani, etc. etc.'; no. 4: 'Sultan Mniiko von Mnowuno in Nguru', 25 Nov. 1884; no. 5: 'Salim Bin Hamid, since four years First Plenipotentiary of his Highness the Sultan of Zanzibar in Nguru', 26 Nov. 1884 [Declaration]; no. 6: 'Sultan of Moomero, Maschai', 26 Nov. 1884; no. 7: 'Kamuende, Sultan of Kimola, Mangubugubu etc. in the Northeast of Usagara', 27 Nov. 1884; no. 8: 'Mangungo, Sultan of Msovero', 29 Nov. 1884; no. 9: 'Sebegul . . . claiming to be Sultan in the northern half of Msovero', 29 Nov. 1884; no. 10: 'Sultaness Mbumi, ruler of the territory Mukondokna in Usagara', 2 Dec. 1884; no. 11: 'Sultan Muininsagara, ruler of Muininsagara etc., sole and absolute sovereign of all Usagara', 4 Dec. 1884; no. 12: 'Sultan Muinhamisi, ruler of the territories Kikundi, kngasi Sultan in Ukami', 14 Dec. 1884.

by a short speech by Peters 'through which I undertook the occupation'. They concluded their ceremony with a cheer for the German Kaiser. Then they fired three volleys 'to demonstrate to the blacks what would happen if they broke the treaty'.[151] After this, the party travelled on. This was Peters's version of the story as he presented it to the German public in 1885.[152]

The texts of these papers were all similar. The so-called treaty with Muinin Sagara, for instance, stated that the Sultan, 'by virtue of his absolute and unrestricted power, transfers the sole and exclusive right to bring colonists to Usagara, to Dr Carl Peters, representative of the Society for German Colonisation'. Furthermore it contained a clause that secured for Peters 'the sole and exclusive right of exploitation under private law' and transferred 'all those rights which, according to German constitutional law, form the essence of governmental sovereignty. Peters listed the right 'to exploit mines, rivers and forests, the right to levy customs and taxes, to establish jurisdiction and administration, and the right to establish a military power'. In return, the German promised protection through the society.[153] With Mafungo, referred to 'as the sole sovereign' of Quaniani, Quatungee in Nguru', Peters concluded two treaties. The first treaty was signed in order to gain 'state sovereignty' and all rights that meant 'the possession of land under private law', while the second paper stated that Mafungo agreed 'to supply labour and military support' at the society's request.[154]

These treaties can only be described as fraud. First, it is obvious that Peters's interpreters could not possibly have translated the treaty text at all. Their language reflected European legal terms (*deutsches Staaatsrecht, privatrechtlicher Besitz, Rechte staatlicher Hoheit*, etc.) and referred to a concept of state sovereignty which was alien to the people of the region. Secondly, it may be argued that Peters deliberately invented the kind of African authority that suited his intentions. A similar process was at work, for instance, when colonial rulers later imposed a system of indirect rule, in which they partly exercised control through invented chiefs.[155] Two

---

[151] Peters, 'Usagara-Expedition', GS i. 302.

[152] His account of the Usagara expedition was published as a series of articles in the *Feuilleton* of the *Tägliche Rundschau*, 7, 8, 15, 19, and 22 March 1885.

[153] Treaty no. 11, Muininsagara, 4 Dec. 1884 (copy), RKolA 390, 56–8.

[154] Treaty no. 3, 23 and 24 Nov. 1884 (copy), RKolA 390, 42–5.

[155] For a recent discussion of this argument see T. O. Ranger, 'The Invention of Tradition Revisited: The Case of Colonial Africa', in T. O. Ranger and O. Vaughan (eds.), *Legitimacy and the State in Twentieth Century Africa: Essays in Honour of A. M. H. Kirk-Greene* (London, 1993), 62–111; for a different picture of the situation in Tanganyika see J. Iliffe, *A Modern History of Tanganyika* (Cambridge, 1979), ch. 10: 'The Creation of Tribes', 318–41.

requirements were thus essential for Peters's deal: first, the individuals who signed had to possess absolute authority over their people and the land they lived on; secondly, the area which was transferred needed to be specified in some way. It seems that neither of these requirements corresponded to actual local structures.

European accounts of the pre-colonial period suggest that the hinterland of Bagamoyo and Saadani (by which is meant here the area described as Uzigua, Nguru, Ukami, Ukaguru, and Usagara) was highly fragmented in political terms. These were not centrally organized kingdoms as they were encountered in Buganda, for instance. In general terms, one might speak of stateless societies in which different clans formed the central political units.[156]

However, there is a persuasive thesis suggesting that the rise of long-distance trade had enhanced a concentration of political power in the hands of certain chiefs.[157] Those who managed to exploit commercial links with the coast to their own ends achieved influence which obviously exceeded the boundaries of their own clan. Between the Kingani and Wami rivers, missionaries observed the existence of chiefs controlling larger regions and subordinate village headmen.[158]

With regard to Peters's treaties, it remains difficult to identify the importance of the local leaders he claimed to have met. There were even serious doubts that Peters had been to the Nguru region at all.[159] A British missionary who had some knowledge of the mainland claimed that the people who had signed the treaties were village headmen only.[160] Thus, Peters may well have exaggerated when he called one of them, Muinin Sagara, 'the overlord of Usagara'.[161]

On the whole, it seems that local political organization was difficult for Europeans to judge. Some of them were well aware of that problem, even if they formulated it in their usual arrogant manner. Toeppen, for instance,

---

[156] See T. O. Beidelman, *The Matrilineal Peoples of Eastern Tanzania* (London, 1967), 28, 42, 58, 68. [157] See ibid. 41, 51.
[158] 'Eine Reise nach Udoe und Usigova an der Ostküste Afrikas. (Nach den Mitteilungen P. Bauers, des apostolischen Vice-Präfekten von Sansibar)', *Katholische Missionen*, 1883, 10 ff. Similar observations were made further north: J. L. Giblin, 'Famine, Authority and the Impact of Foreign Capital in Handeni District, Tanzania, 1840–1940' (University Wisconsin-Madison, Ph.D. thesis, 1986), 171.
[159] Rohlfs to AA, 29 June 1885, RKolA 382, 10 ff., BAB. Rohlfs spoke with the French scientist Bloyet about Peters's acquisitions on 25 and 27 June 1885. Bloyet had lived for several years at Kondoa.
[160] N. R. Bennett, 'The Arab Power of Tanganyika in the Nineteenth Century' (University Boston, Ph.D. thesis, 1961), 127, referring to the account of UMCA missionary J. P. Farler.
[161] Peters, *Gründung*, GS i. 170.

stated that one could not rely on what the people themselves were telling you. On being asked, they would all claim to be the most important one.[162] Somebody like Peters spending less than a month in the area could not have judged these statements at all. If any Europeans had a grasp of what was really going on, it was those people who had spent some time in the region, such as the missionaries.

Established Europeans were convinced that the Sultanate of Zanzibar exerted considerable influence along the trading routes in the interior. Some of them, such as the French scientist Bloyet, went so far as to state that the land visited by Peters 'belonged to the Sultan of Zanzibar'.[163]

While judgements of this kind largely reflected a European concept of territorial states and sovereignty, they failed to grasp the real nature of Zanzibari control on the mainland. Zanzibar had established a rather loose and flexible network of agents, whose major purpose was to secure the commercial mainstay of the Sultanate: caravan trade. This system also included policing the trade routes when necessary. On various occasions Zanzibari soldiers intervened on the mainland. For instance, they would force local chiefs to abandon resistance, as in the reported case of chief Tongo at Mswera.[164] Furthermore, the Sultan assisted French missionaries to establish a station at Mrogoro.[165] He provided letters by which the local chiefs were instructed to receive the French priests well.

In Mamboya, the Sultan had established a garrison, which numbered up to 200 soldiers.[166] He had also installed a local kadi, and a teacher for the Arab children in the area.[167] The Arab presence there had enhanced the power of their allied local chief, Senyagwa Chimola, who later adopted the Arab name of Saidi.[168] The Peters group had not visited Mamboya or met with Saidi Chimola, but they had met with the Arab Salim bin Hamid, whom Peters described as the 'First Plenipotentiary of his Highness the Sultan of Zanzibar in Nguru'. Peters carried home a declaration which allegedly carried a handsign by Salim as his signature. The paper stated that the Sultan of Zanzibar possessed 'no sovereignty and right of protection in Nguru and Usagara'.[169] It is highly unlikely that Salim had signed this

---

[162] Peters, *Gründung*, GS i. 170.   [163] Ibid.   [164] Ibid.

[165] Ibid.; see also Le Roy's report of a trip to Mrogoro in November 1884: *Katholische Missionen*, 1886, 96 ff. (here p. 118).

[166] T. O. Beidelman, 'A History of Ukaguru: 1857–1916', *Tanganyika Notes and Records*, 58/59 (1962), 21.

[167] See Toeppen, 'Nachträgliche Bemerkungen', RKolA 392, 73.

[168] Beidelman, 'History', 18.   [169] RKolA 390, 60, BAB.

paper at all; being asked later about it he said that he had welcomed the German, but he also denied having signed anything.[170]

Peters's account suggests that he did not encounter any hostilities on the way and that people received him well. There is no reason to doubt this. Missionaries who settled in the area had had a similar experience, although they may not have been received everywhere with an equal degree of hospitality.[171] What interests, then, did local people have in establishing a link with visiting Europeans? After all, Peters tells us that he even concluded blood brotherhood with one of the village leaders of Nguru.[172] Among the first Europeans in the area were the French priests, who resorted to the authority of Said Bargash to establish themselves. It is therefore most likely that a man like Peters was somehow associated with Zanzibari authority as well, particularly if he indeed carried a letter from Bargash. Europeans were a potential source of imported goods and potential buyers of surplus production. This may also have been a consideration which influenced Muinin Sagara, of whom Peters reported that he had long wished to see Europeans settle in his area.[173] When the Germans established their first station near Mbusini in Uzigua, the local representative, Claus von Anderten, reported in 1886 that local chiefs welcomed his presence 'as the most powerful sultan'. They obviously hoped that German presence would offer them effective protection against hostile neighbours.[174] Thus in the early and mid-1880s Europeans were either perceived as new patrons or as agents of Zanzibari authority.

After their first two weeks on the mainland, Peters's and his associates made a rather miserable impression. Pfeil and Jühlke suffered from fever, and Otto seems to have been constantly drunk.[175] Peters had already complained about Otto's taste for alcohol on the steamer,[176] but obviously it did not bother him enough to cause him to separate from him after their arrival at Zanzibar.

In the valley of Mkondogua, Peters burnt his foot with some acid, so that he could no longer walk on his own, and had to be carried. From now on he would conclude his treaties lying in a hammock.[177] In Muinsagara he decided to leave Pfeil and Otto behind, allegedly with the task of building

---

[170] Bennett, *Arab versus European*, 130.
[171] See Le Roy's account in *Katholische Missionen*, 1886, 96 ff.
[172] Peters, 'Usagara-Expedition', GS i. 304–5.   [173] Ibid. 301.
[174] Von Anderten's report, 9 Aug. 1886, *KPK* no. 42, 16 Oct. 1886, 298–9.
[175] Ibid.
[176] Peters to his mother, 31 Oct. 1884, PP 85, BAB.
[177] Peters, 'Usagara-Expedition', GS i. 306.

the headquarters for the German society there. In fact this may have been a pretext. The relations between Pfeil and Otto on one side, and Peters and Jühlke on the other, had deteriorated to a point of open hostility. The conflict at some stage escalated. Pfeil apparently fired his revolver at Peters, but missed.[178]

On the morning of 7 December Peters and Jühlke left Muinsagara to return to the coast.[179] Jühlke's fever became more serious, so the porters had to carry him in a hammock as well. Peters forced his African caravan to march for fifteen hours a day, threatening his porters with his revolver. The two Germans suffered from anxiety and fever, and they ran out of food. The more desperate their situation appeared, the more violent Peters became in his treatment of his porters. Apparently, he was still fit enough to slash them with his horse-whip when they were exhausted and wanted to rest.[180] It was only the help of their interpreter Ramassan, and that of a French priest, that ultimately secured their survival. In the end they had only the 'Jesuit's vegetables' left, from which they ate once a day.[181]

On 17 December, they reached the coastal town of Bagamoyo, where French priests took care of them. As a cure they provided high doses of quinine and plenty of red wine.[182] After a few days' rest the two Germans returned to the island of Zanzibar. Jühlke continued to suffer from fever, while Peters was so weak that he could not even hold a pen to write by himself. They recovered only gradually, eating 'giant portions of raw beef'. However, they had taken so much quinine that their ears were seriously affected. They had to shout at each other to make themselves understood.[183]

On 24 December 1884, the two Germans sat on the veranda of the Hotel Oriental, secretly celebrating their colonial coup. Two hundred kilometres west, in Usagara, the merchant Otto died from fever in a goat shed. Count Pfeil was seriously ill, too. He only survived because the French scientist Bloyet found him 'helpless and alone in his hut'. He had neither medication nor food, because 'Dr Peters had left them nothing at his departure'.[184] Pfeil was cured by the scientist in Kondoa, from where he later returned to the coast. Relations between Peters and Pfeil never recovered after their expedition.

[178] See F. F. Müller, *Deutschland—Zanzibar—Ostafrika. Geschichte einer Kolonialeroberung* (Berlin, 1959), 117.   [179] Peters, 'Usagara-Expedition', 307.
[180] Ibid. 307, 309.   [181] Ibid. 310.   [182] Ibid. 312.
[183] Ibid. 315.
[184] Toeppen to consul-general, [no date], DKG, R8023, 265, 101 ff.; Rohlfs to AA, 29 June 1885, RKolA 382, 10 ff., BAB.

Peters returned to Europe via Bombay, reaching Venice on 1 February 1885.[185] Jühlke stayed in Zanzibar as the society's local agent. Peters's so-called treaties allegedly proved the acquisition of some 2,000–3,000 square miles of the East African mainland. He hoped that the Kaiser would place these territories under the protection of the Reich.

Interestingly, nobody in Europe defended Peters's treaties as being legally correct. Krauel, the colonial expert in the Foreign Office, noted that they were 'very non-juristic'.[186] Jühlke, having studied law himself, did not need the judgement of other experts to know that the whole affair was a fraud. He openly conceded that the meaning of the treaties might not have been entirely clear to the Africans.[187] Even Peters admitted some years later that 'such acquisition of land is always and overall fiction'.[188] Herbert von Bismarck commented on Peters's treaties: 'What is meant by acquisition? A piece of paper with some negro crosses at the bottom. Securing it . . . requires agreement with England.'[189]

The practice of treaty-signing was adopted by all European powers which sought to secure a share of the African continent. Treaties were regarded as the most convenient vehicles with which to achieve territorial claims. Although Bismarck ridiculed Peters's treaties in later years, they proved a welcome opportunity for him in 1885. After Peters had requested that his claimed territory be placed under the sovereignty of the Reich,[190] Bismarck received Kusserow to report on the matter. His official praised 'the wonderful beauty and fertility' of the land and spoke of 'a bearable climate'. According to Stanley this was the 'paradise of Africa', Kusserow claimed. He also pointed to the urgency of the matter, since the Congo Association was about to send an expedition to the interior and might acquire the same regions.[191]

Bismarck now wanted to see further data on 'the extent' of the claimed

---

[185] Peters, 'Usagara-Expedition', 317.

[186] Krauel's note, 9 June 1885, FP 18, BAK.

[187] Jühlke to German Consulate, 3 Feb. 1885, RKolA 390 122–3.

[188] Peters, *Gründung*, 170.

[189] H. von Bismarck's [?] marginal note on Bennigsen to Herbert von Bismarck, 30 Dec. 1888, RKolA 370, 169–72. This marginal note has been attributed to the Chancellor himself, but this is doubtful. Bennigsen addressed his letter to Herbert von Bismarck, whose handwriting is indeed difficult to distinguish from that of his father. In general, Herbert seems to have written in a slightly smaller hand. I am grateful to Dr Keipert from the Foreign Office Archives for this information.

[190] Lange to AA, 23 Dec. 1884, Kusserew to Lange, 28 Dec. 1884, Kusserow's note, 2 Jan. 1885 on conversation with Lange, RKolA 382, 1, 2, 4/5; Peters to AA, 8 Jan. 1885, RKolA 390, 33; treaty copies in RKolA 390, 42–64, BAB.

[191] See Kusserow's note, 15 Feb. 1885, RKolA 390, 82–4, BAB.

territories and 'their economic value',[192] but all that Kusserow supplied was a twenty-page memorandum written by Peters. The Chancellor was obviously satisfied with it; at least he did not request further material thereafter. Peters painted the most favourable picture of the claim.[193] He estimated its size at 2,000–3,000 square miles, a figure which could only be arbitrary. He then referred to the judgement of experts, such as Stanley, according to which the area was suitable for cultivation of a whole series of crops: 'coffee, tea, opium, fine tobaccos, rice, sugar, cotton, corn etc.'. Burton had allegedly stated that it was also rich in metals. 'Overall the territory is likely to be particularly suitable for a plantation colony.' Peters characterized its population as 'cowardly, peaceful, and at times very lazy Swahili'. One could introduce European colonization gradually without danger. The East India Company should serve as a model for their venture. He also assured the Chancellor that they would not require any further assistance for exploiting the country, and that they could defend themselves in the interior. One could also bring settlers into the region. What was needed now was free import and export through Bagamoyo, for which purpose they needed the support of the Reich. Bismarck found it 'good' that Peters had requested a provisional charter of protection, and that he wanted to take the East India Company as a model 'to build a polity out of their own resources'.[194]

The Chancellor wanted to know from Kusserow whether the envisaged 'etablissement' extended into the Congo state and, if this was not the case, whether it was still part of the Congo basin, for which the principles of free trade had been agreed by the European powers.[195] As Peters's claims did not violate the borders of the Congo Free State Bismarck saw no further obstacles to issuing a protective charter. Now he acted swiftly. Two days later a draft of an Imperial Charter was presented to the Kaiser. Wilhelm signed the document on 27 February 1885. It was published in the *Reichsanzeiger* on 3 March.[196] In fact, the charter was a *carte blanche* for Peters and his associates, granting them the right to carry out all rights

[192] Kusserow's note to Bismarck, 23 Feb. 1885, RKolA 390, 102–4, BAB.

[193] Carl Peters, 'Ein Memorandum über die Erwerbungen der Gesellschaft für deutsche Kolonisation in Ostafrika in Bezug auf geographische Beschaffenheit, politische Verhältnisse etc. und einige Gesichtspunkte für die dort zu schaffende Verwaltung' [February 1885], RKolA 390, 67–76, BAB.

[194] Kusserow's note, 23 Feb. 1885, and Bismarck's remarks thereon, RKolA 390, 102–4, BAB.

[195] Herbert von Bismarck to Kusserow, 24 Feb. 1885, RKolA 390, 105, BAB.

[196] Drafts and the final version of the Imperial charter in RKolA 359; copy in RKolA 390, 110–11; for a printed copy see Müller, *Deutschland*, 525–6.

which had been transferred to them through their treaties, including jurisdiction, although Wilhelm maintained the right to issue further orders and
amendments. Furthermore, the association had to remain a German one,
and its directors had to be of German nationality.

The course of events and Bismarck's handling of the Peters treaties
reveal two things. First, the Chancellor acted with some haste in order to
prevent a *fait accompli* by other colonial pioneers. He did not bother much
about a more careful analysis of the economic potential, relying on
Kusserow's and Peters's judgements. Secondly, it was an essentially spon-
taneous move in direct response to Peters's request. Hence Peters's activities as such were more important for the establishment of the colony than is
often assumed. If he had not made his trip in 1884 it is unlikely that there
would have been a German East Africa at all. Whatever may have induced
Bismarck to send Rohlfs to Zanzibar, it was clear that British interests there
were paramount. This would have made it difficult for Germany to annex
the island without provoking a serious crisis with Britain. This was not in
Bismarck's interest, but it is possible that the sending of Rohlfs was
intended to consolidate German ties with the Sultan in order to forestall or
discourage potential moves by the British. As long as multiple interests
were involved it would have been difficult for one nation to achieve an
exclusive claim. Furthermore, there is insufficient evidence to suggest that
the Rohlfs mission and Peters's trip had in some way or other been coordi-
nated by the German government. The thesis that Rohlfs's 'trip to
Zanzibar had been disguised as a mission to West Africa in order to ensure
Peters more time to collect his treaties'[197] is not very persuasive and lacks
documentary support.

The acquisition of German East Africa came as a surprise to most
contemporary observers. Bismarck suddenly saw a chance to crown his
colonial efforts at the end of an African conference. The attractiveness of
Peters's scheme lay in the fact that it made a further colonial claim possible
without provoking an imperial showdown over Zanzibar itself. Certainly it
was naive to assume that a German protectorate could flourish as Peters
envisaged in the neighbourhood of the Sultanate. However, Bismarck did
not grasp the nature of Zanzibari rule in the region, or the way in which
commerce was organized and carried out. Nor would this have been of any
interest to him.

The course of events revealed the significance of colonial activism as

[197] M. Reuss and G. R. Hartwig, 'Bismarck's Imperialism and the Rohlfs Mission', *The
South Atlantic Quarterly*, 74 (1975), 84.

such, and of the ideological forces which underpinned these activities. German East Africa was the manifestion of a national desire, a symbol of Germany's commitment to *Weltpolitik*. Many people in Germany now came to see Peters as the man to whom they owed this national asset.[198]

This colonial acquisition had little to do with the imminent threat of Germans being excluded from economic opportunity. The Berlin conference had just asserted the principles of free trade in the Congo basin, and East Africa had been incorporated for that purpose. Bismarck's move can hardly be explained on grounds of primary economic concern. Rather, the Chancellor sought to make himself popular in those circles on which he depended. He satisfied ambitions which sought to compensate for a widespread feeling of national inferiority and of endangered German prestige. In this political climate minor economic concerns were blown up into issues of national importance. This is what Bismarck had in mind when he told Boetticher that 'the whole colonial business is a swindle.'[199]

---

[198] See Bennigsen to Herbert von Bismarck, 30 Dec. 1888, RKolA 730, 169–72, BAB.
[199] Holstein's diary, 19 Nov. 1884, *Die Geheimen Papiere Friedrich von Holsteins*, ed. Norman Rich and M. H. Fischer, ii (Göttingen, 1957), 174.

3

'From the Nyassa to the Nile':
Peters and the German East Africa
Company (1885–1887)

> If Africa, that dark country, did not exist,
> we diplomats would have little to do.
>
> Count Münster, German ambassador
> to London, 1885[1]

BISMARCK, PETERS, AND THE HAMBURG MERCHANTS

With the publication of the imperial charter Peters overnight became a famous man. Official recognition did a lot to strengthen his self-confidence. His belief that he was swimming 'with a historical current' seemed to be confirmed. He saw 'the better part of the nation' standing behind him.[2] With the *Schutzbrief* in his pocket, he was confident that Bismarck would sanction a further series of *faits accomplis*,[3] a hope which—at least in part—was later to be frustrated. Correspondence with his family indicates how much Peters enjoyed public attention in those days.[4] More than twenty years later, he was still to recall his reception by the old Kaiser as one of the few 'brightly shining' moments 'from a grey past'.[5]

In the course of the following months Peters's self-confidence reached a stage that came 'close to megalomania'.[6] On a map which he sent to his brother he had marked the borders of his envisaged 'vast German colonial empire'. It stretched 'from Nyassa (Zambezi) to the Nile' and would 'quickly overtake the Congo state'. 'It will be the centre of the whole African system of states of the future, a source of wealth and power for our German nation.' This was the vision of a 'pan-African colonization

---

[1] Cited in H. Schneppen, *Why Kilimanjaro is in Tanzania* (Dar es Salaam, 1996).
[2] Peters to his mother, 29 March 1885, FP 2, BAK.
[3] Ibid.   [4] See ibid.   [5] Peters, *Gründung*, GS i. 177.
[6] Fabri's Promemoria to Bismarck, 5 July 1889, RKolA 6925, 42–8, BAB.

project', as Richard Krauel, the colonial expert in the Foreign Office, noted.[7] Sometimes, Peters wrote, 'proud images arise in front of me'. In such moments he saw himself 'entering Cairo from the south, like Napoleon I'.[8]

Peters's finances, however, presented a less proud picture. In fact, the Reich had chartered a venture which was to remain on the verge of bankruptcy for two more years. After his return to Berlin Peters worked to form a new organization which was to carry out the task of colonial development under imperial protection, the Deutsch-Ostafrikanische Gesellschaft. Carl Peters und Genossen (DOAG). It entered the Berlin Commercial Register on 2 April.[9] Peters exerted complete control over the company's affairs, having received a full power of attorney from the five-man board, which was composed of Behr, Lange, Jühlke Sen., and Consul Roghé. 'My position is almost that of a dictator', he wrote to his mother with great pride.[10] It was a peculiar situation. The establishment of Germany's empire in East Africa lay in the hands of a 28-year-old academic, who had neither entrepreneurial nor administrative experience. The only commercial task he had ever had to fulfil was to settle his uncle's last will.

In the first three months of its existence, the company sold 310 shares with a value of 270,000 marks[11]—a ridiculous amount to realize Peters's grand designs. The bulk of this money was spent on new expeditions into the African interior, so that by the middle of June only 63,000 marks were left.[12] Thus Peters had good reason to propose on 13 June 1885 that the company should now start seriously on 'the capitalist foundation' as its 'foremost and most urgent task'.[13]

The disastrous finances did little to undermine his Napoleonic ambitions. On the contrary. In a letter to his brother he mentioned a plan to establish a loan company to function as a sleeping partner in his East African enterprise. 'You will understand that for such a manipulation full confidence in the board is essential, so that I have to win over names like Bleichröder, Rothschild, etc. as members of the same.'[14] Many years later, Peters attempted to explain that he saw this form of organization, in which 'the board had all the rights and the subscribers all the duties', as a 'provisional

[7] Krauel to Herbert von Bismarck, 26 Oct. 1886, Bismarck Papers, B 64, 263 ff., BAF.
[8] Peters to Hermann, 16 Aug. 1885, FP 2, BAK.
[9] Peters, *Gründung*, GS i. 185.
[10] Peters to his mother, 29 March 1885, FP 2, BAK.
[11] AA note, 26 June 1885, RKolA 392, 80.
[12] Peters to Hermann, 14 June 1885, FP 2, BAK; Peters to Elli, 14 June 1885, FP 2, BAK.
[13] DOAG proceedings, 13 June 1885, FP 24, BAK.
[14] Peters to Hermann, 16 Aug. 1885, FP 2, BAK.

arrangement'.[15] Contemporary letters nevertheless indicate that in the summer of 1885 Peters was still naive enough to believe that he could attract large-scale capital without granting financiers some control over the use of the funds. Neither Peters's papers nor the company files indicate whether the DOAG board indeed approached Bleichröder and Rothschild for support, although there is some evidence of contacts with the Deutsche Bank.[16] In any event, none of these attempts to raise money came to anything.

In this critical situation, one man saved Peters's venture from collapse: the young banker Carl von der Heydt from Elberfeld. In July 1885 he invested 100,000 marks in the company and became a member of the board.[17] His was not one of the big banking houses, but his contribution made it possible for current activities in Germany and Africa to continue. It is quite clear that, given Peters's authoritarian leadership and exclusive control of the venture, von der Heydt took a risky step. He was not driven by pure financial reasoning. If Peters's venture had really been attractive for German capital, one would have expected a much stronger response to his fund-raising activities. But this was not the case. In fact, von der Heydt's enthusiasm for the venture seems to have been fuelled by a strong national-ist zeal which came close to Peters's own.[18]

One month before von der Heydt invested in Peters's enterprise, Bismarck had already started to look for ways in which the financial basis of the venture could be consolidated. It will be argued below that government intervention played a decisive part in the way in which the East African venture was to develop in the coming two years. State action was taken both within Germany and on the East African coast, as the present and the following chapters will reveal.

The early involvement of the state meant that Bismarck did precisely the opposite of what he had outlined as his colonial policy in the Reichstag in 1884: that the flag follows trade. With regard to East Africa, the Chancellor's proclaimed colonial strategy existed only on paper.

Two factors were largely responsible for this gap between concept and reality. First, the Chancellor lacked an understanding of how East African

---

[15] Peters, *Gründung*, GS i. 186.

[16] See Peters to Mathilde, 27 June 1885, FP 2, BAK; DOAG executive board meeting, minutes, 29 June 1885, 33 ff., 80 Ge 1, vol. 1, BAB; see also Kayser's Promemoria, 11 Oct. 1886, 18 f., RKolA 360, BAB.

[17] DOAG board meeting, minutes, 11 July 1885, DOAG Papers, vol. 1, 35, BAB.

[18] See *KPK* leaders, nos. 1, 2, and 3, 1886; they were published anonymously, but Peters refers to von der Heydt as the author: see GS iii. 282 (note).

trade functioned in general, and how European merchants operated within the Zanzibari commercial empire in particular. Secondly, his policy was not really designed to protect the established interests of the Hanseatic merchants. On the contrary, it concentrated on the rescue of the notoriously underfunded, but increasingly aggressive, venture under Peters.

Bismarck's initial idea was that he could bring about a fusion of interests. He sought an 'association' between the Peters group and the main Hamburg trading houses operating in Zanzibar.[19] In June 1885 the Chancellor instructed his envoy to the Hanseatic cities, Kusserow, to approach the merchants for this purpose.[20] The two major German firms operating in Zanzibar were O'Swald and Hansing. Both had started their commercial activities more than a generation earlier, at first engaging in the trade of cowrie shells from East to West Africa where they were used as currency. When this trade broke down, the firms successfully modified their commercial activities. Now they imported cloth, firearms, gunpowder, and steamers to Zanzibar. Their exports comprised mainly ivory, skins, spices, and copal.[21] The Sultan himself was a major customer of the merchants, but more importantly he had established a system of control and influence which secured long-distance trade on the major caravan routes to the interior. As a consequence, the Hamburg merchants' commercial profits relied heavily on friendly relations with the Sultan, as they repeatedly pointed out. The relationship between European businessmen on the one hand, and the Sultan and Indian merchants on the other, had secured mutual benefits; rising business profits for the traders meant increasing customs revenues for the Sultan.

Peters, with his grand designs for Africa, did not fit into this picture at all. However obscure the eventual size of the German territory may still have been, the basic goal of the charter of protection was obvious: it had sanctioned Peters's colonial acquisitions and given the green light for the company to establish control over the mainland. Since the territorial claims of the DOAG cut right across the major caravan routes to the interior, the Sultan's protests were not surprising. He realized that the German protectorate threatened the fragile political and commercial balance in the region.

Peters's first memo about the future development of the German colony emphasized that the company must aim 'at gaining the maritime coasts',

---

[19] Bismarck's marginal comment on Keudell to Bismarck, 15 June 1885, RKolA 421, 1, BAB.   [20] Ibid.
[21] H. Washausen, *Hamburg und die Kolonialpolitik des Deutschen Reiches, 1880 bis 1890* (Hamburg, 1968), 85, 91.

maintaining that this was an 'actual question of survival'.[22] But most coastal towns lay under the influence of the Sultan, so that DOAG priorities made a conflict with Said Bargash inevitable. How this conflict developed will be treated in some detail in the following chapter. For the moment it will suffice to recognize that DOAG claims provoked the Sultan's opposition.

Seen against this background, there was no possible scenario which could have secured what Bismarck sought: fusing Peters's enterprise with the Hanseatic firms *and* securing friendly relations with the Sultan. Bismarck's envoy to Hamburg, Kusserow, may have regarded the prospects for an association of German interests as 'not unfavourable',[23] but he had a tendency to be overenthusiastic in colonial matters anyway. As we will see, the Hanseatic merchants themselves had no real interest in such cooperation.

Scholars have offered different views on the attitudes and goals of the Hamburg merchants. Washausen has challenged Müller's assumption that the Zanzibar merchants had generally been hostile to colonial policy.[24] He argued instead that, although they did not initiate or take part in the first acquisitions, they still 'supported the German colonial endeavours'.[25]

If this was so, however, there remain important questions for which Washausen has not produced a satisfactory explanation. Why, for instance, did the Hamburg merchants continue to emphasize the importance of friendly relations with the Sultan if they ultimately supported the *Schutzbrief* policy which was a major threat to them? What could have suddenly converted them to the belief that Bismarck's policy opened a more promising prospect for their business and for securing higher profits than the established order? Or, if such a change in conviction did not occur, what other factors could have been responsible for their alleged support of Bismarck's course?

It seems that one possible key to the answer to these questions lies in the way in which the government handled Peters's venture on the one hand, and the Hanseatic interests on the other. However, before looking in closer detail at Bismarck's policy, two other points should be considered.

It is quite clear that the merchants distrusted Peters, who, in their eyes, lacked the commercial skill to run an enterprise.[26] However, this is only

---

[22] Peters's memorandum, 2 May 1885, RKolA 391, 38, BAB.

[23] Kusserow to Bismarck, 6 July 1885, RKolA 421, 2 ff., BAB.

[24] Washausen, *Hamburg*, 96

[25] Ibid. 86.

[26] Kusserow to Bismarck, 4 Dec. 1885, RKolA 421, 74; Kusserow to Bismarck, 26 March 1886, RKolA 359, 114; O'Swald to Bismarck, 25 Sept. 1888, RKolA 360, 126 ff.

part of the story, and arguably not the most important one. Even if Peters had not been DOAG leader, the *Schutzbrief* would still have been a blow to the Sultan's authority and provoked his opposition. Therefore, pointing to Peters alone does not sufficiently explain merchant opposition. The reasons were more profound. In fact, the German protectorate as such raised vital questions about the future of Hamburg commerce.

Early Hanseatic reactions to the *Schutzbrief* contain fierce criticism of Bismarck's colonial coup. O'Swald wrote in a memorandum of September 1885: 'The pioneers of German trade have been entirely ignored.' The government made its decision 'without taking into account that such action would damage certain interests, in order to pave the way for a problematic and, even more so, a dubious future'.[27] This was a clear statement, but it was not meant for publication.

It may be argued that the merchants shied away from expressing their criticism in public because they feared that Bismarck might ignore their interests altogether. With the granting of the charter Peters's East African venture had become a national undertaking, sanctioned by the Kaiser himself. The merchants soon had a taste of how Bismarck handled those who dared to question the East African venture in public. In August 1885 the Chancellor learned about newspaper articles in the *Magdeburger Zeitung* and the *Hamburger Correspondent* which were critical of DOAG activities.[28] He immediately instructed Kusserow, his Hamburg envoy, to issue a warning to Hamburg firms which he suspected of standing behind the criticism. The Chancellor threatened that if no quick settlement between the interests involved were reached, he was determined 'to drop the side which opposed an understanding'. He stressed that 'if this hit the merchants, existing trade relations would suffer seriously'.[29] In other words, if the merchants did not give in, the Reich would no longer consider their interests and would support the DOAG at their expense.

This must have been a bitter pill for the Hamburg merchants. For them, long established businesses were at stake. They were quick to deny that they had anything to do with the articles. Furthermore, they agreed to continue negotiations with Peters,[30] fearing they would be brushed aside if they did not comply with the policy of the government.[31]

[27] O'Swald & Co., Die Annexionen der Deutsch Ostafrikanischen Gesellschaft und die Wirkung auf die bestehenden Deutschen Handelsinteressen, (note), 621-1 Firma O'Swald, vol. 71, HStA (hereafter cited as O'Swald, Annexionen).

[28] Rantzau to [AA], 8 Aug. 1885 (copy), RKolA 393, 43–4, BAB.   [29] Ibid.

[30] Kusserow to Bismarck, 16 Aug. 1885, RKolA 393, 79–86, BAB.

[31] O'Swald, Annexionen, 621-1 Firma O'Swald, vol. 71, HStA Hamburg.

Unlike the Hamburg merchants, Peters had little to lose. He gambled high and was confident that the Chancellor was secretly in favour of his ideas of establishing a vast German empire.[32] His attitude displayed an extraordinary arrogance, which may have been fostered by his conviction that it was he, rather than the Hamburg merchants, who enjoyed the backing of the *Schutzbrief*. He suggested that Hansing and O'Swald should incorporate their businesses into the DOAG. Not surprisingly, this offer was not well received in Hamburg,[33] but Bismarck urged Kusserow to continue his efforts. The Chancellor also made it clear that all these negotiations had to be conducted under 'official leadership'.[34]

It is interesting to notice that after the Chancellor's threat the two merchant houses adopted different strategies in their dealings with the government. Whereas O'Swald chose to keep as much distance as possible, Hansing obviously felt that he had to demonstrate a more cooperative attitude. In response to Peters's scheme he suggested to the government that a large joint stock company should be formed, which was to be capitalized at 50 million marks. He also suggested the establishment of a subsidized steamship line, which he offered to run.[35] Hansing, unlike O'Swald, was quick to conform to official policy. Obviously he sought new opportunities in changing circumstances. On the other hand, Hansing's proposal is not sufficient evidence to suggest that he had become an imperialist at heart. His proposal for reorganization had been made in direct response to Peters's scheme, which simply aimed at swallowing the merchant businesses. Since Hansing's suggestions came immediately after Bismarck's threat to drop their interests altogether, it was meant to appease the Chancellor and to display a willingness to cooperate. As the correspondence of the following weeks shows, Hansing did nothing to push for the realization of his alternative scheme.

On 28 August 1885 Peters came forward with another proposal, which proved entirely unacceptable to the merchants. He estimated that O'Swald operated with a capital base of 500,000 marks, and Hansing with some 700,000 marks, both sums being insufficient to establish a large-scale colonial venture. He offered to take over the two companies, and to provide the merchants with a seat on his board. Kusserow noted that O'Swald and Hansing were surprised by such naivity. They even took offence at Peters's scheme. They would virtually be compelled to liquidate their businesses.

[32] Peters to Hermann, 16 Aug. 1885, FP 2, BAK.
[33] Kusserow to Bismarck, 16 Aug. 1885, RKolA 421, 19, BAB.
[34] Marginal note on ibid. 21.
[35] Kusserow to Bismarck, 20 Aug. 1885, RKolA 421, 24–7, BAB.

Furthermore, they pointed out that Peters was operating with incorrect figures, asserting that their operating capital was about four times higher than DOAG estimates. Finally, they made clear that 'many millions of marks' would be necessary to make them relinquish their businesses on the East African coast.[36]

To resolve the deadlock, Kusserow invited the parties to further negotiations. On 12 September talks began under the auspices of the Hamburg envoy and the two consuls Arendt and Raschdau.[37] The talks dragged on until December before an understanding was reached. This involved no more than a division of their commercial activities in the region. By no means did it constitute a fusion of interests, as Bismarck had envisaged. The DOAG agreed to confine its business to the mainland and to conduct its imports and exports through the agency of O'Swald and Hansing, except those goods that were needed for the development of their own venture. The two firms, on the other hand, agreed to operate as agents without charging fees during the first two years. Thereafter they would receive a commission of 2 per cent on all traded goods.[38] However, the agreement did not come into effect until April 1887 when a contract containing slight modifications was signed by both sides.[39]

The Hamburg merchants had been playing for time, and eventually they managed to maintain their independence. In a way, this was easier to achieve precisely because Peters's proposals were so unrealistic and impudent. The government could do little to pressurize the merchants into a fusion as long as Peters maintained his unrealistic demands.

Throughout 1885 Hanseatic concerns focused on maintaining good relations with the Sultan. Hansing had already found that simply running financial operations for the DOAG on the spot had caused the Sultan to become increasingly reserved towards the firm.[40] Any closer alliance with the declared enemy of the Sultan would have endangered their businesses even further. In May 1886 the German consul in Zanzibar observed that 'the strong antagonism between the Hanseatic firms and the representatives of the company [i.e. the DOAG] continues.'[41]

---

[36] Kusserow to Bismarck, 2 Sept 1885, RKolA 421, 39 ff., BAB.

[37] Kusserow's report, RKolA 421, 49 ff., BAB.

[38] O'Swald and Hansing to DOAG, 19 Nov. 1885 (copy), O'Swald to DOAG, 5 Dec. 1885 (copy), O'Swald to Delbrück, 14 Feb. 1887, 621-1 Firma O'Swald & Co, vol. 71, HStA Hamburg.

[39] Contract of 16 April 1887, copies in 621-1 Firma O'Swald & Co, vol. 71, HStA and RKolA 421, 109–10, BAB.   [40] See Washausen, *Hamburg*, 105.

[41] Arendt to Kayser, 13 May 1886, Kayser Papers 3, Staats- und Universitätsbibliothek Hamburg.

BISMARCK, PETERS, AND THE GERMAN BANKS

In autumn 1885 von der Heydt worked out a plan for reorganizing the DOAG into the legal form of a corporation.[42] Peters still indulged in grandiose ideas. He envisaged the emergence of 'German East Africa' as a 'protected state of the empire'. He saw himself as 'president of the government with monarchic competences', with 'full rights over the civil service, finance . . . and, in case of emergency, the right to decide over war and peace'.[43]

It has been argued that von der Heydt's reorganization plan was designed to push Peters aside.[44] However, there is insufficient evidence to support this view. In fact, there was no real alternative to this step. Peters, in his private correspondence, never mentioned any quarrel with the banker, nor is there any indication that he objected to von der Heydt's organizational plans. One later episode demonstrates that the two men worked hand in hand. In December 1885 the relationship between Lange and Peters deteriorated. Lange had suggested selling the whole company, which made Peters furious, triggering a serious dispute in the DOAG board meeting.[45] von der Heydt clearly supported Peters in this case, and there were other occasions later on where he continued to do so.[46] The quarrel eventually resulted in Lange's resignation. He left after securing compensation of 10, 000 marks.

On 14 December the general assembly of the DOAG eventually adopted the plan to reconstitute itself as a corporation. A 'provisional organization' was established, whose control still lay with Peters. The issue of shares, however, now lay in the hands of the banking house von der Heydt, which was also in charge of running the accounts. This was to enable a 'quicker and easier financing of the enterprise'.[47]

In February 1886 Peters submitted his proposals to the Foreign Office,[48] seeking to reconstitute the DOAG as a corporation according to Prussian state law. However, the Foreign Office was highly sceptical of the constitutional terms (*Präsident der Regierung, Regierung, Landesrat*, etc.) employed in the draft.[49] Peters's proposal looked as if this was the constitution of a state and not of a private venture. 'Such a view has to be opposed',

---

[42] Peters to Hermann, 16 Oct. 1885, FP 2, BAK.   [43] Ibid.

[44] Müller, *Deutschland*, 153.

[45] Minutes of DOAG meeting, 14 Dec. 1885, DOAG Papers, 80 Ge 1, vol. 1, 54/55, BAB.

[46] See Ch. 5.   [47] Wagner, *Deutsch-Ostafrika*, 99–100.

[48] Grundverfassung der Deutsch Ostafrikanischen Gesellschaft, RKolA 409, 3–6, BAB.

[49] H. von Bismarck to von Schelling, 15 Feb. 1886, RKolA 409, 7–10, BAB.

Bismarck wrote to the State Secretary in the Imperial Ministry of Justice.[50] The company had no relations with foreign powers, as Article 35 of the draft implied. Consequently it could not declare war or make peace, nor could it conclude treaties with any foreign power. Bismarck also objected to the implication that the Charter of Protection constituted a contract with the Kaiser or the Reich. Rather, it was an act of grace, which could be withdrawn or changed at any time. The Foreign Office recommended the use of the statutes of the New Guinea Company as a model and asked the ministry to formulate an appropriate draft for the DOAG. Since the new statutes were important to secure the financial basis, a swift settlement was required, as Bismarck emphasized.

But the issue was a quite complex matter which touched upon the responsibilities of other departments as well. During the summer, it was to involve eight representatives from the Ministries of Trade, Justice, and the Interior.[51] On the basis of the DOAG draft the Hamburg merchants had formulated their own demands, without which they would not be prepared to provide any capital for the reorganized venture.[52]

At the same time the attempt to find German investors in London failed. In January Peters went on a three-week trip to London to seek the support of German firms for the DOAG.[53] Herbert von Bismarck even instructed the German consulate to assist him in this matter,[54] but nobody was willing to make a financial commitment. Peters also approached British circles around the shipping magnate Mackinnon and Sir Donald Currie, who were interested in East Africa. He invited them to invest in the DOAG, but they were not to be seduced either.

Faced with such difficulties, Peters gradually increased his demands for state support for his venture. In a memorandum to the Foreign Office of 3 April 1886 he asked for some 'moral support from the state', in order to facilitate the financing of the company. He suggested that the Preussische Seehandlung, a state bank, should be the place where DOAG shares were to be issued in the future.[55] Bismarck instructed the Foreign Office to forward

[50] H. von Bismarck to von Schelling, 15 Feb. 1886, RKolA 409, 7–10, BAB.

[51] See invitation for consultations in the Foreign Office, 23 Aug. 1886, RKolA 409, 193, BAB.

[52] See copy of statute draft with comments, 21 May 1886, RKolA 409, 160 ff., BAB.

[53] See Peters, 'Vorläufiger Bericht über die Resultate der im Interesse der Detusch-ostafrikanischen Kolonialunternehmens in London gepflogenen Verhandlungen', 3 Feb. 1886, RKolA 395, 18–21.

[54] See H. von Bismarck to Hatzfeldt, 4 Feb. 1886, RKolA 395, 22, BAB.

[55] Memorandum of 3 April, encl. in Peters to Foreign Office, 4 April 1886, RKolA 359, 118 ff., BAB.

Peters's request to the Seehandlung. The Chancellor proposed to the bank that it should arrange a meeting with Peters and seek to cooperate with him.[56] Eventually a commissioner from the Seehandlung was sent to attend consultations between Kayser and the DOAG in the Foreign Office. As a result, the bank agreed to Peters's proposal.[57]

Three months later, after having campaigned for the DOAG in southern Germany and the Rhineland, Peters modified his previous request. Now he proposed that the Seehandlung should actually approach potential financiers and seek to win them over for the East African venture.[58] Krauel noted: 'This goes further than originally intended.'[59] Nevertheless, Bismarck again supported Peters's proposal, which was quickly forwarded to the Seehandlung, with the approval of the Chancellor.[60]

Peters also reported on the results of his fund-raising campaign.[61] He assured the Foreign Office that it would be easy to raise a million marks, once the government had approved the reorganization of the company. But Peters was bluffing. When the Seehandlung later asked him to supply more detailed information on those people interested, he did not send them anything.[62] At one point he stated that the Deutsche Bank would be willing to supply a quarter of a million marks, but Director Siemens, when approached by the Seehandlung, said that he had never given such a promise.[63] On 4 November 1886 Peters eventually had to admit to the Foreign Office that prospective investment amounted to a mere 170,000 marks.[64]

This episode was important in so far as it triggered an eventual shift from Peters's fund-raising activities towards an exclusive engagement by the state to secure the necessary funds. The DOAG was instructed to refrain from any further attempts to contact potential investors.[65] Bismarck, it may be argued, had by then drawn two major conclusions. First, the only way out of the problem was a stronger involvement of the Seehandlung in order to mobilize private capital. Secondly, he became willing to provide a sort of state guarantee for the East African venture, without which potential investors were not to be attracted.

[56] AA to Seehandlung, 7 April 1886, RKolA 359, 125, BAB.
[57] Seehandlung [to AA?], 12 April 1886, RKolA 359, 141, BAB.
[58] Peters to Berchem, 26 July 1886, RKolA 360, 8, BAB.
[59] Marginal note, ibid.
[60] AA to von Scholz, 28 July 1886, RKolA 360, 9–11; von Lenz to Rötger, 31 July 1886 (copy), RKolA 360, 13; AA to Peters, 2 Aug. 1886, RKolA 360, 14, BAB.
[61] Peters to Berchem, 3 June 1886, RKolA 359, 159–61, BAB.
[62] Kayser's memo, 11 Oct. 1886, RKolA 360, 18 ff., BAB.   [63] Ibid.
[64] Peters to Foreign Office, 4 Nov. 1886, RKolA 360, 27, BAB.
[65] AA note, 29 Oct. 1885, RKolA 360, 25, BAB.

Eventually the Kaiser enabled the Seehandlung to invest 500,000 marks in the DOAG.[66] Furthermore, the bank contacted potential financiers, and this was an equally important step. A Foreign Office memorandum provides interesting insights in this respect. Leading representatives of the bank pointed out that they were faced with a difficult task. They had concluded that potential financiers were only likely to invest if they could expect other advantages, privileges, and benefits in return.[67] For this reason it was seen as essential at the Seehandlung that the president of the bank should approach potential financiers.[68] The implication of this internal assessment is important: the mobilization of capital for East Africa involved an implicit deal. Investors who helped to finance the DOAG would be rewarded by the Seehandlung's support on other occasions. This suggests that the East African venture had no intrinsic attraction for most banks and industrialists. If they supported the venture, they expected to benefit in other ways in return for their loyalty.

The activities of the Seehandlung succeeded in enlisting a number of banking houses and industrialists to provide new capital for the reconstitution of the DOAG, amounting to a total sum of 2,080,000 marks. Apart from the Seehandlung (500,000 marks) and von der Heydt (who increased his share to 400,000 marks), the largest sum was invested by the banking house Mendelssohn-Bartholdy (100,000 marks). The list of stockholders contained 102 names, who together had bought 208 shares at 10,000 marks each.[69] As Müller has rightly pointed out, most investors had bought no more than one share.[70] This again supports the thesis that an investment in the DOAG was made in order to demonstrate patriotism and loyalty to the state. It was not seen as a lucrative investment.

The reorganization of the DOAG had important consequences for Peters's future role. He had lost his previous position of exclusive leadership, which was incompatible with the need to acquire large-scale capital. Control over the new venture now lay largely in the hands of the newly

---

[66] *Kölnische Zeitung*, 7 Feb. 1887, enclosed in RKolA 410, 54; *NAZ*, 7 Feb. 1887, evening edition; *NAZ*, 31 July 1887, enclosed in RKolA 360, 100; list of stockholders, RKolA 410, 131–9; Scholz to Caprivi, 3 May 1890, RKolA 361, 85 ff.; DOAG to Kaiser, 28 Sept. 1888, RKolA 360, 136 ff., BAB. It should be noted that it is not entirely clear from the sources whether the invested sum was indeed Wilhelm's private money (this is assumed by Bair, 'Peters', 143, and Müller, *Deutschland*, 165), or came from some other fund.

[67] Kayser's memo, 11 Oct. 1886, RKolA 360, 19, BAB.　　　　　　　　　　[68] Ibid.

[69] Seehandlung certificate, 7 March 1887, and list of stockholders, RKolA 410, 130–9, BAB.　　　　　　　　　　　　　　　　　　[70] Müller, *Deutschland*, 173.

formed board of directors and its standing committee. Peters, on the other hand, did not vanish from the scene. On the contrary, he was appointed director of the corporation and thus assigned the leading post in the executive. He was also granted free shares amounting to 100,000 marks.[71]

Oechelhäuser, one of the major new financiers, felt after his first meeting with Peters that 'in professional terms he made quite a good impression'.[72] He saw no reason to oppose Peters's aspiration to the post of DOAG director in Zanzibar.[73] Peters could also still count upon the support of his early associates, such as von der Heydt, Grimm, and Behr. It seems that after his intensive campaigning throughout Germany Peters had become a quite popular figure who could not easily be thrown overboard without damaging the colonial movement as a whole. He was still president of the second-largest colonial association, which grew rapidly in comparison with the longer-established Kolonialverein.[74]

Reorganization of the DOAG also involved other significant changes.[75] The new board of directors consisted of 21 to 27 members, three of whom were appointed by the Chancellor himself. The rest were to be elected by the general assembly. The board of directors controlled the executive and could remove its members. A government official was appointed commissioner. He was entitled to attend every meeting of the board and had unlimited access to all accounts and correspondence. This post was taken by Kayser, who was to function as a major channel between the company and the government in the future.

It is interesting to notice that the leading investors themselves had proposed that the Chancellor should appoint members to the board of directors.[76] Whether they wanted all of them to be chosen by Bismarck is not quite clear, but they argued that a number of firms would make their contribution dependent on appointments being made by the Chancellor.[77] Mendelssohn-Bartholdy, the third-largest shareholder, saw in such an arrangement a 'guarantee . . . for the operation of the DOAG'.[78] A ministerial note, probably from the Foreign Office, likewise concluded 'that these were proposals which would strengthen the leadership and the prestige of the company, and would thus also be in the interest of this department'.[79] Kayser, as the government's representative, came to play an active part in

[71] See RKolA 410, 129, BAB.
[72] Oechelhäuser to ?, 4 Dec. 1886, RKolA 360, 42–3.   [73] Ibid.
[74] See pp. 86 ff.
[75] See statute of 26 Feb. 1887, 1 ff., DOAG, 80 Ge 1, vol. 2, BAB.
[76] Kayser's note, 11 Jan. 1887, RKolA 410, 28, BAB.   [77] Ibid.
[78] Ibid.   [79] No date, RKolA 410, 34 ff., BAB.

shaping the activities of the company.[80] From the very beginning he became involved in setting future agendas for East Africa.[81]

There is sufficient evidence to suggest that the reorganization of the DOAG marked another milestone on the road to colonial rule through the state. Müller's conclusion that the DOAG had become 'the prey' of a pro-colonial 'financial oligarchy'[82] is misleading, as it implies that capitalist circles had been the driving force behind the process of reorganization. This, however, was not the case. Rather, state intervention was crucial to bail the venture out of trouble. The case of East Africa clearly supports the view that most German banks remained reserved towards colonial projects in the Bismarckian period.[83] Von der Heydt was by no means representative of the German financial world. His impetus to participate in the DOAG hardly resulted from a pure calculation of costs and benefits. As we have seen, he was driven by a strong nationalist zeal and his commitment to pan-German ideas.

Looking at the development of the DOAG in the years 1885–7, a certain pattern emerges with respect to Bismarck's policy. There was a consistent effort to prevent the DOAG from collapse. However, the policies to achieve this aim were modified in the course of the two years. It is true that Bismarck once remarked in anger that he would watch the breakdown of Peters's venture in silence.[84] However, the foregoing analysis suggests that this statement is misleading. The Chancellor's actual policy aimed at the opposite.

State support for financing the East African venture proceeded in two major steps. First, there was official coordination and promotion of a fusion of all German interests with the ultimate goal of enlisting the Hanseatic merchants to finance Peters's mainland venture. When this approach had failed, the Prussian Seehandlung was urged to look for potential investors. The Kaiser's decision to provide the state bank with 500,000 marks was to provide a significant incentive. It signalled to potential investors that by lending support to the East African venture they could count on other benefits and privileges.

---

[80] See Ch. 4.

[81] See Delbrück to ?, 25 March 1887, commenting on the setting of the new DOAG agenda, March 1887, I HA, Rep. 109, 5360, 12 ff., GStA-PK.

[82] Müller, *Deutschland*, 174.

[83] B. Barth, *Die deutsche Hochfinanz und die Imperialismen* (Stuttgart, 1995), 43.

[84] Berchem's note, 18 July 1886, RKolA 360, 4 ff.; see also Rantzau to Herbert von Bismarck, 12 Oct. 1886, Bismarck Papers, F3, BAF.

'FUROR TEUTONICUS':[85] PETERS, THE MISSIONS, AND THE
GERMAN NATIONAL LEAGUE OF WOMEN

Besides trading and banking circles, missionary societies also became a
focus of Peters's activities. He was guided by the idea that missionary work
could be exploited for his own ends, both in Germany and in the new colony
itself. He hoped that integrating missionary interests would widen public
support for his own colonial venture at home.

The correspondence of the Neukirchen missionary Julius Stursberg
from November 1885 provides interesting insights in this respect.
Stursberg had sought to contact the DOAG to discuss the establishment of
a mission in East Africa. He instructed a friend from Barmen to speak with
von der Heydt and Peters. Both DOAG men made clear that they wanted to
have a 'big and well-known Protestant missionary society'. The phrasing of
the letter further implies that they were mainly interested in the potential
publicity effect, and in financial investments on the ground.[86] Such expectations could not be met by the tiny Neukirchen Mission, so that no further
cooperation resulted from the meeting.

However, the large missionary societies responded with some reluctance
to a potential involvement in East Africa. In part, financial considerations
may have played a role.[87] Above all, however, there was a debate about their
future position towards politics and the supranational or international
character of mission work. This was also a major theme at the Bremen
mission conference of 27–9 October 1885, in which the delegates discussed
their attitudes towards the German colonial movement. With regard to
East Africa, there was particular confusion about Peters's 'exorbitant' land
acquisitions. Doubts were raised as to whether all that land had in fact been
secured in a decent way.[88] (In fact, the land question was put on ice until the
early 1890s when repeated disputes arose between governor Soden and the
reorganized DOAG about East African land rights.) In the event, established societies such as the Berliner Missionsgesellschaft decided to take a
wait-and-see attitude for the time being.

[85] Gustav Warneck, in *AMZ* 1886, 317.

[86] See Schlurmann to Stursberg, 9 Nov. 1885, cited in B. Brandl, *Die Neukirchener Mission*
(Cologne, 1998), 161-2.

[87] H. J. Niesel, *Kolonialverwaltung und Mission in Deutsch Ostafrika 1890–1914* (Diss. FU
Berlin, 1971), 51.

[88] See 'Eine besondere Missions-Konferenz', *Allgemeine Missions-Zeitschrift*, 1885,
545–63, here 553, 559, 561.

Nevertheless, there was a small Protestant circle in Berlin who had started to discuss the possibility of missionary work as early as April 1885.[89] From the very beginning there were personal links to the inner circle of the DOAG. Among Peters's friends was the Berlin pastor Ludwig Diestelkamp, who had introduced him to the Konservative Club in 1884, shortly after his return from London.[90] Diestelkamp was a driving force behind the idea of an East African mission.[91] As the existing Berliner Missionsgesellschaft remained hesitant, the idea of a new society for East Africa was born. This may not have matched von der Heydt's and Peters's initial intentions. But it was a way to secure at least some public attention.

Beside Julius Diestelkamp and his son-in-law, pastor Berlin, there were also two women with links to the DOAG who were involved in the initial talks: Countess Pfeil, the wife of Peters's early associate, and Baroness von Bülow, the sister of a young DOAG member and an acquaintance of Peters.[92] On 26 October 1885 a provisional executive committee was formed to prepare the founding of the new society. In spring 1886 a statute was adopted, stating the two major purposes of the Deutsch-Ostafrikanische Evangelische Missionsgesellschaft (which became known as Berlin III): (1) the spiritual and physical care of German emigrants; (2) an evangelical mission in German East Africa.[93]

Whether Peters himself had in fact organized the first meetings is not entirely clear. Missionary Inspector Büttner stated that Peters had 'keenly supported' the new society in its early phase. Peters had certainly seized the initiative for founding the new society by early 1886.[94] With a series of co-options, he made sure that the DOAG was strongly represented on the new executive board. Furthermore, his colonial venture also administered the finances of the new society through DOAG treasurer Hollmann.[95] Thus the Protestant mission for East Africa emerged in close cooperation with the Peters group. In public, the new society was in fact seen as a DOAG creation; in 1887 a journalist from the newspaper *Daheim* asked

[89] 'Die Genesis der Deutsch-Ostafrikanischen Evangelischen Missionsgesellschaft' [1886], M 171, Archiv der Bethel-Mission, Wuppertal (hereafter cited as ABM).

[90] See Peters, *Gründung*, GS i. 149.

[91] Büttner [to Redaktion *Daheim*], 27 Nov. 1887, M 167, ABM.

[92] Ibid.; see also 'Genesis der Deutsch-Ostafrikanischen Missionsgesellschaft' [1886], M 171, ABM.

[93] 'Genesis der Deutsch-Ostafrikanischen Missionsgesellschaft' [1886], M 171, ABM.

[94] See minutes of the executive board meetings, 25 and 29 March 1886, 12 and 27 April 1886, 13 May 1886, M2, ABM.

[95] Minute of executive board meeting, 29 March 1886, M2, ABM.

Mission Inspector Büttner: 'is yours identical with the one founded by Peters?'[96]

Peters did not hesitate to exploit the society for his own ends. A case in point was the use of pastor Greiner as an interpreter in his negotiations with the Sultan of Zanzibar.[97] Peters saw missionaries as a welcome means of educating the natives to work, and he was the one who pushed for a revision of the statutes. Under §17, the new version listed the 'education for work' as the primary goal of missionary work. It was adopted without dissent.[98]

The close connection of DOAG and missionary interests in Berlin III met with criticism in other Protestant circles. Above all, the prominent missionary publicist and editor of the *Allgemeine Missions-Zeitschrift*, Gustav Warneck, criticized his missionary colleagues for drawing too close to politics and for being influenced too much by the national idea.[99] Despite attempts by pastor Diestelkamp to solve the embarrassing dispute, the gulf remained. Peters and Warneck were not on good terms with each other. Nevertheless, this did not prevent Berlin III from continuing on its established basis. When Diestelkamp considered a closer cooperation with the older society, Berlin I, the plan was again blocked by Peters. The latter still hoped to manipulate the newly founded society for his own purposes.

In 1887, however, the intimate relationship between Peters and Berlin III cooled, and eventually there was a split. Although there is a gap in the sources for the relevant period, we have reason to assume that this had to do with Peters's mobilization of a German Catholic mission for East Africa. Peters's aim in this move was to rally further support in southern Germany. Hitherto, only French Catholic missionaries had been active in the region. Through his Bavarian agent, Freiherr von Gravenreuth, Peters contacted Pater Andreas Amrhein, from the Catholic mission at St Ottilien, southwest of Munich. A German official portrayed Amrhein as a 'German-minded man' who would focus on 'Germanizing' the new territories and who opposed an expansion of French influence. The plan for a new mission was welcomed by the Bavarian bishops of Munich and Augsburg, and the young Bavarian Prince Ludwig was enthusiastic as well.

When Peters left for Zanzibar as DOAG director in spring 1887, he

[96] Redaktion *Daheim* [to Büttner], 26 Nov. 1887, M 167, ABM.
[97] See DOAG confidential report, 80 Ge 1/2, 35 ff., BAB.
[98] Executive board minutes of 27 April 1886 and 29 July 1886 and enclosed copy of the adopted statute, M2, ABM.
[99] G. Warneck, 'Nachschrift', *AMZ* 1886, 226–31; for the Peters–Warneck dispute cf. also 'Modernste Missionsgeschichtsschreibung', *AMZ* 1886, 297–317.

travelled via Rome, where he signed an agreement with Amrhein.[100] It laid down the borders of two territorial strips within the German sphere of influence, where the Catholics were to work. The two areas stretched from the Indian Ocean right across to the borders of the Congo Free State. In fact, the arrangement implied a future geographical separation of the two Christian denominations. Furthermore, the treaty envisaged close cooperation between the DOAG and missionary work. A company agent was to be based at each mission station, and the arrangement committed the Fathers 'not to damage the German-national interests of the DOAG'.

When the agreement became known in Germany,[101] it alarmed both the German government and Protestant missionary circles. Apparently Peters had acted without prior consultation with the DOAG board, and he had not informed the Foreign Office about his plans. The Protestants complained to the government that implementation of the agreement would put their own denomination at a disadavantage.[102]

The German government, on the other hand, wanted to keep French influence in the new colony to a minimum. Hitherto, the Apostolic Prefecture of Zanzibar had been led by a French bishop, and the Germans were particularly suspicious of Cardinal Lavigerie of Carthague. Bismarck's envoy in Rome called him an ambitious *Kirchenfürst*, who had succeeded in controlling more or less all missionary work in the northern half of Africa.[103] Lavigerie had already expanded his activities as far as the western half of the German sphere, i.e. the region of the Great Lakes. The eastern half, on the other hand, was the responsibility of Bishop Courmont of the French Congregation of the Holy Ghost.[104] Bismarck urged his envoy to impress on the Pope that the Curia should not take any steps 'in favour of France', as far as German territory was concerned.[105] The pope should also consider whether a vicar of German nationality could be chosen. 'It remains of importance to us that the influence of Cardinal Lavigerie is excluded from German territory, and that an independent Apostolic Prefecture is established.'[106] This German concern was not ignored in the Vatican. In November, the Propaganda Congregation

[100] Contract of 16 April 1887, copy and two maps, RKolA 854, 14–18, 29, BAB.
[101] *Deutsches Tageblatt*, 21 April 1887; *Germania*, 26 April 1887, 4 May 1887, 16 June 1887, 2 Oct. 1887; *Kölnische Zeitung*, 8 May 1887.
[102] EMDOA to Bismarck, 9 May 1887, RKolA 854, 34–5, BAB.
[103] Schlözer to Bismarck, 21 April 1887, RKolA 854, 10–13, BAB.
[104] Ibid. 13.
[105] Bismarck's marginal note on Schlözer to Bismarck, 21 April 1887, RKolA 854, 12; AA to Schlözer, 4 May 1887, RKolA 854, 30, BAB.
[106] AA to Schlözer, 21 May 1887, RKolA 854, 44, BAB.

decided to split the Zanzibar vicarate and to found a new prefecture (South Zanzibar) for the German Benedictines.[107]

Furthermore, the German government blocked the geographical separation of the two denominations implied in the arrangement between Amrhein and Peters. The Foreign Office argued that such provisions violated article 6 of the Congo Act and that the DOAG did not in general plan to regulate missionary work through such agreements.[108]

Although Peters's agreement was rejected, he had nevertheless ensured that a German Catholic mission would start its work in East Africa soon. In fact, the first Benedictines departed for East Africa in November 1887, founding a station at Pugu, near Dar Es Salaam. Thus, by 1888 two German missionary societies had entered the field, both starting in close cooperation with Peters's DOAG.

Another factor which alienated Berlin III concerned Peters's acquaintance, Frieda von Bülow, and the founding of a German National League of Women. From the very beginning, medical care for the German community in East Africa had been a primary interest of Countess Pfeil and Baroness von Bülow. Von Bülow had agreed to go to Zanzibar at her own expense, and to establish a hospital on the mainland. This was originally planned under the auspices of the missionary society. In the course of 1886, however, a dispute arose over the emphasis of the confessional character of the venture. Von Bülow wanted to accept donations from Catholic circles. She also emphasized the nationalist character of the project. Eventually, the differences led to a split and the foundation of a separate German National League of Women.[109] Again, Carl Peters was the *spiritus rector* of the new association.[110] He published passionate articles in the *Kolonial-Politische Korrespondenz* (*KPK*), advertising the new organization. Von Bülow managed to secure from the missionary society all those funds which had been donated for her project,[111] but Berlin III now pursued its own plans for a hospital in East Africa. This rivalry eventually led to a break between Peters and Büttner. In December 1887 the DOAG director was excluded from the board of the missionary society.[112]

These episodes reveal that Peters's enthusiasm for the missions did not

[107] Verdict of the Congregation of Propaganda, 16 Nov. 1887 (copy), RKolA 854, 62–3, BAB.

[108] AA to Schlözer (draft), 21 May 1887, RKolA 854, 43–4, BAB.

[109] EMDOA to ?, 27 Feb. 1887, 27 April 1887, M 167, ABM.

[110] See Frieda von Bülow to Pastor?, 22 March 1887, M 167, ABM.

[111] EMDOA to ?, 27 April 1887, M 167, ABM.

[112] [EMDOA] to Peters, 29 Dec. 1887, M 170, ABM.

result from a genuine sympathy for their spiritual objectives. Unlike the rest of his family, which mainly consisted of pastors, he seemed a less than committed Christian. He spoke with some contempt about the clergy,[113] calling Fabri a 'goat of heaven'.[114] Nevertheless, he was clever enough to seek their support when it served his own purposes. At least some missionaries seem to have had no objections to Peters's colonizing agenda, particularly his ideas about the recruitment of African labour. Since the DOAG and Berlin III were so closely intertwined in the early days, Peters's ideas about enforced labour in the new colony cannot have been unknown to them.

THE DRUMMER: PAN-GERMAN AGITATION FOR THE COLONIAL CAUSE

Peters's failure to raise capital did little to discourage him. He was driven by enormous energy and strong confidence in his eventual success. Between May 1885 and February 1887 he made at least fifty-seven speeches in thirty-three different German cities.[115] Peters proved to be a restless agitator who was popular enough to fill local assembly halls and captivate his audience. As Irmer put it, he was an 'eminent force of agitation'.[116]

What gave him such confidence that the venture would eventually overcome its major obstacles? Certainly, Peters's character may provide part of the answer, as he was not a man to give up quickly. More importantly, however, official backing seems to provide an important key to understanding Peters's self-confidence. Supplied with the Imperial Charter, he counted upon Bismarck's support. This conviction was reinforced in the summer of 1885 when Bismarck ordered German warships to line up in front of Zanzibar town. As we will see later, flexing German muscles forced Sultan Said Bargash to accept the German claim to the mainland. From then on, Peters had no doubt that the Chancellor would eventually step in to prevent the company's final collapse. The course of events proved him right.

Peters's aim was to achieve a leading position within the organized colonial movement. As early as May 1885 he envisaged a new central organization which was 'to represent the general interests of German

---

[113] See Peters to his sister Mathilde, 16 Feb. 1895, note in FP 5, BAK.
[114] Peters to brother Hermann, 16 Aug. 1885, PP 92, BAB.
[115] These figures have been collected from Peters's private letters and from *KPK* editions.
[116] Irmer to Bennigsen, 2 Aug. 1890, note in FP 13, BAK.

colonization'.[117] Clearly, these activities challenged the position of the established Kolonialverein. Peters's plan was supported by a number of other associations, such as the Deutscher Exportverein (Berlin), the society Deutsche Kolonie Süd-Afrika (Leipzig), and Friedrich Ratzel's Verein zum Schutze deutscher Interessen im Auslande (Munich). A commission of five members was founded to take the necessary steps in this direction.[118]

In May 1885 Peters also set up his own journal, the *Kolonial-Politische Korrespondenz* (*KPK*). By 1887 its circulation amounted to 6,000 copies and it was delivered to members of the GfdK and to all major newspapers in Germany.[119] The *KPK*, being closely controlled by Peters himself,[120] provided news about the East African venture and functioned as a mouthpiece for his nationalist agitation and colonial ideas.

In his first *KPK* essay[121] Peters stated: 'The German colonial movement is the natural continuation of the German efforts for unification.' It was natural, he continued, that the German *Volk*, after having established its European power position on the battlefields of Sedan and Königgrätz, felt the need to terminate its 'miserable and almost contemptible position overseas'. It had felt the necessity to 'participate in the material advantages which the development of mastery on a large scale has always offered'.

Significantly, Peters remained extremely vague as to what these material advantages would be. In fact, he did not yet know himself what direction economic exploitation in East Africa would take, or in what ways it could be realized. In the first number of the *KPK* he announced that the journal would function as a forum where 'statistical material' would be presented as hints for 'German export production'. However, subsequent editions did not fulfil this promise, and indeed the *KPK* completely neglected trade figures. The reason for this was simple: encouraging figures did not exist. German exports to East Africa were minimal, and prospects appeared, at the least, dubious.[122] There was no large-scale market for German goods, and as long as the financial foundation of the German East African company was not secured, this would remain the case. 'Overall this is a fairly sad picture', Toeppen summed up.[123]

Hence, whenever Peters used economic arguments they remained vague

---

[117] See Wagner, *Deutsch-Ostafrika*, 66.   [118] Ibid. 66–7.

[119] *KPK*, no. 7, 19 Feb. 1887, 53.

[120] Peters to Mathilde, 27 June 1885, FP 2, BAK.

[121] 'Die deutsche Kolonialbewegung, die Gesellschaft für deutsche Kolonisation und die Deutsch-Ostafrikanische Gesellschaft', *KPK*, no. 1, 16 May 1885.

[122] See K. Toeppen, 'Einige Beobachtungen und Erkundigungen in den deutschen Schutzgebieten Ostafrikas', *Deutsche Kolonialzeitung*, 3 (1886), 518–23.

[123] Ibid. 523.

and stereotyped, without much relevance to the realities of East Africa. His statements were so vague that they could not easily be attacked by insiders, such as the Hamburg firms. It was even more difficult to oppose Peters's nationalist agitation, as one could quickly be accused of being hostile to the Reich. This weapon had been exploited by the parties loyal to Bismarck in the election campaign, and it seems that it had worked well to defeat the Left Liberals. Peters lost no opportunity to play the nationalist card. It is notable that his programme grew increasingly aggressive after the German fleet had threatened the Sultan in August 1885.[124] Once the government had demonstrated its determination to protect DOAG claims, Peters became more daring than ever.

KPK leading articles argued on a very general political level. They tied colonial policy into a wider pan-German movement, whose final goal was Germany's mastery of the earth. Two essays by Peters stand out in this context. On 16 May 1886 he published an article with the title 'All-Deutschland',[125] in which he observed that 'a powerful struggle between nations runs through our epoch'. All of these nations sought to coalesce within the boundaries of their *Volkstum*. This idea would draw the east into the dangerous swirl of pan-Slav greed, for instance. However, Peters saw the most glorious manifestation of the idea in the pan-Anglo-Saxon concept encapsulated in Dilke's prophecy: 'The world is rapidly becoming English.'

'How radically different are all these wishes from the political and idealistic cosmopolitanism, which up until this century has mainly been sustained by *Deutschtum*', Peters continued. He referred to Goethe's works to show that the 'best spirits' have constructed 'something like an ideal *Weltbürgertum* instead of a universal empire'. 'It required deep humiliations and the greatest economic and political damage before our people woke up from such dangerous dreams.' In Peters's eyes only the policy of 'blood and iron' which had unified Germany was a decisive historical turning point. It led away from the idea of a nation of *Dichter und Denker*, a notion which he dismissed as 'airy spheres of weak abstraction and obscure humanitarian sentimentalism'. With the victories of Königgrätz and Sedan, Germany had again joined the real struggle of peoples: 'The German movement to unity has, of natural necessity, to be followed by a struggle for a position of power overseas. Our European position as a great power has to be followed by a position as a world power.'

Peters justified the German struggle for world power by the ongoing

---

[124] See pp. 99ff.　　　[125] *KPK* ii. no. 20.

'Anglicization' of the world. Only through this policy would it be possible to guarantee that the Germans would not be completely overtaken by the Anglo-Saxons. 'Every year of hesitation in the assumption of such a task upsets the relationship between both races to our disadvantage.'

A month later Peters extended his nationalist ideas further, linking them to what he saw as the red thread of historical development. In 'Nationalismus und Kosmopolitismus'[126] he maintained that nature worked according to general laws everywhere, including in the development of mankind. Two great ideas would alternate in the course of history, the cosmopolitan and the national. Medieval times had witnessed the rise of the national idea and ended with the victory of the former over the latter; Oliver Cromwell and Richelieu are advanced as the victorious representatives of the national idea, Wallenstein and the Emperor Charles V as perhaps the last representatives of universalism.

As a result, Germany was pushed back from her European supremacy. While western powers flourished and struggled for world supremacy, Germany lapsed into a contemptible weakness. In Peters's eyes only the hard and pragmatic state-building of the Hohenzollerns had turned the national idea into a reality. 'Bismarck's tough and ingenious policy' had brought Germany to the point where Richelieu and Cromwell had left their nations. Not only had the national idea led to restoring Germany's power position on the continent. It had also led to Germany's entry into the competition between peoples for mastery over the world. At this point Peters referred to his Society for German Colonization, which had entirely devoted itself to this idea.

We are determined to fan and strengthen the German national spirit. What we know is this: for centuries, cosmopolitanism has brought our people humiliation and virtual ruin. For our nation nationalism at the end of the nineteenth century means power, wealth, and happiness, and the more so, the more proudly and ruthlessly it is written on our banner.

Interestingly, Peters's critique of cosmopolitanism differed from statements by his academic teacher, Heinrich von Treitschke. In his series of lectures 'Politik', for instance, the professor stated that 'cosmopolitanism has receded too far'.[127] Peters, however, turned this view upside down, claiming that the cosmopolitan concept had driven Germany almost to ruin.

---

[126] *KPK* ii. no. 24, 12 June 1886.
[127] H. von Treitschke, *Politik. Vorlesungen gehalten an der Universität zu Berlin*, ed. Max Cornicelius, 4th edn. (Berlin, 1918), 31.

In various respects, Peters revived the line of thinking he had elaborated prior to the acquisition of East Africa. Once again he praised the foundation of the Reich through military victory which, in his eyes, had laid the basis for Germany's entry into the struggle between nations. Peters thus transferred his earlier notions on Darwin and the struggle for survival from an individual level to the level of states. Pan-Germanism is introduced as the political doctrine with which Germany should master this challenge. As in his earlier articles, the British are the major opponent, but there is no more talk of a possible balance between the two. 'Anglicization' is portrayed as a fundamental threat, and Germany's world policy is thus presented as a strategy for survival. In comparison with his earlier essays, Peters's ideology had become more radical, aggressive, and militant.[128]

Using pan-Germanism as a vehicle to achieve German world power had domestic implications too; German nationalism had to shape all spheres of life if a world political programme was to succeed. The universal claim of Peters's nationalism became obvious as he extended his ideas beyond the purely political realm into the fields of language, culture, art, and family. Peters's *KPK* complained about the German addiction to the use of foreign words in daily life, which was seen as a sign of national weakness: 'It takes some time for a foreigner to study our classical authors; but the miserable *Kauderwelsch* of our menu cards and shop signs . . . is inevitably forced upon him.' The article pointed to the good example of the Deutscher Sprachverein in Dresden, which had succeeded in 'Germanizing' the menu cards in local restaurants. So successful was this practice that the German Association of Innkeepers, who held their annual assembly in neighbouring Görlitz, unanimously adopted the same line.[129]

Another *KPK* article focused on the theme 'Der Kosmopolitismus und die deutsche Kunst'.[130] This criticized classicist artists such as Karstens, Mengs, and their 'academic parrots', because they had failed to exhaust the 'bubbling spring of their own *Volksart*'. The article also speaks of degenerate French art, which was blamed for having demoralized a powerless Germany over centuries, and which had done more damage than all the pillaging of France's soldiery. French contemporary painting was portrayed as an 'artistic home for the sick', 'full of impressionist lepers'. This aggressive attack, employing images of disease and degeneration, anticipated the defamations employed by the Nazis in their persecution of modern art.

---

[128] See also *KPK*, ii, no. 5, 5 Feb. 1887, 35–6.
[129] *KPK* no. 23, 5 June 1886, 143.
[130] *KPK* no. 22, 29 May 1886, 129–31.

In Peters's eyes, the most crucial realm for promoting nationalist think-ing was the family.[131] This was the place where the German woman could create a truly German home, with German cuisine, German clothes, and, last but not least, German art: 'Away with Italian tooting and French blare! German tones for the German house!'[132]

Nationalist education at home had to be promoted by the woman, whose contribution was essential if the man's struggle was not to remain a Sisyphean task.[133] This was Peters's attempt to rally support for his newly founded *Frauenbund*, which was to be another element in the network of societies which he envisaged.[134]

Peters's nationalist ideas have been called 'totalitarian',[135] thus placing them in the immediate context of twentieth-century dictatorships, above all the Third Reich. However, this judgement needs to be treated with caution. Peters had not developed his ideas as part of a domestic political programme. He simply believed that all areas of life had to be addressed to stimulate popular enthusiasm for a vigorous pursuit of world policy. Geoff Eley has rightly criticized 'the desire to make Wilhelmine intellectual history obey an iron logic of proto-Nazi development'.[136] This point may also be made in the case of Peters. Classifying his agenda as 'totalitarian' obscures the actual political context and the intellectual environment in which these ideas were created.

Looking more broadly at Peters's ideology in the years 1883–6, two points may be emphasized. First, the question of colonial expansion was dramatized as a matter of life and death. By employing a pseudo-Darwinian framework of a 'struggle between nations' he claimed that Anglicization of the world posed a threat to the survival of *Deutschtum*. Since he equated the German nation with the *Volk*, it was a scenario in which a lack of imperial activity allegedly resulted in the marginalization or even extinction of the Germans as a people.

To counteract this threat, Germany had to give up its cosmopolitan attitudes and to follow an energetic nationalist course, as encapsulated in the doctrine of pan-Germanism. In this context, the experience of national unification through war was of central importance. It provided

---

[131] 'Deutsch-nationaler Frauenbund', *KPK* no. 4, 29 Jan. 1887, 25.
[132] 'Deutsch-nationaler Frauenbund', *KPK* no. 5, 5 Feb. 1887, 35–6.
[133] 'Deutsch-nationaler Frauenbund', *KPK* no. 4, 29 Jan. 1887, 25.
[134] On women and the colonial movement see also L. J. Wildenthal, 'Colonizers and Citizens: Bourgeois Women and the Woman Question in the German Colonial Movement, 1886–1914' (University of Michigan, Ph.D. thesis, 1994) and idem, *German Women for Empire, 1884–1945* (Durham 2001).
[135] Krätschell, *Peters*, 36.   [136] Eley, *Reshaping*, 185.

the confidence that the German state was powerful enough to achieve that agenda. The nation-state provided the platform from which imperial activities had to operate. Simultaneously, state power was to guarantee the success of expansionist aspirations.

Secondly, the constant preoccupation with the British, both as a model and as a rival, suggests that Peters's colonial ideology was at heart concerned with German national identity. He linked the issue of colonization to the question of what it meant to be a true German. As national identity may be seen as 'fundamentally multi-dimensional',[137] it is not static and immutable, so that new elements may be integrated into it in certain circumstances. Peters portrayed the acquisition of an overseas empire as a vital prerequisite for Germany's self-image on its path to become a leading world power. As the British Empire in the nineteenth century gradually expanded, the perceived status gap between the two peoples grew. German imperial activity was to make sure that the Germans would at least draw level with the British. Pan-Germanism formed the doctrine for this projected identity, which was essentially imperial. Put simply, Peters's credo was that to be a German *required* one to be a colonizer. On the broader level of the nation-state, a colonial empire provided a vital status symbol, which was to compensate for a kind of inferiority complex felt towards the British. Peters himself must have had some sense of the appeal of ideas which were linked to national identity, once stating that pan-Germanism, being a national interest, was such an important element of his agitation that it could not seriously be questioned by anybody.

If Peters's ideas are seen in the context of identity, then it seems possible to interpret his agitation as the mobilization of what one scholar has recently defined as the 'national identity dynamic'.[138] On the basis of an interpretation of Freud, Mead, Parsons, Erikson, and Habermas, Bloom has established a theory of identification which is meant to provide an analytical tool for the study of international relations. His purpose is to illuminate the 'interaction between the national identity dynamic and foreign policy decisions'.[139] Bloom argues that 'if a mass of people who share the same national identity perceive that identity to be threatened, or perceive the possibility of enhancing it, then they will mobilize so as to defend and enhance it.'[140]

This appears to be a very general proposition and it certainly needs to be

---

[137] A. D. Smith, *National Identity* (London, 1991), 14.
[138] W. Bloom, *Personal Identity, National Identity and International Relations* (Cambridge, 1990).   [139] Ibid. 89.   [140] Ibid. 113.

tested against the evidence of a specific historical or political setting, as the author concedes himself. If we apply Bloom's framework to the case of German colonial acquisitions, then at least one qualification needs to be made: the colonial movement in the Bismarckian period cannot be described as a political mass movement. However, given that many political notables and prominent figures of the establishment stood behind the colonial movement, it certainly had a voice in public which could not be ignored.

Peters's voice, in particular, fits well into Bloom's framework. The colonial agitator presented images 'in such a way that either (1) national identity is perceived to be threatened, or (2) the opportunity is present to enhance national identity'.[141] The issue of German colonization made both variants possible. The failure to acquire colonies was dramatized as a threat to the survival of *Deutschtum*. To embark on colonial policy, on the other hand, provided an opportunity to enhance national identity. In line with Bloom, this prospect may be seen as an important stimulus for the government to take some initiative in this direction; acting as the custodian of national identity and fulfilling nationalist demands, Bismarck was bound to further his own popularity. On the other hand, inaction was likely to expose the government to increasing criticism since it would be failing to protect what was perceived as a national interest. The way in which the bankrupt DOAG was rescued through the intervention of the state points to a similar mechanism. Bismarck felt obliged to take that step because giving up East Africa would have meant too heavy a blow to his own and Germany's prestige.

It may be argued that Peters's restless activities helped to consolidate his position within the colonial movement. Although the split between the Kolonialverein and Peters's GfdK continued until 1887, a number of prominent figures came to support Peters and his pan-German agenda, helping to pave the way for an eventual merger of the two colonial organizations.

One of these men was Friedrich Fabri, known as the 'Father of the German Colonial Movement', who came to cooperate with Peters in the summer of 1885. In the spring Fabri had still been critical of Peters's risky settlement schemes for East Africa. However, once Bismarck had demonstrated his support, he was quick to give up his critical distance and began to back the young DOAG leader. Certainly, the two were not bound together by a great deal of mutual sympathy. While Peters privately noted

---

[141] Ibid. 79.

how ridiculous it was to march along with a 'goat of heaven' at one's side,[142] Fabri secretly criticized Peters's 'vanity coming close to megalomania'.[143] Both, however, realized that such cooperation was the only way to bridge the gulf between the various colonial interest groups.

From Peters's perspective, Fabri held a key position within the move-ment, as he was the leader of the West German Colonial Association, the most powerful branch of the Kolonialverein. This was sustained by a number of industrialists whom Peters hoped to tap for the financing of the DOAG. Furthermore, Fabri maintained close contacts with leading members of the Kolonialverein itself. Finally, he was a potential channel to missionary circles, which Peters hoped to engage for East Africa as well. Fabri, on the other hand, recognized Peters's talent for agitation and his dynamic manner. He saw Peters as a useful drummer for public support.[144]

Only a few days after the German fleet had threatened Said Bargash, Fabri invited Peters, Saint Paul-Illaire, and Behr to an assembly of the West German Colonial Association.[145] He praised Peters's acquisition as the 'most important and most promising'[146] venture, in order to rally support among the leaders of the association. The meeting still failed to convince industrial capitalists to invest larger amounts;[147] only a small contribution was made by Krupp, who supplied 50,000 marks for equipping East African expeditions. Nevertheless, Fabri continued to lend his support to Peters in the following months. He favoured Peters's plan for a central colo-nial association and worked towards a merger of the Kolonialverein and the GfdK. He even threatened that his West German branch might act inde-pendently if the Kolonialverein leadership refused to negotiate about the creation of a central committee through which links to the other societies could be established.[148] Above all, this was an attempt to draw closer to Peters's GfdK. The same was true for Rudolf von Bennigsen, leader of the National Liberals and member of the Kolonialverein. He brought forward a motion to initiate closer cooperation between the different colonial asso-ciations.[149] As a result, it was agreed between the rival groups to hold a

[142] See Peters to brother Hermann, 16 Aug. 1885, PP 92, BAB.

[143] Fabri's memo, 5 July 1889, RKolA 6925, 45–8, BAB.

[144] 'Deutsch-Ostafrika. I', *Kölnische Zeitung*, 16 July 1886, enclosed in RKolA 360, 6.

[145] Peters to Hermann, 16 Aug. 1885, PP 92, BAB; Wagner, *Deutsch-Ostafrika*, 67 f.

[146] Cited in Wagner, *Deutsch-Ostafrika*, 68.

[147] Bade (*Fabri*, 293) sees von der Heydt's entry in the context of the August meeting. In fact, however, von der Heydt had invested in the DOAG already a few weeks earlier.

[148] Fabri to KV executive board, 22 Oct. 1885, DKG 899, 250–1.

[149] Bennigsen's motion (*Anlage 6c*) for the executive board meeting on 3 Nov. 1885, *DKG* 899, 252, BAB.

'conference of delegates' on a regular basis, and the new committee met first in January 1886.

Peters was also keen to move closer to Fabri, who was appointed an honorary member of the GfdK committee.[150] The missionary also functioned as a judge in a competition organized by the GfdK; participants were asked to write a treatise on the question: 'How do we best educate the negro for work?'[151]

Fabri supported the DOAG in public, too. In a series of articles in the *Kölnische Zeitung* he praised the East African possessions as 'one of the greatest facts of modern history'. German East Africa had a size of roughly 30,000 square miles, if one included the Somali coast. 'That is three times as much as Germany's own land mass', the author noted, although the extention of the territory had not yet been delimited with respect to rival British claims. In a short period its size could be doubled to cover the entire region, stretching as far as Lake Nyassa and Lake Tanganyika. German East Africa 'stood in the foreground of all German overseas possessions', and 'with it, a new India had fallen Germany'. The article raised hopes of building a German equivalent of the centrepiece of the British Empire. All this was the work of a young German scholar, whose action was 'daring, swift, and completely unbloody'. Here was 'a young prophet' who had successfully embarked on his first 'colonial political crusade'.[152]

How much Fabri had adopted the tone of Peters's propaganda in this article may be indicated by the Foreign Office's suspicion that the series had in fact been launched by the DOAG leader himself. The newspaper had not named Fabri as the author. Two weeks later, however, Fabri published a booklet under his own name which turned out to be an extended version of the newspaper articles.[153]

The Foreign Office felt that the article was important enough to inform Bismarck about. The Chancellor's reaction to it is particularly interesting: 'This is misleading the public', he scribbled in the margin.

What has the German East African Company achieved so far? Mines cannot be set up in its territory. To grow wheat is not in our interest; it would only be competing with our domestic agriculture. Therefore it has to focus on a plantation economy. But who will drink all the coffee which can be grown on 30,000 square miles.[154]

[150] See Wagner, *Deutsch-Ostafrika*, 65.   [151] *KPK* i, no. 9, 16 Aug. 1885.
[152] *Kölnische Zeitung*, 16 July 1886, enclosed in RKolA 360, 6, BAB.
[153] *Deutsch-Ostafrika. Eine colonialpolitische Skizze* (Cologne, 1886); Krauel's marginal note in RKolA 360, 4, BAB.
[154] Berchem's note, 18 July 1886, RKolA 360, 5, BAB.

Bismarck was obviously concerned about the discrepancy between those boastful remarks on the size of territory and the society's lack of capital. In the same context, he repeated his directive that the Reich should follow pioneers, and not pave the way for them. But in fact the government had already partly given up this position, since it had agreed to help the DOAG in finding financiers for the venture. With regard to the article, Bismarck ordered his officials 'to speak severely with Peters'.[155] This remark is interesting in so far as it implied some concern by the government that public propaganda might arouse expectations that had nothing to do with the realities of East Africa.

Apart from Fabri, Robert Jannasch also drew closer to Peters. Like Fabri, the chairman of the Centralverein supported Peters's plan to organize a 'General German congress for the promotion of German interests overseas'. This idea had first been formulated by Peters in late 1885.[156] On 6 February and 20 March 1886 Peters's *KPK* published an invitation to the event, signed by 157 supporters, many of them prominent political figures. Apart from Peters's closer allies, such as Otto Arendt, Wilhelm von Kardorff, and Schroeder-Poggelow, there were a number of other well-known parliamentarians such as Mirbach-Sorquitten, von Kanitz, and Freiherr von Hammerstein. Along with some industrialists, prominent academics were represented as well, including the philosopher Eduard von Hartmann and the biologist Ernst Haeckel.[157]

The Kolonialverein (DKV) was asked to participate, but its committee refused. In public the DKV argued that the congress was insufficiently prepared,[158] but this was hardly more than a pretext. Arguably, the dispute did not so much express differences about colonial questions as such, but rather reflected a struggle for leadership within the colonial movement. Peters, with his megalomaniac tendencies, wanted to be the new man at the top. Hohenlohe, however, did not want to give way to the newcomer. The GfdK maintained its claim to the opening speech at the congress dealing with 'The Present State of German Colonization'. This was unacceptable to the DKV, who made clear that they were not prepared 'to stand back behind the GfdK or any other corporation'.[159] Ultimately, the DKV

---

[155] Berchem's note, 18 July 1886, RKolA 360, 4 ff., BAB.
[156] See Jannasch's speech, *Bericht über die Verhandlungen des Allgemeinen Deutschen Kongresses zur Förderung überseeischer Interessen* (Berlin, 1886), 2, enclosed in RKolA 7010, 12–56, BAB.
[157] A list of signatories is enclosed in RKolA 7010, 2–4, BAB.
[158] Circular of 18 March 1886, *DKZ*, 1886, no. 7; see also *KPK* no. 12, 20 March 1886, 49.
[159] *Delegiertenkonferenz*, session of 19 April 1886, *Anlage*, DKG 255, 54, BAB.

boycott of the congress did not help to curb Peters's influence. On the contrary, important figures chose to move closer to the GfdK. Fabri, for instance, participated, chairing the congress working group on emigration. The range of signatures on Peters's appeal revealed that he had secured support within all parts of the political establishment.

The congress eventually convened from 13 to 16 September 1886 in Berlin, and was attended by more than 600 people.[160] Four working groups were established: (1) practical colonization; (2) questions of German emigration; (3) German missions overseas; (4) maintaining the German language and German manners away from home. In the course of the four-day programme, a wide spectrum of colonial issues was covered. Peters did not adopt the aggressive tone of his recent *KPK* essays. Nevertheless, he repeated his earlier criticism of cosmopolitanism, referring to Goethe, who had thought 'to win our people for the spiritual fraternization of the whole of mankind'. 'This feature of the German character has almost caused our political ruin, and we would be the last to congratulate our people on it.'[161] The idea of *Deutschtum* was not the only issue, but it was certainly an important one at the congress, which displayed the close ideological nexus of colonial and pan-German ideas.

The crucial point about the Berlin congress was that Peters had been able to achieve it despite the Kolonialverein's boycott. This was a clear triumph for the DOAG leader. Hohenlohe, not Peters, was in danger of being isolated in the struggle for leadership. Peters and his GfdK proved to be a force in rallying public support for the colonial cause. In 1886 GfdK membership increased sharply (from 900 to 3,300)[162] while the Kolonialverein's size stagnated with just over 12,100.[163]

At the congress the GfdK, the Centralverein and the Schulverein agreed to set up a new holding organization, called the Allgemeiner Deutscher Verband zur Vertretung deutsch-nationaler Interessen (ADV). The ADV turned out to be short-lived, and it did not meet Peters's initial expectations of becoming an umbrella organization for all societies with a German national interest. Nevertheless, it is misleading to speak of 'a

---

[160] *KPK* no. 38 u.39, 25 Sept. 1886, 266–7. 621 participants had entered their name on the lists, but it was estimated that in fact 800–900 people had attended.

[161] C. Peters, 'Die Kulturhistorische Bedeutung des Deutschtums', in *Bericht über die Verhandlungen des Allgemeinen Deutschen Kongresses zur Förderung überseeischer Interessen* (Berlin, 1886), 81, enclosed in RKolA 7010, 12–56, BAB.

[162] Wagner, *Deutsch-Ostafrika*, 121. More than 1,000 members joined the GfdK immediately after the Berlin Congress.

[163] See *Kassen- und Geschäftsbericht des Deutschen Kolonialverein*, 1887, enclosed in DKG 928, 69–75, BAB.

complete failure'[164] in this context because this tends to obscure two important points. First, it cannot be concluded that pan-Germanism was an insignificant concept within the colonial movement; rather, the established societies already provided a platform for such ideas. Both the DKV and the GfdK advocated a colonial policy in which pan-German thinking was a major factor. So far, both societies had served as a forum for pan-German aspirations, and they continued to do so.

The crucial point, however, is that the ADV appeared largely superfluous as a potential umbrella organization when the DKV moved closer to the GfdK and paved the way for a merger. Arguably, the creation of the ADV had accelerated this movement, as it forced Hohenlohe to take some action if he wanted to prevent his own society from disintegration. Shortly after the congress the DKV signalled to the ADV that it was prepared for negotiations.[165] Interestingly, the decisive initiative for a fusion with the GfdK then came from a local DKV branch. In April, the regional branch at Dresden advocated a merger for the pursuit of a 'practical, German-national colonial policy'.[166] This resembled the tone of Peters's agitation.

Peters himself departed to East Africa in spring 1887, so that others had to conduct the talks with the DKV. Above all, Otto Arendt and Livonius became active in this respect. Negotiations towards a fusion were initiated in May 1887, and at the first meeting six representatives of each side were present.[167] Arendt emphasized that in the future 'the German-national interests' and *Deutschtum* had to be promoted. Hammacher, representing the DKV, agreed to Arendt's demands. He saw 'no principal opposition against a German-national work'. Miquel obviously had some initial concerns about 'the danger of dubious pan-Germanism' but he dropped them in the course of the conversation. Finally, he felt a need to stress 'that, in principle, both societies wanted and aspired to the same thing'. These statements are quite interesting as Arendt had never concealed his support and sympathy for Peters. His booklet, *Ziele deutscher Kolonialpolitik*, published in 1886, more or less repeated Peters's agenda.[168] The meeting of May 1887 indicates that the ideological differences between GfdK and DKV leaders were perhaps not as 'divisive' as previous authors have

---

[164] R. V. Pierard, 'The German Colonial Society, 1882–1914' (Univ. Iowa, Ph.D. thesis, 1964), 87; for a similar view see Bendikat, *Kolonialbewegung*, 105.

[165] DKV to ADV, 29 Dec. 1886, DKG 263, 51, BAB.

[166] Dresden branch, General Assembly, 20 April 1887, DKG 928, 78–80, BAB.

[167] Minutes of the meeting, 16 May 1887, DKG 255, 78–80; GfdK representatives: Arendt, Behr, Credé, Livonius, Regely, Schroeder; KV representatives: Fabri, Hammacher, Kurella, Martius, Miquel, Weber.

[168] O. Arendt, *Ziele deutscher Kolonialpolitik* (Berlin, 1886).

suggested.[169] Personal rivalries and competition seem to have contributed more to the frictions between the two associations. Now DKV leaders were keen to merge, as they feared that they might be overtaken by the Peters group and its followers.

The final merger of the two societies was quite favourable for the GfdK. In the new organization, called Deutsche Kolonialgesellschaft (DKG), Peters's society secured an equal share of the top positions,[170] although it contributed less than a third of the overall membership. At the leadership level, the principle of parity favoured the Peters group, which was much smaller in size. With the final fusion, the Allgemeiner Deutscher Verband was no longer needed. Pan-German aspirations could still be integrated into the *Kolonialgesellschaft*, which provided Peters and his followers with a platform for their ideas and activities.[171] Hence the abortive history of the ADV is no indication of a lack of pan-German forces within the colonial movement. Only three years later, when colonial circles loudly protested against the Heligoland–Zanzibar Agreement, a pan-German league came into existence, serving as a new forum for radical nationalists.

RIVALRY AND PARTITION: GERMANY, BRITAIN, AND THE
SULTANATE OF ZANZIBAR

In Zanzibar the news of the German charter caused 'great excitement' in the Sultan's palace, as Consul Rohlfs reported. Bargash's 'feelings towards me are no longer as favourable as they were in the beginning'.[172] The Sultan repeatedly enquired about the precise location of the German claim, but he received no reply. For the time being, Rohlfs was told by the Foreign Office that the borders of the acquired territories had not yet been precisely defined. The government made clear that it did not want 'to anticipate the development of the emerging enterprise'.[173] By the end of April Bargash had lost his patience, communicating his formal protest to the Kaiser. He claimed that 'these places have been ours from the time of our fathers'.[174] He regarded the German claim to Usagara as 'usurpation' and refused to recognize it. 'Without doubt the answer is inspired by the British consul-general', noted Rohlfs.[175]

[169] Pierard, 'Colonial Society', 92.   [170] Ibid. 93.
[171] See Peters's articles in the *DKZ*, 25 Sept. 1888, 311; 21 July 1888, 225–6; 28 July 1888,
233.   [172] Rohlfs to AA, 13 March 1885, RKolA 390, 125, BAB.
[173] AA to Rohlfs, 13 March 1885, RKolA 390, 115–16, BAB.
[174] Bargash to Kaiser Wilhelm, 28 April 1885, RKolA 391, BAB.
[175] Rohlfs to AA, 28 April 1885, RKolA 390, 130, BAB.

The British consul was indeed alarmed by the unexpected German move. He was aware that the Peters group would sooner or later claim access to the sea, without which their possessions were worthless. This could cause the complete collapse of the Arab state, as he pointed out to his superiors.[176] The British, who for a long time had exerted informal influence on the Sultan to protect their commercial and strategic interests, did not want a serious quarrel with the Germans to be caused by backing up the Sultan's protest. Their bargaining position was relatively weak, since they depended on German support to resolve the Egyptian crisis.[177] London assured Berlin that Kirk had received 'very strict instructions' not to work against the Germans.[178] Although they stated that the 'Sultan's sovereignty over the coast should not be questioned', they made clear that they were not opposed to German actions in the interior.[179]

But how far did the Sultan's dominions extend into the interior? Where were their boundaries? These questions soon began to occupy diplomats in East Africa and officials in European ministries, but they were hardly adequate to shed light on the political reality of East Africa. The very fact that these questions were asked, displayed a great deal of ignorance, or perhaps a deliberate lack of interest in the existing structures. The Sultanate was not an empire which resembled a European territorial state. Bargash's rule was not clearly confined by any fixed boundaries. It had developed on the basis of long-distance trade, the economic mainstay of the Sultanate. The assessment of local agents who had to some extent grasped the flexible nature of Zanzibari rule[180] was not taken into account. As we will see later, they did not fit into the colonial concept.

As far as the Sultan's political power on the mainland was concerned, he relied on a set of commercial and political networks established with local chiefs and members of the coastal elite. In this system, Zanzibari agents shared the exercise of political control with local rulers.[181] The degree of Zanzibari involvement and influence varied from place to place. Overall it served the purposes of securing trade routes, controlling coastal plantations, and collecting customs revenues.

---

[176] Bennett, *Arab versus European*, 131.
[177] P. Kennedy, *The Rise of the Anglo-German Antagonism 1860–1914* (London, 1980), 184 ff.
[178] Münster to AA, RKolA 391, 47, BAB.
[179] Bismarck's memo to the Kaiser, 30 April 1885, RKolA 391, 16 ff., BAB.
[180] Arendt to Bismarck, 20 Dec. 1885, RKolA 597, 47 ff., BAB.
[181] For the nature of Zanzibari rule see J.-G. Deutsch, 'Inventing an East African Empire: The Zanzibar Delimitation Commission of 1885/1886', in P. Heine and U. von der Heyden (eds.), *Studien zur Geschichte des deutschen Kolonialismus in Afrika* (Pfaffenweiler 1995), 211 ff.

Having received the Sultan's formal protest, Bismarck advised Wilhelm not to reply and to avoid 'any direct communication with Bargash'.[182] He had instructed Consul Rohlfs to secure free transit rights through the coastal strip. Without it, the Chancellor believed, 'the matter is hardly practicable'.[183] Given that Bargash's income almost entirely came from the collection of customs,[184] such a permit had serious implications. If free transit was to be granted to all other nations as well, this was likely to ruin the Sultanate's finances. But Bismarck, knowing little about Zanzibar at this stage, failed to recognize these consequences. Otherwise he would not have stubbornly insisted that Rohlfs should link the question of free transit with the promotion of friendly relations and the securing of the 'Sultan's confidence'.[185] Only later would he concede that the Sultan should receive compensation for the loss of customs.

Bismarck's East African policy indicates the underlying concept. The Chancellor obviously believed that the protectorate could be established as a neighbouring state to the Sultanate. He hoped to gain informal influence on Bargash in order to ensure that existing trade relations could be transformed and built into the new protectorate's economy. But anyone who had some practical experience of the system of long-distance trade, such as the Hamburg merchants, was convinced that this would not work.[186]

On 24 April Peters wrote to Bismarck that free transit was essential for 'the energetic ... exploitation and colonization of East Africa'. He declared that this was not to be achieved via 'friendly negotiations with the Sultan'. Rather, the Reich should lend its 'moral support' to the company by permanently stationing a German warship in Zanzibar.[187] In a memorandum of 2 May, Peters extended his demands. He maintained that all efforts had to focus on 'winning the coast'. This was a 'matter of life and death' for the company. He estimated that the Sultan collected roughly 600,000 rupees a year from customs, 'which we are not able to pay off'. It was obvious to him that 'either our efforts succeed, and then the Sultan is ruined, or he succeeds in ruining us'. Their interests were 'diametrically opposed to each other'. 'Any modus vivendi' could therefore only be of a 'temporary nature'. There was only one option: to force the Sultan to give in. Finally he added: 'Should it be in Germany's interest to bring the entire

[182] Bismarck's memo to Kaiser, 30 April 1885, RKolA, 391, 16–22, BAB.
[183] Marginal comment on note by Kusserow, 23 Feb. 1885, RKolA 390, 102–4, BAB.
[184] See Rohlfs to Bismarck, 5 May 1885, RKolA 392, 19, BAB.
[185] Rohlfs to Bismarck, 5 May 1885, RKolA 392, 19, BAB.
[186] See Strandes to Hansing, 4 March 1886, RKolA 359, 156, BAB.
[187] Peters to Bismarck, 24 April 1885, RKolA 391, 11 f., BAB.

Sultanate into German dependency in one form or another, then this moment would be particularly favourable.'[188] When Peters was called for a conference with Krauel, a colonial expert in the Foreign Office, he repeated precisely these points.[189]

While Peters bombarded the government with his aggressive schemes, Rohlfs's double mission—securing free transit and promoting friendly relations—collapsed.[190] The consul made things worse by poking his nose into other issues, which alienated the Sultan even further. Rohlf's suggested that the Reich should intervene because the Sultan had cast an eye on the Comoro islands. If necessary, he wrote, the Sultan's aspirations should be prevented by force. The Chancellor was furious when he learned about Rohlfs's unauthorized efforts,[191] and Herbert von Bismarck noted that the consul was faced with a task 'which exceeded his capacity'.[192] Eventually, Rohlfs was called back to Berlin. His place was taken by Travers, whom the Chancellor explicitly instructed to confine himself to routine business.[193] The question of free transit now had to be handled by Bismarck himself.

Peters's early call for a military presence obviously found a willing ear. At the end of April Bismarck asked for the Kaiser's permission to confer with the admiralty about 'the concentration of several warships in the waters of Zanzibar'.[194] If his diplomats failed to establish friendly relations with the Sultan, then perhaps the German navy could bring him 'to a more correct bearing'.[195] The Chancellor's instructions also included the option of bombarding Zanzibar town, should the mere presence of the navy fail to impress the Sultan.[196] In addition, Bismarck believed he had yet another trump card in his hand. Some years previously, one of Bargash's sisters, Princess Salme, had married the German merchant Hermann Ruete and settled down with him in Hamburg. However, her brothers in Zanzibar had always opposed this liaison. Over several years, Salme had failed to reconcile them to it and to receive the inheritance to which she felt entitled. Now Bismarck saw a chance to employ Salme as a tool to put further pressure on Bargash. He granted her free transport to

[188] Peters's memo [to AA], 2 May 1885 RKolA 391, 38 ff., BAB.
[189] Kusserow's memo, 3 May 1885, RKolA 391, 43 ff., BAB.
[190] Rohlfs to AA, 9 May 1885, RKolA, 65, BAB.
[191] See Bismarck to Rohlfs, 8 April 1885, AL2/23/1, 129, ZNA.
[192] Herbert von Bismarck to Wilhelm von Bismarck, 12 June 1885, Bismarck Papers, D 17, 332–4, BAF.   [193] Hatzfeldt to Travers, 12 June 1885, AL2/24, 1–2, ZNA.
[194] Bismarck's memo to the Kaiser, 30 April 1885, RKolA 391, 16 ff., BAB
[195] Malet to Granville, 30 May 1885, FO 84, vol. 1714, 64 ff., PRO, London.
[196] See Kusserow to Bismarck, 16 June 1885, RKolA 392, 56.

Zanzibar on a German war cruiser, where she was treated 'as secret cargo', as Commodore Paschen pointed out to her.[197] As she was a German citizen, her claims might prove useful to legitimize the use of force, as Bismarck noted in his instructions to Admiral Knorr.[198] However, should Bargash give in before a bombardment, then Salme would have to travel home again.

On 7 August, when Bargash still refused to recognize the German protectorate, the German squadron entered the harbour of Zanzibar. Commodore Paschen gave the Sultan an ultimatum, allowing him twenty-four hours to accept the German demands. He positioned his ships along the shore, from where 'the Sultan's buildings, if necessary, could be shelled and taken easily'. Bargash could see the cannons through the windows of his palace, which was just a few metres from the quay. He could do nothing but capitulate.[199] He signed a formal note in which he accepted the German protectorate.

Nobody was more satisfied with this intimidation than Peters himself. The Reich had taken action to enforce DOAG claims. Now it was clear to everybody that Berlin was serious about the East African venture and that it would back Peters's company, if necessary by military means. The DOAG leader was quick to express his 'most obedient thanks' for the government's 'great and sweeping support of German interests against the pretensions of the Sultan, and of DOAG rights in particular'.[200] At a time when company funds were dwindling and new investors were not in sight, there could hardly have been a better advertisement for the colonial enterprise than naval intervention on its behalf by the Reich.

However, the initial euphoria was misleading. Although the government celebrated the mission as a great success in public, it had in fact achieved little on the ground. True, the Sultan had given up his protest, but the question of transit remained unsettled and the extent of Peters's acquisitions was still vague. At the end of 1885 Bargash at least agreed to sign a new treaty of commerce and friendship. For the Germans, it did not mean a big step forward, as the transit issue was not really resolved, and the original 5 per cent import duty remained. Future DOAG products which had not been grown there before would be duty free, but that point played no practical role for the moment, since DOAG stations were far from producing

[197] See Salme's own recollections: E. Ruete, *Memoirs of an Arabian Princess from Zanzibar* (Princeton, 1989), 282 [original German edition, Berlin 1886].
[198] Bismarck to Knorr, 18 May 1885, RKolA 8895, 19–30, BAB.
[199] Cited in Müller, *Deutschland*, 215.
[200] Peters to Bismarck, 19 Aug. 1885, RKolA 393, 91, BAB.

anything at all. Bargash's monopoly duties on copal and ivory were to be replaced by fixed rates.[201]

All these provisions were certainly painful for the Sultan, but they were far from Bismarck's original goal of free transit. Why did the Chancellor not force this policy through after the arrival of the German navy? He had manoeuvred Germany into a quandary. The DOAG, facing financial collapse, was not in a position to pay compensation to the Sultan, and Bismarck did not want to involve the Reich for this purpose. Without compensation, however, Bargash's rule might collapse, which was not Bismarck's intention either. The Chancellor sought to exploit Bargash's authority and influence for German ends, and he still envisaged some form of informal control over Zanzibar. Consequently, the treaty of December 1885 had only put the major problems on ice.

The Sultan had bowed to the muzzles of German cannons, but he had not capitulated entirely. Rather, he now challenged the Germans with their own weapons. If Peters could gather treaties with a few crosses on them and claim a whole empire, so could the Sultan. He sent out an expedition and secured a treaty with Mandara, one of the Chagga rulers on Kilimanjaro. Perhaps he could at least rescue his authority over the northern caravan routes.

Once the race for the interior had begun, the British government sought to rescue as much of its informal influence as it could. Since they were not in a position to oppose German policy openly, the British adopted a different strategy, that of propping up the Sultanate as far as possible. Above all, the Sultanate had to be shielded against a possible German takeover. Although the German government had earlier assured them that it did not intend to establish a protectorate over Zanzibar,[202] the mounting tension between Bargash and Berlin must have worried officials in London. The British therefore suggested settling the dispute about the Sultanate by means of a commission.[203]

Bismarck welcomed the initiative. He was willing to join the 1862 declaration in which France and Britain had guaranteed the future independence of the Sultanate, once Bargash recognized the German protectorate. But in addition he demanded that the commission, representing France, Britain, and Germany, should bring 'certainty about the extent of the Sultanate'.[204]

[201] 'Freundschafts-, Handels- und Schiffahrtsvertrag zwischen dem Deutschen Reich und dem Sultan von Zanzibar' [20 Dec. 1885], R1501/103845, 116–29, BAB.
[202] See Malet to Herbert von Bismarck, 16 Jan. 1885, RKolA 8892, BAB.
[203] See Hatzfeld's memo, 11 Aug. 1885, RKolA 393, 52–3, BAB.
[204] Bismarck to Travers, 7 Oct. 1885, AL2/25/2, 201, ZNA.

It is interesting that Bismarck did not yet want to fix any boundaries for the young protectorate, but rather sought to define the limits of the Sultanate. The future extent of German territory to the west, north, and south would thus remain open. This meant that Peters and his self-appointed conquistadors had a free hand to expand into the interior. The Chancellor, on his part, signalled a green light when he informed Peters that 'the company should take what it feels confident to take without our encouragement and intervention. We shall see later what we can back officially.'[205]

Rapid expansion had been Peters's priority from the very beginning. On 24 February, three days before the *Schutzbrief* was granted, the first expedition departed to extend German claims.[206] Every month another group of Germans disembarked in the harbour at Zanzibar. In haste they bought equipment and supplies, and then they would sail off to the mainland. By 1887 eighteen DOAG expeditions had set foot on East African soil, only one of them being concerned with what the DOAG called 'exploration'. The rest were to make further treaties with African leaders.[207]

These were costly enterprises, and they absorbed the company's modest budget very quickly. Within the first three months the company's capital declined from 270,000 marks to a mere 63,000 marks.[208] But Peters, intoxicated with his sudden success, wanted 'to gobble up everything around him like a wolf'.[209]

While Peters's agents were busy making one dubious treaty after another, London and Berlin differed widely in their ideas about the Sultan's mainland dominions. According to the British, they formed a coastal strip from Cap Delgado to Somaliland (Warsheikh), extending some sixty nautical miles inland. The Germans, on the other hand, claimed that the Sultan's authority was limited to a few points on the coast, not extending further inland than 5 or 6 nautical miles.[210]

Characteristically, the Sultan was not allowed to have a voice in the matter. As Kirk remarked a little later, he was merely 'an oriental prince to whom are not accorded the usual rights prescribed by international law'.[211] On 11 December 1885 the German consulate simply sent Bargash a note informing him about the establishment of the commission.[212]

[205] Marginal note on Hatzfeldt to Rantzau, 11 July 1885, RKA 393, 8 f., BAB.
[206] Wagner, *Deutsch-Ostafrika*, 75.
[207] List of expeditions in *KPK* no. 3, 22 Jan. 1887, 21–2.   [208] See Ch. 3.
[209] Peters, *Gründung*, GS i. 182.
[210] Hatzfeldt's memo, 11 Aug. 1885, RKolA 393, 52–3, BAB.
[211] Cited in J. S. Galbraith, *Mackinnon and East Africa, 1878–1895* (Cambridge, 1972), 103.
[212] Consulate to AA, 11 Dec. 1885, AL2/25/2, 238, ZNA.

The three commissioners did not question the Sultan's sovereignty over Zanzibar, Pemba, and Mafia. As far as the mainland was concerned, they were to visit the major coastal towns and to investigate whether the Sultan exerted sovereign rights there or not. Since both the British and the German governments had already made up their minds as to the size of the Sultan's possessions on the mainland, it was clear that each commission member would try to find evidence for his government's version. But even if the commission had eventually come to a common conclusion (which it did not), this would never have reflected the real extent of Zanzibari rule on the mainland. As has been pointed out above, the Sultanate's authority did not operate within fixed boundaries, as was common in Europe; hence, whatever size the commission might determine for the Sultanate's mainland dominions, the outcome would necessarily be a European fabrication. In this sense the colonial powers were indeed inventing a Zanzibari empire which would serve their colonial interests.[213] The commission's purpose was to delimit 'spheres of action' for the Europeans, as was pointed out in a German report.[214]

The commission itself never got very far; as Admiral Knorr observed, it soon got stuck 'in a cul-de-sac'.[215] Not surprisingly, the Sultan did his best to present as much visible evidence of his authority on the coast as he could. Every port which the commission visited thus presented its own, allegedly permanent, garrison of Sultanate soldiers. The German commissioner observed that these men 'remarkably resembled' those they had met before at other places. The Sultan obviously moved them every time before the commission arrived at a particular harbour. They were there 'for decorative purposes', Schmidt sarcastically remarked.[216] He saw the British delegate as 'the Sultan's advocate', finding the evidence prepared for his own benefit.[217]

Schmidt quarrelled throughout with his French and British counterparts. Kitchener and Raffray insisted that once the Sultan's authority in two neighbouring coastal towns had been proved the coastal strip in between would automatically belong to his dominion as well. The German member was opposed to this view.[218] Furthermore, Kitchener and Raffray came up with various other suggestions which the German government

---

[213] Here I agree with the argument of Deutsch, 'East African Empire'.
[214] Political report to Bismarck, 15 Jan. 1886, AL2/26/1, 8–15, ZNA.
[215] Knorr to Admiralty, 21 Dec. 1885, RKolA 597, 59 ff., BAB.
[216] Arendt to Bismarck, 6 March 1886, AL2/26/1, 187, ZNA.
[217] Schmidt to Bismarck, 14 Jan. 1886, RKolA, 597, 88–94, BAB.
[218] Schmidt to Bismarck, 20 Dec. 1885, RKolA, 597, 23–30, BAB.

was not willing to accept. First, they wished the Sultan to receive an 'official assurance of the real object of the commission'. According to the British, this was not only to lay down the 'limits of the Sultan's dominions' and thus provide the basis for a territory 'guaranteed' by all three powers. In addition, 'the Sultan's existing rights in territories outside the guarantee' should not be compromised.[219] The latter point would have meant that the commission recognized the existence of Arab claims in the interior, as far away as Tabora or Ujiji. The Germans carefully avoided such a declaration, because it could be used against the extension of the German territory into the hinterland.

Secondly, the French and the British commissioners demanded from the Berlin government that it should officially disavow the flag-hoisting activities of the Peters group at Ghasi on the northern coast. This request was likewise rejected.[220] Finally, the Germans refused to put the Kilimanjaro issue on the commission's agenda.[221] Schmidt then concluded 'that the delimitation of the Sultanate could only be realized in Europe'. If the commission continued its work, 'it would run the risk of reaching a deadlock or a result which would not fulfil expectations'.[222]

Alarmed by the commissioner's reports, Bismarck adopted a new line of policy. Facing French and British opposition in Zanzibar, Germany now considered withdrawing its representative altogether.[223] In practice, this meant the end of the commission. Bismarck wanted to have the issue settled at the green table at home.

In autumn 1886 a German delegation under the leadership of Richard Krauel, the expert on colonial affairs in the Foreign Office, travelled to London to meet his British counterpart Anderson and his staff. Krauel was accompanied by Peters, Behr, and Arendt. This DOAG presence made it clear that Berlin negotiated on behalf of the company, and that it could not afford to ignore their demands.

A closer look at the preparations for this meeting provides interesting insights into German aims at that time. On 12 October Herbert von Bismarck sent a draft instruction to his father at Varzin. This was guided by the thought 'that such a favourable moment' for negotiation 'will not come again so quickly'. He believed that the 'duration of the present British government, as well as its reputation in the Mediterranean, depended only on our attitude towards France'. Therefore, the Germans would now be

[219] Note Verbale, Malet to AA, 17 Jan. 1886, copy in AL2/26/1, 125–6, ZNA.
[220] See Bismarck to Arendt, 26 March 1886, AL2/27/1, 33, ZNA.
[221] Berchem to Arendt, 21 May 1886, AL 2/27/1, 190, ZNA.
[222] Schmidt's report, 12 March 1886, RKolA 598, 127–40, BAB.
[223] Berchem to Arendt, 21 May 1886, AL2/27/1, 190, ZNA.

able 'to get what we want'. He suggested 'bringing the Sultan of Zanzibar into the same position in relation to us as the Kehdive of Egypt holds towards the English government'. The young Bismarck was thus prepared to shift to a policy which Peters had already proposed a year-and-a-half earlier: 'If we take over the handling of the customs system, albeit under the ostensible sovereignty of the Sultan, it is predictable that in the course of time we will gain a colony which will pay well.'

Herbert von Bismarck also stated that 'without the employment of force this goal will not be achieved'. He referred to the British navy, which had threatened the Sultan in the 1860s, forcing him to give in to their demands. He believed that the Germans could achieve the same 'friendly relationship' if 'they showed the Sultan their teeth'. And he added: 'If we had a patriotic majority in the Reichstag, I would already be suggesting installing commissioners and police forces in Dar es Salaam and Ghazi, as we did in the Cameroons and Togoland.'[224]

The father slightly dampened the enthusiasm of the son. He rejected the idea of taking over control over Zanzibar.[225] Nevertheless, he sanctioned a number of points which were to form the guidelines for Krauel's negotiation in London:[226]

1. To secure Dar es Salaam as a duty-free harbour. This should be achieved by leasing the customs administration from the Sultan, who should then ensure free transit to the interior. (This was a quite revealing demand since it implicitly conceded the Sultan's *de facto* authority along the trade routes, and the DOAG's inability to secure duty-free trade with the interior.)
2. The Sultan's claim to Ghazi was to be rejected, as it had been by the German commissioner Schmidt before. The Sultan should recall his troops from Ghazi.
3. To clarify the borders of the Witu region under German protection and to reject any rights by the Sultan to Manda Bay.
4. To achieve a settlement of rival British and German claims (Peters and Mackinnon) on Kilimanjaro. The Sultan's claim to the mountain should be recognized neither by the British nor by the Germans.

Since the British signalled early that they would accept a German customs lease at Dar es Salaam, Kilimanjaro thereafter became the central

---

[224] H. von Bismarck to O. von Bismarck, 12 Oct. 1886, FP 18, BAK.

[225] Bismarck's marginal comment, ibid.; Rantzau to Herbert von Bismarck, 12 Oct. 1886, Bismarck Papers, F 3, BAK.

[226] See draft instruction to Krauel, 12 Oct. 1886, FP 18, BAK.

issue. It was a complicated matter, as three rival claims lay on the table: the Sultan's treaties with Mandara; Jühlke's documents; and a set of treaties which the British had suddenly dug out, concluded in the region in 1885 by Harry Johnston. If Peters's treaties had sufficed to establish a German protectorate, any of these papers could serve the same purpose with respect to the Kilimanjaro region. That Mandara had not in fact yielded his sovereignty to anybody was of no relevance to the diplomats.[227]

Peters had always pointed to the importance of Kilimanjaro for Germany. In January 1886 he had travelled to London[228] to negotiate with the so-called Taweta group around Sir Donald Currie and Mackinnon. The British had also made claims to the mountain area, based on Johnston's treaties of 27 September 1884.[229] Peters obviously hoped that he could now kill two birds with one stone. He suggested that the British should join his DOAG.[230] This was to ensure that the Kilimanjaro region would eventually come under German sovereignty. Furthermore, Peters would have secured new investors and improved the company's financial standing, but these ideas came to nothing, as Mackinnon pursued other goals. In 1888 his enterprise would receive its own Royal Charter from the British government.

To make things worse for Peters, the London episode triggered an embarrassing dispute between the DOAG director and Bismarck. The Foreign Office found out that Peters had allegedly told the Scottish shipping magnate Mackinnon that the Chancellor himself had invested 100,000 marks in the company. Herbert von Bismarck was outraged at this news. Peters gave his word of honour that he had never made such a comment, but Mackinnon, when asked about the issue, maintained his claim. Eventually, however, the Scotsman stated that it might all have been a misunderstanding, so that the German government saw the matter as settled.[231] Nevertheless, the affair must have increased Bismarck's distrust of Peters and his methods.

---

[227] For a convincing discussion of this aspect, see J. C. Winter, 'Identität in Verhandlung, Dissens und Oktroi. Zur juristischen Problematik der Schutzverträge der Carl-Peters-Gruppe in Ostafrika, 1884/1885', *Paideuma*, 35 (1989), 301–15; see also Ch. 6 on Carl Peters on Kilimanjaro.

[228] Peters, 'Vorläufiger Bericht über die Resultate der im Interesse des Deutsch-Ostafrikanischen Kolonialunternehmens in London gepflogenen Verhandlungen', 3 Feb. 1886, RKolA 395, 18–21, BAB.

[229] H. von Bismarck to Consul Arendt, 25 Feb. 1886, RKolA 395, 41–3, BAB.

[230] Galbraith, *Mackinnon*, 106–7.

[231] Peters to Mackinnon, 10 Nov. 1886; Mackinnon to Peters, 17 Nov. 1886; Krauel's note, 10 Dec. 1886; Mackinnon to Peters, 21 Dec. 1886; Krauel to Peters (draft), 28 Dec. 1886; RKolA 374, 3, 7–10, 15, 23–4, 25, BAB; see also Galbraith, *Mackinnon*, 107–9.

As far as Kilimanjaro was concerned, the DOAG maintained a firm stand. In a conference with the Foreign Office on 7 October Peters made clear that he considered Kilimanjaro and Mombasa as *noli me tangere*.[232] But the mountain had long attracted Bismarck's attention as well. In a memorandum from Kusserow the Chancellor marked the following passage: 'Mr Hansing mentioned in passing that the acquisitions on Kilimanjaro were of the greatest value; those regions would be more suitable for lucrative enterprises than any other acquisition of the colonization society.'[233] It seems that Bismarck had kept this assessment in mind, and Kilimanjaro emerged as a *conditio sine qua non* for the Germans.

The British had two counterclaims in their hands, those of Bargash and of Johnston. If the Germans wanted to secure the mountain, they would have to offer substantial compensation, which was of some importance for British enterprise. The *quid pro quo* was Mombasa, a port hitherto claimed by the DOAG. For the British, the coastal town stood at the top of their list. As Sir Percy Anderson pointed out, they needed 'a free way to Lake Nyanza, because the sources of the Nile were located there and secured access to lower Sudan'. 'For political, strategic and commercial reasons' this would be 'of vital importance'.[234]

They also suggested that the Germans should abandon their claim to nearby Ghazi and chose another port further south instead.[235] After having conferred with von der Heydt, Peters agreed, proposing Pangani as an alternative outlet for the Kilimanjaro region (Bismarck: 'good').[236] On 19 October 1886 Krauel could cable to Berlin that Witu (point 3) and Kilimanjaro (point 4) had been secured.[237]

In short, the Germans had thus swapped Mombasa and Ghazi for sole control over Kilimanjaro. To get the mountain, Berlin eventually gave up all claims on the northern coast except Witu. They were all formally assigned to the Sultan, but *de facto* reserved for a lease to the British. London also agreed to support Berlin in reaching a 'friendly settlement' with the Sultan over the Kilimanjaro dispute.[238] In the language of diplomacy this phrase simply meant that London would put pressure on the Sultan to abandon his claim to the mountain.

---

[232] Peters to Lucas, 7 Oct. 1886, Lucas Papers, copy in FP 16, BAK.
[233] Kusserow to Bismarck, 16 Aug. 1885, RKolA 421, 19, BAB.
[234] Krauel's report, 20 Oct. 1886, FP 18, BAK.
[235] Krauel's report from London, 16 Oct. 1886, FP 18, BAK.
[236] Krauel's report, 20 Oct. 1886, FP 18, BAK.
[237] Krauel's cable, 19 Oct. 1886, FP 18, BAK.
[238] Krauel's report, point 4, 26 Oct. 1886, FP 18, BAK.

Many years after the negotiations, Peters held that it was only due to his insistence that Kilimanjaro was not given away. However, the documents suggest that Bismarck himself was keen to acquire the mountain too, and that Krauel consequently defended this claim. At the same time it was clear that the German government could not make a decision without considering the demands and wishes of the DOAG. Otherwise, the delegation would not have constantly conferred with DOAG members while negotiating in London.

Peters, despite his boastful declarations in public, knew that the British would claim their slice of the cake.[239] In fact, he regarded the situation for negotiating with the British as 'very favourable'.[240] It was only later that he blamed his government for not having been tough enough in the negotiations.[241] In 1886 he did not complain loudly about the outcome.

He could be satisfied anyway, since the ascribed sphere of influence was far larger than the DOAG was able to swallow.[242] The Sultan's authority in Tabora and Ujiji was simply ignored, since Britain and Germany had partitioned the interior behind the coastal strip into two spheres of influence. The separating line ran from the Umba river westward, along the northern slopes of Kilimanjaro to the eastern shores of Lake Victoria. In fact, the Anglo-German agreement kept the door open for further expansion inland, and it sanctioned a gradual dismantling of Zanzibari authority in the interior.

With regard to Peters we should bear in mind that he was a gambler, too. He sought to stir up public sentiment in order to put pressure on the government, which he did by always formulating maximum demands. This was not only true of the long list of coastal towns he had claimed for the DOAG; it was also true with respect to the Sultan's dominions. His demand for free transit rights without compensation was as extreme and aggressive as his impatient call for a coastal port. Although these aims were not immediately realized, the outcome of the agreement was a step in Peters's direction. Owing to the insistence of the DOAG, the Sultan was eventually granted just a tiny strip along the coast, not more than 10 miles wide.[243] Furthermore, the British committed themselves to support negotiations between the Sultan and the DOAG for a customs lease in Pangani and Dar es Saalam.[244]

[239] Peters to Lucas, 7 Oct. 1886, Lucas Papers, copy in FP 16, BAK.
[240] Ibid.   [241] Peters, *Gründung*, GS i. 204.
[242] See marginal comment by Bismarck, Krauel's report, 20 Oct. 1886, FP 18, BAK.
[243] See Krauel's report, 20 Oct. 1886, FP 18, BAK.
[244] Krauel's report, point 2, 26 Oct. 1886, FP 18, BAK.

From Peters's point of view the outcome was favourable. He may not have made all the tricks, but he had certainly won an important game. The agreement left plenty of room for further acquisitions in the interior, and access to the sea was now only a matter of time.

'HAVEN'T YOU SHOT A NEGRO YET?':[245] GERMAN STATIONS ON THE MAINLAND

The term 'sphere of influence' which was employed in the Anglo-German agreement of 1 November 1886 may have reflected well upon the future aspirations of the European powers. However, it had nothing to do with the actual situation on the ground. By the mid-1880s most parts of the so-called 'German sphere' had never been visited by a German before. There were only a few places in which the DOAG had settled by the end of 1886. The real state of these stations stood in sharp contrast to the rosy pictures which Peters painted in his propaganda journal *KPK*.

Twenty days' march away from the coast lay Simaberg, the company's first station on the mainland. Its founders were Count Pfeil and the merchant Otto, whom Peters had left behind in Usagara in December 1884.[246] By March 1885 Pfeil had recovered from his fever and started to construct a house at Sima, one and a half hours' walk from Muini Sagara. But only a month later Peters ordered him back to the coast to lead another expedition to the interior ('Pfeil sofort Njassa'[247]). Pfeil returned to Zanzibar via Chutu, making further treaties on the way.[248] The Usagara station (or the beginnings of it) remained unattended. Peters had chosen the gardener Carl Schmidt to replace Pfeil in Usagara, but his departure from Zanzibar was delayed because the Sultan obviously obstructed the recruitment of porters.[249] Many of them then deserted on the way, so that Schmidt reached Sima with great difficulty.

When another expedition arrived at Usagara in the summer of 1885, its leaders, von Bülow and von Derivere, 'found nothing' where 'they had expected a well equipped station'.[250] A short time later, both men became so ill that they had to be carried back to the coast.[251] Schmidt continued construction work, and started to experiment with various crops which the

---

[245] Peters's saying, according to Adolf von Tiedemann, *Der Tag*, 2 Feb. 1908, FP 12, BAK.
[246] See Ch. 2.   [247] Peters, *Gründung*, GS i. 189.
[248] *KPK*, 22 Jan. 1887, no. 3, 21.
[249] Toeppen to Arendt, n.d., DKG 265, 101 ff., BAB.
[250] Ibid. 106.   [251] Ibid.

company wanted to grow on large-scale plantations. The conditions in the fertile valley were promising,[252] but before anything could be produced on a larger scale, Schmidt died from fever in the summer of 1886.[253] The venture had cost two agents their lives, but had achieved hardly anything on the ground.

The story of the Sima station, which the *KPK* stubbornly described as a flourishing venture,[254] was more or less representative of DOAG settlements in the 1880s. None of them had made any significant impact on the local economy, let alone laid the foundation for a colonial economy. They neither sold European goods on any significant scale, nor participated in the trade in local products (apart from a handful of potatoes from Dunda station which were sold in the market at Zanzibar).[255] Few stations had achieved self-sufficiency in food; most of them had to be completely subsidized. Kiora, for instance, another Usagara station, consumed around 7,000 rupees or more than 9,000 marks per year,[256] yielding nothing in return. By 1887 it had been so neglected by the company that its major building collapsed. Peters lamented that Africans from the neighbourhood 'burnt the entire Boma as firewood'. The flagpost was knocked down and sheep and goats occupied the remaining buildings.[257] Whether one looks at Petershöhe in Useguha, at Tanganiko in the north, or at the Kingani stations Dunda, Usungula, and Madimula, none were in a promising state. They were, as the ivory merchant Kurt Toeppen noted of Tanganyiko, 'not worth anything'.[258]

In part, the poor state of the stations had to do with Peters's priorities in 1885 and 1886. He was still *spiritus rector* of the venture, and his agenda was expansion, so that most of DOAG's funds were absorbed by financing treaty-gathering expeditions. The establishment of stations was largely accidental and not based on a consistent economic, political, or administrative agenda. Consul Arendt complained that they were located too far apart, and that Peters had failed to recognize the importance of the central caravan routes, starting from Saadani and Bagamoyo. He wrote that 'the DOAG had done nothing to acquire military posts by establishing stations

[252] See Schmidt's report 'Über das Sima-Thal', RKolA 386, 21–6, BAB.

[253] Wagner, *Deutsch-Ostafrika*, 111; *KPK* no. 38 u. 39, 25 Sept. 1886, 265.

[254] *KPK* no. 14, 17 Oct. 1885.

[255] B. Kurtze, *Die Deutsch-Ostafrikanische Gesellschaft* (Jena, 1913), 81.

[256] Ibid. 82; for currency values see ibid. 103.

[257] Peters to Consulate, 1 June 1887, AL2/107, 187, ZNA.

[258] Toeppen to ?, 17 Dec. 1887, RKolA 387, 3; see Meyer's negative assessment of Dunda, Michahelles to AA, 26 Sept. 1887, RKolA 386, 68, BAB.

in the interior through which they could exercise their rule' over the acquired territories.[259]

Certainly, it was naive to expect from a company on the verge of bankruptcy that it would engage in the establishment of a functioning military network. Financial deficits and a lack of manpower were the central reasons for the situation deplored by Arendt, but there were other factors which also slowed down DOAG activities. One was omnipresent: disease.

Although precise figures are not available, contemporary reports indicate that illness was a decisive factor in this weakness. Many of the nineteen DOAG agents who had been sent to East Africa by 1886 were struggling with disease.[260] Sometimes they were not capable of leaving their beds for weeks. In these circumstances, any agricultural or construction work was impossible. Of the twenty-six DOAG agents who arrived in April 1887, four died from fever within a few weeks.[261]

Peters presented all sorts of explanations for this state of affairs. In a report to Bismarck he spoke of 'a general political confusion' which had prevented him from taking 'practical steps in Usagara'.[262] A year and a half later he sought to convince the Chancellor that 'political considerations' had forced the DOAG 'to split their forces to various points'. (Bismarck: 'nonsense').[263] Peters portrayed the protectorate as 'a newborn baby, struggling for air'. Once it had started to breathe properly, further growth would result more or less automatically, 'following organic laws'.[264]

Since German stations were scarcely involved in commerce or production at that stage, the economic sector was not yet a major area of conflict between DOAG agents and African communities. Nevertheless, various disputes over the supply of labour clearly indicated a major issue for the future. Peters's claim that 'the labour question may be regarded as being solved on all our stations'[265] was just another myth with which he deceived the Foreign Office. It seems that Africans were not opposed in principle to working for the Germans. Otherwise a handful of Europeans, without substantial military support, would hardly have managed to recruit local workers at all. Sometimes agents reported that they could not even employ all those Africans who sought work.[266] Most Africans, however, regarded

---

[259] See Arendt's reports to Bismarck, 6 March and 2 April 1886, RKolA 382, 69 ff., 94 ff., BAB.   [260] See *KPK* editions 1885–7, passim.

[261] See *KPK* no. 33, 20 Aug. 1887, 258.

[262] Peters to Bismarck, 21 April 1886, copy, RKolA 386, 3, BAB.

[263] Peters's report, DOAG to Bismarck, copy, 21 Oct. 1887, RKolA 386, 75, BAB.

[264] Ibid. 73.   [265] Peters's report, copy, 21 Oct. 1887, RKolA 386, 76, BAB.

[266] See Hermes' report 'Bericht über die landwirtschaftlichen Verhältnisse der Station Usungula', 2 Aug. 1886, RKolA 386, 27–8, BAB.

work for the Germans as an occasional opportunity to earn cash with which to buy goods such as cotton clothes.[267] Consequently, they did not want to be employed on a regular basis.

Under such circumstances, the prospect of acquiring a permanent workforce was slight. German frustration about this fact was fuelled by the widespread prejudice that Africans were lazy anyway, and that they had to be educated to work first. This so-called education often involved the use of the whip. Any initial willingness of Africans to work for Germans therefore declined rapidly.[268]

Sometimes the labour question triggered conflicts on a larger scale. This was the case at Usuangula, where the station director, Bülow, quarrelled with a neighbouring chief over the right to employ one of his people. Even the DOAG admitted later that the dispute could have been avoided if local representatives had behaved differently.[269] Their agent Hoernecke declared that 'the unrest was not caused without guilt on the part of their officers'.[270] Fighting lasted three days, causing 'heavy casualties' among the Africans.[271] Eventually, Bülow ordered the burning down of the entire village 'to restore tranquillity' in the region.[272]

Bülow, whom Bismarck seems to have estimated highly for his 'heroic' character,[273] was not the only violent temper around. At Korogwe, in the Pangani valley, Friedrich Schroeder terrorized his African subordinates and the neighbourhood. He had been a tobacco planter in Sumatra and now sought to establish a plantation at Lewa for the German Plantation Company, a subsidiary of the DOAG. The explorer Hans Meyer, who had visited Korogwe as well as a number of other DOAG stations, was so shocked by Schroeder's brutality that he felt obliged to inform the German consul at Zanzibar about what was going on there.

Schroeder often suffered from sleepless nights. At such times he would get up to find his servants. 'He would beat them, then bind their hands together on their back and hang them up from the roof until dawn.'[274] So bad were Schroeder's excesses at Korogwe that for a long time afterwards no African dared to work at the station. A neighbouring chief who had refused to force his people into German service got a taste of Schroeder's

[267] See Schmidt's report, RKolA 386, 21–6, BAB.   [268] Ibid.

[269] DOAG to Bismarck, 15 April 1887, RKolA 386, BAB.

[270] Arendt to AA, 10 March 1887, RKolA 386, 59, BAB.   [271] Ibid.

[272] Arendt to Bismarck, 27 April 1887, RKolA 386, 63, BAB.

[273] See Frieda von Bülow to Elli Peters, 16 Aug. 1891, note in FP 5, BAK. Peters also praised Bülow for his 'pluck': Peters to his sister Elli, 1 Aug. 1892, PP 87, BAB.

[274] Michahelles to Bismarck, 26 Sept. 1887, AL2/107, 273 ff., ZNA.

brutality as well. Three weeks after the beatings, he was not yet able to move his arm. Once Schroeder maltreated a number of workmen whom he had hired to build a house. The Indian contractor who had supplied the Africans took them to Zanzibar to present them to the consul. They had 'broken arms and other serious injuries', reported Michahelles to Berlin.[275]

German atrocities were not only confined to stations and their surrroundings. DOAG expeditions were also widely feared, particularly among those Africans who had been recruited for carrying the loads. For the slightest irregularity porters were punished by heavy flogging, observed the German consul. 'Minor insubordination, perhaps arising from a misunderstanding, was answered with a bullet.'[276] That Germans repeatedly executed porters was no secret in Zanzibar. It was therefore not surprising that Africans frequently deserted from their service, but this increased the brutality of their white masters even more. If somebody ran away, the German caravan leader would arbitrarily pick another porter from the group and beat him half to death, 'as a warning example'.[277]

With a peculiar mixture of brutality and arrogance, DOAG agents not only terrorized the members of their own caravans; they also provoked violent clashes with local African communities. Despite their superior weapons, the Germans did not always get the upper hand in those fights, as the following episode reveals. On their way through the Saadani hinterland, DOAG officers Schmidt and Hentschel bullied a passing African of the Wakamba who had refused to sell his bow and arrows to them. Schmidt started to beat him, but the young black escaped and called on his people for support. They attacked the Germans and wounded both of them seriously. The two whites were lucky, because English missionaries happened to live in the neighbourhood. They helped them to return to Zanzibar.[278]

We have seen that the DOAG had hardly any influence on the local or regional economy in the years 1885–7. In political terms, however, the situation was different. Some Africans regarded the Germans as potentially powerful allies or patrons. Equipped with modern weapons, white people were viewed as useful allies by all those Africans who still had to settle a score with a neighbour, or for those seeking protection against the raids of their enemies. Zelewski at Usuangula, for instance, managed to win over a

---

[275] Michahelles to Bismarck, 26 Sept. 1887, AL2/107, 273 ff., ZNA.   [276] Ibid.
[277] Ibid.
[278] Consul to Bismarck, ZNA, AL2/87, 165 ff.; Kirk to Salisbury, 9 Nov. 1885, AA1/43, ZNA. German records suggest a version of the incident which differs slightly from that given by Bennett (*Arab versus European*, 135) who presents a labour dispute as the trigger.

number of local chiefs who had repeatedly been raided by a neighbouring people from Ukami.[279]

These alliances, however, did not mean that the DOAG was able to establish political control. Its agents were easily drawn into ongoing conflicts whose causes they did not understand and whose players they hardly knew. At this stage German agents functioned like a catalyst for political turmoil. A case in point was the struggle on Kilimanjaro, where Mandara had welcomed Jühlke and Weiss and hoped for their support in his conflict with Sina of Kibosho. A few years later, Carl Peters himself would become involved in the politics of that mountain, as Chapter 6 will show. During the 1880s, however, the German presence was still focused on a few places near the coast.

The inability of German stations to establish political control in their area became most obvious in Usagara. Consul Arendt bitterly complained that the DOAG did nothing to maintain order in the new protectorate. The Sultan had complained to him that 'gangs of robbers' made any caravan trade increasingly risky.[280] According to the Hamburg merchant O'Swald, caravan trade was in heavy decline, since the DOAG had arrived in East Africa and confused the situation everywhere.[281]

In the past the Sultan had made provisions to police the trade routes to the interior. His garrison at Mamboja, for instance, served this purpose. With the proclamation of the German protectorate, however, the Sultan was obliged to abstain from military activities in the Usagara region. The Germans failed to fill the resulting power vacuum, thus perhaps inviting local African leaders to raid their neighbours. Even if the Sultan had not exerted full control in the region either, his presence had at least provided for some security along the trade routes. Two years of Arab–German rivalry had upset the fragile equilibrium, so that fewer and fewer caravans passed through the region.

It is a peculiar feature of DOAG activities in 1885 and 1886 that, despite their limited range and resources, they evoked a widespread anti-German feeling in the region. Among Arabs in Zanzibar, Germans were seen as 'adui Allah', the enemies of God.[282] The few Germans on the mainland provoked the hostility of Africans through their brutal excesses on stations and during their expeditions.

How do we account for this brutality? It is interesting that contemporary

[279] Hermes' report, 2 Aug. 1886, RKolA 386, 28, BAB.

[280] See Arendt to Bismarck, 6 March 1886, RKolA382, 69 ff., BAB.

[281] See O'Swald's complaint about the decline of caravan trade, O'Swald to Bismarck, 25 Sept. 1888, RKolA 360, 126 ff., BAB.   [282] Bennett, *Arab versus European*, 139.

German reports, including those of Peters himself, often stressed that Africans of the Swahili coast were not very aggressive or warlike.[283] Even if we treat these judgements with caution, they seem to suggest that white people did not encounter any initial hostility from the Africans. Hence, one might ask the motives of Peters's agents when they provoked violent clashes or maltreated their porters or employees.

Consul Michahelles, who had collected evidence of the maltreatment of Africans, suspected that DOAG agents sought to manifest their superiority through a certain *Schneidigkeit* (pluck). This, he observed, would be considered 'as good form' among the young DOAG representatives.[284] Peters's followers thus practised a cult of violence which formed part of their identity as true colonizers. Peters's favourite saying 'Haven't you shot a negro yet!?' encapsulated this kind of attitude.[285] Borrowing a hunting metaphor in order to degrade Africans to the level of animals, the phrase portrayed colonial violence as a sort of cultural privilege, reserved for the heroes of colonial conquest. But this was not only a mode of colonial ideology. It had become colonial practice as well.

THE ZANZIBAR MISSION: PETERS AND THE MAKING OF THE
COASTAL TREATY

In his new position as DOAG director, Peters was sent to East Africa to run the company's affairs on the ground. On 17 May 1887 he disembarked at Zanzibar harbour, accompanied by twenty DOAG agents.[286] Three days later, Arendt introduced him to Said Bargash, who declared 'that he would welcome any German whom the consul introduced to him'.[287] In fact, however, the Sultan had good reason to be worried about the group of young Germans. During the past two years he had had plenty of quarrels with the DOAG. It took only two weeks to convince him that the Peters group was no different in this respect.

In the early morning of 25 May the German cruiser *Möwe* took Peters and a few of his associates to the coastal town of Dar es Salaam. Peters had told the German consul that he wanted to collect the necessary materials for

[283] See, for example, Peters, 'Die Usagara-Expedition', GS i. 300; Frieda von Bülow, 'Aus Ostafrika', *KPK* no. 33, 20 Aug. 1887, 200.
[284] Michahelles to Bismarck, 26 Sept. 1887, AL2/107, 273 ff., ZNA.
[285] Article by Adolf von Tiedemann, *Der Tag*, 2 Feb. 1908, FP 12, BAK.
[286] DOAG confidential report, 80 Ge 1/2, 35 ff., BAB.
[287] Arendt to AA, 30 May 1887, RKolA 360, 92, BAB.

the planned customs lease, and to establish a local DOAG agency there.[288] Three days later, he returned to Zanzibar, expressing to Consul Arendt his 'satisfaction about the cooperation displayed by the Wali of Dar es Salaam'.[289]

The Sultan, however, produced quite a different story. He informed Arendt of a number of excesses which had occurred during Peters's visit. Bargash pointed out that turmoil of unpredictable dimensions could break out among the local population if such incidents were not prevented in the future.[290] This was indeed a prophetic statement, as later events on the coast were to prove.

What had happened? Enquiries by German and British officials provide sufficient evidence to trace the real course of events. When Peters entered the town, he was accompanied by a handful of Germans and two dozen Arab soldiers whom he had hired for the trip to the mainland. Not surprisingly, the Sultan's governor was irritated by the appearance of the German military force, which exceeded the number of his own soldiers in the town.[291] Peters had neither come with the German consulate's interpreter, who should have mediated in the purchase of land and houses, nor did he carry Bargash's letter of recommendation which Arendt had arranged.[292]

Peters obviously believed that a demonstration of military strength was the best way of bringing local authorities to heel. With his group of mercenaries, he surrounded the governor's residence. He then seized 'the Sultan's accredited agent for communicating with the neighbouring chiefs'. He 'openly offered to bribe him to make a declaration that he was the virtual ruler of the country under his supervision and consented to place it under the German Africa company. At his refusal a pistol was held to his ear and he was forced to put his signature to the document.'[293]

While Peters threatened the Sultan's agent, Hörnecke bullied two Swahili outside Dar es Salaam to make them sell their land. The Africans stated that DOAG agents had forced them with their pistols to sign a contract whose contents they did not even know.[294] Hörnecke's companion later denied any use of force, but he admitted that Hörnecke had beaten two blacks with his stick; one had allegedly shown him the wrong path, the

[288] Peters to Arendt, 19 May 1887, 7; Arendt to Bismarck, 2 June 1887, 3–6, RKolA 388, BAB.   [289] Arendt to Bismarck, 2 June 1887, RKolA 388, 3–6, BAB.
[290] Ibid.
[291] See Arendt to Bismarck, 5 June 1887, 14–15, RKolA 388, BAB.
[292] Holmwood to Salisbury, 6 June 1887, AA1/52, ZNA; Arendt to Bismarck, 2 June 1887, RKolA 388, BAB.
[293] Holmwood to Salisbury, 6 June 1887, AA1/52, ZNA.
[294] Steifensand to Bismarck, 20 June 1887, RKolA 388, 28, BAB.

other had refused to carry him over a river.[295] In the meantime August Leue, designated station director of Dar es Salaam (he was called 'the poet'[296] by his DOAG fellows), had posted his armed soldiers in the streets. Residents understood the military demonstration as a sign that the Germans now claimed the entire town as their own.[297]

Being questioned by the consul, Peters now explained the events as 'misunderstandings', which had arisen through the absence of Bargash's letter of recommendation, and 'the energetic action' of single DOAG agents.[298] In Germany, an article appeared in the *Kölnische Zeitung*, seeking to play down the rumours of turmoil in Dar es Salaam: 'All that happened was a little quarrel between the lower servants and some natives . . . Apart from that the good relationship with the indigenous population has not been disturbed for one moment.'[299]

But Steifensand, who had been sent to Dar es Salaam to make enquiries, was not able to disprove the charges against Peters. The deputy consul questioned two DOAG members, who admitted that their director had treated the Wali in 'a very energetic way', allegedly because the Sultan's agent had forbidden his residents any German employment.[300]

Sultan Bargash was particularly worried about the German military demonstrations in the town, and Leue was immediately instructed by Steifensand to disarm his mercenaries and withdraw them to Usaramo.[301] Furthermore, the Sultan asked for the punishment of those who had insulted the Wali and maltreated the residents. He also demanded that the land contracts should be cancelled, and that the DOAG should stop further construction work in the town. Peters, under pressure from Arendt, agreed to take back the contracts. He even sent a letter of apology to the Sultan, explaining the incident as due to 'bad interpreting'.[302] As a result, the Sultan withdrew his request for the punishment of Peters. Hörnecke, on the other hand, was sentenced to a fine of 100 marks, because of disorderly conduct.[303]

Supported by his superior, Leue managed to maintain his post in Dar es Salaam, despite complaints that had reached Berlin. It was Peters who intervened on his behalf; he maintained that Leue had not been responsible

[295] Steifensand to Bismarck, 20 June 1887, RKolA 388, 29, BAB.
[296] See Arendt to Bismarck, 5 June 1887, RKolA 388, 15, BAB.
[297] Steifensand to Bismarck, 20 June 1887, RKolA 388, 29, BAB.
[298] Arendt to Bismarck, 2 June 1887, RKolA 388, 4, BAB.
[299] Article 'Africa' of 13 July 1887, copy in RKolA 388, 23, BAB.
[300] Steifensand to Bismarck, 20 June 1887, RKolA 388, 30, BAB.
[301] Ibid. 29.   [302] Ibid. 31.   [303] Ibid. 31–2.

for the conflict and that all doubts about his suitability were unjustified.[304] On the contrary, he praised the exemplary discipline which the agent had established among his followers. A year later it was Leue who impatiently broke off talks with local notables, badly insulted them, and drove them into resistance.[305]

With Peters's foolish show of strength the DOAG had achieved nothing. On the contrary, he had undermined his own position in Zanzibar. The consulate's sentence on Hörnecke was a defeat and must have confused Bargash about who was the real representative of German interests, Peters or Arendt? After the incident in Dar es Salaam the Sultan became more reserved towards Peters than ever before. Bargash was so irritated that he even sought to avoid any further contact. Twice he asked the German consul to act as an intermediary between him and the DOAG director, but Arendt replied that Peters was 'authorized to conduct direct negotiations'.[306]

In the meantime Peters had adopted a new strategy. Since brute force had not yielded the expected results, he now turned to diplomacy. Through his agents Peters intimated to Muhammad bin Salim, the Sultan's secretary, that he was Bismarck's 'special confidant' and crucial adviser in colonial matters.[307] When Consul Arendt, who was not on good terms with Peters, left Zanzibar in the middle of June, the Sultan took this as proof of Peters's influence.[308] He did not know that the actual reason for Arendt's return was his poor health.[309]

As Arendt left the island, another colonial enthusiast arrived in Zanzibar on 17 June 1887,[310] Frieda von Bülow, representative of the Deutsch-Nationaler Frauenbund and one of Peters's close associates. Her task was to establish a German hospital in the protectorate, as illness was a serious problem for most Europeans in East Africa (with the exception of Peters, who always felt that his health improved the longer he stayed in East Africa!). As a British colonel told Bülow on their boat passage, Zanzibar had 'such a feeling of a church-yard about it'.[311]

She came with a good deal of enthusiasm, which was fuelled by her desire to meet Carl Peters again. In Usagara House, the company's centre

---

[304] Peters to DOAG, 29 Aug. 1887, RKolA 388, 41–2, BAB.
[305] See Leue to DOAG, 28 Sept. 1888 (copy), RKolA 407, 41, BAB.
[306] See Michahelles to Bismarck, 22 Oct. 1887, AL 2/107, 290–4, ZNA; see also Arendt to Bismarck, 5 June 1887, London 561, PA-AA, Bonn.   [307] Ibid.
[308] Ibid.   [309] H. von Bismarck to Michahelles, 27 Nov. 1887, FP 18, BAK.
[310] F. von Bülow, *Reiseskizzen und Tagebuchblätter aus Deutsch-Ostafrika* (Berlin, 1889), 21.
[311] Ibid. 9.

at Zanzibar, the DOAG community would come together and hold their dinner parties. They had decorated the hall of the old Arab building with DOAG and German flags. On one side, a bronze bust of the Kaiser stood on a pedestal, decorated with flowers.[312] On clear, star-spangled nights Peters and Bülow would indulge in philosophical discussions, 'which were elevating for our German national spirit'.[313] It was in those days that Bülow and Peters became really close to each other.[314]

Bülow's reports displayed great admiration for Peters and his 'youthful patriots': 'These were the brave men whose names we had often read in the *Korrespondenz*, whose courage and persistence we had admired at home.'[315] DOAG activities were described in glorifying terms: 'It is a true satisfaction for the German national spirit to watch the unanimous, energetic, and serious efforts of our colonial officers.'[316] Bülow's Zanzibar experience was to inspire a series of novels which she later published in Germany; these were largely a glorification of Peters himself.[317]

Peters's attitude towards Frieda von Bülow is less clear, as his correspondence gives no clue. His friend Irmer stated later that Frieda had been 'the only woman for whom he felt real affection'[318] prior to his marriage to Thea Hebers. Whatever the truth behind the rumours which circulated about the pair,[319] their tête-à-têtes in Zanzibar did not lead to a permanent relationship.

Peters's private life may have flourished in Zanzibar. His colonial venture, however, ran into further trouble. To overcome this problem, he decided to turn to the British consul for support. After all, London had promised in the 1886 agreement to help the Germans to gain a customs lease in Dar es Salaam and Pangani. Consul Holmwood indeed conferred with Bargash on the German matter once or twice early in July 1887.[320] After his intervention, Peters and the Sultan quickly agreed on a customs lease in the two coastal towns.[321]

But before this settlement was put into effect, Peters found out that the British had already negotiated a lease of the coastal strip within their sphere of influence.[322] On 14 July Peters again approached Holmwood, informing

[312] *KPK* no. 31, 6 Aug. 1887, 244; *KPK* no. 33, 20 Aug. 1887, 259.

[313] *KPK* no. 35, 3 Sept. 1887, 277.

[314] Frieda von Bülow to Elli Peters, 13 Nov. 1889, FP 5, BAK.

[315] *KPK* no. 33, 20 Aug. 1887, 259.   [316] Bülow, *Reiseskizzen*, 163–4.

[317] See Ch. 5.

[318] Schnee Papers, Schnee, 'Notizen über Carl Peters', 1 HA Rep 92, vol. 24/49, Interview Irmer (p. 107), GStA-PK.

[319] See F. von Bülow to Elli Peters, 13 Nov. 1889, FP 5, BAK.

[320] Michahelles to Bismarck, 22 Oct. 1887, AL 2/107, 290–4, ZNA.   [321] Ibid.

[322] Lucas to Bismarck, 11 July 1887, note in FP 18, BAB.

him that he wished to secure a similar arrangement for the German part. The consul had no objections and promised to assist.[323] Again, it seems that Holmwood paved the way for the Germans, for on 19 July the Sultan sent Peters a copy of the British treaty. The DOAG director accepted this as a model for the German concession.[324] By 30 July, Muhammad bin Salim, the Sultan's secretary, and Peters had both signed a preliminary treaty.[325] In substance, it was identical to the British one.[326] Now, the board of directors in Berlin had to give their *placet*.

But they did not reply as quickly as expected. Peters spent weeks and weeks waiting for confirmation, but there was no message. To kill time, he would sometimes walk up and down on Frieda's veranda, singing for her the songs of his youth.[327] Only on 3 October did he receive an answer.[328] The board was not prepared to accept article IX of the treaty. They refused the following passage:

The Association hereby guarantees to His Highness the whole amount of the customs duties which he now receives, from both the import and the export trade of that part of His Highness's dominions included in this concession. The definite amount of the annual average shall be fixed after one year's experience. For the first year the Association guarantees to His Highness the amount of the customs which He now receives, as shown by his books, . . .[329]

The company leadership in Berlin saw these arrangements as 'a leap into the dark'.[330] They feared that the compensation to be paid to the Sultan 'might result in damage to the company which could lead to immediate liquidation'. When they enquired with Arendt, the former consul, he declared that Bargash's customs system was not suitable for providing statistical data, such as were common in Europe. 'Only a practical experiment could yield concrete data', he told DOAG leaders.[331]

Clearly, the DOAG in Berlin had got cold feet. They refused their signature and told Peters he should seek changes in the treaty. The Sultan should not be guaranteed a fixed sum for a first probationary year. Instead he should be paid the returns from the actual customs collection less all

[323] Correspondence in AL 2/107, 295, 296, and AA 1/52, ZNA.
[324] Michahelles to Bismarck, 22 Oct. 1887, AL 2/107, 290–4, ZNA.
[325] Copy of treaty, AL 2/107, 216–20, ZNA, also in DOAG Papers, 80 Ge 1/2, 43–5, BAB.
[326] See copy of the British treaty, Article IX, RKolA 324, 15, BAB; AA note, 7 Nov. 1887, FP 18, BAK.   [327] See Bülow to Peters, n.d., FP 5, BAK.
[328] Note in FP 18, BAK.
[329] See copy of the treaty in DOAG Papers, 80 Ge 1/2, 43–5.
[330] DOAG to Peters, 3 Oct. 1887, note in FP 18, BAK.
[331] See DOAG proceedings, 30 Sept. 1887, 80 Ge 1/2, 38, BAB.

administrative costs (military and civil administration). This amount should then be fixed as the future sum for the lease. Furthermore, the treaty was to include a clause which would make an adjustment of the actual sum possible every three years.[332] The demanded version now differed significantly from the British one.[333]

For Peters, the refusal of the board of directors was highly embarrassing. How could he explain to the Sultan that his treaty had not met with approval at home? He had spent weeks persuading Bargash that he was Bismarck's major *intimus*, and that his opinion was decisive. And now this! His bold pretensions were now likely to backfire and threaten his entire mission.

Bargash was indeed upset about the new German demands and refused to make any further alterations. To the consul he complained that Peters had deceived him.[334] He also refused to maintain direct contact with Peters or any other company representative.[335] While the negotations were stalled, Herbert von Bismarck emphasized that any future negotiations which extended into the political field should be conducted by the consul.[336] By the turn of the year the DOAG had decided to recall Peters to Berlin without having resolved the customs issue.

Apart from the negotiations over the customs lease, Peters had in fact achieved little on the ground. Stations in Mpuapua and Arusha were founded, but this could not compensate for the miserable state of stations in the interior. Some of them were to be sold, according to the new agenda, but Peters was not successful in finding appropriate buyers. The station at Simatal, for instance, was offered to the Holy Ghost Fathers twice, but the missionaries did not find it worth purchasing.[337] On top of this, the leadership in Berlin had turned down a new initiative from Peters to promote immediate emigration to the colony.[338]

However, as far as the coastal treaty was concerned, the DOAG displayed a good deal of hypocrisy. Peters was made a scapegoat and was blamed for the failure to reach a better deal. In fact, however, the situation had more to do with the intention of DOAG financiers to shift all financial risks onto Bargash. When it came to a further discussion of the draft treaty,

[332] DOAG proceedings, 28 Sept. 1887, DOAG Papers, 80 Ge 1/7, 18–19, BAB.
[333] See copy of the British treaty, Article IX, RKolA 324, 15, BAB.
[334] Michahelles to Bismarck, 18 Nov. 1887, note in FP 18, BAK.
[335] Michahelles to Bismarck, 18 Dec. 1887, RKolA 388, 55–7, BAB.
[336] Bismarck to Michahelles (drafted by Krauel), 27 Nov. 1887, FP 18, BAB.
[337] See J. A. P. Kieran, 'Abushiri and the Germans', *Hadith* 2, ed. Bethwell Ogot (Nairobi, 1970), 157–201.
[338] DOAG proceedings, 6 July 87, 80 Ge 1, vol. 7, DOAG Papers, BAB.

the DOAG leadership maintained their hard line and rejected any official proposals for a compromise. Kayser suggested leaving the collection of customs in the Sultan's hands for another year, monitoring its collection, and then fixing a sum on the basis of the acquired data.[339] But the DOAG did not want to give in. They argued that so far they had 'only made sacrifices' and that 'a powerful word' from the Chancellor would surely suffice to force the Sultan to give in.[340] They counted upon official pressure to secure their maximum demands.

Interestingly, the German government also made enquiries as to how the British had solved the issue. According to Michahelles, the British East African Company had been more obliging in fixing a sum of compensation for Bargash, as they had more capital.[341] German financiers, on the other hand, were not prepared to invest more. They sought to run the venture largely at the expense of Bargash.

Bargash had no confidence whatsoever in the commercial skills of the DOAG which was no surprise after its performance in Dar es Salaam and elsewhere. He told the German consul that Peters and his people were bad administrators and businessmen, who could not secure his income.[342]

When Bargash continued to object and complained to Bismarck, the Chancellor expressed his sympathy for the British approach and was angry that the Germans had not accepted a similar deal. 'They should have let him benefit by granting him part of the good business!'[343] As far as the lease was concerned, he was thus in line with Peters. His son Herbert regarded Bargash's attitude that any leaseholder also had to bear the risk of paying a yearly sum as 'fair'.[344] Eventually the DOAG at least agreed to pay an advance (not more than 150,000 marks) and to fix a maximum administrative cost to be subtracted from the customs income (250,000 marks).[345]

It is important to note that the government had no objection to Peters's deal as such. On the contrary, they opposed the inflexible line of the DOAG financiers. Why, then, did they favour Peters's removal from Zanzibar?[346] Arguably, they were not ready to tolerate Peters's secret diplomacy, in

---

339 Delbrück to Bismarck, 22 Dec. 1887, note in FP 18, BAK.
340 DOAG to Bismarck, 8 Nov. 1887, note in FP 18, BAK.
341 Michahelles to Bismarck, 13 Feb. 1888, note in FP 18, BAK.
342 Michahelles to Bismarck, 21 Nov. 1887, note in FP 18, BAK.
343 Bismarck's marginal comment on Michahelles to Kayser or Krauel?, 13 Feb. 1888, note in FP 18, BAK.
344 Marginal comment on Michahelles to Bismarck, 21 Nov. 1887, note in FP 218, BAK.
345 H. von Bismarck to Michahelles, 27 Dec. 1887, note in FP 18, BAK.
346 See H. von Bismarck's comment on Michahelles to Bismarck, 21 Nov. 1887, note in FP 18, BAK.

which he had represented himself as a close confidant of Bismarck. Peters's moves were too unpredictable to be of real value for the government. In a letter to Michahelles, Herbert von Bismarck indicated this position when he called Peters an unreliable representative.[347] The DOAG, on the other hand, met with Peters's opposition to the treaty modifications, so that they also had an interest in his removal. Thus, his return to Germany was inevitable.

The episode provides interesting insights into the confused state of German colonial affairs. Peters had been given freedom to negotiate, but when he had reached an agreement it was rejected. The German consul in Zanzibar had been told not to interfere in the process, but ultimately it was Arendt's judgement that was crucial in obstructing the Peters treaty. This episode was just another proof that Bismarck's charter system was not suitable for handling East African affairs. This was implicitly conceded by Herbert von Bismarck when he decided to place further negotiations in the hands of Consul Michahelles in Zanzibar. Throughout 1887, however, Bismarck was not yet prepared to admit the failure of his programme. He wanted to preserve the image of a DOAG that managed its affairs on its own,[348] but *de facto* the government had intervened more than once.

The final blow to the charter system was soon to come. In March 1888 Sultan Said Bargash died. The Germans had an easy time with his successor, Said Khalifa, who was not as experienced as his brother Bargash. When the German government threatened to withhold official recognition as long as he objected to the treaty, Khalifa gave way and accepted. The document was signed by Michahelles and the Sultan on 28 April 1888. The Germans now paid an even lower advance than they had offered to Bargash (50,000 rupees, or about 75,000 marks). The maximum administrative cost to be subtracted from the customs collection was fixed at 170,000 rupees (about 255,000 marks).[349]

Now the way was open for a takeover of the coast. But the triumph of German colonial enthusiasts was to be short-lived. As they prepared to take over coastal administration in the summer of 1888 rebellion shattered all hopes for a quick consolidation of company rule. In 1889 German imperial forces under the command of Hermann Wissmann moved in. After eighteen months of fighting, the Germans had put down the uprising on the coast, having caught most of the rebel leaders and executed many of them.

---

[347] H. von Bismarck to Michahelles, 27 Nov. 1887 (draft Krauel), note in FP 18, BAK.
[348] See Bismarck's marginal comments, Consul General to Bismarck, 13 March 1887, note in FP 18, BAK.
[349] Michahelles's telegram, 13 April 1888, note in FP 18, BAK.

Military intervention also marked the collapse of the charter system. German East Africa was turned into a state colony, run by an imperial governor and with a state-financed military and administrative system. It is not possible in this context to deal with the rebellion in great detail. Carl Peters had been back in Europe for more than six months when the uprising started. Nevertheless, it was he who had long been *spiritus rector* of company affairs. Even after the reconstitution of the DOAG in 1887 he maintained a prominent and arguably influential position within the company. His post in Zanzibar was taken over by Vohsen, whom company leaders praised for his commercial experience. But the continuities were perhaps more significant than they appear at first glance. The core of DOAG agents on the ground was still the same. They had been recruited by Peters and often favoured a ruthless policy in his style. Furthermore, the basic pattern of the DOAG scheme for the coast was still the one which had been drafted by Peters himself. Hence this chapter concludes with a brief enquiry into the relevance of DOAG policy to the outbreak of rebellion, an issue which is still open to debate.

There is a wide range of literature on the uprising and its causes.[350] One recent study, however, stands out in this context: Jonathon Glassman's *Feasts and Riot* is the most profound and convincing work on the topic.[351] While previous scholars have employed a rather narrow focus, following a pattern of European imperial intrusion and African response, his explanation is more profound. It sheds light on the growing tensions on the Swahili coast prior to German intrusion, resulting from the growth of long-distance trade. A picture of a fragile equilibrium emerges in which Swahili notables and the Sultan of Zanzibar's representatives shared political power on the coast. At the heart of Glassman's interest, however, lies the plebeian crowd, slaves who manned the caravans or worked on the sugar plantations. He shows that they had their own motives for rioting which differed considerably from the aims of their leaders. He points to the significance of ritual feasts in which plebeians could express their aspirations to status. Urban festivals provided a platform for performing the rituals of dance societies and religious brotherhoods. By chance, the Germans intervened at a time of intense festival activity. In Pangani, their provocations turned feasts into riot.

---

[350] Among the most important works are Müller, *Deutschland*; Kieran, 'Abushiri'; Iliffe, *Modern History*; Bennett, *Arab*.

[351] J. Glassman, *Feasts and Riot. Revelry, Rebellion, and Popular Consciousness on the Swahili Coast, 1856–1888* (Portsmouth, 1995), and idem, 'Social Rebellion and Swahili Culture: The Response to German Conquest of the Northern Mrima' (University of Madison-Wisconsin, Ph.D. thesis, 1988).

Glassman has thus challenged explanations which have portrayed the uprising as a straightforward and unified African response to German aggression.[352] One of the merits of his work is that it destroys the myth of a homogeneous rebel movement. His study shows the variety of interests involved, and the differing motivations of those who participated in armed rebellion. But he goes one step further. He argues that 'the Germans may have been a necessary catalyst for the rebellion, but they were not a sufficient cause.'[353]

Is it really plausible to attribute to the Germans the mere role of a catalyst? Were they just the spark which brought a powder-keg to explode? Or was there perhaps more to the German factor? Glassman is convincing when he argues that early DOAG activities in the interior could not have caused the uprising as such. Their stations played no role in the local economy and their impact on regional politics was still negligible.[354]

However, another point should not be underrated in the context of the German presence. This is the coastal treaty by which Sultan Khalifa leased the coastal strip to the DOAG.[355] Arguably, this step posed a serious threat to the economic and political structure on the coast. More precisely, it endangered the position of Swahili notables in coastal towns. As Glassman himself has shown, the Sultanate was not the only political authority in these towns. Urban notables, the *majumbe*, and Zanzibari representatives shared the exercise of political control. Whatever may have been the tensions arising from that sharing of power, the system was flexible enough to ensure that coastal Swahili elites maintained commercial and political privileges and could benefit from the growth of long-distance trade as well. For example, they still had a right to collect *ada*, duties paid by caravans arriving from upcountry or upon other occasions.[356]

The prospect of a German takeover destroyed any hopes of preserving such a position. Certainly, coastal elites were not hostile to foreign initiatives as such, as long as they could benefit from them as well. However, the German deal with the Sultan had been concluded largely at their expense. The reason why the *majumbe* resisted thus cannot be separated from the German advance itself. Whatever may have motivated the crowd to follow their patrons, the rebel leadership aimed largely at a reversal of the German deal with the Sultan. In that sense it originated precisely from

[352] See Glassman, *Feasts*, 177.   [353] Ibid. 11.   [354] Ibid. 178.
[355] This point is also recognized in Bennett, *Arab*, 174.
[356] See 'Bericht über die augenblicklichen politischen Verhältnisse an der Ost-Afrikanischen Küste von Dr. Franz Stuhlmann, z.Z. in Zanzibar', [1888], RKolA 693, 41–51, BAB; see also Glassman, *Feasts*, 204.

German intrusion. This point cannot be ignored in any explanation of the rising.

As early as 1887 Peters's performance in Dar es Salaam had caused a lot of excitement among local notables. Given the good communications on the coast, it is very likely that Peters's outrages had become known in other coastal centres as well. At that time, the DOAG had been punished for their actions and the situation calmed down again. But a year later, when Zelewski entered Pangani, things were to develop differently.

Glassman himself has narrated the events in Pangani with great skill, and this is not the place to tell the story again. However, it is important to bear in mind that Emil von Zelewski and his group acted with an amazing degree of arrogance and contempt. They desecrated the mosque when Zelewski forced his way into the prayer room, wearing boots and accompanied by his hunting dog.[357] German marines terrorized people in the town and the surroundings, seizing women at will and raping them. When they were questioned about their behaviour they would reply: 'This is the way things are done in Europe'.[358]

Interestingly, the only existing written source in which the Pangani rebels explain their situation to the Sultan makes explicit references to the German outrages as mentioned above.[359] Not all notables may have decided to rebel against the Germans for these reasons. However, the petition of 13 September 1888 suggests that those Pangani notables who joined the resistance movement did so to remove the Germans from the coast.

A look at Bagamoyo and Dar es Salaam reveals a similar picture, despite the different local conditions. As Glassman indicates, in Bagamoyo the *majumbe* constituted the core of the rising. There is evidence that they objected to German administration as it meant a further reduction of their political power.[360] German brutality there should not be overlooked either. Marines carried out a massacre in Bagamoyo at the very beginning of the tensions, killing some 100 people.[361] Such actions made it clear that the Germans were not willing to compromise or negotiate. Many of the Bagamoyo notables thus chose the option of armed resistance. They regarded the Sultan and the Germans as allies who acted at their expense. Another rebel leader, Bwana Heri at Saadani, chose to resist because he feared that German intrusion might endanger his commercial and political

---

357 Glassman, *Feasts*, 215 ff.   358 Ibid. 217.

359 For an English translation of the document see Glassman, 'Social Rebellion', 649 ff. A German translation is to be found in RKolA 406, 110 ff. For a printed version see Müller, *Deutschland*, 544–6.   360 Glassman, *Feasts*, 204.

361 Ibid. 210–11.

influence in the caravan trade.[362] This motive could also have played a role
for Swahili caravan traders in Pangani. The situation at Dar es Salaam,
which was fairly quiet at the beginning of the uprising, still deserves
further research. At least one author has suggested that Peters's early associate August Leue and his group drove the local *majumbe* into opposition,
causing them to flee the town and join the rebel forces.[363] The *majumbe*
were indeed 'the soul' of the uprising, as the German scientist Stuhlmann,
a careful observer of the scene, suspected in 1888.[364]

The simple but crucial point about the German factor was that it was
perceived as a fundamental threat to the position of coastal Swahili elites.
German administration meant a further loss of power for the notables,
without providing sufficient compensation. There were both moderate and
radical forces opposing the German presence. Bushiri, for instance, was
known for his hostility towards the Sultan.[365] He may have calculated that
driving out the Germans could secure a degree of autonomy which was
beneficial to all those who had been at odds with Zanzibari rule. Others
were obviously willing to negotiate, as Vohsen learned from Arab interme-
diaries. They believed that restoration of the *status quo ante* was the best
way to protect their interests.[366] On the whole, however, there is sufficient
evidence to suggest that German intervention persuaded many coastal
leaders to resist. In this sense, the German intrusion remains a crucial
factor for the uprising. This is not to question the skill and originality of
Glassman's work, but it tends to attribute too little importance to the
impact of the German takeover.

As a final point in this context it should perhaps be noted that the
DOAG officers who were active in 1888 had mostly been recruited by
Peters himself. They were all quite close to him in ideological terms, and
their methods and attitudes resembled those of their early leader. They
made sure that 'a ruthlessly brutal policy—*à la* Peters'[367] left its traces even
after his departure.

---

[362] See Glassman, *Feasts*, 195.   [363] See Müller, *Deutschland*, 432.
[364] 'Bericht über die augenblicklichen politischen Verhältnisse an der Ost-Afrikanischen
Küste von Dr. Franz Stuhlmann, z.Z. in Zanzibar', [1888], RKolA 693, 41–51, BAB.
[365] See Kieran, 'Abushiri', 167.
[366] See Vohsen to DOAG, 13 Nov. 88; RKolA 407, 64–8, BAB.
[367] Peters to Lange, 29 Jan. 1885, note in FP 15, BAK.

4

Rescuing Emin Pasha
(1888–1890)

I will attempt . . . to carve
my name deep into world history.

Carl Peters on his planned Emin
Pasha expedition, 1888[1]

EXPANSIONIST DESIGNS AND IMPERIAL POLITICS:
THE MAKING OF THE EMIN PASHA COMMITTEE

The failure to negotiate a final treaty with Said Bargash was a heavy blow
for Peters. As his sister observed, he was 'crushed in body and soul' when
he returned to Europe in early 1888.[2] In fact, his future colonial career
was seriously threatened. 'The fight against Dr Peters . . . starts with
heavy guns', Count Behr observed at the time,[3] and Schroeder remarked
to Palezieux: 'I doubt that they will be willing to send out Peters again,
and he will have to operate very skilfully if he does not want to fall altogether.'[4]

Opposition against Peters was mounted not only within the board of
directors but also at the Foreign Office, which criticized Peters's dubious
finances. It turned out that the Zanzibar agency had exceeded its budget by
almost 100,000 marks, without providing any records. Some of the money
had been spent only after Peters's departure from Zanzibar, but he was still
responsible for an excess expenditure of almost 50,000 marks.[5] Arguably,
however, the Foreign Office was less concerned about the financial issue as

---

[1] Peters to Elli, 18 Dec. 1888, PP 87, BAK.
[2] Schnee Papers, 'Notizen über Karl Peters', vol. 24, 49/109, 1 HA, Rep 92, GStA-PK
(Krätschell, *Peters*, 41, mistakenly refers to Arendt).
[3] Behr to Palezieux, 5 Feb. 1888, Palezieux Papers, vol. 1, 33–4, BAK.
[4] Schroeder to Palezieux, 27 Jan. 1888, Palezieux Papers, vol. 7, 26–7, BAK.
[5] Behr to Palezieux, 31 Jan. 1888, Palezieux Papers vol. 1, 31–2, BAK; AA to Delbrück, 8
April 1888, RKolA 403, 30 f.; meeting of the Board of Directors, 26 March 1888, minutes,
RKolA 375, 67–70; Anlage (General-Vertretung Zanzibar), RKolA 375, 76, BAB.

such, but rather about a man who cared little for directives from above and who was difficult to control.

While Peters was still on his way home, the DOAG chose a new representative for East Africa, who had more experience in commercial matters. This man was Ernst Vohsen, who was to function as DOAG agent 'for trade and customs administration'.[6] On the other hand, Peters was not fired altogether. His post as a DOAG director remained untouched.[7]

It seems that a key figure shielding Peters was his friend von der Heydt. Aware of the problems that would arise, the DOAG chairman sought to catch Peters on the way before he returned to Berlin.[8] At the beginning of February the two men met at Nervi, near Genoa, where von der Heydt had a holiday house. There they could discuss the situation and agree on a future strategy. Von der Heydt outlined a plan which seemed to provide a way out of the problem. He suggested that Peters should set out to find the mysterious Emin Pasha in Upper Sudan and take over his position there.[9]

Emin Pasha's fate had occupied the minds of colonial enthusiasts for some time. His real name was Eduard Schnitzer. He came from Neisse in Silesia, and he had embarked on an unusual career for a medical doctor. Since 1878 Schnitzer had ruled the Equatorial Province in Central Africa as governor for the Egyptian khedive. When the Mahdi's rebellion broke out in Sudan in 1883 and General Gordon was killed in 1885, Emin Pasha was cut off from his Egyptian superiors. With his military force, he retreated south and established himself at Wadelai, near Lake Albert. When Emin was cut off from supplies through Buganda in summer 1886 and asked for help, the famous explorer Henry Morton Stanley started a relief expedition up the river Congo.[10] The main promoter of the enterprise was the Scottish shipping magnate William Mackinnon, who sought to develop the British sphere of influence in East Africa into a large trading colony. The British hoped that Emin would garrison the interior stations of a trading chain reaching from Wadelai, north of Lake Victoria, to Mombasa on the coast.[11]

What von der Heydt now suggested was a rival German expedition.

---

[6] Board of directors, standing committee meeting, 20 Jan. 1888, FP 24, BAK.

[7] Peters to Palezieux, 29 March 1888, Palezieux Papers, vol. 5, 16, BAB.

[8] Schroeder to Palezieux, 2 Feb. 1888, Palezieux Papers, vol. 7, 28–9.

[9] See Schroeder to Palezieux, 21 Feb. 1888, Palezieux Papers, vol. 7, 34–5, BAK.

[10] I. R. Smith, *The Emin Pasha Relief Expedition* (Oxford, 1972) is a profound study of the subject.

[11] M. J. De Kiewiet, 'History of the Imperial British East Africa Company, 1876–1895' (Ph.D. thesis, London University, 1955).

Although Peters initially hesitated to commit himself to the project,[12] he soon became convinced that this was an opportunity by which he could restore his former glory. In April 1888 the Nuremberg branch of the DKV began to push for a German relief expedition,[13] which was hardly a coincidence as Peters's brother was the secretary there. At the same time, Peters made progress in the Berlin branch. His motion 'to approach the matter of Emin-Bey' was adopted with only one dissenting vote.[14] From then on he stood firmly behind the project.

In spring 1888 Peters worked hard to restore his standing in colonial circles.[15] For this purpose he also travelled to Weimar, where the Grand Duke, a shareholder in the DOAG and a supporter of the colonial cause, received him warmly. Peters enjoyed the opulent dinners, where he could show off with his African stories in the presence of the ladies.[16] Briefly, he even thought about becoming engaged to an 18-year-old countess,[17] but this was just a short-lived flirtation; he preferred the loose and frequent affairs for which he became well known in Berlin.[18]

It seems that the Weimar visit stimulated Peters's fantasies in a different direction, too. On the basis of the Emin enterprise he outlined a new scheme for his own future and that of East Africa which he communicated to Palezieux. He believed that in the course of his 'Nyanza-Nile expedition' he could annex the 'Nyanza regions', which meant that German territory would be extended far into the area of the Nile sources. Furthermore, he saw himself 'at the top of our administration out there'.[19]

How this could be realized he made clear in a subsequent 'Promemoria' meant for the Grand Duke himself. The kernel of Peters's plan was that the sovereign rights of the *Schutzbrief* would be transferred to a German prince, who would act as a sort of viceroy of East Africa.[20] This *Generalstatthalter*, as Peters called him, would be responsible only to the German Kaiser, and the colony would follow the principle of 'self-government'. The DOAG in

---

[12] See Schroeder to Palezieux, 27 Feb. 1888, 3 March 1888, Palezieux Papers, vol. 7, 37, 38–41, BAK.

[13] See Sachse's speech at the directory board meeting of the Colonial Society, 11 Sept. 1888, RKolA 249/5, 85, BAB.

[14] See Peters to Palezieux, 14 April 1888, Palezieux Papers vol. 5, 19–20, BAK.

[15] Peters to Elli, 15 April 1888, PP 87, BAB; Peters to Palezieux, 29 March 1888, Palezieux Papers vol. 5, 16, BAK.   [16] Peters to Elli, 15 April 1888, PP 87, BAB.

[17] Ibid.

[18] See Schnee Papers, 'Notizen über Karl Peters', 1 HA, Rep 92 Schnee, 49/103, 107, GStA-PK.

[19] Peters to Palezieux, 14 April 1888, Palezieux Papers vol. 5, 19–20, BAK.

[20] Peters's Promemoria (highly confidential!), 22 May 1888, Palezieux Papers vol. 5, 21–21a, BAB.

its present form would be dissolved, and its private rights to land etc. transferred to purely commercial companies which would not have to carry the burden of administrative tasks. The colonial government would initially cover its costs through a loan, the interest on which would be financed via customs and tax income. Unfortunately we do not know the Grand Duke's reaction, or what Palezieux thought about the scheme. In any event it is unlikely that the Reich would have engaged a single German state for the task of colonization. Not only would this have destroyed the national character of colonial policy; it was also bound to affect the federal balance within the Reich.

In Berlin, things were changing in Peters's favour again. By June 1888 he had regained ground in the DOAG. Delbrück, his arch-opponent, stepped down from the board of directors, officially for health reasons.[21] Furthermore, Hasenclever, the man who had brought Peters's chaotic finances to light, suddenly lost his job.[22] Peters interpreted these changes as a partial victory for himself,[23] although to what extent they were triggered by his own manoeuvres is difficult to say. There is evidence that prior to these changes Schroeder and his associates had been working behind the scenes to see 'whether one could get rid of Delbrück'.[24] Peters himself had always been a master of intrigue, as a close associate remarked later.[25]

Peters became more and more involved in DOAG matters again. In collaboration with Kayser and von der Heydt a number of decisions were taken concerning the future of the venture. For example, they agreed to allow the establishment of new subsidiary companies, which Peters hoped to use for mining ventures and railway construction. Furthermore, small DOAG shares of 1,000 marks should again be issued in order to attract a wider circle of people. As Peters pointed out, he worked 'hand in hand' with Kayser, much to the surprise of some others.[26] This is an indication that the Foreign Office representative had made peace with Peters, and now sought to involve him rather than pushing him aside.

At that stage, however, Peters's primary concern became the Emin Pasha venture. On 27 June a provisional executive committee was formed to prepare a German relief expedition; apart from Peters, who chaired the

[21] Peters to Elli, 8 June 1888, PP 87, BAB; board of directory, standing committee meeting, 7 June, FP 24, BAK; Peters to Palezieux, 5 June 1888, Palezieux Papers vol. 5, 22, BAK.
[22] Peters to Elli, 8 June 1888, PP 87, BAB.   [23] Ibid.
[24] Schroeder to Palezieux, 16 April 1888, Palezieux Papers, vol. 7, 45–7, BAK.
[25] Schnee Papers, 'Notizen über Karl Peters' (Interview with Irmer), 1 HA, Rep 92, 49/107, GStA-PK.
[26] Peters to Palezieux, 10 June 1888, Palezieux Papers vol. 5, 24–7, BAB.

group, it comprised his closest associates: Arendt, Livonius, Schroeder, and the senior ministerial official Sachse (Imperial Post Office).[27] A little later they were joined by the prominent scientist Schweinfurth, the former Prussian minister Hofmann, the DOAG director Lucas, and the explorer Hermann Wissmann, who had already crossed the African continent twice.[28]

The *Kölnische Zeitung*, well known for its pro-colonial line, welcomed the planned expedition. It also mentioned rumours that Stanley's enterprise had failed to reach Emin Pasha.[29] On 7 July Peters and his associates wrote to Herbert von Bismarck in the Foreign Office, informing him of their plan and expressing their hope that the Chancellor would support the expedition out of his funds for exploration in Africa.[30] At the same time they formulated a confidential circular which outlined the major goals of the enterprise. This stated that 'Stanley's expedition must be considered as having failed'. Emin 'held the last outpost of a front line which everywhere else had been overrun by Islam'. According to the paper, the Equatorial Province was, in terms of trade policy, 'the key to opening up the actual heart of Africa, the upper lakes region'. It was obvious that 'the future in the whole of Central Africa belonged to that people which succeeded in establishing a firm connection from the coast, via Lake Victora and Lake Albert, to the territories occcupied by Emin Pasha.' The trade of the region would fall to those who controlled the area.

The circular emphasized that Emin had supposedly gathered huge amounts of ivory, and that he was in a position to acquire even more from regions in the north. In more concrete terms, the enterprise would pave the way for a 'trading route to the east', which would be based on a chain of newly founded stations. For this purpose the circular envisaged the foundation of a German East African Lakes Company, which would link Lake Victoria with Lake Albert.[31]

The paper made clear its ultimate aim: the Equatorial Province should be placed under German control. It implied the extension of the *Schutzbrief* to Emin's territory. As Peters mentioned later, the aim was not to bring Emin to the coast, but to utilize his position in central Africa for German ends, and to strengthen his position there. Peters held that whoever possessed that region would automatically dominate East and

[27] See Peters, *Die Deutsche Emin-Pascha-Expedition* (Munich, 1891), reprinted in GS ii. 10.
[28] See ibid.   [29] Note from *Kölnische Zeitung*, 1 July 1888, FP 18, BAK.
[30] Emin Committee to Herbert von Bismarck, 7 July 1888, FP 18, BAK.
[31] Confidential Circular, n.d., FP 18, BAK.

West Africa.[32] In this sense, the Equatorial Province was the potential core of a large-scale African empire in German hands, stretching from the Atlantic coast to the Indian Ocean, a vision which later became known as German *Mittelafrika*. This concept was to conflict with British schemes to establish an axis from the Cape to Cairo.

Behind the German Emin Pasha Committee stood a number of prominent political figures. Its composition mirrored support among all three parties of the so-called Kartell which backed Bismarck in the Reichstag, particularly the National Liberals and Free Conservatives. Among the signatories were leading political figures such as Rudolf von Bennigsen, Count Mirbach-Sorquitten, Count Arnim-Muskau, and von Kardoff-Wabnitz. Overall, there were 13 Reichstag members and 40 representatives of the Prussian Parliament in the Emin Pasha Committee.[33] Within a few weeks it had attracted 105 members.[34]

On 20 July the committee submitted its petition to the Chancellor.[35] This repeated, more or less, the major points of the circular, emphasizing that the expedition could provide a 'further hinterland' for German East Africa. The enterprise was not only a 'humanitarian act' but also a venture in the 'German national interest'. Both propositions—hinterland and German national interest—were marked in the margin with question marks, indicating that Bismarck was sceptical about the aims of the expedition.

The committee also sought direct support from the new Kaiser, the young Wilhelm II. It was Wissmann who succeeded in getting an audience with the Kaiser on 6 August. In this conversation, Wilhelm signalled 'his interest in the aims of the expedition'.[36] On the next day, the committee wrote to the Kaiser and asked for his support, 'encouraged by the reception which was granted yesterday to . . . Wissmann'.[37] This would be necessary to interest potential financiers.

Wilhelm now asked Under-secretary, Graf Max von Berchem for a comment on the proposal.[38] Berchem referred to Bismarck 'who had received a similar petition' and had declined the request for financial support from government funds. It would hardly match the intentions of His Majesty, Berchem reported Bismarck as noting, if official cooperation

[32] Peters, *Expedition*, in GS ii. 486.
[33] List of members, printed in GS ii. 465–6.   [34] Ibid.
[35] FP 18, BAK.
[36] See Berchem to Wilhelm, 11 Aug. 1888, RKolA 249/3, 23–6, BAB.
[37] Committee to Wilhelm, 7 Aug. 1888, FP 18, BAK.
[38] See Berchem to Wilhelm, 11 Aug. 1888, RKolA 249/3, 23–6, BAB.

'leads to the impression that the government had accepted political or military resposibility for the German expedition'. For the same reasons the British refused any official support for Stanley's enterprise. Bismarck also noted that, from a political viewpoint, 'the rescue of Emin Bey would be primarily an Egyptian–English interest'.

In conclusion, Berchem stated that a written reply would 'hardly be necessary', since the Kaiser had already expressed his interest during the conversation with Wissmann. Interestingly, the Kaiser did not follow this advice. On 13 August the Foreign Office wrote to the committee and informed them of the Kaiser's 'warmest sympathy for the success of the enterprise'.[39] Obviously Wilhelm was not bothered by Bismarck's remarks, or the fact that the expedition opposed British foreign policy interests.

Two days later the Chancellor replied to the petition. He acknowledged the 'high-minded purpose' behind the project but also pointed out that it would be 'alien to our colonial interests'.[40] The Chancellor's experiences with the East African venture had been disillusioning. The DOAG was still struggling financially, and Bismarck had worries enough about the future of the existing possessions. Expansionist dreams did not contribute to a consolidation of the colonial venture, but rather meant further financial burdens. In fact, Bismarck had good reason to entertain doubts similar to those of the British government. As a British official had noted with respect to Stanley's expedition, the cabinet did not want to run the risk of 'having to rescue the rescuers'.[41]

However, Bismarck shied away from making his concerns really explicit. Instead he emphasized his wish 'that the patriotic efforts of the committee may succeed in carrying out this difficult venture'.[42]

This statement not only obscured his concerns about the state of colonial affairs in East Africa; it also contradicted his own arrangements with Britain. In 1887 the Chancellor had committed himself to the so-called Anglo-German hinterland agreement. London and Berlin had exchanged notes committing both governments to discourage annexations in the rear of the other power's sphere of influence.[43] If Bismarck nonetheless signalled that he wished the venture to succeed, this was an opportunist gesture to the colonial enthusiasts in the committee, who were all closely connected with the parties of the Kartell. Moreover it should be borne in

[39] Berchem to Committee, 13 Aug. 1888, FP 18, BAK.
[40] Bismarck to Committee, 15 Aug. 1888, RKolA 249/3, 30–1, BAB.
[41] Memo by Iddesleigh, 25 Nov. 1886, FO 84/1794, 184, PRO, London.
[42] Bismarck to Committee, 15 Aug. 1888, RKolA 249/3, 30–1, BAB.
[43] See E. Hertslet, *The Map of Africa by Treaty*, iii (London, 1908; repr. 1967), 888–9.

mind that the young Kaiser had already expressed his enthusiasm for the enterprise. If Bismarck wanted to avoid the impression that there was friction between him and the new Kaiser, then he had to communicate his good wishes as well.

Both Wilhelm's and Bismarck's answers must have been encouraging to the organizers of the expedition. Peters had found in 1885 that he could get an imperial charter for large stretches of land, even though the Foreign Office had denied any support and interest prior to the venture. Now, they had 'the warm sympathy' of the Kaiser on paper, and good wishes from Bismarck. Peters and his associates probably understood this as a green light.

Peters was now facing another problem. Wissmann, who had been successful in securing the Kaiser's support and who had more African travel experience than Peters, was himself eager to rescue Emin Pasha. He travelled to Egypt to check whether the expedition could reach Emin from the north, but soon realized that this would have meant a full-scale military campaign.[44] Thus the decision was taken to advance from the East African coast.

The rivalry between Peters and Wissmann was eased by adopting a scheme which comprised two expeditions. Wissmann would take 200 to 300 men and proceed to Lake Albert. There he would meet with Peters and the main caravan, which would then advance further to Wadelai.[45]

The committee launched a public campaign in order to collect the necessary 600,000 marks, which was the calculated cost of the operation.[46] In a public appeal they presented Emin's rescue as a point of honour for every German. Again, he was viewed as holding the last remaining outpost of European civilization in the heart of Africa. 'Should our heroic compatriot . . . be left exposed to ruin, should his province which has been won for civilization with German enterprise, fall to barbarism?'[47] A public meeting in Hanover on 20 September 1888 attracted some 3,000 people. Peters, usually in favour of forced labour for Africans, had now discovered the use of humanitarian arguments: in his speech he said that the expedition could also prevent slave hunting in the interior.[48]

---

[44] German Consul General (Alexandria) to Bismarck, 1 Sept. 1888, RKolA 249/3, 43–4, BAB.

[45] Note from *Kölnische Zeitung*, 20 Sept. 1888, FP 18, BAK; Emin Committee to Bismarck, 5 Oct. 1888, FP 18, BAK; see also Peters, *Expedition*, GS ii. 13.

[46] See petition of 20 July, FP 18, BAK.

[47] Printed in Peters, *Expedition*, GS ii. 9–10.

[48] *DKZ* special edition, 25 Sept. 1888, cited in Bair, 'Peters', 184; see note from *Nationalzeitung*, 22 Sept. 1888, FP 18 BAK.

In the middle of September the Emin euphoria was suddenly overshadowed by news that violence had broken out on the East African Coast. Von der Heydt immediately urged Bismarck to receive Peters in his position as DOAG director, and have him report on the situation on the ground.[49] On the same day the Chancellor received another telegram. Hohenlohe-Langenburg, president of the Kolonialverein, informed Bismarck that his organization had decided to back the Emin venture. He expressed his hope that 'the enterprise will not lack the powerful support of Your Excellency at the proper time'.[50]

The combination of the two telegrams pointed to the problem that Bismarck faced in autumn 1888. On the one hand, violence on the coast seriously threatened the success of his proclaimed charter policy; on the other, he was confronted with increasing enthusiasm for the Emin expedition, the aims of which were expansionist and seemed to ignore the crisis on the coast.

This time the Chancellor sought to avoid a situation such as had emerged in August, when the Kaiser had rushed in, without leaving Bismarck a chance to intervene. Now he wanted to make sure that 'the Kaiser would not give too much backing to the Emin project'.[51] He compiled a lengthy memorandum for Wilhelm which argued against the use of the expedition for Germany.[52] Bismarck expected the Emin venture to fail, and its failure would endanger German colonial policy. Eugen Richter and his friends (i.e. the Left Liberals) would use this crisis to justify their opposition, so that it would hardly be possible to rally support for colonies in the Reichstag in future. Bismarck also pointed to the fact that, in terms of international law, a German occupation would be dubious, since the Equatorial Province had hitherto belonged to Egypt and indirectly to Turkey. But even if its status in international law were secure, Bismarck could not see the advantage 'of such an eccentric extension' of African claims. Germany, he held, 'could not even fulfil its adopted civilizing task in the thousandth part' of its current possessions. The Emin enterprise would make this even more difficult.

Bismarck made clear to the Kaiser that occupying the Equatorial Province was likely to antagonize Britain, which regarded Egypt, with its Suez Canal, as a vital interest. At the same time, he was worried about the

---

[49] Von der Heydt to Bismarck, 11 Sept. 1888, RKolA 349/3, 54, BAB.
[50] Hohenlohe to Bismarck, 11 Sept. 1888, RKolA 249/3, 77, BAB.
[51] Note by Rantzau, 15 Sept. 1888, FP 18, BAK; see also Herbert von Bismarck to Otto von Bismarck, 16 Sept. [1888], Bismarck Papers, D 2, 279–80, BAE.
[52] Bismarck's memo, 14 Sept. 1888, RKolA 249/3, 61–8 (draft with Bismarck's corrections), 69–76 (final memo), BAB.

future of the existing possessions and how this would affect the government's position at home. Considerations of both foreign and domestic policy were thus advanced against the venture.

Interestingly, however, Bismarck was not prepared to inform the Emin Pasha Committee of his foreign policy concerns. This indicates that Bismarck was anxious not to appear openly as a brake on colonial policy. Thus he put a good face upon matters, although he obviously disagreed with the expansionist aims of the committee.

With the outbreak of rebellion, Peters was to face 'disgusting weeks'[53] in Berlin. Bismarck became more and more convinced that the DOAG director was mainly responsible for the violence on the coast. In his reply to von der Heydt of 11 September he criticized the company for having failed to come to an understanding with the Sultan, an approach which 'the Hanseatic merchants had employed for some decades'.[54] This attack was peculiar in so far as it was Bismarck himself who had always protected DOAG interests against those of the merchants.

Four days later Bismarck directed his criticism explicitly against Peters. He informed the DOAG that he would 'take no further interest' unless the company stopped 'placing Dr Peters in the foreground'.[55] According to the Chancellor, Peters was 'entirely incapable of leading such a difficult venture, not through lack of talent, but through lack of caution, and excessive self-confidence'. This was not the last attack. In the *Schlesische Zeitung* the Chancellor discovered an article critical of the Emin Pasha expedition and of the prospect of Peters being its commander. Having secured Wilhelm's consent, Bismarck arranged for a shortened version to be reproduced in his mouthpiece, the *Norddeutsche Allgemeine Zeitung* (*NAZ*). This article questioned Peters's qualification for leading an expedition of such a kind and doubted its practicability.[56]

The Chancellor was confirmed in his view about Peters by a letter from O'Swald.[57] The merchant complained bitterly about the state of affairs in East Africa, stating that the DOAG had achieved 'hardly anything' in four years, because it 'lacked organizational power and had made a wrong judgement of the existing situation'. And who is mainly responsible for that? he asked: 'Overall, Dr Peters'.

    [53] See Peters to brother Hermann, 25 Jan. 1889, PP 92, BAK.
    [54] Bismarck to von der Heydt, 11 Sept. 1888, FP 18, BAK.
    [55] 15 Sept. 1888, RKolA 687, 45, BAB.
    [56] *Schlesische Zeitung*, 16 Sept. 1888, Berchem to Kaiser, 20 Sept. 1888, *NAZ*, 20 Sept. 1888, RKolA 249/3, 78–80, BAB.
    [57] O'Swald to Bismarck, RKolA 360, 126 ff., BAB.

In the meantime, the DOAG director gave a new demonstration of his agitational skills. In an interview with *The Times* he stated that there was no doubt that the Reichstag would grant the necessary money for the Emin expedition, since the leaders of the three Cartel parties were in favour of the enterprise.[58] This statement clearly contradicted the government's declared position. By 8 October, Bismarck had no more doubts: 'Peters corrupts'.[59] And therefore he wanted him to be pushed aside.

In late September Bismarck briefly thought about using the press to discourage the enthusiasm for the Emin expedition,[60] but although he had managed to gain the Kaiser's approval for this move, he decided to postpone the campaign until he had worked on Hohenlohe and Bennigsen.[61] Interestingly, the *NAZ* did not carry any articles critical of the Emin expedition during the following days, so that Bismarck must have dropped the idea altogether.

It seems that the wave of enthusiasm for Emin did not fail to have an impact on the Chancellor's policy. By early October he had devised another tactic. Instead of working against the enterprise, he now attempted to divert its resources for other purposes and thus to manipulate the nationalist euphoria for his own ends. Violence on the East African coast continued, so that Bismarck had to think seriously about how to handle the crisis. The DOAG had no idea how to act in this matter. More than a month after the first news of the rebellion had reached Berlin, the board of directors had got no further than taking the decision 'to discuss with outstanding Africa travellers in what ways order could be restored on the coast'.[62] Their reluctance to respond was calculated. They counted upon help from the government, after Bismarck had told von der Heydt in the middle of September that he would 'be happy to support the company with my whole influence with the Kaiser and the Reichstag'.[63] However, Bismarck still hesitated to engage the Reich financially. Instead, he now tested another option: why not combine the resources of the Emin Committee with those of the DOAG in order to restore order on the coast?[64]

Bismarck believed that the new plan could only function if Wissmann

[58] Note from *The Times*, 6 Oct. 1888, FP 18, BAK.
[59] Bismarck's marginal comment on a note by Krauel, 8 Oct. 1888, FP 18, BAK.
[60] Berchem's note, 20 Sept. 1888, FP 18, BAK.
[61] Berchem's note, 25 Sept. 1888, FP 18, BAK.
[62] Standing committee meeting, 12 Oct. 1888, FP 24, BAK.
[63] Bismarck to von der Heydt, 11 Sept. 1888, RKolA 249/4, 5, BAB.
[64] See Bismarck to Michahelles, 6 Oct. 1888, RKolA 249/4, 6, BAB; letter by Rottenburg, 30 Sept. 1888, FP 18, BAK. This early reference to the plan makes it unlikely that Bismarck had got the idea from Fabri, as argued by Bade, 'Antisklavereibewegung', 39.

was given the sole command of the enterprise.[65] This conviction was not only rooted in his aversion to Peters. Wissmann was a trained officer, whereas Peters had not even been accepted for military service. Peters simply lacked the military background that was seen as essential for the job. Bismarck had his plan communicated to various members of the Emin Committee, but he carefully avoided discouraging the aim of advancing to Emin's province. He suggested using the resources to restore order on the coast, in order 'to make the routes passable which lead to Emin Pasha'.[66] The Emin Committee agreed to this idea, but emphasized that the ultimate aim of the enterprise remained the rescue of Emin Pasha. Bismarck wondered: 'but how? by air or the Nile?'.[67]

On 19 October, Bismarck ordered an expert opinion on the practicability of an Emin expedition.[68] This was written by the scientist Wilhelm Juncker, who had spent some time with Emin in Central Africa. Juncker stated that an advance through Uganda would be dangerous but not impossible. However, war was unavoidable in order to establish a link with Emin. He suggested that two British and two German expeditions should advance on different routes from the east and the south to Uganda and occupy the country.[69] However, Krauel concluded that this was 'not very suitable for practical purposes'.[70] Despite this sceptical remark, the Foreign Office, after having asked for Bismarck's permission, forwarded Juncker's paper to the Emin Committee.[71]

To the committee it must have looked as if the Chancellor had agreed in principle to the aims of the venture. This impression was reinforced by an article in the *Militär-Wochenblatt*, which was reprinted in the *Deutsches Tageblatt*.[72] The article quoted a major named Liebert, who outlined a programme for East Africa: first, the coastal rebellion had to be put down; then a military expedition had to march to Wadelai. The British press immediately reproduced Liebert's scheme.[73]

Bismarck was not happy with this unauthorized comment, and he immediately asked for information on Liebert.[74] He was told by the General Staff

---

[65] See marginal note by Krauel, 8 Oct. 1888, RKolA 249/4, 12–13, BAB.
[66] Ibid.
[67] Marginal comment on Krauel's note, 12 Oct. 1888, RKolA 249/4, 17–18, BAB.
[68] Rottenburg to Krauel, 19 Oct. 1888, RKolA 249/4, 33, BAB.
[69] Juncker's expertise, RKolA 249/4, 34–50, BAB.
[70] Krauel's note, 6 Nov. 1888, RKolA 249/4, 33, BAB.
[71] See Krauel to Bismarck, 6 Nov. 1888, Rottenburg to AA, 10 Nov. 1888, Krauel to Juncker, 13 Nov. 1888, Krauel to committee, 15 Nov. 1888, RKolA 249/4, 51, 53, 54, 58, BAB.
[72] Enclosed in RKolA 249/4, 57, 60, BAB.
[73] *Standard*, 15 Nov. 1888, *Daily News*, 16 Nov. 1888, notes in FP 18, BAK.
[74] Note one Rottenburg's letter, FP 18, BAK.

that the man was one of their most capable officers, albeit a very enthusiastic speaker (marked in the margin by Bismarck).[75] The reported speech, Bismarck learned, was held in a closed circle of officers, but this did not appease the Chancellor: 'That does not matter. Once it is in the paper, it is always an official position.' Bismarck approached Waldersee[76] to make clear that Liebert's plan was not the government position. Nevertheless, he explicitly refused to publish an official denial, in order to avoid the impression that there was a friction between the government and the General Staff.[77]

The episode suggests that Bismarck wanted to keep his assurances to the Emin Committee confidential. His primary aim was to rally support for action on the coast, and to achieve this he obviously regarded it as necessary *not* to discourage expansionist designs in Central Africa.

On 6 December Peters and his associates informed the Chancellor that Wissmann should be sent to East Africa in the near future. He should investigate the best way to realize the 'major purpose' of the enterprise, the support of Emin Pasha. Peters was to command the second expedition. Furthermore, they asked whether Bismarck would issue a letter of recommendation for Wissmann to the consulate on the ground.[78]

'S'abstenir' Bismarck wrote on the top of the letter. He was alarmed by the fact that Peters was still part of scheme ('Peters will not be useful there'). Moreover, he commented: 'I have nothing to do with the Emin question and I say nothing about it.'[79] Bismarck now talked to Wissmann directly,[80] in order to win him for the suppression of the coastal rebellion and to persuade him to drop his agitation for the Emin expedition. In their conversation he told Wissmann that 'in view of the situation in European politics he would like to avoid opposing Britain'.[81]

By the beginning of December Bismarck had decided that he would approach the Reichstag with a bill for financing a military operation on the East African coast. This had become necessary because the DOAG was threatened with liquidation unless the Reich supplied financial support for the military operation.[82] As Herbert von Bismarck pointed out in a

75 Note on letter (by General Staff?), 15 Nov. 1888, RKolA 249/4, 61, 62, BAB.

76 Rottenburg to Krauel, 16 Nov. 1888, RKolA 249/4, 65, BAB.

77 Herbert von Bismarck's note with comment's by his father, 17 Nov. 1888, RKolA 249/4, 66, 67, BAB.

78 Petition of the Emin Committee, 6 Dec. 1888, RKolA 249/4, 84–8, BAB.

79 Marginal comments, ibid.

80 See Rottenburg to Herbert von Bismarck, 7 Dec. 1888, Bismarck Papers, B 99, 151–2, BAB.

81 Rottenburg's private letter (extract), 7 Dec. 1888, RKolA 249/4, 98, BAB.

82 See Bade, 'Antisklavereibewegung', 39.

memorandum, the loss of East Africa would have been a serious blow to Germany's international prestige. If this was to be avoided, the DOAG would need 'vigorous backing' by the state.[83]

By portraying the intervention primarily as a measure to fight the slave trade, the Chancellor hoped to rally support among the Centre Party and to ensure that the bill would meet with broad agreement in the Reichstag.[84] With this emphasis on a supposedly humanitarian mission, the government also protected itself against accusations that the state was intervening only to rescue a bankrupt company from collapse.

Under the new scheme Wissmann would be sent out as an imperial commissioner. This also had the advantage that he would have to follow official instructions, rather than pursuing the scheme adopted by the Emin Committee. Bismarck succeeded in gaining wide Reichstag support for his East African scheme[85] and in enrolling Wissmann for the task. However, if the Chancellor hoped that this had automatically solved the Emin issue, he had not reckoned with Carl Peters.

'The main thing is that I now have sole command of the Emin expedition', Peters wrote to his brother Hermann in January 1889, full of new enthusiasm.[86] The Committee was by no means prepared to drop the Emin plan, as Bismarck may have hoped. Thus the year 1889 not only saw a continuation of the quarrels; these were to become even more intense and serious.

THE GERMAN EMIN PASHA EXPEDITION

Peters's Landing, the Neera-Dispute, and a Chancellor under Pressure

In the early afternoon of 31 March 1889, Peters disembarked at Zanzibar harbour.[87] His original plan had been to organize an expedition of 600 porters and a military force of 100 Somali soldiers.[88] However, Bismarck and Salisbury had agreed to establish a joint blockade on the East African coast, and this interfered with Peters's plans. Naval patrols were to make sure that the rebels on the mainland would be cut off from arms supplies. Thus the British confiscated all the weapons which Peters had shipped

---

[83] H. von Bismarck to O. von Bismarck, 5 Nov. 1888, RKolA 360, 165–85, BAB.

[84] Bade, 'Antisklavereibewegung', studies this policy in detail.

[85] See ibid. 54.

[86] Peters to brother Hermann, 25 Jan. 1889, PP 92, BAK.

[87] Peters, *Expedition*, GS ii. 22.   [88] Ibid. 27.

from Aden to Zanzibar. The German government was not willing to lend him any official support. On the contrary, Bismarck instructed his London ambassador to inform Lord Salisbury that Peters and his associates were considered as private travellers and had nothing to do with the Reich. 'I would find it natural if England prohibited passage for armed units', he added in his instruction.[89] The Somali soldiers Peters had hired in Aden were eventually disembarked at Bagamoyo, after they had been refused landing at Lamu and Zanzibar.[90]

However, Peters was not easily forced to capitulate. He hired a little steamer from an Indian businessman and went to Bagamoyo which, as Tiedemann observed, was 'a heap of ruins'.[91] The ship charter alone cost 75,000 marks, so that Peters had to cut down the intended size of his expedition by two-thirds.[92] Eventually, he took seventy-four of his Somali soldiers back to Zanzibar and discharged them, paying them 5 rupees each.[93] The mercenary troops then complained to the British consul about their sudden dismissal, charging Peters with having broken their contract. Eventually Peters's associate Borchert arranged for their return to Aden, paying them another 3 rupees each. Thus a legal dispute before the court of the German consulate was avoided.[94]

Peters managed to persuade Wissmann, the new imperial commissioner, to provide the expedition with guns—a hundred muzzle-loaders and fifty breech-loaders—from his depot in Dar es Salaam, as well as seventeen magazine rifles. A French misssionary at Bagamoyo, Brother Oskar, arranged for sixty Central African porters for the venture.[95] Eventually, Peters even succeeded in persuading the British admiral, Freemantle, to return his hunting weapons, which he had confiscated.[96]

However, the major problem remained unsolved. The British navy would not allow Peters to land his armed expedition anywhere within their blockade-line, or anywhere else within the British concession.[97] They expected Peters to land at Lamu, which was 'still under arbitration'

[89] Bismarck's note, 28 March 1889, RKolA 249/5, 20, BAB.

[90] See note on Deinhard's telegram to Admiralty, FP 18, BAK; captain Capelle's report, 17 March, FP 18, BAK; A. von Tiedemann, *Tana—Baringo—Nil*, 3rd edn. (Berlin 1907), 9.

[91] Malet to AA, 6 July 1889, Copy, Al 31/2, German Consular Records, ZNA; Tiedemann, *Tana*, 9.   [92] Peters, *Expedition*, 27.

[93] Portal to Michahelles, 30 May 1889, AL 31/2, 167, German Consular Records, ZNA; Peters, *Expedition*, 29, refers to seventy-three Somalis.

[94] Portal to Michahelles, 30 May 1889; reply by German Consulate, n.d., AL 31/2, 167, 168, German Consular Files, ZNA.

[95] See Admiral Deinhart's report, 6 May 1889, FP 18, BAK; Peters, *Expedition*, 29; see Tiedemann, *Tana*, 20.   [96] See Peters, *Expedition*, 30.

[97] Malet to AA, 6 July 1889, Copy, AL 31/2, German Consular Files, ZNA.

between Britain and Germany, so that from a British point of view it was 'evidently undesirable that he should be allowed to do so'.[98]

Peters considered marching through the German territory instead,[99] but it must have been Wissmann who convinced him that this plan was doomed to failure. The imperial commissioner, as well as the German navy, had instructions not to let Peters and his armed expedition march to the interior.[100] Peters and Wissmann may have maintained quite friendly relations,[101] but the newly appointed imperial commissioner could hardly afford to ignore the instructions of his superiors. Nothing would have been more embarrassing for Peters than being stopped by Wissmann, his own compatriot. The latter had also made it clear to the Emin Committee in Berlin that he could not grant Peters permission to pass through the German territory.[102] Consequently, Peters dropped the idea of taking the route from Dar es Salaam via Usagara, although the track was reported not to be blocked by rebels.[103]

In the meantime, the press in Germany took up the issue again. The *Post*, closely associated with the Free Conservatives, had shifted its position from enthusiastic support of the government line; it now warned against wasting the money collected for the Emin expedition, and asked whether it would not be better used for Wissmann's enterprise. This clearly resembled Bismarck's position.[104] The *Nationalzeitung*, however, published a statement from the Emin Committee, maintaining that Peters's venture had not lost its importance. The committee rejected the idea of making the resources available for Wissmann's military campaign.[105] The semi-official *Norddeutsche Allgemeine Zeitung* joined in, denying that Bismarck had recognized Peters's enterprise as a patriotic venture, as the Emin Committee had declared. It emphasized that Bismarck did not favour Peters's landing. His expedition would only establish a fourth power in the rebellious region, in addition to Germany, Britain, and the Arabs, and this could only lead to further complications. For example, it would be very difficult for the Reich to help members of the expedition if they were

[98] Portal to Michahelles, AL31/2, 169, German Consular Files, ZNA.
[99] Peters to Lucas, 5 May 1889, FP 16, BAK.
[100] Herbert von Bismarck to Admiral von der Goltz, 17 March 1889, FP 18, BAK; Peters to Lucas, 5 May 1889, FP 16, BAK; Admiral von der Goltz to Herbert von Bismarck, 3 April 1889, FP 18, BAK.
[101] See Admiral Deinhart's report, 6 May 1889, FP 18, BAK.
[102] H. von Bismarck to Admiral von der Goltz, 17 March 1889, FP 18, BAK.
[103] See Peters to Lucas, 5 May 1889, FP 16, BAK.
[104] *Die Post*, 28 April 1889, note in FP 18, BAK.
[105] *Nationalzeitung*, 30 April 1889, note in FP 18, BAK.

captured, the article explained. It also denied the view of committee members that it was Wissmann who could decide whether Peters was granted access or not. This question would be decided not in Bagamoyo, but in Berlin.[106]

While the public in Germany quarrelled over the issue, in Zanzibar Peters formed a new plan with which he hoped to outsmart his British opponents. He released the news that he intended to travel to Mozambique to recruit further mercenaries.[107] In fact, however, he wanted to land in a little bay north of Lamu, which was difficult to reach and which the British ships might not guard as closely as other places. From there he planned to march up the river Tana towards Baringo and then carry on towards the Equatorial Province, where he hoped to meet with Emin Pasha.

After having recruited another handful of porters in Dar es Salaam,[108] Peters headed south, then made a U-turn northward, passing the eastern coasts of the islands of Zanzibar and Pemba, and reaching the little bay of Kwaihu on 15 June 1889.[109] There he managed to slip ashore, undetected by the four British ships on patrol in the area. For the previous six weeks Peters had been playing cat and mouse with the British navy. Now he had won, but what was left of his original plan for a large-scale expedition?

Peters rested in Witu for some time, still hoping to secure further equipment and to augment his manpower—without great success. All his barter goods had fallen into British hands after he had landed, together with his steamer *Neera*.[110] This was perhaps the most serious problem, since it was known that the more powerful African communities on the way would claim tribute for safe passage. For this purpose, Peters was hardly equipped at all. Every experienced European traveller would have shaken his head, in view of the tiny group and their poor supplies, but Peters was driven more by his extreme ambition than by rational considerations.

His expedition now comprised eighty-five porters, thirteen African women (carrying their husbands' private belongings), twenty-five Somali soldiers (including four camel drivers), eight private servants, and one guide from Lamu. He had also bought sixteen camels, eight donkeys, and one Arab horse for himself. His beloved dogs, two pointers, were also part of the expedition.[111] There were two more Germans with him: Adolf von Tiedemann, a young officer in the Prussian army, and Lieutenant Rust,

[106] *Norddeutsche Allgemeine*, 4 May 1889, note in FP 18, BAK.
[107] Michahelles's report, 2 May 1889, FP 18, BAK; see Peters, *Expedition*, 30, 32.
[108] Peters, *Expedition*, 32.   [109] Ibid. 32–5.
[110] Tiedemann, *Tana*, 54; Peters, *Expedition*, 49.
[111] Peters, *Expedition*, 63; Tiedemann, *Tana*, 54, 55, 58.

whom Peters ordered to stay in Witu for the time being in order to await further supplies.

Peters had no idea what heated debates his venture had triggered in Germany in the meantime. The dispute between Bismarck and the Emin Committee had not been resolved. On the morning of 11 May Hofmann, a former Prussian minister and a leading member of the Emin Committee, met with Consul Arendt to discuss the issue. Both must have been dissatisfied with the course of the conversation; Hofmann learnt that the Chancellor had refused to allow Peters a passage through Witu, while Arendt was to test the limits of his diplomatic skills. Hofmann was in a state of 'extreme nervous excitment', as Arendt noted, and could not be pacified. Several times, he hammered on the desk with his fist, claiming that the article in the *NAZ* had presented him as a liar. Arendt chose to adopt a 'yielding attitude as I had learnt it in the Orient in order to appease an overheated temper', but it brought only 'a brief success'. Hofmann was by no means satisfied with Arendt's proposal to await the success of Wissmann's operation first. He threatened to go to see Wilhelm directly 'in order to find out whether a Kaiser's or a Chancellor's word may be doubted'. When Arendt mentioned that a scientist like Juncker might be more suitable for the venture, Hofmann insisted that Peters was still the best person to undertake the expedition.[112] Hofmann's reaction was not surprising if one bears in mind the statements made by Bismarck and Wilhelm the previous summer. Wilhelm had expressed his 'warm sympathy' for the venture, while Bismarck had sent 'his best wishes for success'. And now the *NAZ* claimed that Bismarck had never regarded the venture as patriotic.

The Foreign Office was aware of the difficult situation into which Bismarck had manoeuvred the government with his zig-zag policy. When Hofmann asked Herbert von Bismarck for a meeting, the latter gave an evasive response, claiming that the proposed expedition would 'lie outside the portfolio of my department'.[113] Two days later the government thought it necessary to employ the *NAZ* again to find a way out of the tricky situation. The newspaper published Bismarck's letter to the Emin Committee of 15 August 1888, stating that 'this benevolent refusal' had been meant for the respected person of Wissmann. The paper further argued that the situation on the coast had changed since then, so that Germany had to adopt a wait-and-see attitude.[114]

[112] Arendt's note, 11 May 1889, FP 18, BAK.
[113] 12 May 1889, FP 18, BAK.
[114] *NAZ*, 14 May 1889, note in FP 18, BAK.

This was a clear blow against Peters, but his supporters did not hesitate in producing another article to support their case. This time it was Peters's close friend Otto Arendt, a member of the Prussian parliament, who took the initiative. He praised Peters, to whom alone Germany owed her entire possessions in East Africa (Krauel's comment in the margin: 'nonsense'). The *NAZ*, Arendt stubbornly insisted, must have been badly informed 'when it denied that Prince Bismarck had recognized the Emin Pasha Expedition as patriotic'.[115]

The official press campaign to discredit Peters did not fail to have an impact on parts of the Emin Committee. Director Sachse, from the Imperial Post Office, had already left the group in March.[116] He regarded the expedition under the leadership of Peters as only an 'adventure'. On 22 May Count Mirbach wrote to Herbert von Bismarck that he had left, since he did not want to participate in something which lacked 'your father's full consent'.[117] Nevertheless, the core group maintained its position despite Bismarck's anti-Peters campaign. Hofmann argued in a letter to the Foreign Office that a cancellation without providing substantial reasons would 'ridicule the expedition in front of the nation' and cause a 'setback to the entire colonial movement'. Herbert von Bismarck simply replied with a reference to Bismarck's earlier letters.[118]

In the middle of July the gulf between the goverment and the Emin Committee widened further when it became known that Peters's steamer *Neera* had been confiscated by the British. The *Kölnische Zeitung* reported that the *Neera* case was to come before the prize court in Zanzibar on 18 July,[119] speculating that the court would give the ship to the British and demanding reprisals by the German government: the German navy should snatch every British ship which carried weapons for the British East African Company. 'A more rigorous safeguarding of German interests in East Africa against the British would be appropriate', the article stated. A day later, the *Berliner Börsenzeitung* published a letter from Peters dated 29 March which spoke of further British expeditions to rescue Emin. He mentioned a certain Mr Martin, who supposedly had been provided with porters by the British consulate and had departed to Mombasa. Peters also complained about the British navy, who had informed him that they had orders not to let him land. Since the blockade applied to war materials and

[115] *Deutsches Wochenblatt*, 16 May 1889, note in FP 18, BAK.
[116] Sachse to Krauel, 14 March 1889, FP 18, BAK.
[117] Mirbach to Herbert von Bismarck, 22 May 1889, note in FP 18, BAK.
[118] Hofmann to Herbert von Bismarck, 14 May 1889, Herbert von Bismarck's reply, 18 May 1889, FP 18, BAK.   [119] *Kölnische Zeitung*, 16 July 1889, note in FP 18, BAK.

slaves only, Peters held that these orders violated the terms of the Anglo-German collaboration.[120]

As a result of the confiscation, protest assemblies were organized in various German towns, directed against 'the outrage upon the leader of the Emin Pasha Expedition by the English Admiral Freemantle'.[121] The Emin Committee appealed to the public to lend the venture further financial support.[122] The *Kölnische Zeitung*, in particular, continued to attack the government: appeasement would only lead to a loss of British respect for Germany; the German consulate in Zanzibar was accused of not having reacted to the measures against Peters; such weakness towards England would damage German authority in the region.[123]

The Foreign Office reacted with instructions to Hatzfeldt, the German ambassador in London. They urged that the British admiral should explain why he had intervened in this way, since the confiscation of the steamer was hardly justified by the terms of the blockade. They also emphasized that the British action 'had caused extreme excitement among the German public' and had 'triggered a press campaign against England'. If the British concluded that Admiral Freemantle's approach had not been correct then the German government would appreciate it if Salisbury 'could immediately take remedial measures'.[124] In response, the Prime Minister promised appropriate compensation if the admiral's actions turned out to have been unjustified.[125] On 6 August the prize court in Zanzibar ordered the return of the ship to its owners.[126]

By that time, however, the tide of national indignation in Germany was not easily stemmed. This was particularly embarrassing for the government, since the Kaiser had just started a visit to London. The Deutsche Kolonialgesellschaft, which had joined with the Emin Committee in organizing public protests, had scheduled a big assembly for 8 August, to be directed against the British actions in East Africa. The prominent scientist Georg Schweinfurth was to give a speech entitled 'Germany's duty towards Emin Pasha'. The Foreign Office urged the organizers to cancel the event: it would be 'tactless' to hold the meeting in the German capital at a time when His Majesty was visiting England, particularly a rally in which 'our

---

[120] *Berliner Börsenzeitung*, 17 July 1889, note in FP 18, BAK.
[121] See *Deutsches Tageblatt*, 19 July 1889, note in FP 18, BAK.
[122] See Appeal published in the *Nationalzeitung*, 3 or 4 Aug. 1889, note in FP 18, BAK.
[123] *Kölnische Zeitung*, 22 July 1889, note in FP 18, BAK.
[124] H. von Bismarck to Count Hatzfeldt, 27 July 1889, FP 18, BAK.
[125] Hatzfeldt to Bismarck, 3 Aug. 1889, FP 18, BAK.
[126] See note in FP 18, BAK.

leading scientists' participated and which gave 'the impression of official connivance'. Berchem summoned the organizer, Dr Ebert, to convince him that such a meeting could only strengthen the position of their British rivals. He argued that the British were likely to pay compensation after the ruling of the prize court. Therefore the German public should refrain from putting pressure on the British government. After threatening the Kolonialgesellschaft 'with the expression of the highest disapproval', Berchem secured no more than Ebert's promise to postpone the meeting by two weeks.[127] The Kaiser was outraged by this stubbornness, demanding that the meeting should be 'totally prevented'.[128] Count Berchem therefore informed the Kolonialgesellschaft that no German colonial interest was so strong that, in order to assert it, the government would accept being exposed to serious British resentment.[129] The Chancellor decided to employ the *NAZ* to comment critically on the planned meeting. He drafted his argument as follows:

The Emin Pasha Expedition never informed the government about its purpose and its goals, and it had never asked the Kaiser or any of the government's organs for official support. If it had done so, it would have been told that there were important objections to the venture, which England regards as an interference in her sphere of interest. English friendship, however, is far more valuable for us than anything which the expedition could hope to achieve. . . . As the expedition did not ask for support from the government, either it intends to establish commercial relations, for which purpose it must carry all the risks itself; or it wants to make annexations in the Sudan, in which case the enterprise is criminal, even if it cannot be prosecuted under our law. If Mr Peters, with his or Emin Pasha's weapons, intends to snatch a province from the Egyptian empire which belongs to it according to the treaties, then this is a criminal undertaking. Then Mr Peters is a filibuster.[130]

With this draft, Bismarck clearly contradicted his and the Kaiser's early correspondence with the committee. It could not be denied that the group had repeatedly asked for official support. Therefore, Herbert von Bismarck had to eliminate the relevant section. He also formulated certain other passages in a more moderate way. In the published article the word 'criminal' did not appear any more. Instead, it spoke of a venture 'of questionable justification'. The reference to the 'filibuster' Peters was crossed out too. Clearly, the Foreign Office did not want to emphasize the expedition's

[127] Berchem's note, 7 Aug. 1889, FP 18, BAK.
[128] Ibid., marginal comment by Herbert von Bismarck.
[129] Berchem's note, 8 Aug. 1889, FP 18, BAK.
[130] Rottenburg to Herbert von Bismarck, 11 Aug. 1889, FP 18, BAK.

criminal character too openly, since the venture still enjoyed wide support in the Kartell.[131]

The *Kölnische Zeitung* criticized the *NAZ* statement as 'a weak declaration', and pointed to the fact that the article had 'sent the entire press of the unified opposition parties into raptures'. The Catholic *Kölnische Volkszeitung* interpreted this as 'a new sign of the deep resentment which the nationally minded, i.e. the specific colonial policy circles, entertained against the Imperial Chancellor'.[132] They noted that this might also relate to Bismarck's objections to the person of Dr Peters. The *Nationalzeitung* took a similar position to the *Kölnische Zeitung*, denying that the Foreign Office had warned against the expedition, and insisting that Bismarck had recognized it as a patriotic venture.[133] The left-liberal *Vossische Zeitung* commented that the Chancellor had failed to express his position openly at an early stage, when it would still have been possible 'to nip the headless enterprise in the bud'.[134]

Interestingly, government pressure did not succeed in cancelling the protest assembly in Berlin. During the meeting a letter from Heinrich von Treitschke was read out in which he favoured steps against the British as 'politically necessary and legally justified'. Schweinfurth made his announced speech criticizing the scepticism towards the expedition and praising the 'heroic performance of the *Führer*'; without him, the German nation would hardly have acquired its possessions in East Africa. Peters was presented as a brave pioneer for German glory. A resolution was adopted which asked Bismarck and the imperial government 'to provide protection and satisfaction for the Germans abroad' and 'to find ways and means of terminating conditions which were heavily damaging German interests'.[135] The *NAZ* reacted to the meeting with an article in which it pointed out that the leadership of the expedition had changed, and that the government had declared as early as 15 August 1888 that 'the extension of territory in East Africa had already exceeded the resources available for its exploitation.'[136] The quarrel between the *Kölnische Zeitung* and the *NAZ* continued for a few more days.[137] The semi-official newspaper repeated its statement that the shift of policy derived from the change of leadership in

---

[131] Herbert von Bismarck to his father, 13 Aug. 1889, FP 18, BAK; *NAZ*, 14 Aug. 1889, note in FP 18, BAK.

[132] See *Kölnische Zeitung*, 14 Aug. and 15 Aug. 1889; *Kölnische Volkszeitung*, 15 Aug. 1889, notes in FP 18, BAK.   [133] *Nationalzeitung*, 14 Aug. 1889, note in FP 18, BAK.

[134] *Vossische Zeitung*, 14 Aug. 1889, note in FP 18, BAK.

[135] Report in *Nationalzeitung*, 18 Aug. 1889, note in FP 18, BAK.

[136] *NAZ*, 19 Aug. 1889, note in FP 18, BAK.

[137] See *Kölnische Zeitung*, 20 Aug. 1889, *NAZ*, 23 Aug. 1889, notes in FP 18, BAK.

the expedition. As long as Wissmann had been its head there had been no reason to discourage the operation, but this changed when Peters took over, the paper held.[138] To any British reader, these comments must have been irritating, since they again called into question Bismarck's earlier assurance that he was not at all in favour of the venture. This was a further manifestation of a zig-zag course.

By the end of August the quarrel had escalated to the point where the *NAZ* stated that the foreign policy of the Reich 'would be determined by the responsible Imperial Chancellor, and not by the chairman of the Emin Pasha Committee'.[139] A day later a more distant observer, the *Neue Freie Presse* in Vienna, commented on the issue: 'The dispute about the Emin Pasha Expedition is now among the most important affairs of the Reich, in terms of both domestic and foreign policy.' It observed that the National Liberals were threatening to leave the Cartel. And it asked: 'Have these retired ministers, *Oberpräsidenten*, and *Oberbürgermeister* some kind of secret backing in which they can trust? Do they feel that the time has come in which one can revolt against the ageing Chancellor without punishment?'[140]

To the Interior

By the end of August, Peters had already advanced far up the river Tana. He had departed from Witu on 25 July 1889, leaving half of his Somali force behind with Rust.[141] From the very beginning, he adopted very cruel measures to keep his group together. Physical punishment was rigorously applied. Porters who had dropped their load were put in chains and whipped with the *kiboko*, made of hippoptamus skin. As a deterrent he threatened to shoot anyone who attempted to run away.[142] A little later he made his threat good when his Somalis shot two porters who had attempted to escape.[143] On 6 August Peters ordered all porters from Lamu and Witu to be put in chains to prevent them from fleeing.[144] Nevertheless, at least nineteen managed to escape by the end of August.[145] Apart from the brutal

---

[138] *NAZ*, 23 Aug. 1889, note in FP 18, BAK.

[139] *NAZ*, 29 Aug. 1889, note in FP 18, BAK.

[140] *Neue Freie Presse*, 30 Aug. 1889, note in FP 18, BAK.

[141] See Peters to Bennigsen, 1 July 1889, FP 13, BAK; Peters, *Expedition*, 63, 66; Tiedemann, *Tana*, 55.   [142] Peters, *Expedition*, 52, 55, 74.

[143] Ibid. 90; Tiedemann, *Tana*, 79.

[144] Tiedemann, *Tana*, 68; Peters, *Expedition*, 77.

[145] Peters, *Expedition*, 74, 75, 76, 90. The real number was probably higher. Peters stated at one point that his porters from Witu were leaving him daily 'in pairs' (p. 75).

treatment, the main reason for the desertions was probably a lack of food, since the country they crossed in July and August was afflicted by famine.[146] (As Peters put it: 'In Africa, as everywhere, discipline is primarily a question of the stomach.'[147])

As early as the beginning of August many porters were sick. Six of the sixteen camels had died.[148] This was not a good start, but Peters still believed that 'ahead of me, there lies middle Africa and a great, proud task',[149] as he wrote to a German friend. Tiedemann noted in his diary that Peters's 'fire' was 'irresistible' and 'swept everybody along'.[150] Peters sought to console himself with reading Goethe and Schopenhauer's ideas about the 'seemingly intentional nature of fate'.[151] He also enjoyed the 'pretty and warlike impression' that their camps gave to the observer.[152] At night the two Germans would engage in long discussions about national economy, protective tariffs, and free trade, or Peters would get excited with terrifying ghost stories, theosophy, and metaphysics.[153] For the local people, the expedition was a disaster, as everywhere the porters plundered the available food.[154]

By the end of September Peters had reached a group of Galla people who had settled on the Tana island of Oda-Boru-Ruwa. Scholars have traced the origins of the Galla people to the region around Lake Stephanie and Lake Shamo. They are believed to have spread widely in the sixteenth century, mainly to the north, east, and south-east. Through these movements they came to compete with the Somali.[155] When Peters arrived at the Tana, he observed that the Galla were in conflict with various neighbours. Above all, they had to confront groups of Somali who were pushing south.[156] Peters had no great difficulty settling nearby. It is possible that the Galla welcomed the Europeans as potential allies who might shield them against Somali attack. The Germans were allowed to build a station which Peters named 'Von der Heydt-Haus'. They also secured a treaty by which

---

[146] Peters, *Expedition*, 73, 78; Tiedemann, *Tana*, 63, 67.   [147] Peters, *Expedition*, 74.
[148] Ibid. 77.   [149] Cited in ibid. 78–80.
[150] Tiedemann, *Tana*, 67.   [151] Peters, *Expedition*, 91.
[152] Ibid. 84.   [153] Tiedemann, *Tana*, 66, 67.
[154] Peters, *Expedition*, 89.
[155] See H. S. Lewis, 'The Origins of the Galla and Somalis', *Journal of African History*, 7 (1966), 27–46; E. S. Wakefield, *Thomas Wakefield. Missionary and Geograhical Pioneer in East Equatorial Africa* (London, 1904), 192; see also J. Stursberg, *Ferdinand Würtz, Missionar und Missionspionier im Pokomoland in Brit.-Ostafrika* (Neukirchen, 1910), 50.
[156] Peters's remarks about continuing war between Galla and Somali agree with missionary reports: see *Der Missions- und Heidenbote*, Beiblatt, 9 Juni 1887, as cited in Brandl, *Neukirchener Mission*, 166; P. Paulitschke, *Ethnographie Nordost-Afrikas. Die materielle Cultur der Danakil, Gall und Somal* (Berlin, 1893), 24; *Der Missions- und Heidenbote*, Dec. 1894, 296.

the Galla allegedly accepted Peters's protection and ceded all rights of exploitation, 'above and below the ground'.[157]

The initial harmony did not last long, despite the fact that Peters was impressed by the 'aristocratic' appearance of his African hosts.[158] Peters had a few Somalis in his own column and this soon led to tension.[159] He also claimed that conflict arose over a slave community from the coast which the Galla had under their control.[160] If Peters's version is correct, the coastal people had asked him for protection. Possibly they deceived him to achieve their aim, telling him that the Galla were planning to attack the German camp. In any event Peters decided to strike first. Accompanied by ten Somali soldiers and twenty-five porters, he took a few boats and crossed the river to the island. The attack left seven Galla leaders shot dead. Peters took 'prisoners of war' and a number of women hostages. In addition, he secured eighty boat-loads of grain, which he piled up in his camp.[161]

On 16 October Peters forced the defeated Galla to accept another treaty.[162] Tiedemann fell ill, so that the expedition had to stay at the islands until he recovered. They were still waiting for Rust, the third man of the expedition, who had been left behind in Witu. Rust had sent a message confirming the arrival of the barter goods from the coast.[163] In the meantime, however, disturbing news came from downriver. Five thousand Somalis had gathered on the Tana shores and cut off Peters's column from Rust's party in Witu.[164] Knowing about the trouble between Galla and Somali, Peters decided to depart, leaving instructions for Rust in the newly built station.[165] They also had to abandon their machine-gun, which was no longer working. (For Africans further down the route, this was a fortunate defect of German quality products.)

Some years after the expedition, the *Fortnightly Review* cited a letter of the Danish traveller Scavenius who had moved up the river Tana on the same route as Peters:[166]

When I had rowed some 200 kilometres upstream the population began to retire. On every side I came across traces of war. In the neighbourhood of Obangi I found eleven villages that had been destroyed by fire, and everywhere skeletons of men,

---

[157] Peters, *Expedition*, 116. [158] Ibid. 108. [159] Ibid. 114.
[160] The existence of slavery among the Galla was also observed by the Methodist missionary Wakefield; see Paulitschke, *Ethnographie Nordost-Afrikas*, 261.
[161] Peters, *Expedition*, 119–21. [162] Ibid. 124. [163] Ibid. 92.
[164] Ibid. 122; Tiedemann, *Tana*, 97, speaks of 'large amounts' of Somali.
[165] Peters, *Expedition*, 126–8.
[166] E. Sellers, 'Dr. Carl Peters. The Leader of the Recent Anti-English Agitation in Germany', *Fortnightly Review* 61 NS [67 OS] (1897), 125–38; 134.

women and children, those of the women and children being especially numerous. ... The natives were terrified at my white face, for the last white man they had seen was Dr Peters.

The account seems to suggest that Peters himself wiped out all these villages, but such conclusions should be treated with caution. This is not to overlook Peters's violent temper. However, the military strength of the two Germans may easily be exaggerated as well, particularly as they had had to leave their machine-gun behind. The reported devastation could also have resulted from inter-African conflict, as Galla and Somali seem to have been fighting in this area over many years. In 1887 the Neukirchen missonaries had made observations which were quite similar to Scavenius's report.[167] A German ethnographer noted in 1893 that the Galla population along the Tana had sharply diminished as a result of these conflicts.[168]

Peters's rearguard under Rust never caught up again. In November 1889 he was still camped around the Neukirchen Mission station at Ngao. Apparently, he spent most of his time drinking, and he mistreated the local people. 'His journey through Pokomoland has done a lot of damage', the missionary Weber noted; 'the people are very much afraid of him.'[169] Borchert, Peters's other associate, reached the upper Tana in December, finding the German house untouched.[170] Lacking food and suffering from illness, he had to return to the coast as well.[171]

Violent clashes with the local population continued as Peters's caravan proceeded further upriver towards the Kikuyu. Shortage of supplies remained a major problem. On the upper Tana, Peters took eleven young Wandorobbo women hostage, only turning them loose in exchange for some sheep. After the Africans had given in, he attempted to secure further animals by force. The quarrel resulted in open fighting, during which Peters was able to capture the leader of the group. The latter was only freed when the expedition was supplied with further sheep.[172] Eventually Peters carried out what he called a cattle raid,[173] stealing 250 goats and sheep from the Wandorobbo.[174] From then on, the expedition was always accompanied by a large herd of animals.

[167] See *Der Missions- und Heidenbote*, Beiblatt, 9 Juni 1887, cited in Brandl, *Neuchkirchner Mission*, 166; Stursberg, *Ferdinand Würtz*, 64.
[168] Paulitschke, *Ethnographie Nordost-Afrikas*, 24; see also Stursberg, *Ferdinand Würtz*, 50.
[169] Wilhelm Weber's diary 124, 127, as cited in Brandl, *Neukirchener Mission*, 280.
[170] Peters, *Expedition*, 118.   [171] See *Der Missions- und Heidenbote*, März 1890, 6.
[172] Peters, *Expedition*, 140–5.   [173] Tiedemann, *Tana*, 113.
[174] Peters, *Expedition*, 149.

Further upriver, he forced people to exchange grain for some of his own goods. When a few Africans tried to get hold of Peters's five donkeys, he ordered his Somali force to capture as many African cattle as possible; they took another 600 sheep and 60 oxen. Peters and his soldiers then shot a number of African warriors who approached to fight for their lost cattle. They had had no previous experience of European firearms. But Peters was not satisfied with this victory. He wanted to teach the people a lesson, he said. 'C'est la guerre', he noted, proudly describing the event in his account. He ordered his people to burn six African villages and to take all valuable goods away. Thereafter his people came to call him 'Kupanda Sharo' ('Climbing fortifications').[175]

With his cattle raids, Peters had solved his own food problem. For those who had been deprived of their entire livestock, this was a disaster, which possibly endangered their survival. Nevertheless, Peters could not prevent his party from shrinking further and further. People still deserted, and others died of disease. By the middle of December only fifty to sixty people were left.[176] A number of camels and donkeys, his horse, and the two dogs had died, too.[177]

Initially the expedition had suffered mainly from heat and heavy rain.[178] Now, as they were ascending to Leikipia Plateau, they confronted increasing cold. The temperature fell below zero at night. Peters heard his men screaming, as they had no clothes or blankets to protect them. The expedition leader was better off; he had a tent, woollen underwear, four woollen blankets, and his winter coat, but even this did not suffice. He woke up at night, freezing cold.[179]

Having reached the plateau, Peters had his first encounters with the Maasai.[180] He seems to have been well received at first. Soon, however, he provoked them by shooting one of their bulls, which looked as if it wanted to attack him. Since Peters was determined not to pay any tribute for passing through, negotiations with the Maasai reached a deadlock. He made things worse by saying that 'they could also have war, if they did not want

[175] Ibid. 155–9; Tiedemann, *Tana*, 115.
[176] Peters, *Expedition*, 181; Tiedemann, *Tana*, 137–8.
[177] Peters, *Expedition*, 181, 172, 169; Tiedemann, *Tana*, 116, 119, 121, 122.
[178] See Peters to Bennigsen, 1 July 1889, note in FP 13, BAK.
[179] Peters, *Expedition*, 183; Tiedemann, *Tana*, 132.
[180] For the Maasai, see J. L. Berntsen, 'Pastoralism, Raiding and Prophets: Maasailand in the Nineteenth Century' (Univ. of Wisconsin-Madison, Ph.D. thesis 1979); idem, *Maasai and Iloikop: Ritual Experts and their Followers*, Occasional Paper 9 (University of Wisconsin-Madison, 1977); A. H. Jacobs, 'The Traditional Political Organization of the Pastoral Masai' (University of Oxford, D.Phil. thesis, 1965).

to comply with his peaceful suggestions'. The Maasai left in silence; Peters's Kikuyu interpreter said to him that this meant war.[181]

Peters had no interest in a peaceful solution, as the idea of beating the Maasai evidently gave him personal satisfaction. During the following night, the Maasai secretly carried away two loads from the camp. The guard fired after them and the Maasai shot back with poisonous arrows. On the next morning, 22 December 1889, Peters decided to attack. He took a force of thirty-five people, divided them into three wings and marched against the Maasai kraal of Elbejet. On the way they shot a young shepherd. While the Maasai sought to defend the kraal entrance, Peters shot one of the elders with whom he had negotiated on the previous day. Six other Maasai also fell.

The Massai now headed towards Peters's camp, so that he decided to retreat. On their way back, they lost three people. Shortly after the expedition had departed in haste from their camp, they met a large number of Maasai warriors, approaching through the forest. Heavy fighting left more than 120 Maasai dead, according to Peters's estimates.[182] His own party lost at least seven people,[183] who were mutilated by their enemies. Peters's soldiers now cut off the heads of the dead Maasai and threw them down the hill to where the remaining Masai had retreated. Tiedemann wrote: 'The whole area around us is covered with dead or dying Maasai warriors, their massive spears and the large white shields are lying everywhere.'[184]

Peters gave orders to loot the kraal which they had attacked before, and to set fire to the huts. He had captured 2,000 head of cattle, but he had lost a substantial part of his people and used some 900 cartridges. There were only 600 left for the remaining part of the journey. Furthermore, he lacked a guide for the trail to Lake Baringo, which he had hoped to find on the plateau.[185]

But the Maasai had not yet given up. They accompanied the caravan at some distance, waiting for a chance to strike again. On 23 December a large force gathered close to the camp, but a solar eclipse apparently persuaded them to wait. The Germans believed that the Maasai attributed this natural phenomenon to special powers of the white people.[186] In any case, the

---

[181] Peters, *Expedition*, 195, 196.

[182] Ibid. 200; Tiedemann, *Tana*, 137–8 speaks of at least 150 Maasai who had been killed, maybe more.

[183] Peters, *Expedition*, 200; Tiedemann, *Tana*, 138, speaks of eleven casualties on their own side.   [184] Tiedemann, *Tana*, 137–8.

[185] Peters, *Expedition*, 197–202; Tiedemann, *Tana*, 136–8.

[186] Peters, *Expedition*, 206; Tiedemann, *Tana*, 139.

alleged deterrent did not last very long. On 24 December, the Maasai eventually attacked. Although Peters succeeded in defending his party without
losing further people, the fight again cost him a lot of ammunition. He
knew that if the Maasai continued with their tactics he would be defeated
sooner or later. Furthermore, he had to worry about Tiedemann. His young
associate was suffering from dysentery, being afflicted by feverish visions.
He could no longer stand on his feet. On 31 December he passed out three
times.[187]

However, since the Maasai had suffered many casualties during their last
attack, they changed tactics. Now they offered to guide Peters, leading the
expedition on a wrong track, where they could not find any water.
Suddenly, the guides disappeared, having 'lured us into the desert', as
Tiedemann noted.[188] Eventually, Peters caught one African, whom he
forced with his revolver to show him the next river.[189] As the expedition
continued to march westward, he eventually succeeded in shaking off the
Maasai warriors. Peters forced two young local people to take him to Lake
Baringo which he reached on 12 January 1890.[190]

It seems that Peters quite deliberately provoked a violent clash with the
Maasai. European rumours about a notoriously aggressive people who
attacked passing caravans presented a distorted picture. Certainly, the
Maasai raided their neighbours for cattle and also harassed travellers at
times. But during the nineteenth century there are only two recorded
instances of an attack on a caravan, as one scholar of the Maasai has pointed
out.[191]

As far as Leikipia was concerned, two earlier European expeditions,
those of Thomson and Teleki, had passed shortly before Peters without any
fighting.[192] However, they had accepted Maasai terms of passage, paying
the usual *hongo* (tribute). No doubt Peters was not as well equipped as other
caravans for such a deal. A lot of the barter goods that were intended for the
Maasai route had been confiscated on the coast. Nevertheless, he still had
plenty of material with which he could have sought to reach an agreement.
But this was not Peters's way of doing things. He despised a character such
as Thomson for his yielding attitude and the acceptance of *hongo* payments.
He also ridiculed the 'clowning about' with which the British traveller came

---

[187] Tiedemann, *Tana*, 147.   [188] Ibid. 145.

[189] Peters, *Expedition*, 206–16; Tiedemann, *Tana*, 139–47.

[190] Peters, *Expedition*, 222, 229.   [191] Berntsen, 'Pastoralism', 263.

[192] See L. von Höhnel, *Zum Rudolph und Stephanie-See. Die Forschungsreise des Grafen
Samuel Teleki in Ost-Aequatorial-Afrika 1887–1888* (Vienna, 1892); J. Thomson, *Through
Masai Land* (London, 1885).

to be recognized as a white medicine-man among the Maasai.[193] At one stage, Thomson wrote in his book: 'I have a couple of artificial teeth, which at this juncture were perfect treasures. These I manipulated to the astonishment of the Maasai, and as they thought I could do the same thing with my nose or eyes, they hailed me at once as a veritable "lybon n'ebor" (white medicine-man).' Peters preferred other methods: 'I have found that in the end only the bullets of a repeater . . . make an impression on these wild sons of the steppe, when applied to their own bodies.'

Indeed, Peters's massacre seems to have left a lasting impression on the Maasai. When the German traveller Georg Kolb met some Maasai near Mount Kenya in 1894, they immediately asked him about Carl Peters.[194] Many years later the last governor of East Africa, Heinrich Schnee, remembered an invitation to Peters's London flat in 1905. The walls in the dining room were decorated with a number of African spears, and Peters explained that he had selected only the weapons of those Africans whom he had shot himself.[195]

Having reached Baringo, Peters persuaded the local people to sign another of his notorious treaties. This was a piece of paper which stated that the elders accepted Peters as their patron and that they asked for the incorporation of their land into the German *Schutzgebiet*.[196] The territory clearly lay north of the line of demarcation which London and Berlin had agreed upon in 1886, but this did not worry Peters. He saw Baringo as a good place for trading in ivory.

From Baringo the expedition headed towards Kavirondo, on the northeastern shores of Lake Victoria. On the way they met another caravan which had been organized by a well-known coastal Arab, Juma Kimameta. This carried exciting news for the two Germans. A white person was reported to be staying at Kavirondo, 'with a lot of women and soldiers'.[197] He had supposedly not come from the coast, so that there was some reason to assume that it might be Emin Pasha. However, a few days later their hopes were shattered when they learned that there were two British in Kavirondo, Mr Jackson and Mr Martin, accompanied by two other whites.[198] They had recently left their camp to go hunting elephants. During the following days Peters was confronted with much contradictory

[193] Peters, *Expedition*, 186.
[194] See G. Kolb, 'Von Mombasa durch Ukambani nach Kenya: zwei Expeditionen 1894–1896', *Petermanns Mitteilungen*, 42 (1896), 224; see Berntsen, 'Pastoralism', 322.
[195] Schnee's manuscript, Schnee Papers 1 HA, Rep 92, vol. 22, 75, GStA-PK.
[196] Treaty text printed in Peters, *Expedition*, 231.   [197] Ibid. 238.
[198] Ibid. 253.

news. Then, on 13 February 1890, two local Africans gave Peters some letters which were addressed to the British expedition. One of them carried the name of Stanley on its back. Peters did not hesitate to open the envelope. The few lines brought certainty about Emin Pasha's fate; he had left the Equatorial Province even before Peters had started his march into the interior. He had met Stanley and had now—the letter dated from 4 September 1889—reached the southern shore of Lake Victoria. 'In a few days the expedition will depart from here to the coast via Mpuapua', the letter concluded.[199] This news marked the sudden end of Peters's grand schemes in the heart of Africa.

His immediate reaction was to burst into tears. However, he did not yet want to give up altogether. After all, there was still Uganda, where war had been raging for a few years, and where both Catholic and Protestant missionaries hoped to maintain a foothold and to widen their influence. If Emin had left, perhaps there was a chance to 'work in Uganda for the benefit of German national interest'.[200] This could always be justified as making Uganda a 'bastion' of Christianity in order to contain the Muslim 'tidal wave' from the north.[201]

In Europe the news of Emin's march to the coast had already become known months earlier. It had reached Berlin on 14 October 1889 and put an end to the long dispute between the government and the Cartel parties about the usefulness of Peters's operation. The simple news of Stanley's success suddenly solved a crisis which had caused Bismarck such great difficulties. With Emin's departure any further support for Peters's venture had become unsustainable. The Emin Committee informed the government that their plan was now 'frustrated'.[202] They wanted to instruct Peters to return to the newly acquired Somali coast. However, the Foreign Office objected to this plan since it was not clear 'what effect the sudden appearance of an armed column could have' upon the local 'warlike' population.[203] Obviously the government feared that Peters might trigger another coastal rebellion further north. Therefore the Emin Committee was asked to instruct Peters to halt his expedition and to await further instructions 'at a suitable place'. However, no such message ever reached Peters in the interior.

---

[199] Letter printed in ibid. 302.   [200] Ibid. 303.   [201] Ibid.
[202] Hofmann to Bismarck, 31 Oct. 89, RKolA 251, 116, BAB.
[203] AA to Emin Committee, 4 Nov. 1889, RKolA 251, 121, BAB.

In Uganda

In February 1890, Peters left Kavirondo, marching along the northern shores of Lake Nyanza towards Mengo, the Bugandan capital. As they drew closer, they gathered their own first impressions of the state of affairs in Buganda: 'We came into a perfectly desolate country', noted Peters.

Not only were the villages burnt, and the groves of bananas destroyed, the whole landscape was simply burnt up, and lay there a black expanse. By the roadsides lay skeletons and corpses still in process of decomposition, poisoning the air. . . . An oppressive desolation filled our hearts.[204]

A few months earlier, a French missionary stationed in Buganda had noted in his diary:

Even Mengo, Mwanga's capital, has disappeared in the long grass. There now remains only the post of a lightning conductor. Rubaga and Mengo have fallen prey to the flames. At every step one comes across dead and wounded. Swarms of vultures hover in the air and swoop down on corpses which nobody troubles to bury.[205]

For the last two years internal conflict had been raging in Buganda and threatening to tear the Central African kingdom apart. Among the various kingdoms in the region, Buganda had gained considerable power and size by the middle of the century. It was a well-organized state, at the head of which stood the *kabaka*, who ruled with almost absolute power. He could appoint and depose local chiefs at will. He held court in his capital, judging cases, appointing the leaders of military campaigns, and receiving envoys from his neighbours.

In many respects, however, Buganda was in a state of profound transition. A number of factors came to challenge the established political, economic, and social order in the nineteenth century. With the growth of long-distance trade, Arab communities and their Islamic faith gained increasing influence within the kingdom. King Mutesa (1856–84) welcomed the Arab presence, partly because he sought to secure assistance in case of an Egyptian invasion from the north. He counted on Arab traders to provide him with new ammunition and arms.[206]

---

[204] Peters, *Expedition*, 315; Tiedemann, *Tana*, 175.

[205] Lourdel's diary, 7 Oct. 1889, cited in J. M. Gray, 'The Year of the Three Kings of Buganda, Mwanga—Kiwewa—Kalema, 1888–1889', *Uganda Journal*, 14/1 (1950), 45.

[206] D. A. Low, *Religion and Society in Buganda, 1875–1900* (Kampala, 1958), 1; J. Brierley and T. Spear, 'Mutesa, the Missionaries, and Christian Conversion in Buganda', *IJAHS* 21/4 (1988), 601–2.

By the late nineteenth century European missionaries had also entered the scene. The first CMS missionaries appeared in 1877, and the Catholic White Fathers from Algiers followed two years later. Their presence not only opened up new ideological and religious perspectives, but also offered further access to technology and knowledge. New religious beliefs—be they Islamic or Christian—were thus bound to be drawn into the field of politics. The missionaries became as much political actors as they were proponents of their faith. They were also to play an important role when Peters, as an agent of a reportedly powerful country, approached in 1890 and attempted to exploit the missionaries as mediators for his own purposes.

After Mutesa died in 1884, his son Mwanga, some 20 years old, succeeded to the throne. Although his accession was not accompanied by any immediate bloodshed, his rule did not remain unchallenged. Rival factions soon attempted to depose Mwanga and to install their own candidate. Friction between political groups in Buganda was reinforced by their respective religious ties. There was a significant Muslim group; there were those who still adhered to traditional beliefs and customs, remaining suspicious of any outside influences; finally, there was a growing number of Christian converts, Protestant or Catholic, many of whom had political ambitions. Some occupied important positions within Bugandan politics. Mwanga's *katikiro* (prime minister), for instance, was a Protestant.

Political opposition to Mwanga's rule gathered mainly around the Muslim faction. On the other side, there were the two Christian parties who supported the king. Their unity, however, was threatened by Catholic–Protestant divisions. The years 1888 and 1889 witnessed fierce fighting between the rival groups. Mwanga was displaced twice, but always managed to re-establish his power.[207] By February 1890 Mwanga had recaptured his capital Mengo, on the western shores of Lake Victoria, and his Muslim enemies had retreated to the Bunyoro border in the north.

Such was the situation when Carl Peters and his column entered Mengo on 25 January 1890. There was only a handful of Europeans in the region at that time. At the station of Ukumbi there were sixteen Roman Catholic missionaries; the Protestants had sent out only two people to Usambiro.[208] There was also an Irishman named Charles Stokes, who had embarked on a quite extraordinary career in the African interior. A civil engineer by

[207] See Gray, 'Year', 15–52.
[208] Mackay's letter of 30 July 1889, printed in *The Times*, 6 Dec. 1889; Uganda Mounted Cutting Book One, 1889–1893, MSS Lugard 82/1, Rhodes House, Oxford.

profession, he took service with the CMS in 1878 to work in East Africa. In 1886, however, he married the daughter of an African chief, left the missionary service, and established himself as a trader,[209] supplying Mwanga with arms and ammunition.[210] The King himself had converted to Catholicism in Bukumi in 1889, after Kalema, his rival and leader of the Muslim party, had forced him into exile. Mwanga's refuge with the White Fathers turned out to be an important episode in Bugandan history, since it lay the foundations of close ties between the White Fathers and the King. There is some evidence to suggest that, apart from Stokes,[211] the French Catholic Father Lourdel became the most influential European at Mwanga's court. The British missionaries suspiciously observed that Lourdel 'now has very great authority with Mwanga and fears that any white men resident in the country will interfere with his power and influence'.[212]

'Where do you have your cannon?', Mwanga asked as he welcomed Peters and his group, making clear that his prior concern still lay with his enemies further north.[213] Mwanga had heard that Peters had beaten the Maasai. Thus he had some reason to assume that the German could be useful as a military ally. He and the missionaries had previously asked Jackson for help, without any success. The British company had no instructions to enter Uganda, and Jackson believed his forces to be too small to make any military intervention successful.[214]

Peters's group was not in a position to provide much help for Mwanga either. His party had diminished in number, and he had no extra supplies of arms. All he could do to put Mwanga in a favourable mood was to give him 120 pounds of powder,[215] a present which certainly delighted the King since his army was confronted with a shortage of powder.[216] In any case Peters did not really want to be drawn into the domestic struggles of the country. His primary aim was to secure a treaty from Mwanga, and for this purpose he hoped to bring onto his side the Catholic missionaries who entertained close relations with the *kabaka*.

---

[209] Gray, 'Year', 31–2.

[210] See Mackay's letter, 30 July 1889, printed in *The Times*, 6 Dec. 1889, Uganda mounted Cutting Book One, 1889–1893, MSS Lugard 82/1, Rhodes House, Oxford; Gordon to Euan Smith, 25 Oct. 1889, MSS BRIT. EMP. S 43, 174–81 (enclosed in Lugard Papers), Rhodes House, Oxford.

[211] Extract from Walker to Euan Smith, 21 Oct. 1889, MSS BRIT. EMP. S 43, 221–6.

[212] Ibid.; see also Gordon [to Jackson], 23 Nov. 1889, in MSS BRIT. EMP. S 43.

[213] Peters, *Expedition*, 319.

[214] See Jackson to Mwanga, 8 Nov. 1889, MSS BRIT. EMP. S. 43, 191; Jackson [to CMS], 6 Dec. 1889, MSS BRIT. EMP. S 43, 197–9.   [215] Peters, *Expedition*, 321.

[216] Gordon to Euan Smith, 25 Oct. 1889, MSS BRIT. EMP. S 43, 174–81; see Tiedemann, *Tana*, 172.

Mwanga welcomed Peters's arrival, but he was still deeply worried that an outside power would deprive him of power altogether. In 1885 he had received disturbing news from the coast that the Germans had annexed a large stretch of territory, challenging the Sultan's supremacy. A little later he had given the order to murder Bishop Hannington upon his arrival in Buganda. As the missionaries suspected, Mwanga obviously associated the bishop, who had been described to him as the representative of the Queen, with a general advance of the Europeans in order to take over power in his country.[217] He was by no means prepared to sign a treaty of protection such as Peters may have had in mind, although this intention is not explicitly stated anywhere. Mwanga had refused Jackson's overtures for accepting the governance of the British company, despite his fragile domestic position.

The King's primary aim was to channel European influence in a way which would strengthen his own position without paving the way for foreign rule. He wanted to establish a small European settlement under his control which could also be helpful in protecting Buganda from a potential attack from Bunyoro.[218] In general, however, he was convinced that sooner or later Buganda could not escape the fate of being ruled by the Europeans. 'I am the last King of Buganda. The whites will take over the country after my death. While alive I will be able to prevent it, but I will be the last of the black kings of Buganda', Lourdel reported on Mwanga's attitude.[219]

Mwanga's policy towards Peters was in line with his plans for European settlement. He gave Peters a house near his own palace,[220] and also discussed military issues with him. Peters, believing his military skills to be outstanding, offered to train the King's people, and to lead them in battle should Mengo be attacked.[221] Obviously this was one of the occasions upon which Peters sought to compensate for the humiliation he had felt when he had been refused for military service.

Peters seems to have been on good terms with Father Lourdel, who arranged for a separate meeting with the King just two days after their arrival. Peters succeeded in gaining Mwanga's signature on a treaty of friendship which committed the King to the principles of the Congo Act, guaranteeing Europeans free trade, free access, and the right to settle in

---

[217] See D. A. Low, 'The British and Uganda, 1862–1900' (Oxford University D. Phil. thesis, 1957).

[218] See Mwanga to Consul-General (copy), 26 April 1890, MSS BRIT. EMP. S 43, 214.

[219] Lourdel to Lavigerie, Nov. 1885, *Les Missions Catholiques* (1886), 314–15, printed in D. Robinson and D. Smith, *Sources of the African Past* (London, 1979), 100.

[220] Peters, *Expedition*, 337.   [221] Ibid. 322.

Buganda and its tributary countries. According to the treaty, Mwanga entered into friendship with the German Kaiser and enjoyed the same rights in Germany as he had granted to Europeans in Buganda.[222]

In fact, this agreement largely matched Mwanga's ideas of a limited European presence in his kingdom. At the same time, he obviously believed that the treaty might shield him against the imminent threat of a British protectorate. Otherwise, the sharp protest of the Protestant faction against the treaty would be incomprehensible. On the whole it seems that Peters's move into Buganda made Mwanga's position even more precarious instead of strengthening it, since it deepened the gulf between Protestants and Catholics. Eventually, however, the Protestants gave in and accepted. After all, Peters did not stay in Buganda, so the future role of the Germans in the region was still vague.

Father Lourdel's intentions are far from clear with respect to the establishment of European rule. The Protestants, at least, suspected that he wanted to preserve the King's position since it gave him a most influential role. They also believed that Lourdel feared that a British intervention might favour the Protestant party and threaten the prospects of the Catholic missions.[223] However, there is no clear evidence to suggest that he in fact worked towards a German protectorate. If Mwanga could consolidate his rule again after his victory over the Muslims, the Catholics would be in a good position, and it is difficult to see why they should have worked towards a takeover of control by the Europeans, particularly after the experiences on the coast, where the German intrusion had sparked off a rebellion.

Thus it is a myth that Peters in fact secured a protectorate over Buganda, although this may well have been his idea in entering the country. Since nothing more was to be gained, Peters left Buganda in the middle of March. Next it was important to return to the coast and to see what might be gained politically from the newly established friendship with Mwanga. At least Peters hoped that with his treaty he could prevent the outright annexation of Buganda by the British.[224]

Peters and his party crossed Lake Nyanza by boat, and reached the Catholic mission station at Nyagezi on the southern shore by the middle of April. From there they marched back towards the coast.

On the way, Peters longed for further military success, so he decided to

[222] Treaty text printed in Peters, *Expedition*, 326.
[223] Gordon [to Jackson], 23 Nov. 1889, MSS BRIT. EMP. S 43; Walker to Euan Smith, 21 Oct. 1889, MSS BRIT. EMP. S 43, 221–6; cf. also Jackson to Walker, 27 March 1890, MSS BRIT. EMP. S 43.   [224] See Tiedemann, *Tana*, 180.

fight the people in Ugogo in order to show them 'who the Germans are'.[225] In the past the Wagogo had demanded *hongo* from passing caravans, and Stanley had complained bitterly about their ability to 'annoy and molest' travellers. Peters had no mercy with them. He burnt twelve villages and captured some 200–300 head of cattle, shooting all herdsmen who could not flee in time. 'Well, Mr Tiedemann, I think this will suffice until we reach Mpwapwa.'[226]

On 19 June they marched into Mpwapwa.[227] Here they met the man whom they had sought to rescue, Emin Pasha. The doctor had already been to the coast with Stanley. However, Emin eventually chose to take service under the Germans, much to the annoyance of the British.

In Mpwapwa another surprise awaited Peters; this was the news that Bismarck had been dismissed in March 1890. The evidence presented in this chapter lends further support to the thesis that growing dissatisfaction with a moderate course in colonial policy had weakened Bismarck's position within the Kartell and thus contributed to his final downfall.[228] The National Liberals turned increasingly against Bismarck in 1889, and this was partly a result of his opposition to the Emin Pasha Expedition and the expansionist programme behind it. In this sense, Peters himself, acting as the spearhead of colonial expansionism, became a factor in undermining Bismarck's authority. The Emin Pasha expedition marked the first significant incident in which the government was confronted with a nationalist opposition.

---

[225] Peters, *Expedition*, 436.   [226] Ibid. 438.   [227] Ibid. 444.
[228] Pogge, 'Domestic Origins', 159; see also J. C. G. Röhl, 'The Disintegration of the Kartell and the Politics of Bismarck's Fall from Power, 1887–1890', *HJ* 9 (1966), 75.

5

After Bismarck:
The Heligoland–Zanzibar Agreement
and its Consequences
(1890–1891)

IMPERIAL POLITICS AND THE MAKING OF THE PAN-GERMAN LEAGUE

When Peters arrived at Bagamoyo on 16 July 1890,[1] he realized that all his efforts to extend claims in East Africa had been in vain. Two weeks earlier the British and German governments had concluded the so-called Heligoland–Zanzibar Agreement, which was to settle their colonial disputes. Above all, it meant the final partition of East Africa. It fixed the borders of the British territory in the north and the German one in the south. Britain secured Witu, Uganda, a protectorate over Zanzibar, and the Stephenson Road between Lake Nyassa and Lake Tanganyika. In return, it ceded the island of Heligoland to the Reich. Finally, Britain committed itself to assisting the Germans in obtaining the coastal strip from the Sultan, who had not been granted a voice in the matter at all.[2]

This is not the place to concentrate on the diplomatic negotiations leading to the agreement, which other scholars have examined in some detail.[3]

---

[1] Peters, *Gründung*, GS i. 281.

[2] For the full text of the agreement see E. Hertslet, *The Map of Africa by Treaty*, iii (London, 1909; repr. 1967), 899–906.

[3] For the German side see R. Lahme, *Deutsche Außenpolitik 1890–1894. Von der Gleichgewichtspolitik Bismarcks zur Allianzstrategie Caprivis* (Göttingen, 1990). Salisbury's motives have been far more debated by historians: see D. R. Gillard, 'Salisbury's African Policy and the Heligoland Offer of 1890', *EHR* 75 (1960), 631–53 and idem, 'Salisbury's Heligoland Offer: The Case against the "Witu Thesis"', *EHR* 80 (1965), 538–52; G. N. Sanderson, *England, Europe and the Upper Nile, 1882–1899* (Edinburgh, 1965) and idem, 'The Anglo-German Agreement of 1890 and the Upper Nile', *EHR* 78 (1963). More recently, it has again been questioned whether Salisbury's motives in East Africa were primarily strategic: J. Darwin, 'Imperialism and the Victorians: The Dynamics of Territorial Expansion', *EHR* 112 (1997), 614–42.

Rather, we will focus on the reactions it provoked in Germany. A good deal of criticism was expressed in public in Germany, so that it is misleading to state that 'enthusiastic approval of the treaty in the press was the rule'.[4]

True, the acquisition of Heligoland was welcomed, and it was also stated that British friendship was a desirable thing in principle.[5] But the loss of African claims was seen as unfortunate, in both the National Liberal and the Conservative camps. The *Kölnische Zeitung*, for instance, commented on 19 June 1890: 'Hardly anybody who has a heart and some understanding for Germany's colonial efforts has read the agreement with the English government without dismay. The yielding of the Germans is entirely unexpected.'[6] The paper also reported at length on the assembly of the Colonial Society in which Fabri strongly opposed the agreement. He deplored that Zanzibar and Witu had been given away and that Germany had failed to secure Walvis Bay. In his eyes, the government's colonial inclinations had slackened. Only in this way was it possible that the German Emin Pasha Expedition had been sacrificed to British admirals and officials.[7] The *Kolonialzeitung* likewise criticized the treaty and quoted in full a letter by Carl Peters, which referred to the treaties he had concluded in the area now being recognized as belonging to Britain.[8]

The *Münchener Allgemeine Zeitung* was even more pronounced in its criticism. It stated that it would take a long time for the German spirit of exploration to recover from that blow 'which we all hope future history will not point to as the Olmütz of the German colonial movement'.[9] Conservative papers reacted sceptically, too. *Die Post* stated that Germany had lost 'not only the best in the whole of Africa, but also one of the most promising possessions of the entire world, a second East India'.[10] The *Kreuz-Zeitung*, although stating that the government had done the best it could, also deplored the fact that Britain had got 'the lion's share' in Africa.[11]

There were more positive assessments as well, but they largely came from the opposition party, the Left Liberals.[12] This was also recognized in

[4] J. R. Dukes,'Heligoland, Zanzibar, East Africa: Colonialism in German Politics, 1884–1890' (University of Illinois Ph.D. thesis, 1970), 203.

[5] *National-Zeitung*, 18 June 1890, note in FP 19, BAK.

[6] Quoted in M. Sell, *Die öffentliche Meinung und das Helgolandabkommen im Jahre 1890* (Diss. Bonn, 1926), 82.   [7] *Kölnische Zeitung*, 2 July 1890, note in FP 19, BAK.

[8] See *DKZ*, 28 June 1890.

[9] 18 June 1890, quoted in Sell, *Öffentliche Meinung*, 65–6.

[10] *Die Post*, 28 June 1890, quoted in Sell, *Öffentliche Meinung*, 77.

[11] *Kreuz-Zeitung*, 18 June 1890, quoted in Sell, *Öffentliche Meinung*, 73.

[12] See Sell, *Öffentliche Meinung*, 90 ff.

a press report by the Foreign Office,[13] which found it quite 'extraordinary' that the *Berliner Tageblatt* favoured the position of the government.

The discontent about the conduct of colonial policy lent wings to the pan-German movement. After the *Reichsanzeiger* had announced the basic points of the agreement, a circle of nationalists from Zurich sought to rally support against any concessions in the colonial field. This was a group around the medical doctor and university lecturer Adolf Fick, who was related to Wislicenus, a chemistry professor at Leipzig and an ardent colonial enthusiast. They published a pamphlet of protest under the title *Deutschland wach' auf!*

We are prepared to follow our Kaiser's call to walk in rank and file, and to be led towards the bullets of the enemy, silently and in obedience. But in return we can claim a reward that is worth the sacrifice. And this reward is to belong to a *Herrenvolk* which takes its part of the world, without depending on the goodwill of other peoples.[14]

Here again was a reference to the German wars of unification, which were only seen as worthwhile if Germany became a world power. The Anglo-German agreement, it was stated further, would destroy all hopes for a large German colonial empire. Hence, a mass petition should be submitted to the Reichstag. It should give a voice to the feeling that the treaty 'has called forth the pure desperation of thousands who cling to Germany with every fibre of their hearts'.

Although the envisaged mass petition did not come into existence and the Colonial Society in Cologne shied away from taking the lead in the opposition movement,[15] the pan-Germans were not discouraged. They observed that 'the nationally minded bourgeoisie cannot understand that their government sacrificed promising countries without any reason.' The reason why parts of the bourgeoisie nevertheless followed the government was 'a lack of will-power'.[16] This assessment indicates that pan-German circles also perceived their movement as a form of political emancipation which provided an alternative to established forms of *Honoratiorenpolitik*, the politics of notables. Nationalist societies were regarded as a platform for giving their political demands a voice, as the current opportunities for political participation were not seen as sufficient for the promotion of their goals.

---

[13] Lindau's press report, 30 and 31 July 1890, notes in FP 19, BAK.
[14] 24 June 1890, ADV Papers, vol. 1, 11, 13, 14, BAB.
[15] See confidential letter by Hubartsch, Felix, Fick, and Müller to ?, 15 July 1890, ADV Papers, vol. 1, 22, BAB.   [16] Ibid.

Peters was still on his way from Africa to Europe when he was first approached by pan-German circles which sought to win him over as a leader.[17] An address to him was drafted by Hugenberg and signed by sixty-three supporters, including prominent colonial writers such as Hübbe-Schleiden and Jannasch.[18] Peters seemed the ideal person for the job, as he was the man who had expressed German aspirations to world power in the most uncompromising terms. He had organized the General German Congress in 1886, he was known as an able agitator, and he was no 'armchair imperialist' but a man of action.

It may be argued that the criticism of the Heligoland–Zanzibar Agreement and the revival of the pan-German movement had an important impact upon the shaping of Germany's East African policy. In July 1890 a new colonial department was formed within the Foreign Office, and Paul Kayser was chosen as its director. He was confronted with a number of difficult tasks, particularly with regard to East Africa. The government had decided that the state was to take over control from the DOAG, which had proved incapable of managing colonial affairs out of its own resources. Wissmann had put down the coastal uprising and the Sultan was forced to sell the coastal strip; now a colonial administration had to be set up, which would make it possible for the commercial companies to turn the possession into a profitable enterprise.

As the administrative head of the new colony, a governor had to be chosen. Wissmann, having led the East African military operation, was one possible candidate for the job. However, he was opposed by Chancellor Caprivi,[19] probably because he saw him as an opponent of his moderate colonial policy. Hence the government appointed Julius von Soden, who had been Germany's colonial administrator in the Cameroons since 1886.

What, however, should be done with the famous *Afrikaner*, Wissmann, Peters, and Emin, who all counted upon some sort of reward for their colonial achievements? The most uncomfortable candidate in this respect was Peters. Not only was it clear that he had primarily political ambitions; he had also demonstrated more than once that his actions were difficult to control from above. His skill as a political agitator and his connections to the press were well known.[20] Furthermore, the aura around Peters as a colonial hero was still growing. He began to feature prominently in colonial novels

[17] See Kayser [to Marschall], 20 Aug. 1890, note in FP 21, BAK.
[18] Address to Carl Peters [1 Aug. 1890], ADV Papers, vol. 1, 36.
[19] See Kayser to Marschall, 20 Aug. 1890, note in FP 21, BAK.
[20] See, for example, Kayser to Marschall, 20 Aug. 1890; Kayser [to ?], 7 Aug. 1890, notes in FP 21, BAK.

and his own account of the Emin Pasha Expedition was soon to be published.

Most importantly, however, the government was confidentially informed about pan-German attempts to recruit Peters for their movement.[21] This was a worrying prospect, as the government was anxious to contain growing agitation against their Anglo-German agreement. After Peters returned to Zanzibar in the middle of July, he immediately cabled to Wissmann that the latter should prevent the cession of Uganda. However, his intervervention came too late, as the agreement had already been signed. Fearing that Peters's activities were bound to create trouble, Caprivi agreed to Kayser's proposal to send him a telegram in order to appease him. This was done through an intermediary, who signalled on behalf of the Foreign Office that Peters could count upon a decoration by the Kaiser and on the government's goodwill if he displayed 'good behaviour' in return. This was a quite remarkable step, as the Emin expedition had been undertaken against the explicit wish of the goverment. Kayser was satisfied with his policy of appeasement. On 20 August he observed that Peters had so far resisted any temptation to accept pan-German offers.

When Peters arrived back in Germany, he stopped first at Nuremberg, home town of his brother Hermann. The citizens of the town organized a great welcome for him. A few years ago they had presented him with a replica of Charlemagne's sword.[22] The symbolism of this gesture indicates that Peters was recognized as an empire-builder, following in the steps of the great medieval king. But Peters's speech in Nuremberg may have been disappointing to ardent colonialists; adopting an explicitly conciliatory tone, he stated that it was up to the Kaiser and the government to determine what was best for the nation. This was precisely what Kayser had hoped for. Obviously Peters had taken the bait.

At the same time, the colonial director was aware that the Foreign Office had to continue its efforts if it wanted to draw Peters firmly to its side. 'It lies in the hands of the government either to guide the movement behind Peters to their own benefit, or to let it grow against them', he wrote to Marschall on 20 August 1890.[23] Kayser therefore sent a welcoming telegram to Peters in Nuremberg, stating that he would 'be extraordinarily pleased to see you soon'.[24] The men arranged to meet in the following week.[25]

---

[21] Kayser [to ?], 7 Aug. 1890, note in FP 21, BAK.
[22] *The Times*, 25 Aug. 1890, 5.
[23] Kayser to Marschall, 20 Aug. 1890, note in FP 21, BAK.
[24] 23 Aug. 1890, note in FP 21, BAK.
[25] Kayser to Marschall, 20 Aug. 1890, note in FP 21, BAK.

Kayser also urged Foreign Minister Marschall to prepare a favourable reception in Berlin. Otherwise, he believed, 'the whole thing could still be spoilt'. He suggested that Marschall should arrange to receive Peters as soon as possible to tell him about his decoration. Moreover, the Foreign Minister should give him a hint that there were no obstacles to later employment in the colonial service in East Africa.[26]

After the Kaiser had consented,[27] Kayser's scheme was quickly realized. On 30 August Wilhelm decorated Peters with the 'Kronen-Orden, III. Klasse'.[28] This was not to be the only recognition for the expedition leader; he also received the 'Ritterkreuz, 1. Klasse des Albrechtsorden' from the King of Saxony, and the 'Ritterkreuz, 1. Klasse des Hausordens der Wachsamkeit' from the Grand Duke of Saxony–Weimar–Eisenach.[29]

The government's attempt to manipulate colonial enthusiasm for its own ends is also reflected in its attitude towards the so-called Karl-Peters-Stiftung. The foundation was established on 14 August 1890 by a circle of Peters's associates, 'as a sign of recognition'. They included Schweinfurt, Arendt, Bennigsen, Arnim, Hugenberg, Krupp, Kardorff, Schroeder, Woermann, and Wislicenus.[30] Hohenlohe was chosen as its president. The foundation was meant to collect money for a 'Peters steamship' on Victoria Nyanza, and for other measures to improve communications in the new colony. Kayser was quick to jump on the bandwagon. He suggested to Marschall that the project should be publicly supported.[31] This was to demonstrate to Peters and his friends that the government was ready to recognize his achievements in the colonial field. Hence the appeal for contributions was also published in the newly established official *Kolonialblatt*.[32]

The government's strategy seemed to work. In September pan-German circles deplored the fact that 'despite the Zanzibar treaty, Peters is again placing himself at the disposal of the government'.[33] At the same time, however, his decision did not yet seem to have been a firm commitment. Rather, it was a decision 'for the time being',[34] as Peters clearly wanted to assess his options first before taking a final decision.

[26] Ibid.   [27] Ibid.

[28] Wilhelm's decree, 30 Aug. 1890, note in FP 21, BAK.

[29] See Herrfurth to AA, 17 Oct. 1890, and Kayser's marginal note; note by the Legation of Saxony, 15 Nov. 1890, FP 21, BAK.

[30] Report of the Carl Peters Foundation [1890], Promemoria, 13 May 1891, RKolA 978, 15, 6–9, BAB.

[31] Kayser to Marschall, 20 Aug. 1890, note in FP 21, BAK.

[32] Appeal of 1 April 1891, RKolA 978, BAB.

[33] 'Notizen', 29 Sept. 1890, ADV Papers, vol. 1, 59, BAB.   [34] Ibid.

The government now had to decide what post it should give to Peters in East Africa. This was the birth of the so-called 'imperial commissioner system'. Peters, Emin, and Wissmann were to occupy prominent official posts in the new colony,[35] so that each of them should contribute to the opening-up of the new territory. However, all three were to be placed under the authority of the governor, and this was the point where the trouble started, as will be demonstrated later.

Peters accepted the post,[36] but he did not break with the pan-Germans. On the contrary, he revived his activities. In January 1891 he agreed to work towards 'a large-scale movement', and in April the new Allgemeiner Deutscher Verband was constituted. The executive board included the core group of the colonial movement: Fabri, Arendt, Behr, von der Heydt, Hübbe-Schleiden, Kardorff, Ratzel, Schroeder, and Peters.[37] Its manifesto was remarkably similar to that of the GfdK in 1884. Peters also communicated a copy to the Foreign Office and stated: 'The society will become a pillar of the government, I hope.' It would make propaganda in the country and in parliament for bills 'that aim at a strengthening of our foreign policy'.[38]

Arguably, however, Peters had involved himself in the new league in order to keep a path open for future agitation. He regarded this as a potential trump card for himself, and he believed that it would be a suitable instrument for putting pressure on the government if things did not work out according to his plans. Kayser, on the other hand, had resolved the Peters issue for the moment. However, by incorporating the agitator the government had taken a first step towards association with the pan-German movement. Kayser's hope of using the movement behind Peters for his own ends was but one side of the coin; the other was that pan-Germans had received official recognition and thus improved their own political standing. This was bound to raise further expectations in the field of colonial policy, and to expose the government to even more pressure than before.

In this chapter I have argued that the formation of the Pan-German League was triggered by dissatisfaction with the moderate official line in colonial policy. Those who have denied that link[39] have failed to take into account the fact that colonial circles were predominant among the founding members of the Pan-German League. Moreover, the League's programme contained an explicit demand for furthering the colonial cause,

[35] See Caprivi to Peters and Emin, 17 Feb. 1891, note in FP 21, BAK.

[36] Peters to Caprivi, 24 Feb. 1891, letter of appointment, 7 March 1891, notes in FP 21, BAK.   [37] Note in FP 23, BAK.

[38] See note in FP 21, BAK.   [39] See, for example, Dukes, 'Heligoland', 225.

so that it is implausible to ignore the colonial dimension of the pan-German movement. The League was designed as a new political platform through which its activists hoped to put pressure on the government and to influence foreign policy decisions. Geoff Eley has therefore rightly stressed that radical nationalism aimed at developing a structure of politics that differed from the conventional practice of party politics.[40] In this sense, the pan-German movement, which sought to gather behind Peters as its 'heroic figure' (Eley), can be seen as the political manifestion of an emerging nationalist opposition.

However, Eley went further and argued that radical nationalism was 'thoroughly hostile to the conventional way of doing things and was formed from a protracted conflict with the old governing establishment'.[41] With regard to the late 1880s and early 1890s, however, this thesis does not seem to fit the case. Rather, the available evidence suggests that this view should be modified. Certainly, the pan-Germans saw the League as an additional platform for political activity, but it is doubtful whether this activity was meant to undermine existing forms of political practice. If we take the circle of Peters's supporters, for instance, we see that various people, such as Kardorff, Arnim, Arendt, or Bennigsen, were in fact firmly established in party politics. Peters himself never expressed any serious doubts about the domestic political system. The crucial point in our context seems to be that extra-parliamentary organizations were used as additional ways of giving political demands a stronger voice. By building a network of local chapters, which was one of Peters's central aims, wider circles of the population could be mobilized. However, this did not mean that he and his followers opposed party politics in principle. Indeed, as we will see later, he aimed to gain a Reichstag seat himself. Thus it seems doubtful that, as Eley has suggested, 'the internal disputes in the pressure groups between moderate and radical nationalists normally followed the distinction between those members who were simultaneously active in conventional party politics and those who were not'.[42] In fact, party politics and extra-parliamentary agitation or participation in societies did not mutually exclude each other.

This is not to say that there were no tensions between moderate and more extreme forces within the nationalist societies. Nor should one play down the significance of agitational politics for the nationalist opposition. But what these groups really seem to have opposed was not so much a

---

[40] Eley, *Reshaping the German Right*.
[41] Ibid. 351.   [42] Ibid. 47.

system or a political structure; they mobilized against what they perceived as a lack of national concern on the part of the government. In the late 1880s and early 1890s this opposition manifested itself largely in the field of colonial and foreign policy, and it could be quite uncomfortable for the government, as the dispute about the Emin Pasha Expedition and the protest against the Anglo-German Agreement illustrated. For Peters, the existence of an alternative political structure opened the way to oscillate between cooperation with the government and opposition politics in the form of agitation.

Finally, some remarks will be made about what Eley has called the 'antagonism between old and new right' in the post-Bismarckian period.[43] 'Old' here refers to the moderate nationalist forces, while 'new' is attributed to the radicals. Eley argues that 'the dominant ideologies of the Wilhelmine Right were actually generated by specific political conflicts inside the Wilhelmine period itself'.[44] 'The post-Bismarckian period—inaugurated by processes of accelerated capitalist development, the end of the depression and the passage to imperialism'—is conceived as 'one of far-reaching political change in which the entire structure of the public domain was reordered. The particular history of the nationalist pressure groups makes sense only in the context of change.'[45]

But how 'new' was this radical Wilhelmine Right, if we look at its ideology? Is it really sufficiently explained within a framework that limits itself to the time after 1890? Eley's study has been important in improving our understanding of the way in which right-wing dissidence operated in the particular setting of Wilhelmine politics. He has also drawn our attention to the increasing mass mobilization from the 1890s onwards. However, the present study indicates that the substance of what the so-called radical nationalists wrote on their banner—further colonial expansion, pan-Germanism, an energetic overseas policy—was already a feature of nationalist euphoria in the Bismarckian period. The case of Carl Peters makes this clear. In fact, his career would not have been possible without the support of precisely those groups which in Eley's model were part of the old moderate Right. This casts some doubt on a principal antagonistic pattern of old and new nationalist forces. Consequently, if we seek to understand the origins of this nationalist dynamic, a wider focus may be required than is suggested by Eley's study.

As mentioned before, colonial aspirations already flourished in the nationalist movement before 1848. Fenske, in his pioneering article, has

---

[43] Eley, *Reshaping the German Right*, 166.   [44] Ibid. 186.   [45] Ibid. 15.

gone as far as to argue that after 1870 the arguments for imperial expansion were essentially the same as those expressed various decades earlier.[46] If we test this thesis in the case of Peters, it seems that in at least two respects his ideology differed from older imperial aspirations. Firstly, his agenda was formulated in an unprecedentedly aggressive tone and, arguably, received a strong new impetus through pseudo-Darwinist ideas. Secondly, Peters placed great emphasis on the actual experience of German national unification, which had considerably changed the map of political power in Europe. The achievement of national unity through military victory was an encouragement that writers in the 1840s had not yet possessed. However, it is important to note that imperial aspirations had emerged hand in hand with the nationalist movement, and this had occurred *before* unification. This is an important element of continuity, linking Bismarck's colonial policy and Wilhelmine *Weltpolitik* with the liberal nationalist movement in the middle of the century. By seeking to explain the radical Right exclusively within the Wilhelmine period itself, this continuity is not given sufficient weight.

The attempt by pan-German circles to win Carl Peters as their leader gives an indication of the prominent position which he had acquired within that political spectrum, largely resulting from his agitational skills and his pioneering efforts as an imperialist. The ideas which Peters presented between 1883 and 1891 thus had a model character for other pan-German writers. A case in point is Fritz Bley, an ardent early supporter of Peters, who in 1897 published *Die Weltstellung des Deutschtums*. In his book he explicitly refers to Peters's writings, and his ideas display a similar concern with the British Empire. Bley, too, employs pseudo-Darwinist arguments to claim that only the stronger peoples in the world will ultimately survive.[47] Like Peters, he sees no contradiction between divine will and the Darwinian struggle for existence. Most striking is Peters's influence on another Social Darwinist writer, Alexander von Tille. In the 1890s Tille was a lecturer at Glasgow University, and in 1900 he became a member of the Pan-German League.[48] In his anonymously published book *Volksdienst. Von einem Sozialaristokraten* (1893) Tille seems to have taken over whole passages of Peters's writings on the relationship between the British and the Germans, and the Darwinian struggle.[49]

---

[46] Fenske, 'Imperialistische Tendenzen', 379.

[47] F. Bley, *Die Weltstellung der Deutschen* (Munich, 1897), 31, 24.

[48] For Tille's life see W. Schungel, *Alexander Tille (1866–1912). Leben und Ideen eines Sozialdarwinisten* (Husum, 1980).

[49] See *Volksdienst*, p. 25 (as cited in Schungel, *Tille*, 68) and Peters's article: 'Deutschtum und Engländertum' (1883).

Rather surprisingly, Roger Chickering's more recent study on the Pan-German League, *We Men who Feel Most German*, has not examined Peters's ideology at all. Perhaps this is one of the reasons why significant elements, such as his picture of the British, the struggle between peoples and nations, or the quest for the domination of *Deutschtum*, play a rather subordinate (and thus insufficient) role in his analysis. Chickering has certainly provided valuable insights into the symbolism of the League, its social composition, and its operation on the local level. However, the claim that pan-German ideas 'were anchored in a socially conservative populism' seems to overemphasize a concern with 'preserving social order',[50] at least as far as the early phase of the League is concerned. Chickering argues that 'the imagery in the ideology of the Pan-German League betrayed a paramount concern for order'. In his view, '*Deutschtum*, the German nation, the language, empire, Bismarck, and the navy all symbolized order'.[51] The League is said to have called 'for aggressive defence of these symbols, in the creation of a great Central-European nation state with a worldwide empire'. The latter 'represented the ultimate dyke against the flood, that counter-symbol of disorder in all its ethnic, social and psychological manifestations'.[52]

However, it is quite difficult to see why the terms mentioned should symbolize order in the first place, instead of what could be associated with them otherwise: the empire as a symbol of power, for instance, Bismarck as a symbol of authority, and the navy as a symbol of military strength and modern technology. On the basis of his psychological model, Chickering explains the preoccupation with order by the supposed marginality of many pan-Germans. However, a look at the social composition of the Pan-German League, in which the educated bourgeoisie was strongly represented,[53] seems to contradict this view.[54] Most of the members were firmly established in society, and one therefore wonders why they should be perceived as 'marginal groups disoriented during periods of rapid social change'.[55] In many ways these groups were major beneficiaries of that change, so that it is difficult to believe that insecurities and anxieties played such an overriding role as Chickering seems to suggest. The author himself concedes at some point that the imagery of the Pan-German League 'was very rich'. The attempt to force almost everything into a frame of order therefore appears too reductionist.

---

[50] Chickering, *We Men*, 92.   [51] Ibid. 86, 96.   [52] Ibid. 96–7.
[53] See Chickering's ch. 5, 'Social Foundation of Ideology', 102–21.
[54] A similar point is made in Jarausch's review of the book, *JMH* 57 (1985), 585–7.
[55] Ibid. 130.

Peters's ideas certainly provide no evidence that order was a paramount concern. The images which are advanced by Chickering to illustrate that general concern, such as the flood, dykes, fortresses, or forts, do not appear in Peters's writings at all. It may be that these became more important after the turn of the century, as Chickering's material seems to suggest, but in the early phase of the Pan-German League, they played no major role. Moreover, Peters himself can hardly be seen as somebody who belonged to a marginal group. On the contrary, he seems to have been at the centre of social life, and his contacts with prominent figures in the political establishement can hardly be taken as indicators of cultural or social marginality. In many ways, then, Peters does not fit well into the general picture that Chickering has drawn of the pan-Germans.

Finally, the historical dimension within pan-German ideology, of which Bley's book is a good example, seems to be neglected in Chickering's study. Arguably this kind of approach provided much of its appeal, given the predominance of historicist thinking at the time. More recently, the importance of historical arguments for political mentalities and orientations have been emphasized in a different context, namely with regard to the causation of the First World War.[56] For the question of colonial expansion, a similar pattern is discernible where historical legitimations were advanced. As was shown in Chapter 4, Peters envisaged a glorious pan-German future in a world empire. This vision was developed with explicit reference to the German past, which he portrayed as a miserable, weak, and sentimentalist phase of cosmopolitanism. Only through the war of unification of 1870–1 had the Germans embarked on that promising path of future development.

LITERARY IMAGES OF COLONIAL HEROISM

Peters's Expedition Account

Shortly after his return from Africa Peters met with the Munich publisher R. Oldenburg, who admired the 'founder of our most important colonial empire'.[57] In the spring of 1891 Oldenburg brought out Peters's 560-page account, *The German Emin Pasha Expedition*. The book contained a series of paintings by Rudolf Hellgreve, a well-known painter of colonial

[56] See J. Burkhardt, 'Kriegsgrund Geschichte? 1870, 1813, 1756—Historische Argumente und Orientierungen bei Ausbruch des Ersten Weltkrieges', in idem and J. Becker, *Lange und Kurze Wege in den Ersten Weltkrieg* (Munich, 1996), 9–86.

[57] Oldenburg to Peters, 4 Sept. 1890, FP, vol. 8, BAK.

scenes,[58] and a printed portrait of Peters by the Munich painter Franz Lenbach. With a price of 16 marks the first edition was quite expensive, obviously one of the reasons why the book did not go into a second edition during the 1890s.[59] An English edition was soon published,[60] and in 1907 a cheaper edition (*Volksausgabe*) was printed, followed by another one in 1909.[61]

Max Koch, a professor of philology and a committed pan-German, praised the 'epic tone' of Peters's book in his history of German literature,[62] seeing it as 'the most outstanding product of recent German travel and discovery literature'.[63] The account 'excited and affected' him like 'a great epic tale'.[64]

It seems that Peters also wrote his book with a view to the general political climate that had emerged after the Heligoland–Zanzibar Agreement. The text deals at length with his attempt to land on the coast, reminding the reader of David and Goliath—the strong British navy that fails to catch the clever little German—and takes up in detail the *Neera* affair, which had excited nationalist circles in Germany in 1889 and 1890.

As far as his advance to the interior is concerned, the book appears as a literary celebration of violence. In most of the battles that the author describes the expedition does not act in self-defence. Rather, Peters appears as a brave conqueror who teaches the local people who the Germans are. The use of brutal force is motivated by alleged European virtues such as 'ruthlessness' or 'strength to act'. A combination of will and force constitutes the ideal mind of a successful colonizer, and a man is not misled by any sentimental feelings.[65] The Emin Pasha book is a literary manifesto of

---

[58] Later, Peters praised Hellgrewe for having made the East African venture popular 'with his genius brush'; see Peters, *Gründung*, GS ii. 189.

[59] See Kolonial-Verlag, Theodor Mumm, advertisment for its *Volkausgabe* of the book (1907), enclosed in Hübbe-Schleiden Papers 908, NSG.

[60] Arnim's statement (Sten. Ber. IX/IV/60, 14 March 1896, 1451) that the book had gone through eleven editions must be an error. I have not been able to find any reference to further German editions between 1891 and 1907. According to the publishing house Oldenburg, Munich, the remaining copies of the first German edition were sold in 1894 to the Antiquariat Griesbach, Gera, which no longer exists. I am grateful to Johannes Woll, Oldenburg Verlag, for this information.

[61] Kolonial-Verlag Theodor Mumm, advertisement of the *Volksausgabe*, 1907, enclosed in Hübbe-Schleiden Papers 908, NSG; see also GS i. 501.

[62] Max Koch, *Geschichte der deutschen Literatur*, 4th edn. (Leipzig, 1900), 270.

[63] Koch to Peters, 14 March 1896, PP 21, 4, BAB.

[64] Koch to Peters, 22 April 1891, PP 21, 2–3, BAB.

[65] Peters's repeatedly argued against 'sentimentalist phrases' circulating in Germany with regard to black people; see Peters, *Gefechtsweise und Expeditionsführung in Africa* (Berlin, 1892), reprinted in GS ii. 520. This was one of the major points with which he antagonized missionary circles.

'ruthless, brutal politics—*à la* Peters', as he called it in 1885.[66] Some of the images in the book appear as a perverse combination of destruction and salvation. At one point, for example, Peters described how they burnt a Maasai kraal in December 1889: 'As the bells summoned the faithful to church for Advent in Germany, the flames were crackling towards the sky over the great kraal.'

It seems that the literary celebration of violence was seen by Peters as a promising vehicle for creating a heroic myth around himself. Having studied literary texts for a long time, Peters certainly had a sense for language and the way in which it could be used to affect a reader. He wanted to appear as the subduer of the warlike Maasai, who allegedly terrorized the caravan routes to and from the interior.

For those who were convinced pan-Germans this was obviously a great book, but it should be noted that the account also provoked less enthusiastic remarks, as a review in a geographical journal illustrates. The author deplored the book's frequent presentation of Peters's brutality, because of which it could not be attributed a high moral value.[67]

Frieda von Bülow's Colonial Novels

In 1891 Peters also emerged as the hero of a colonial novel, when *Der Konsul*, written by Frieda von Bülow, appeared in German bookshops. This book was 'a patriotic novel of our times', as the subtitle declared. It strongly reflected the author's own East African experiences, and there is little doubt that its major protagonist was modelled on Peters himself. To contemporary readers, at least, this link seems to have been obvious.[68]

The story is situated in the fictitious Arab town of U, somewhere on the African coast, which served as 'the starting point of important German trading enterprises'.[69] The description of the town,[70] with its Indian, African and Arab people, points to the place which Frieda von Bülow had visited in 1887: Zanzibar.

The local population plays a minor role in the novel, being mainly present in the form of black servants with big smiles on their faces,[71] as 'black children of nature who knew how to laugh and sing',[72] or as a crowd

[66] Peters to Lange, 29 Jan. 1885, note in FP 15, BAK.
[67] *Deutsche Rundschau für Geographie und Statistik*, ed. Friedrich Umlauft (1891), 13/8, 343–51.   [68] ? to Peters, 28 Jan. 1897, FP 8, BAK.
[69] Frieda von Bülow, *Der Konsul. Vaterländischer Roman aus unseren Tagen* (Berlin, 1891).
[70] See ibid. 36, 60.   [71] Ibid. 9, 10.   [72] Ibid. 37.

whose favourite occupation was to watch other people at work.[73] The German missionary Schrotmüller sees blacks 'walking around in mental apathy, not much better than animals, and not knowing what they lack'.[74] At times general European contempt for the Africans turns into romantic contemplation about supposed native happiness: 'If any people on earth may be called happy, then it is these children of the sun . . . ! Their needs are small and their ability to enjoy is great. With us it is the other way around.'[75]

The Peters of the novel is called Baron Max von Sylffa. As the new German consul he arrives in town with the aim of promoting German consciousness and of enhancing German trade. Of course, there is a snobbish German merchant already established there, who prefers to socialize with the British rather than with the other Germans, who are plebeians in his eyes.[76] Sylffa also encounters Germans who prefer to change their names, for example from Johann Friedrichs to John Fredericks[77] (like the real Hamburg merchant Oswald who had changed his name to O'Swald).

The local shop is run by a Galician Jew named Lindenlaub. (The name was hardly chosen innocently: it was a leaf of a linden-tree falling on Siegfried's shoulder when he bathed in dragon's blood which marked the only place where he was to remain vulnerable.) Lindenlaub is 'a shrewd scoundrel', but 'immensely rich'[78] and capable of coping with the haggling of the Indians and Arabs in town. The Jewish restaurant also serves as a sort of local brothel with a Bohemian girl named Josepha: she is 'beautiful as sin', but Catholic.[79] Sylffa's first honourable deed is to tell Lindenlaub to rename his business from 'Restaurant' (too French-sounding!) into 'Wirtshaus'.

Like Peters, Sylffa is driven by a strong will. Moreover, he is anti-Semitic: 'Where do the Jews get this dog-like obsequiousness from, this dreadful self-contempt which allows them to crawl, while cunning and malice lurk at the base of their souls?'[80]

While Sylffa falls in love with Nelly, the young daughter of a Hamburg merchant, political trouble arises in U. The British are suspicious of the new consul's activity. From his superior in Berlin, the Geheimer Legationsrath K. (Kayser!), Sylffa receives advice to abstain from any bold action; a conflict with the British has to be avoided at all costs.[81] But Sylffa

[73] von Bülow, *Der Konsul*, 20.   [74] Ibid. 51.   [75] Ibid. 37.
[76] Ibid. 27.   [77] Ibid. 22.   [78] Ibid. 30, 40.
[79] Ibid. 61, 62.   [80] Ibid. 42.   [81] Ibid. 195.

feels that Berlin erred greatly. 'Where would our Church be if Luther had obeyed?'[82] Without the consent of his government he arranges for a new trade treaty with the local ruler. The British are alarmed and secretly work against Sylffa. In Germany, the press launches a campaign against the consul's megalomania.[83] Eventually, he is dismissed from his post in U and has to leave. This puts a dramatic end to the love story as well. Sylffa loses his post and his love, but he has secured a moral victory. The Germans in U thank him for his brave work.

Quite clearly, *Der Konsul* is a fictitious adaptation of the real Peters story of 1887 which in literary form displays features of emerging German naturalism (see, for instance, the use of dialect). The underlying political theme of the novel is the growing tension between ardent nationalists and the state. Sylffa eventually has to bow to his orders, but the dramatic ending makes it clear that the moral victory is on his side. Sylffa is the one who pursues the right goals.

The anti-Semitic tones attributed to Sylffa seem to reflect more Bülow's own attitudes than Peters's. In Bülow's letters we find strong anti-Semitic tones,[84] whereas in 1902 Peters obviously intended to marry a rich Jewish woman in England. Bülow commented: 'It is terrible that this ghost-like people manages again and again to refresh its senile and foul blood through ties with the strong and outstandingly powerful Teutons.' Peters's anti-Semitism, on the other hand, is less obvious. Although he is at times named in connection with anti-Semitic circles,[85] he also opposed the exclusion of Jewish members from the Pan-German League, arguing that this would split the movement.[86]

Some years later Peters again became the model for a Bülow novel. *Im Lande der Verheißung* (1899) was first published as a journal series in *Velhagen & Klasings Monatshefte*. This time, the hero is a certain Dr Ralf Krome, whose lover, Maleen von Dietlas-Waltron, sets up infirmaries in the colony. (Frieda von Bülow had made a similar attempt in 1887.) As might be expected, Krome is at odds with the imperial government, which disagrees with his colonization activities. Eventually he decides to work for the British, turning his back on his fatherland, and with this decision the end of the love story is sealed as well. This book contains a more dramatized

---

[82] Ibid. 197.   [83] Ibid. 271.

[84] Frieda von Bülow to Peters, 10 March 1902, FP 5, BAK.

[85] See Götz to Peters, 1 May 1891, PP 41, who speaks of 'Zelewsky's, Bley's and your anti-Semitic inclination'.

[86] See 'Erklärung des geschäftsführenden Ausschusses des Allgemeinen Deutschen Verbandes' [1892], ADV Papers vol. 2, 85–6, BAB.

version of a theme familiar from *Der Konsul*, and had a real background, in so far as Peters was dismissed from the imperial service in 1897 and then moved to Britain. *Im Lande der Verheißung* became Bülow's most successful book, which by 1914 had already gone into its sixth edition.[87]

---

[87] See J. Warmbold, *Germania in Africa. Germany's Colonial Literature* (New York, 1989), 235.

6

King or Pawn? Peters on Kilimanjaro (1891–1892)

> I have always found that here in East Africa
> the early and energetic use of the horse-whip
> can save you some charges of gunpowder.
>
> Peters to Kayser, 1891.[1]

MAREALLE'S NEW ALLY

On 2 June 1891, Carl Peters arrived in Tanga, 'booted and spurred',[2] to meet the newly appointed governor, Baron Julius von Soden. The two Germans disliked each other from the very beginning. Soden, a full-blooded bureaucrat whom the Africans soon nicknamed *Bwana Karatasi*[3]—Mr Paper—had served six years in the Cameroons before he was appointed governor of East Africa in April 1891. He thus ranked among Germany's more experienced colonial administrators and he was highly suspicious of Peters's grand designs.

However, Soden's superiors in Berlin had instructed him not to antagonize Peters upon his arrival, and the new governor attempted to be as accommodating as possible. Soden had to brief Peters about his future work as a commissioner. He gave him a short memorandum on the tasks of district officers and commisioners of 28 April 1891, a speciaL instruction for his personal use and a collection of orders by the governor as a 'guideline'.[4] A month earlier he had already informed Peters that he should at all costs avoid any 'declarations of war and military operations of a larger scale without the prior permission of the governor'. Before such activities could be sanctioned, the commissioner would have to produce sufficient grounds.[5]

---

[1] 8 Aug. 1891, FP 18, BAK.
[2] Soden to Caprivi, 5 June 1891, FP 21, BAK.
[3] J. Koponen, *Development for Exploitation. German Colonial Policies in Mainland Tanzania, 1884–1914* (Helsinki and Hamburg, 1995), 100.
[4] Soden to Caprivi, 5 June 1891, FP 21, BAK.
[5] Soden to Peters, 6 May 1891, FP 21, BAK.

After the suppression of the coastal rebellion, Soden sought to establish an administrative framework which would guarantee tight control over the coastal belt and secure the major caravan routes through a chain of military stations in the interior. On the whole he wanted to avoid new conflicts in the inner regions where German rule was not yet established. This was a fairly cautious approach; it was not an ambitious scheme for the rapid achievement of German control. Soden wrote to station leaders in late 1891 that 'the role which you have to play towards the natives is by necessity rather more that of a diplomatic intermediary than that of a military dictator.'[6] He instructed his district officers that they should 'establish peaceful relations with the tribes and chiefs in the hinterland' and 'use money and good words' to bring them into a condition of dependence.[7]

For his time Soden was 'a pacifist', as Marcia Wright has remarked.[8] He was puzzled by Peters's manner and his far-reaching claims. 'The plans of the commissioner are characterized more by diversity than by clarity', Soden reported to Caprivi after their first meeting. According to the governor, Peters first spoke about an 'exploration of the Maasai steppe', then about 'works on Victoria-Nyansa' and 'the supervision of the railway construction in Usambara', not to mention various other schemes. Soden pointed out that Peters's plans clearly exceeded his actual administrative responsibilities on Kilimanjaro and that every single project which he had in mind would 'in fact commit a single person for years'.[9]

Peters's primary objective was to oversee the railway project in Usambara. He immediately rejected Soden's instructions for Kilimanjaro, maintaining that they were not in line with what he had discussed with Kayser in Berlin.[10] In a letter to Kayser, head of the colonial department, Peters emphasized his deep disappointment about the meeting with Soden.[11] He was backed by the banker Carl von der Heydt, who sought to persuade Kayser that Peters should be given control of the railway construction.[12]

Peters finally gave in only after Kayser had made it clear that the beginning of the railway construction could not yet be determined. At the same time the *Kolonialdirektor* expressed 'his hope that there will be ways and

---

[6] Cited in Koponen, *Development*, 101.

[7] 'Denkschrift an die 5 Bezirksämter und die Station Mpapua, Tabora und Bukoba', 28 April 1891, TNA G1/1, 114.

[8] Marcia Wright, 'Local Roots of Policy in German East Africa', *JAH* 9 (1968), 624.

[9] Soden to Caprivi, 5 June 1891, FP 21, BAK.   [10] Ibid.

[11] Peters to Kayser, 5 June 1891, FP 18, BAK.

[12] Von der Heydt to Kayser, 25 June 1891, ibid.

means to meet your wishes'. For the moment, however, Peters would have to put up with 'provisional employment' in a different field.[13] As the question of railway construction had to be put on hold, Peters agreed to take over the German station on Kilimanjaro. Soden was quite relieved about this interim solution, through which Peters would at least be occupied for a while and could not interfere in his work on the coast. Kayser had gained time, too. He had expressed his concern that Peters's aspirations would 'cause difficulties' in Berlin, which were usually 'hard to overcome'.[14] Late in June Peters departed from the coast and marched inland.[15]

Having arrived at Moshi on the southern slopes of Kilimanjaro, Peters took over from the German official Eltz, who had been stationed there since February 1890.[16] He encountered an environment with which he was totally unfamiliar, since his earlier expeditions had not taken him to Kilimanjaro; it was his friend Karl Jühlke and Lieutenant Weiss who had obtained treaties for the DOAG there in 1886.[17] Peters, therefore, could not rely on any personal experience, but only on information supplied by others. The sources make it difficult to assess the extent to which Peters had been briefed about the situation on the spot. Soden gave him some information on the conditions in the area,[18] but its content remains unknown. No previous German agent had in fact spent much time in the region, so that the German picture of local conditions was necessarily sketchy and vague.

Another point may be mentioned in this context. Whatever Peters may have found out about local structures on the ground, it was channelled through African means of communication, and thus inevitably exposed to potential African manipulation. Peters's insight into regional politics thus depended largely on what his African allies were willing to tell him. He had no real chance to look behind the scenes. This was even more true since he refused to establish closer links with the British missonaries in the region. They probably were the best-informed Europeans, having established their station as early as 1885.[19]

Moreover, Peters's belief that he was superior to all these 'miserable tribes'[20] did not make him very eager to overcome his fundamental ignorance. He was interested in ruling the place, and the idea of creating his own

[13] Kayser to Peters, 3 July 1891, ibid.　　　　[14] Kayser to Soden, 3 July 1891, ibid.
[15] Soden to Caprivi, 5 June 1891, FP 21, BAK.
[16] *Koloniales Jahrbuch*, iii (1890), 191. See N. R. Bennett, 'The British on Kilimanjaro: 1884–1892', *Tanganyika Notes and Records*, 63 (1964), 240.
[17] C. Peters, *Das Deutsch-Ostafrikanische Schutzgebiet. Im amtlichen Auftrage* (Munich and Leipzig, 1895), 121.　　　　[18] Soden to Peters, 6 May 1891, FP 21, BAK.
[19] See Bennett, 'The British on Kilimanjaro', 236.
[20] Peters to Soden, 8 Aug. 1891, FP 18, BAK.

personal empire in the African interior had excited him repeatedly in the past. 'I will undertake to maintain law and order with ease in my region with forty soldiers',[21] he wrote to Soden with great naivity. And he assured his sister Elli: 'Here I want to imprint the mark of my work for centuries to come.'[22] The last German who had left his mark there was Wissmann, and it had been bloody; in February 1891 he had led a punitive expedition against Chief Sina of Kibosho, who was not prepared to raise the German flag—a skirmish to which we will return later.

What political situation did the Germans encounter when they appeared on the mountain in the 1880s? Geographical conditions have been seen as important for the shaping of political organization in the history of the local people, the Chagga.[23] The mountain slopes are dissected by a number of streams flowing down from the dense rain forest belt, which is partly why numerous small, self-sufficient communities could develop on the ridges. Despite this early segmentation, Chagga people also established forms of wider cooperation among each other, such as defence, trade, and marriage.

Bantu peoples had settled on the mountain in various waves of migration at least since 1400, perhaps much earlier.[24] At that time Kilimanjaro is said to have been already populated by Wakonyingo or Wateremba pygmies. By the nineteenth century the Chagga were organized in a number of small, politically autonomous chiefdoms. The number of these, however, decreased throughout the century through processes of centralization, the underlying causes of which are not yet entirely clear.[25] Possibly the emergence of long-distance trade, particularly in ivory and slaves, provided new sources of wealth to certain communities, and became the key to the rise of more powerful chiefdoms.[26] By the time the Germans arrived there were about forty chiefdoms, in place of a hundred at the beginning of the century, while smaller communities often functioned as dependencies of more powerful ones. From time to time chiefdoms fought and raided each other, breaking old alliances and forming new ones.[27] In the 1880s two chiefs competed for paramountcy on the mountain, one of them the above-mentioned Sina, whom Wissmann had fought in 1891, and the other Rindi, at Moshi, who was also known as Mandara.

---

[21] Peters to Soden, 8 Aug. 1891, FP 18, BAK.

[22] Peters to Elli, 16 Sept. 1891, FP 5, BAK

[23] See A. M. H. Sheriff, 'Tanzanian Societies at the Time of the Partition', in N. H. Y. Kaniki (ed.), *Tanzania under Colonial Rule* (London, 1980), 23.

[24] The following sketch is mainly based on S. F. Moore and P. Puritt, *The Chagga and Meru of Tanzania* (London, 1977), 5 ff., and K. Stahl, 'Outline of Chagga History', *TNR* 64 (1965), 35 ff.   [25] See Sheriff, 'Tanzanian Societies', 24.

[26] See Moore and Puritt, *Chagga*, 12 ff.   [27] See ibid. 28.

Chagga chiefs were usually by no means hostile to newcomers from the coast. On the contrary, they had invited Swahili traders to settle in the area, and Europeans—be they German, American, French, or British—were accepted, too, because local chiefs expected to benefit from such contacts. This may be illustrated by the account of Hans Meyer, the first European to reach the top of Mount Kilimanjaro. Chief Mandara welcomed the German scientist with the words: 'You have brought me a number of very fine things from Europe and are my honoured friend. But I still want some gin and a good double-barrelled rifle, and above all a few cannons.'[28]

Why, then, did Chief Sina of Kibosho decide to resist the German presence and fight Wissmann's troops in 1891? One possible answer to this question may be derived from the local struggles for power on the mountain. The Germans had signed a treaty with Rindi, who had also invited the Church Missionary Society to stay at Moshi. These new alliances represented a potential threat to Sina's power. The latter had also previously signed a treaty with the British, but he remained more reserved about any closer links with the Europeans. The very fact that Sina adopted an uncompromising attitude towards the newcomers shows that he was obviously convinced of his superior power. As Marcia Wright has shown in the case of Chief Merere, African leaders in the interior had to make a choice in the face of German intrusion: 'With intelligence sources aplenty and with an eye to their own inter-tribal rivalries they assessed German intention and power.'[29]

Sina was confident of his power, particularly after his experiences with Peters's predecessor, the German agent Eltz. With his small force of only twenty Sudanese, Eltz did not make a strong impression on the chief in Kibosho. On the contrary, Sina taught him a lesson: when Eltz visited him at Kibosho demanding that he should comply with German orders, the Chagga leader kept him blockaded for a few days and told him that he should leave his dependencies alone. He told him that all German flags would be torn down. With respect to his rival Mandara, Sina 'did not see at all why that king should have everything'.[30]

The Germans had built up links with Mandara, who was an able diplomat, and he had encouraged Europeans to settle at Moshi. Hence the Germans provoked Sina's opposition. It was either Eltz or Wissmann who exacerbated the situation. In complete neglect or ignorance of existing

---

[28] H. Meyer, *East African Glaciers* (London, 1891), 97.
[29] Wright, 'Local Roots', 625; idem, 'Chief Merere and the Germans', *TNR* 69 (1968), 41–9.   [30] Cited in Bennett, 'The British on Kilimanjaro', 240.

hierarchies, one of them demanded that Sina should accept the overlord-ship of the chief of Uru—the latter had been installed by Sina himself as his subordinate. This was 'as if one had compelled the King of Prussia to acccept the Prince of Lippe-Detmold as his lord', the German scientist Georg Volkens commented some years later.[31]

Eltz, as we have seen, had burnt his fingers at Kibosho, and apparently he was not too keen to do it again before his departure. However, Wissmann, who had eventually succeeded in putting down the Bushiri rebellion on the coast, wanted to restore peace in the interior as well as keep the caravan routes open. Supported by Mandara's troops, Wissmann attacked Sina's massive stone fort. After fierce fighting the African chief eventually had to capitulate in the face of the Germans' superior weaponry. Sina lacked the machine-guns which Wissmann and his troops had at their disposal. Two hundred Kibosho warriors were killed, and sixty were wounded. Sina signed a treaty and left the Germans with the impression that he would in future accept their mastery in the region. Wissmann wrote that 'in my twelve years' experience in Africa never have I met negroes so brave as Sina's men.'[32]

By the time Peters arrived on the mountain six months later everything seemed calm and quiet to him. 'There are no wars here any more!' Peters enthusiastically declared in August 1891.[33] His sister must have gained the impression that her brother had become the ruler of paradise. In poetic vein, he wrote:

It is so beautiful here, 1,530 metres above sea level, with a view over the wide steppe dotted with burnt-out craters, and over Lake Jipe, in the clearest September air, that I can hardly describe it. A sanatorium of the first class, air and climate like Madeira. You would not recognize me, so fresh have I become with this lively work up here.[34]

Kilimanjaro, with its permanent covering of snow at its peak, impressed Peters as much as it did many other Europeans: 'Like a gigantic revelation of the earth's titanic strength, Kilimanjaro stands there, broad and massive in the sunny and light atmosphere of the African tropics, as if in defiance of eternity itself.'[35] During the 1880s no fewer than forty-nine Europeans had visited the mountain,[36] a substantial number given its remoteness and the difficulties of access.

[31] G. Volkens, *Der Kilimanjaro* (Berlin, 1897), 361.
[32] Quoted in Iliffe, *Modern History*, 100.
[33] Peters to Soden, 8 Aug. 1891, FP 18, BAK.
[34] Peters to Elli, 16 Sept. 1891, FP 5, BAK.
[35] Peters, *Schutzgebiet*, 113.
[36] Meyer, *Glaciers*, 20.

In a letter to Elli, Peters described his newly built station: 'I wish you could see my station garden. How it all sprouts: cucumbers, beans, peas, kohlrabi, radish, etc. etc.'[37] The image of Peters as a committed gardener may have amused his family at home; Chagga people, however, were soon to learn about another side to Peters's 'lively work'.

Peters's interest in vegetables was not purely private; it had a political dimension as well. He built his own irrigation system around the station,[38] obviously modelled on the system the Chagga had established in their garden groves, called *kihamba*.[39] He grew a whole range of crops to assess their potential use for future German farming. 'Apart from papaya and oranges I grew all sorts of European vegetables; the results must be regarded as extremely promising,'[40] Peters wrote in his book *Das deutsch-ostafrikanische Schutzgebiet* (1895). On the attached map, the slopes of Kilimanjaro were marked as a region for German settlement. Less fertile areas, such as the plains, would be left to the Africans.

The map seems to suggest that Peters aimed at a complete separation of European from African agriculture, drawing clear boundaries all over German East Africa. This thesis is strongly supported by statements by British missionaries on the ground. Albert R. Steggall, a CMS missionary stationed at Moshi, complained about 'the apparent eagerness of the German authorities to depopulate Kilimanjaro so as to make room for European settlers'.[41] Bishop Tucker, who visited the region in February 1892, noted that it is 'the avowed policy of the Germans . . . to drive out the native population of the Chagga on Kilimanjaro and introduce in large numbers German colonists.'[42] According to Steggall, 'Dr. Peters stated in Taveta that he would like to see the natives on the mountain replaced by Chinese labourers working under European colonists.'[43] Peters's radical schemes alarmed the missionaries, who had baptized the first young people at Moshi and taught them the Gospel. Steggall stated that 'such is the attitude of the people that it seems cruel to leave them without a teacher.'[44] The missionaries provided medical treatment for the local population and wanted to establish an 'industrial mission station' in the region, where the natives would grow crops, fruit, and trees for timber. This scheme would

[37] Peters to Elli, 16 Sept. 1891, FP 5, BAK.   [38] Peters, *Schutzgebiet*, 125.

[39] Moore and Puritt, *Chagga*, 25.   [40] Peters, *Schutzgebiet*, 125.

[41] Steggall to Lang, Moshi, 24 Feb. 1892, G3/A5/O 1892, Church Missionary Society Archives, University Library, Birmingham.

[42] Tucker to Lang, 9 March 1892, G3/A5/O 1892, CMS Archives.

[43] Steggall to Lang, Moshi, 24 Feb. 1892, G3/A5/O 1892, CMS Archives

[44] Steggall to Lang, 13 April 1891, Steggall to Lang, 2 Jan. 1891, G3/A5/ O 1891, CMS Archives.

also provide the opportunity for 'experimenting generally with agriculture'.[45] The pursuit of Peters's plans, on the other hand, was likely to put an end to all misssionary work on the mountain.

A German debate developed about the suitability of the area for European settlement. Peters was strongly in favour, while others opposed it, partly because they regarded the Chagga as 'unsuitable for wage labour',[46] and they obviously did not contemplate the removal of the Chagga from the mountain. The fact that Peters's ideas were not carried through in the end certainly prevented a major upheaval on Kilimanjaro. Widenmann, doctor of the German colonial forces, the *Schutztruppe*, argued for a less radical solution: 'The colony and the fatherland will benefit more if the living conditions of the local population, who are very modest and diligent, are raised and if they become accustomed to greater needs and higher production.' He opposed schemes of German settlement, since those people 'would not find what they hoped for in this Promised Land'.[47]

Soon after his arrival Peters shifted the German headquarters away from Moshi to Marangu some miles further east.[48] One of Peters's officers, Lieutenant von Pechmann, later declared that they wanted to be closer to Taveta in order to observe British movements there.[49] However, other considerations may have also influenced this decision. Peters wanted a free hand on the mountain, and it was therefore not in his interest to be closely observed by the missionaries. This may explain why the Peters group did not cultivate any relations with the CMS station in Moshi.[50]

This lack of communication marked a significant change from previous practice. Hitherto the few Europeans—be they officials, travellers, hunters, or missionaries—had entertained close and mostly friendly relations. The British missionary Dr Abbott, for instance, looked after the German station at Moshi when the agent of the German East African Company was recalled to the coast in the late 1880s. The station had been decorated 'in the

   [45] See Steggall's 'A few ideas about the desirability of having an industrial mission station in the neighbourhood of Kilimanjaro', G3/A5/O 1892, CMS Archives; Steggall to Lang, 13 April 1891, G3/A5/O 1891, CMS Archives; Baxter to Hooper, 23 June 1891, G3/A5/O 1891, CMS Archives.

   [46] Dr Brehme in *Mittheilungen aus den deutschen Schutzgebieten*, 7 (1894), 130, quoted in Volkens, *Kilimanjaro*, 360.

   [47] Dr Widenmann in *Mittheilungen aus den deutschen Schutzgebieten*, 8 (1895), 307, quoted in Volkens, *Kilimanjaro*.

   [48] Steggall to Lang, 5 Dec. 1891, G3/A5/ O 1891, CMS Archives.

   [49] Testimony of Pechmann, 7 July 1892, FP 21, BAK.

   [50] Ibid.; Steggall to Lang, 24 Feb. 1892, G3/A5/ O 1892, CMS Archives.

national colours of black, white and red' and 'the earnest face of the Emperor Wilhelm II' looked down from the wall.[51] The British kept it in its original state. Peters did not cultivate such friendly contacts. His self-chosen isolation also meant that the Germans could not take advantage of missionary knowledge concerning the local African environment. This did not bother Peters much, since he was arrogant enough to believe that he knew best of all how to deal with the local communities.

Moreover it may be suspected that the young chief at Marangu, Marealle, played some role in Peters's choice of location. Obviously, Peters was well received by the young chief on his first visit, noting in a report that Marealle made 'a very pleasant impression' on him.[52] Certainly it was an important concern for the newcomer to find a safe location for his station, as even a man like Peters would have appreciated the advantage of settling in a place in which he felt secure. Hence it is quite possible that Marealle's gestures influenced Peters's decision to move.

From an earlier expedition account it is evident that Marealle was a talented diplomat. He was keen to establish friendly relations with arriving Europeans, as Höhnel's account of Count Teleki's expedition in 1887 reveals. The European explorers were quite impressed by Marealle, who was then in his mid-twenties: 'Polite as a Spaniard',[53] the Marangu leader received his guests in 'excellent Swahili'.[54]

According to Stahl's interpretation, Marealle sought to use the Germans to strengthen his own position against neighbouring rival chiefs to the east.[55] This would have improved his standing against his rival Mandara at Moshi. Höhnel's expedition account supports this view in so far as it provides further evidence for the tensions between Marealle and Mandara. The latter was alarmed by Marealle's attempt to win Count Teleki as his ally, and he sought to ridicule Marealle as the 'donkey-drover' of the Europeans after Teleki had refused to accept Mandara's presents. The preference of Teleki's party for Marealle had a specific reason: they had made plans to use Marangu as a starting point for climbing the Kibo, the highest peak of Kilimanjaro, and were therefore keen to establish a friendly contact with the Marangu leader.[56]

---

[51] See Meyer, *Glaciers*, 94.

[52] 'Bericht des Reichskommisars Dr. Peters an den Kaiserlichen Gouverneur für Deutsch-Ostafrika über die zu gründende Kilimanjaro-Station', printed in *Deutsches Kolonialblatt* (1891), 456–8; A similar point is made in K. Stahl, *History of the Chagga People* (The Hague, 1964), 322. Unfortunately, Stahl has failed to produce precise references to the 'oral traditions' and the other unpublished sources she has used.

[53] Höhnel, *Zum Rudolph- und Stephanie-See*, 120.   [54] Ibid. 121.
[55] Stahl, *History*, 322 ff.   [56] Höhnel, *Rudolph-See*, 116.

MACHINE-GUN DIPLOMACY AND ILLUSIONS OF CONTROL:
PETERS'S MARCH AGAINST THE WAROMBO

Soon after Peters had arrived, the period of tranquillity on Kilimanjaro was
to cease again. Late in August Peters was informed that three African
messengers, who were on their way from Useri to Marangu, had been killed
by one of the Warombo leaders. Peters sent two of Marealle's people to
Useri with the message that the commissioner himself would come to
'settle the case'.[57] In general, he was convinced that the Germans had to use
force to preserve their position. Otherwise, he believed, Africans would
perceive them to be weak, which would encourage them to be more aggressive and recalcitrant. Displays of weakness, as Peters remarked some time
later, would lead 'the impudent tribes to say to themselves that the
Germans have turned into women'.[58]

On 30 August Peters, Lieutenant Pechmann, and Sergant Schubert left
the station, accompanied by fifteen Sudanese troops and twenty-five Swahili
askaris, and marched north-east towards Useri. On the way they were told that
the two messengers Peters had sent to Useri had been brutally murdered.[59]
After this, the commissioner came to the conclusion that the Africans on the
eastern side of the mountain had to be taught a lesson. He ordered a 'march
against the Warombo'. First, he turned on a chief called Matendera, who,
according to Peters's African advisers, had a 'wavering' character. The
Germans obviously caught him by surprise in his fort, and encountered no
major resistance. Peters forced the chief to raise the German flag, after his
troops had flogged some of 'his warriors who were shaking their lances'.[60]

On the next day Peters and his troops reached the residence of Chief
Kinabo. There they were joined by 300 more askaris, supplied by other
'friendly sultans'.[61] Kinabo, a Warombo chief himself, entertained good
relations with Marealle,[62] and was known for his trade in slaves, which he
captured in his eastern neighbourhood.

Peters stated in his report that he now wanted 'to occupy the lower
approaches to the land, and to order the three sultans there to enter into
discussions about the murder of his two messengers'.[63] Soon, however,

[57] Peters's report, 8 Sept.1891, FP 18, BAK.
[58] Peters to Kayser, 5 Sept. 1892, FP 18, BAK.
[59] Peters's report, 8 Sept. 1891, FP 18, BAK.
[60] Ibid.   [61] Ibid.
[62] Stahl, *History*, 326, 328.
[63] Peters's report, 8 Sept. 1891, FP 18, BAK.

Pechmann and Schubert became involved in a fight. The Germans captured part of the African fortifications, burnt twenty to thirty houses, and started chopping down the banana groves. 'Every concession at this moment would have been interpreted [by the Warombo] as weakness and fear on our side',[64] Peters wrote, justifying his scorched earth policy. Suddenly, however, Sergeant Schubert was ambushed and killed by seven or eight lances. Two of Peters's Swahili askaris were speared, too.[65] Warombo warriors had hidden in a number of holes, which they had dug between the thick banana groves. Such subterranean chambers were a typical part of their defence system, as well as other constructions. Peters described it as an 'ingenious system of fortification, which through a series of narrow corridors, walls, and palisades reduced the effectiveness of the firearm and favoured the lance'. Peters ordered his men to proceed slowly, cutting all the banana trees in order to gain a field of fire for their arms. Two major attacks by the Africans were beaten back without further losses on Peters's side. In total he claimed to have burnt down 'fifty villages' before darkness came, by which he probably meant fifty African households with their adjacent gardens.[66] On 3 September Peters marched back to Marangu to bury Schubert with 'military honours'.[67]

Historians have not yet dealt with the story of Peters's war against the Warombo. There is some evidence to suggest that he was drawn into a conflict that had started long before his arrival. In 1887 Höhnel had learned that the Chagga chiefs on the southern slopes, some of whom were supplied with firearms and thus had an advantage, repeatedly raided their neighbours to the east.[68] It may be assumed that Marealle himself had a strong interest in Peters's advance to Rombo, as there was much to gain for the Marangu leader in the eastern chiefdoms.[69] His own chiefdom was still fairly poor, with few livestock, in 1891.[70] It is interesting that Peters was informed in great detail about the fate of the murdered messengers. He learned that their 'hands had been chopped off first, then their eyes torn out, and then they had been killed'.[71] Possibly Marealle deliberately exaggerated the story in order to provoke Peters's anger. Certainly Peters had no

---

[64] Ibid.   [65] Ibid.

[66] There were no Chagga villages. Their huts were grouped together rather loosely, each of them forming the centre of its own banana grove; see Johannes's report, Marangu Station, 31 May 1893, G1/18, 119, TNA.   [67] Peters's report, 8 Sept. 1891, FP 18, BAK.

[68] See Höhnel, *Rudolph-See*, 216–17.

[69] See Stahl, *History*, 329, on Marealle's later exploitation of the eastern chiefdoms.

[70] Ibid. 325.   [71] Peters's report, 8 Sept. 1891, FP 18, BAK.

chance to check whether Marealle's messengers had indeed been murdered or not, and he could easily have been manipulated in this respect.

On 26 September Peters launched a second attack on the Warombo, this time supported by 500 of Sina's warriors.[72] This is an interesting detail of Peters's account. Having been defeated by Wissmann, the Kibosho leader was obviously aware that he could only lose further if he continued to oppose the German intruders. Cooperation, on the other hand, might yield some benefits for him. Above all, it might again strengthen his own position against his rival Mandara at Moshi.

On his second march Peters decided 'to eliminate everything living in the subterranean fortifications where they kept large numbers of cattle, women, and so on'. He wanted 'to demonstrate to all these tribes that we can also deal with their peculiar national fortifications',[73] so he ordered his troops to block the entrances to the caves with hay, wood, and stones. They then set fire to both entrances, as well as to the houses in the area. 'Ten men died, among them two sons of the Sultan; four women and many cattle suffocated.'[74] The German party was attacked again as they retreated, but they shot about 100 men 'through their volleys'. On that day, Peters noted, they had killed 124 Africans.[75]

In his report to Soden, Peters proposed reporting to the Kaiser the 'glorious conduct of his officers Johannes and Pechmann', and 'decorating some of the coloured with war medals, notably Shawish Seliman and Ombshi Achmed Ibrahim Sudani', who had saved Peters's life during the battle on 2 September. He also suggested that one of the allied 'sultans' should be decorated for fighting bravely despite a head injury; according to Peters, he had 'set a good example' to his people.[76]

Soden was shocked when he learned about Peters's latest 'military and civilizing achievements'. He told him 'to cultivate, if possible, peaceful relations' and above all to stop his war against the Warombo.[77] He also forwarded Peters's report to Chancellor Caprivi in Berlin, as the Foreign Minister, Adolf Marschall von Bieberstein, had instructed the governor to keep them informed about Peters's activities.[78] After he had reported the issue to the Kaiser, Caprivi noted that no decorations should be made at present. This was 'to avoid the impression that one gains honours for suffocating non-combatant people'. But the Chancellor also added that 'the relevant persons

---

[72] Peters's report, 6 Oct. 1891, FP 18, BAK. [73] Ibid.
[74] Ibid. [75] Ibid.
[76] Ibid. [77] Soden to Caprivi, 9 Nov. 1891, FP 18, BAK.
[78] Marschall to Soden, 18 March 1891, FP 21, BAK; Kayser to Soden, 11 May 1891, G1/1, 138, TNA.

may be suggested another time' for decorations.[79] Furthermore, Peters's report on his first advance against the Warombo was chosen for publication in the official *Kolonialblatt*.[80]

After Peters's march against the Warombo, things did not get any easier for the Germans. At night strange noises increasingly caused 'a sense of insecurity' within the station.[81] They started to fortify their station in Marangu with fences made of barbed wire, brier, and spears, and to dig trenches around the station, so that Peters claimed that his new fortress could beat back thousands of African warriors and 'make the firearm more effective'.[82]

DETERRENCE THROUGH EXECUTION: THE HANGINGS OF
MABRUK AND JAGODJO

It was against this background of high tension that, one night, a black youth named Mabruk was caught by the Germans after he had broken into the house where Peters's black concubines slept. Apparently, the young man had stolen some of Peters's cigars and he was also said to have had sexual intercourse with one of the girls named Jagodjo. According to one white witness, Peters said: 'This pig will be hanged today . . . if the boy had broken into the house of Marealle's women, Marealle would have hanged him as well.'[83] Another officer recalled Peters's reaction in a similar way: 'Such impudence in using the woman of the bana mkubwa (ruler) deserves capital punishment.'[84] The Germans discussed the case and came to the conclusion that severe measures had to be taken. Otherwise their reputation among the Africans would be at stake. Peters, Jahncke, and Pechmann held court and sentenced Mabruk to death. 'Peters and the white gentlemen sat inside in the mess having their meal when the execution was carried out', a member of the station recalled. 'The first cord broke, so they had to find another one.'[85] At breakfast on the following morning one of the officers is reported to have said: 'I think it was good that Mabruk was hanged. It did indeed make a good impression.'[86]

[79] Caprivi's marginal note on Soden to Caprivi, 9 Nov. 1891, FP 18, BAK.
[80] *Deutsches Kolonialblatt* (1891), 488–91; the printed date of 8 Aug. 1891 is wrong; Peters wrote this report on 8 Sept.1891.
[81] Testimony by Pechmann, 11 April 1896, FP 21, BAK.
[82] Peters's report, 11 Nov. 1891, FP 18, BAK.
[83] Testimony by Kuhnert, 27 March 1895, FP 21, BAK.
[84] Testimony by Bronsart von Schellendorf, 27 March 1896, FP 21, BAK.
[85] Testimony by Bronsart von Schellendorf, 16 Sept. 1896, FP 21, BAK.
[86] Testimony by Peters, 20 Nov. 1896, FP 21, BAK.

Some weeks later a second incident sharpened the tension around the Kilimanjaro station. A small group of African women,[87] among them Jagodjo, fled the station and took refuge at the fort of the Rombo chief Malamia.[88] Jagodjo had originally been one of Marealle's wives.[89] The origins of the other women are unknown, although some German statements indicate that they were from Marangu, too. The Germans at the station claimed that all the girls had been given to them as presents by local chiefs,[90] and they were treated as if they were prostitutes by the whites.[91]

The Germans decided to recapture the girls. 'After Malamia's huts had been burnt down they were eventually returned.'[92] Then the girls were whipped until 'the blood trickled down through their loin-cloths'. Peters 'sat in his bamboo chair and watched'.[93]

What happened after this is difficult to reconstruct, since the statements of the station members contradict one another. As Peters himself stated later, he sentenced Jagodjo to six months' hard labour in chains for espionage and high treason.[94] Why was her punishment more severe than that of the other girls, two of whom had returned to Peters's household as concubines? When the Germans questioned the girls, they said that Jagodjo had persuaded them to flee, since she had claimed that 'all whites would be killed during the course of the following night'.[95] Thus they may have concluded that only Jagodjo was a spy. However, one could argue for a more cynical scenario as well. One member of the station stated that Jagodjo suffered from syphilis,[96] and her punishment was possibly aimed at isolating her from the rest of the station.

According to Peters, the girls were threatened with the death penalty to deter them from fleeing again.[97] Jagodjo, however, escaped a second time and sought refuge with Marealle, her former chief, who refused to protect her and sent her back to the station.[98] When she was brought back, Peters and his officers were playing cards. They interrupted their game and held

[87] The sources differ on their number, ranging from three to five girls; see testimony by Wiest, 23 May 1892 and Jahncke, 7 Aug. 1896, FP 21, BAK.
[88] Testimony by Wiest, 23 May 1892, FP 21, BAK.
[89] Testimony by Marealle, 18 Aug. 1892, FP 21, BAK.
[90] Testimony by Pechmann, 27 March 1896; testimony by Bronsart von Schellendorf, 27 March 1895, FP 21, BAK.
[91] See, for example, testimony by Bronsart von Schellendorf, 27 March 1895, FP 21, BAK.
[92] Testimony by Wiest, 23 May 1892, FP 21, BAK.
[93] Testimony by Kuhnert, 27 March 1895, FP 21?, BAK.
[94] See Sten Ber IX/IV/60, 14 March 1896, 1449–50.
[95] Testimony by Pechmann, 11 April 1896, FP 21, BAK.   [96] Ibid.
[97] See Sten Ber IX/IV/60, 14 March 1896, 1449–50.
[98] Testimony by Marealle, 18 Aug. 1892, FP 21, BAK.

court again.[99] They carried out their previous threat. Jagodjo was to face the same fate as Mabruk three months earlier. Wiest had to perform the task. 'The captive Jagodjo was indifferent until the end. She even climbed up onto the platform herself', the medical assistant recalled.[100] The animal painter Kuhnert is remembered as saying: 'I must see this. I have never seen anybody hanging.'[101] Peters apparently commented: 'It is a strange feeling to see such a girl swinging.'[102]

Stahl's study of the Chagga also mentions Peters's dispute with Malamia and the hanging of the African girl. Her version seems largely based on the recollections of Chief Malamia himself, who was still alive in 1959. Stahl concluded that the women's flight from the German station had been ordered by Marealle in order to discredit his rival Malamia of Mamba: Marealle told the girl 'to flee secretly from Peters and to take refuge with Malamia. This she did and Malamia was happy to take her in. Marealle then told Peters where the girl was hiding. In his anger Peters deposed Malamia and hanged Ndekocha from a roadside tree near the river Una.'[103]

We may assume that the German documents and Stahl's account both in fact refer to the same girl. The two names (Ndekocha and Jagodjo) may have resulted from different pronunciation and spelling. (In the German files the version 'Jagodja' also appears.) But was Marealle really the great manipulator behind Jagodjo's flight and Peters's dispute with Malamia, as Stahl has suggested? It seems that this was at least Malamia's own view of the events. Moreover, it is quite suggestive that Marealle obviously came out as the major beneficiary of Malamia's defeat. Ultimately, however, it should be emphasized that these are reasoned speculations, not conclusive answers.

After the girl's execution, Peters ordered the construction of a gallows in front of the station, 'as a warning sign, so that the surrounding tribes will be kept in fear'.[104] He expected a major attack by the Warombo; indeed, he related his fear of such an eventuality to Albert von Bülow, his deputy.[105] According to Wiest, the medical assistant, there were approximately 6,000 Warombo facing the twenty-eight members of the German station. They

[99] Testimony by Schroeder, 25 July 1897, FP 21, BAK.
[100] Testimony by Wiest, 23 May 1892, FP 21, BAK.
[101] Testimony by Jancke, 25 March 1896, FP 21, BAK.
[102] Testimony by Schroeder, 25 July 1897, FP 21, BAK.
[103] Stahl, *History*, 322.
[104] Testimony by Jancke, 27 March 1896, FP 21, BAK.
[105] Bülow to Soden, 23 May 1892, FP 21, BAK.

thought that Malamia might ally with the Warombo, with whom Peters had fought some weeks before.[106]

Another fact made it even more difficult for the Germans to assess the situation. The great Mandara at Moshi died in October,[107] and he was succeeded by his son Meli, 'a youth of seventeen or eighteen'.[108] Meli's messengers appeared at the German station, where they declared that Malamia now stood under Meli's protection. Malamia himself called the Germans 'women' and started his war-dance.[109]

German policy on the mountain increasingly alarmed the CMS missionaries at Moshi: 'Dr Peters is there, and the barbarity which he seems to delight in showing towards the natives, and the immorality of almost the whole party of Germans would furnish, I think, material for a report which would be hardly credited in Europe.'[110] One missionary concluded that 'the story of his rule on this mountain is so black, and his estimate of the value of African lives so low' that he had no great hopes that Peters would change his policy in the future.[111] Missionary Alfred Steggall heard from one African 'who was spoken to by Dr Peters . . . in these words: "God sent me to Kilimanjaro to exterminate the black man" '.[112]

GERMAN DEFEAT AND THE SUBJUGATION OF MELI:
THE 'BÜLOW-DISASTER' AND ITS AFTERMATH

These were gloomy prospects for Peters, who, only six months earlier, had declared that he saw it as mere child's play to keep the Africans on the mountain in check.[113] Now he was under pressure from two sides, from Meli in the west and the Warombo in the east. Peters reacted to the mounting crisis with a boastful threat against Meli. He wrote to the British missionaries at Moshi: 'I beg to inform you that I shall propose to the German government to crush these people by war in order to have peace in the Kilimanjaro district. . . . I shall ask the German Government to send

[106] Testimony by Wiest, 23 May 1892, FP 21, BAK.
[107] Steggall to Lang, 5 Dec. 1891, G3/A5/O 1892, CMS Archives.
[108] Ibid.
[109] Testimony by Peters, 10 April 1895, FP 21, BAK.
[110] Steggall to Lang, 5 Dec. 1891, G3/A5/O 1892, CMS Archives.
[111] Steggall to Lang, Moshi 28 Jan. 1892, G3/A5/O 1892, CMS Archives.
[112] Steggall to Lang, Moshi, 21 May 1892, G3/A5/O 1892, CMS Archives.
[113] Peters to Soden, 8 Aug. 1891, FP 18, BAK.

me approximately 150 soldiers in order to finish this young fellow.'[114] Peters marked his letter 'confidential', apparently because he did not want Meli's people to learn about his plan, but it was obviously difficult to keep anything secret on the mountain. It is not known whether the missionaries warned Meli of German intentions, but in any event he found out that the Germans were planning to take action against him. When Bishop Tucker visited Moshi in February 1892, Meli asked him whether he had 'heard anything of a proposed attempt by the Germans to depose him and . . . crush his people'.[115] However, Peters never carried out his threat. It is not even clear whether he actually called for further support from the coast.

Secretly, Peters may have been much more worried about his own life than his letters of the time suggest. He had already lost Schubert, one of his officers, and he might well have reflected on the fate of the Prussian commander Zelewski, whose column was ambushed by the Hehe in August 1891. Zelewski himself, riding a donkey, had been speared by a sixteen-year-old boy. Of the thirteen Europeans, only three survived. Moreover, some 250 of Zelewski's 320 askaris were killed in the fight, while the Hehe lost more than 250 of their warriors.[116]

Hence Peters may have welcomed a message from the coast which ordered him back 'to delimitate the frontier with Consul Smith',[117] as certain sections of the Anglo-German border still needed to be settled in detail. After Peters's departure his deputy, Bülow, was left in charge on Kilimanjaro, but he too left some weeks later, so that the German officer Wolfrum had to run the station. During this period no major attack on the station occurred, but tension continued between Meli at Moshi and Wolfrum at Marangu. When one of Wolfrum's Sudanese soldiers stole some potatoes from children in Kirua, a chiefdom near Moshi, the thief

[114] M. Reuss, 'The Disgrace and Fall of Carl Peters: Morality, Politics and Staatsräson in the Time of Wilhelm II', *CEH* 14 (1981), 118. Reuss has produced a useful account of events, but leaves plenty of room for further analysis, particularly with respect to the political implications and consequences of Peters's activities in the Kilimanjaro region. For a brief narrative see E. Groth, 'Galgen am Kilimanjaro', *Die Zeit*, 20 Jan. 1989, 41–2; unfortunately Groth does not give any references to primary sources.

[115] Extract from a letter by Tucker, 19 Feb. 1892, Occasional Papers no. 10, Diocese of East Equatorial Africa, enclosed in G3/A5/O 1892, CMS Archives.

[116] Iliffe, *Modern History*, 109. For a detailed account of the battle see B. Arnold, 'Die Schlacht bei Rugaro 1891 (Tansania, Iringa). Verlauf der Kämpfe und Ursachen der Niederlage des Expeditionskorps der kaiserlichen Schutztruppe für Ostafrika', in P. Heine and U. van der Heyden (eds.), *Studien zur Geschichte des deutschen Kolonialismus in Afrika* (Pfaffenweiler, 1995), 94–114.

[117] Steggall to Lang, Moshi, 24 Feb. 1892, G3/A5/O 1892; Peters to Steggall, 24 Jan. 1892 (copy), G3/A5/O 1892, CMS Archives.

was killed by local Chagga warriors.[118] The chief of Kirua sent cattle and ivory to Wolfrum to appease him, but the German rejected the offer and maintained that the negroes had to be punished.[119] In May Bülow returned to Kilimanjaro. Although he did not feel much inclination to fight the Kirua, he ultimately decided to do so for the same reason that Peters had advanced before. After the German threat had been made by Wolfrum, Bülow did not want to appear too yielding, so he decided to lead a punitive expedition against the Africans, which resulted in what became known as the 'Bülow-disaster'. It was the second major defeat of the Germans in the East African interior.[120]

The British missionaries attempted to convince Bülow that his charges against Meli were based on false information, invented by Meli's enemies. 'I can assure you that Meli always has been, [and] still is, most anxious to preserve friendly relations with German authorities', wrote Baxter, in an effort to avoid armed conflict in Moshi.[121] Steggall visited the German station and discussed the matter with Bülow, but 'nothing I could bring forward could alter their position as to the existence of the plot', he noted with resignation.[122] The missionaries recognized that Bülow had no less violent a temper than Peters. Africans referred to Bülow as the 'man with the bloody hand'.[123]

On 6 June the Germans marched against Moshi, but Meli ambushed Bülow's troops in the banana groves. With newly acquired British-made breech-loaders, Meli's men surrounded the German party, shot down its officers, and forced it to flee to the coast.[124] 'The Germans brought a ridiculously small force considering that they had to fight in the bush', Steggall wrote after the fight. They 'ensured [their own] defeat by making their soldiers volley away hundreds of cartridges at an all but invisible enemy lurking under cover'.[125]

Stahl has argued that Marealle had encouraged the Germans to teach

---

[118] Baxter to Bülow, 16 May 1892, G3/A5/O 1892, CMS Archives.
[119] Testimony by Wittstock, 25 April 1896, FP 21, BAK.　　　　　　　　[120] Ibid.
[121] Baxter to Bülow, 16 May 1892, G3/A5/O 1892, CMS Archives.
[122] Steggall to Lang, 21 May 1892, G3/A5/O 1892, CMS Archives.
[123] See Steggall to Lang, 24 Feb. 1892, G3/A5/O 1892, CMS Archives. According to the historian Gwassa, the same name was also used for Carl Peters ('mkono wa damu': man with the bloody hand). Unfortunately, no documentary evidence is produced. Therefore, it remains unclear when and by whom this name was given to Peters; see G. C. K. Gwassa, 'The German Intervention and African Resistance in Tanzania', in I. N. Kimambo and A. J. Temu (eds.), *A History of Tanzania* (Nairobi, 1969), 98.
[124] Iliffe, *Modern History*, 101.
[125] Steggall to CMS Secretary, 22 June 1892, G3/A5/ O 1892, CMS Archives.

Meli a lesson in order to enhance his own position.[126] German sources neither support nor disprove this interpretation, but British missionary letters do in fact suggest that Meli's enemies supplied reports 'which have been nothing but a series of falsehoods got up by his enemies for the purpose of harming him'.[127] Furthermore, Stahl's thesis seems plausible since Marealle continued to maintain close relations with the Germans, even after Peters had left. This view is supported by the fact that Marealle eventually secured all the German belongings in the Marangu station, which had been abandoned in haste following Bülow's death. Marealle transferred them to Kinabo's fort in order to hide them from Meli's warriors. Later he gave them back to the Germans.[128]

Peters himself never returned to Kilimanjaro. After having finished his work on the coast he went to South Africa for a holiday. It was Captain Johannes who reoccupied the German station three months after Bülow's defeat. He maintained a close alliance with Marealle, and Meli's triumph was short-lived. In August 1893 the Germans led new troops into Moshi and captured Meli's fort.[129] He had to give up three of his dependencies and cede them to Sina and Marealle. The latter became the most powerful chief that Kilimanjaro had ever seen, making gains through Meli's defeat. Furthermore, he syphoned off the wealth of Malamia's territory in the east, and that of other Warombo chiefs. Sina died in 1897, allegedly poisoned by Marealle, so that the Marangu chief no longer faced any rivals of equivalent strength and power.[130]

In the light of this account one may draw some preliminary conclusions about Peters's role on Kilimanjaro. First, the course of events brought home an important message, namely that the use of the commissioner system to build up German control in the interior had been a disaster. The German public was shocked by the 'Bülow-disaster' and the loss of German officers.[131] Soden had been critical of the practice from the very beginning,[132] terming it an 'expensive evil'. However, he failed to convince his superiors in Berlin, who had chosen this system largely for reasons of domestic policy. It soon became clear that the governor had no means of controlling Peters's activities in the interior.

[126] See Stahl, *History*, 323.
[127] Baxter to Bülow, 16 May 1892, G3/A5/O 1892, CMS Archives.
[128] See Volkens, *Kilimanjaro*, 68.
[129] See Iliffe, *Modern History*, 101. For a contemporary account see A. Becker, *Aus Deutsch-Ostafrikas Sturm- und Drangperiode* (Halle, 1911).
[130] Iliffe, *Modern History*, 101.
[131] See various notes from the German press in FP 21, BAK.
[132] See Soden to Caprivi, 25 July 1891 and 24 Sept. 1891, FP 21, BAK.

Secondly, German actions on Kilimanjaro shed some light on the nature of the relationship between the colonial intruders and African communities on the ground. Was Peters in full command of the situation, as he always made himself and others believe? Or was he, as has been suggested by African historians, rather used as a pawn in an African political game?[133] The latter interpretation seems convincing in many ways, particularly when one considers the role of Marealle and his consequent rise to power. The story of Peters and Marealle makes two things fairly clear: first, the Germans were heavily dependent on African support; and second, even with African support, they were by no means in a position to control the outcome of events at this early stage of colonial intrusion.

However, an emphasis on the manipulative nature of African politics tends to obscure the Europeans' military superiority. The machine-gun furnished the Germans with a degree of independence which made attempts at manipulation on the African side inherently dangerous. To use a metaphor, Peters was like a blind giant, equipped with powerful resources, but incapable of employing them without the guidance of those with sight. In this respect he became a tool for those African leaders who were able to win him over. However, African attempts at control were limited by the superiority of Peters's weaponry, as well as his lust for power.

Ultimately, rivalry between the various chiefdoms gave Peters a potential trump card. It is clear, however, that he failed to play it effectively, since he was unfamiliar with the region's particular circumstances. Thus his announced policy of 'divide and rule' was more a myth than a reality.[134]

Manipulative strategies on the African side were risky, as in case of failure they could provoke German retribution. Marealle's policy, however, did not fail, as is demonstrated by his rapid rise to the position of paramount leader on Kilimanjaro.[135] Once Marealle had embarked on this course, however, he also became irreversibly dependent on German support, without which one cannot explain his rise to a dominant position.

---

[133] Gwassa, 'The German Intervention and African Resistance in Tanzania', 95.
[134] Peters to Kayser, 7 July 1892, FP 21, BAK.
[135] Stahl, *History*, 330–2.

7

Colonial Scandal
(1892–1897)

THE UNCOMFORTABLE CANDIDATE

In late 1892 Peters returned to Berlin. He continued his work on the Kilimanjaro boundary negotiations with the British representatives which were concluded by the summer of 1893.[1] Peters's social activities indicate that he again drew closer to government circles. Along with other officials, Peters repeatedly dined in Kayser's house, and the young Kaiser invited Peters as well.[2] Obviously the government was keen to secure Peters's loyalty, but this did not solve the issue of his future position. In fact, his career was on ice. In the summer of 1893 Peters took a four-month holiday in the United States, leaving Kayser with the same problem he had faced back in 1890: what should the government do with a difficult person like Peters? They considered sending him back to Africa again, but the new governor, Schele, refused to accept Peters as an subordinate officer. Schele, like his predecessor, believed that Peters would be a threat to his own position in the colony.[3]

Eventually, Kayser found a temporary solution by appointing Peters to write an official study on the development of German East Africa. This was only an interim measure which gave both Peters and the Colonial Department time to rethink their options. His study, entitled *Das Deutsch-ostafrikanische Schutzgebiet* and published by Oldenbourg, kept Peters busy until the beginning of 1895.[4]

While Peters was working on this book, controversy arose in the Foreign Office over whether he should be decorated for his work on Kilimanjaro. Schuckmann, official in the Foreign Office, strongly opposed the idea of

[1] See Hohenlohe to Wilhelm II, 6 Nov. 1895, note in FP 21, BAK.
[2] Notes from Kayser's guest book, FP 14, BAK; telegram from Eulenburg to Marschall, 1 July 1893, note in FP 21, BAK.
[3] Caprivi to Peters (draft by Kayser), 30 Nov. 1893, Caprivi to Schele, 30 Nov. 1893, Hohenlohe to Kaiser, 6 Nov. 1895, notes in FP 21, BAK.
[4] Peters to Kayser, 21 Jan. 1895, FP 21, BAK.

giving Peters further credit for his battles on Kilimanjaro, pointing to his executions. Kayser was not prepared to accept such criticism, standing firmly behind Peters and claiming that Schuckmann's view was 'tendentious'.[5] He was anxious not to encourage feeling against Peters, since he feared that his agitational skills might then be turned against the government. He also stated that Marschall was in favour of the decoration. The quarrel continued for some time, but Humbert, dealing with personnel matters in the Foreign Office, did not give in. He insisted that the circumstances of the executions were not sufficiently clear to permit a decoration. He also pointed to the excitement which atrocities by Leist and Wehlan, two officials in the Cameroons, had recently caused in the Reichstag and the press. In the circumstances, he argued, one could not decorate a person like Peters. Eventually the idea of a further decoration seems to have been dropped again.[6]

In the course of 1894 controversy also sharpened between Soden's successor, Schele, and Kayser in the Colonial Division. In Kayser's view, Schele had worked from the very beginning to turn the governor into a sort of viceroy, who would be largely independent of the Colonial Division and the Chancellor.[7] Since Kayser had to defend colonial policy in the Reichstag and had to keep a majority in favour on colonial questions, he was not ready to accept a governor who operated beyond his control. 'The present situation, of the governor's omnipotence and central impotence, is not acceptable', he complained to his superior Marschall.[8] There was also disagreement about the role of the protection force, which was still under the command of the Naval Office, thus giving the whole administration a rather militaristic outlook, as Kayser put it. Kayser wanted to turn the protection force into a colonial police force under the command of the governor, which would have put an end to the dualism in colonial matters between the two different ministries, the Naval Office and the Foreign Office. Kayser believed that a reorganization of this kind would lead to more cautious financial planning, since the same office that drafted the budget would also have to defend it in the Reichstag. As it was, the colonial division had to justify and defend demands which were made by the Naval

[5] Humbert to Kayser, 16 Feb. 1894, Kayser's note, 24 Feb. 1894, Schuckmann's report, 14 Feb. 1894, notes in FP 14, BAK.

[6] Humbert [to Kayser?], 9 March 1894; Kayser [to Humbert?], 10 April 1894; Humbert [to Kayser?], 30 April 1894, notes in FP 14, BAK. The Peters Papers in Altena contain Peters's medals. There is no indication that Peters had been awarded the swords in addition to his Kronen-Orden, III. Klasse, which he had received for his Emin Pasha Expedition.

[7] Kayser to Marschall (draft), 21 Nov. 1894, note in FP 14, BAK.   [8] Ibid.

Office. The governor faced an increasing gulf between the colony's income and its costs. The government in Berlin pointed out that military expenditure under Schele had reached its 'climax'.[9] As the gulf between Schele and Kayser widened and the colonial director threatened to resign ('It's now a matter of Schele or myself'), Hohenlohe persuaded Wilhelm to recall Schele and appoint a new governor for East Africa. However, Kayser came to see this as a 'Pyrrhic victory'.[10] Not only would this damage his relations with the Kaiser, since Schele was known to be one of Wilhelm's favourites and was also supported by military circles, it also provided Peters with the kind of opportunity he had been awaiting for so long. On the other hand, Kayser was satisfied with the new Chancellor, Hohenlohe, who in his view was more supportive than his predecessor Caprivi.[11] Kayser also believed that Hohenlohe would back his plan for an independent colonial ministry, in order to secure his position against the governor.[12]

Peters, on the other hand, still lacked any long-term prospects. Early in 1895 an attempt to enter parliamentary politics failed, when he ran unsuccessfully for a Reichstag seat in a by-election in the constituency Eschwege-Schmalkalden. There the candidate of the anti-Semitic party won.[13] Hence Peters's attention again turned back to the field of colonial administration.

The dispute over the colonial protective forces was also an important factor in the appointment of a new governor. Wissmann, who had put down the Bushiri rebellion and was a popular *Afrikaner*, had previously failed with a proposal to place the protection force under the control of the future governor. Caprivi had refused to turn the *Schutztruppe* into a civilian police force and was anxious to avoid Wissmann's appointment to the governorship. Although we lack explicit evidence in this question, it seems that Kayser placed his hopes on Wissmann as the future governor, although Wilhelm had only limited sympathy for the man. For Kayser, the decisive point must have been that he could count on Wissmann's support in the dispute over the protection force, and that he was much less of a political figure (i.e. an agitator) than Peters. Overall, Wissmann was a more loyal and convenient prospect.

    [9] Kayser's draft 'Die Schutztruppe und die Kolonialverwaltung', 12 Dec. 1895, Votum by the Prussian Prime Minister, regarding the Protective Forces in the Colonies of the Empire, Dec. 1895, note in FP 14, BAK.
    [10] Kayser to Baron, 26 March 1895, FP 14, BAK.
    [11] Kayser to Baron, 15 Dec. 1894, FP 14, BAK.   [12] Ibid.
    [13] See O. Perst, 'Carl Peters Reichstagskandidat im Werraland 1895', *Das Werraland*, 19 (1967), 53–5.

In the meantime Peters had sent clear signals that he saw himself as the appropriate candidate.[14] In fact, he had hoped to secure this post since he returned from the Emin Pasha Expedition in the summer of 1890.[15] For various reasons, however, Peters did not match Kayser's requirements. First, Kayser was aware that administrative work was not one of Peters's assets. He had had plenty of opportunity to witness Peters's performance in the reorganized DOAG. The financial chaos which Peters left upon his return from his negotiations with Sultan Bargash certainly did not favour his appointment. Secondly, Peters was not an officer, and his voice in military matters was not likely to be authoritative. Wissmann had pursued a military career, while Peters had not even been accepted for military service, so that military circles were not likely to take Peters seriously in this field. Most importantly, however, Kayser suspected that Peters's agitational skills and his connection with influential political figures were bound to be damaging to the government in colonial matters. Peters's line was as unpredictable as it was uncontrollable, since he employed channels largely outside the control of the governmental framework. Therefore, it was clear to Kayser from the beginning that Peters was not a suitable candidate for the governorship. At the same time, he knew that he had to face a battle with Peters, who would not silently accept defeat.[16]

In the middle of March another factor undermined Peters's chances. The story of his atrocities on Kilimanjaro gained new attention when the Social Democrats claimed in the Reichstag that Peters had hanged two blacks because they had had a sexual relationship. Kayser was quick to deny the charges and to protect Peters against the attack. However, the fact that he had failed to close the embarrassing chapter once and for all posed a potential threat to the government, which promised to make further enquiries into the issue.

Kayser now became convinced that Peters's 'honourable removal from Germany to a post which does not attract the world's attention appears to be the best thing for the government'. He saw this as a way to 'calm down a restless spirit'.[17]

It is clear that the Colonial Director was not worried about the hangings as such. No moral concerns were expressed. In 1892 Caprivi had ordered

[14] Kayser to Baron, 26 March 1895, FP 14, BAK.

[15] This is implied by a letter by Francis Parry, member of the legislative council of Hong Kong, who, apparently in response to Peters's request, wrote to a high German official to persuade him that Wissmann's idea of a black police force had originally been Peters's concept. Parry expressed his hope that Peters would be appointed governor; Parry to Peters, 4 Aug. 1890, PP 41, BAB. [16] Kayser to Baron, 26 March 1895, FP 14, BAK.

[17] Kayser to Hohenlohe, 17 May 1895, FP 21, BAK.

that the charges should not be investigated further, 'for political reasons' as he put it.[18] Not only was such an investigation likely to antagonize the Peters clique; it could also be exploited by the political opposition in their attacks on the government's colonial policy. In May 1895, however, Kayser does not seem to have worried very much about the opposition. Rather he started to consider whether the charges against Peters could perhaps be used for the government's own ends. At that stage, he concluded that the investigation of the atrocities would *not* suffice to eliminate Peters or to diminish him.[19]

PETERS'S CAREER ON ICE

At the end of April 1895 Hohenlohe, probably following Kayser's advice, appointed Wissmann to the governor's post. It was then necessary to calm Peters down and to find a position for him which he would be ready to accept. Peters himself made three major proposals: (1) to be a consul in San Francisco or Cape Town; (2) to return to East Africa, if he was given an independent administration; or (3) to head a department for emigration in the Foreign Office, which was his favourite option.[20]

Kayser warned against complying with the latter proposal, or even using Peters at all in the colonial administration in Berlin. He suspected that Peters aspired to gain a leading position in a future Colonial Office. Although Kayser claimed that this did not bother him personally, it was quite clear that it would put Peters into direct competition with Kayser himself. It is therefore not implausible to assume that the cooling relationship between the two also related to Peters's aspirations in Berlin. Seen in this light it is also possible to understand why Kayser was no longer prepared to back Peters in the question of the Kilimanjaro killings.

The colonial department had in fact collected further evidence against Peters in the Kilimanjaro matter as a result of Vollmar's accusations in the Reichstag. They had questioned the animal painter Kuhnert, who had visited Kilimanjaro in 1891, and Bronsart von Schellendorf, one of the officers at the German station. Both backed the claim that sexual motives were involved.[21]

[18] Soden to Caprivi, 24 June 1892, marginal note by Kayser, FP 21, BAK.
[19] Kayser to Hohenlohe, 17 May 1895, FP 21, BAK.
[20] Peters to Arendt, 15 May 1895, Kayser [to Hohenlohe], 17 May 1895, FP 21, BAK. Peters states in his letter that his friends in the Reichstag would enter a motion to establish the relevant post.
[21] Note on Kuhnert's and Bronsart's testimonies in the Foreign Office, 27 March 1895, FP 21, BAK.

Nevertheless, this did not persuade the government to take any disciplinary measures. Instead they sought to place Peters as far away as possible. It was decided to offer Peters the post of a regional head (*Landeshauptmann*) in the Tanganyika province of East Africa.[22] Wissmann signalled that he would accept Peters only if he were placed under his control.[23]

Not surprisingly, Peters did not like the idea, because it placed him in a similar position to 1891. He would still be subordinate to the governor, and he could see that the post would not give him enough room for manoeuvre. In a note which he channelled via Arendt to Hohenlohe he made clear his conditions: he wanted to work independently from Wissmann as he did not agree with the governor in essential issues of colonial administration. Rather, he wanted to test his own colonial system in his territory.[24] To those who had previous experience with Peters such ideas must have rung the alarm bell. Hohenlohe indeed suspected that such a constellation could only lead 'to entanglements of all kinds'.[25]

The issue continued to occupy both sides for several months. Peters tried to improve his position by employing Arendt and Kardorff as mediators in the dispute.[26] However, Kayser and Hohenlohe were not prepared to give in. An independent position for Peters was bound to undermine Wissmann's authority. It would only have fuelled the permanent administrative crisis in the young colony. After all, the government had already gone through three governors in the first four years. This was both a symptom and a new cause of the fundamental inability of the colonial power to put an efficient administrative system in place. As regards Wissmann, it was no secret that the new governor did not enjoy 'a bed of roses', facing opposition in naval and court circles.[27]

After much argument about Peters's future position, Hohenlohe eventually lost patience and issued an ultimatum. Peters had to make up his mind within the next three days.[28] He immediately replied that the conditions were unacceptable to him, and he therefore asked to be kept available for another occupation in the imperial service.[29]

[22] Hohenlohe to Peters, 31 May 1895, FP 21, BAK.
[23] Note by Kayser, 28 May 1895, FP 21, BAK.
[24] Peters's note, 18 May 1895, FP 21, BAK.
[25] Hohenlohe's note, 25 May 1895, FP 21, BAK.
[26] See Arendt to Kayser, 26 Oct. 1895, FP 21, BAK.
[27] See Arendt to Kayser, 10 July 1895, FP 21, BAK.
[28] Hohenlohe to Peters, 5 Nov. 1895, note in FP 21, BAK.
[29] Peters to Hohenlohe, 6 Nov. 1895, note in FP 21, BAK.

'ALWAYS FULL STEAM AHEAD':[30] NAVAL AGITATION AND THE
TRANSVAAL CRISIS

A deadlock was reached. In this situation, Peters again turned to what he knew best: agitation. On 28 November 1895 the *Berliner Börsenkurier* carried a short note on Peters; at a dinner in Lüneburg, he had let it be known that he did not expect a position in German East Africa 'in the foreseeable future'. Instead he 'would dedicate himself to German politics'.[31] A development in the coming weeks was to provide a fruitful opportunity for Peters's attempt at a political comeback. In South Africa, the unsuccessful attempt by Leander Starr Jameson to topple the Kruger government in Transvaal resulted in an Anglo-German crisis of unprecedented scale. In his famous Kruger Telegram, Wilhelm congratulated the president of the Boer Republic for succeeding 'in restoring peace and in upholding the independence of his country against attacks from without.'[32] It was the second part of the telegram which caused anger in the British government, and even more among the British public. In London it was seen as an illegitimate intervention in the affairs of the British Empire, and as proof 'of hostile designs against this country', as *The Times* wrote.[33]

In Germany there was wide public support for Wilhelm's policy. Marschall noted in his diary: 'Our press is wonderful. All the parties are of one mind, and even Auntie Voss wants to fight.'[34] So enthusiastic were the German people that Wilhelm considered whether he should not use this wave of nationalist emotion immediately to launch a programme for the enlargement of the fleet.[35] In his famous speech of 18 January 1896, the twenty-fifth anniversary of the proclamation of the Reich, the Kaiser committed himself to a course of *Weltpolitik*. The *Kolonialzeitung* was thrilled: 'These impressive, pithy words from the Kaiser direct attention to the higher goals of *Deutschtum*. Not only a "united Germany", no a

[30] 'Die deutsche Marine und koloniale Aufgaben', *DKZ*, no. 26, 29 June 1895, 201–2.
[31] Note in FP 21, BAK.   [32] GP xi, no. 2610.
[33] W. H. Langer, *The Diplomacy of Imperialism* (New York, 1956; 2nd edn. 1960) 242; for this topic see also H. Rosenbach, *Das Deutsche Reich, Großbritannien und der Transvaal 1896–1902* (Göttingen, 1993).
[34] Marschall's diary, 3 Jan. 1896, cited in J. C. G. Röhl, *Germany without Bismarck* (London 1967), 166.
[35] See H. Hallmann, *Der Weg zum deutschen Schlachtflottenbau* (Stuttgart, 1933), 171 f.; W. Deist, *Flottenpolitik und Flottenpropaganda* (Stuttgart, 1976), 52 f., 58 f.; Röhl, *Germany*, 164 ff. For naval policy in general, see also G. Eley, 'The German Navy League in German Politics, 1898–1909' (Ph.D. University of Sussex, 1974); V. Berghahn, *Der Tirpitz-Plan: Genesis und Verfall einer innenpolitischen Krisenstrategie unter Wilhelm II* (Düsseldorf, 1971).

"greater Germany" it shall be!'[36] The speech encouraged naval and colonial enthusiasts alike, who now loudly demanded a larger fleet for the German Empire.[37] The *Kolonialzeitung* embarked on a whole series of leading articles on 'Deutschlands Flotte und Aufgaben'.[38] This was precisely where Peters saw his chance; jumping on the bandwagon, he could perhaps win the Kaiser's sympathy and give his political career a new impetus.

Peters was in his element again. Only four days after the Kaiser's speech, he agitated for the enlargement of the fleet in the Berlin branch of the Colonial Society.[39] 'If necessary, Germany must make itself respected with warships and their cannon. In case of war it also has to be able to attack, and not limit itself only to the defence of its coastlines.' For all this, Peters argued, a larger fleet was indispensable. He continued to agitate at public meetings in the capital,[40] but he also spoke in Magdeburg and took part in a large rally in Dresden on 3 March 1896.[41] It should be noted here that Peters's interest in naval questions was not entirely new. In fact, he had long seen a larger fleet as a necessary element for a growing colonial empire.[42] The general enthusiasm of 1896 could only serve his purposes.

In the eyes of his critics, Peters's naval ambitions were boundless.[43] There is some evidence to suggest that Peters's came to lead a public movement which was also encouraged by parts of the Foreign Office. Arguably, the key figure in this was Kayser, who knew of Wilhelm's passion for the navy and who obviously sought to consolidate his own position by supporting propaganda for this purpose. Holstein, who seems to have favoured a more cautious naval policy, repeatedly spoke of Kayser's activities, suspecting him to be the 'nodal point' of the agitation. 'The little Kayser, who aspires to an independent Colonial Office, has made himself useful to the navy and is agitating in the press for projects of naval enlargement.'[44] In Holstein's opinion the Kaiser had been stimulated by this.

[36] 'Ein Ruf des Kaisers', *DKZ*, no. 5, 1 Feb. 1896, 33.

[37] Pierard, 'Colonial Society', 169

[38] *DKZ*, no. 5, 1 Feb. 1896, 33; no. 6, 8 Feb. 1896, 41; no. 7, 15 Feb. 1896, 49; no. 9, 29 Feb. 1896, 67; no. 11, 14 March 1896, 83.

[39] 'Mitteilungen aus der Gesellschaft', *DKZ*, no. 6, 8 Feb. 1896, 44.

[40] *DKZ*, no. 7, 1896, 50.   [41] Pierard, 'Colonial Society', 171.

[42] 'Alltagspolemik und Kolonialpolitik', *Tägliche Rundschau*, 9 May 1884, as printed in Peters, *Deutsch-National. Kolonialpolitische Aufsätze* (Berlin, 1887), 48–58, here 51.

[43] See Lieber's speech, Sten. Ber. IX/IV/60, 14 March 1896, 1473; Werner's speech, Sten. Ber. IX/IV/ 61, 16 March 1896, 1477. *Vorwärts*, 14 March 1896, speaks of Peters's 'Milliardenflottenpläne', note in FP 21, BAK.

[44] Holstein to Eulenburg, 13 Jan. 1896 (no. 1188), Holstein to Eulenburg, 14 Jan. 1896 (no. 1189), *Phillip Eulenburgs Politische Korrespondenz*, iii, ed. John Röhl (Boppard am Rhein, 1983), 1636, 1637.

Indeed, a major crystallization point of the public naval movement became the Colonial Society, which organized the first large rally on 25 January 1896, in the aftermath of the Kruger Telegram and the Kaiser's anniversary speech.[45] This was precisely the meeting which Holstein associated with Kayser's activities.[46] It was after this meeting that Peters was assigned the task of agitating for the navy by the executive board of the society.[47] Thereafter, Peters emerged as a major figure in naval propaganda.[48]

On 14 January Hohenlohe consulted various party leaders in order to find out whether they would sanction a motion for the naval expansion as envisaged by Wilhelm. Both the Conservatives and the Centre signalled their opposition to such plans,[49] and as a result the Kaiser postponed his naval demands until the following session.[50]

However, the tide of public enthusiasm rolled on. Peters's agitation did not fall on deaf ears in colonial circles. The naval issue secured him support within the Berlin branch of the Colonial Society and pushed aside those who were critical of such costly ventures. At their annual meeting Peters attacked the president of the branch, Prince Arenberg, for having opposed his call for a larger fleet. After all, Peters argued, the executive board of the Colonial Society had asked him to give a speech on that topic, and 'he had not envisaged any greater enlargement of the fleet than one must have expected from the Kaiser's words.'[51] The reference to Wilhelm put Arenberg on the defensive. Peters recommended that Arenberg should not be re-elected, since he no longer represented the position of the Colonial Society in naval questions. Instead, he presented himself as a suitable candidate, and a large majority voted for him.[52]

This victory must have reassured Peters that he was on the right track. By March 1896 he had risen to be a leading protagonist of the fleet movement.[53] His name was now again on everybody's lips. Things did not look bad for him in the spring of 1896. He had as yet no clue as to what was to happen in the Reichstag proceedings of 13 March, which marked a decisive turning point in his life.

As far as the rise of naval agitation is concerned, this chapter suggests that

[45] *DKZ*, no. 4, 25 Jan. 1896, 25, 26.
[46] Holstein to Eulenburg, 14 Jan. 1896, *Phillip Eulenburgs Politische Korrespondenz*, iii. 1637.   [47] *DKZ*, no. 9, 29 Feb. 1896, 68.
[48] See Lieber's speech, Sten. Ber. IX/IV/60, 14 March 1896, 1473.
[49] Holstein to Eulenburg, 13 January 1896, *Phillip Eulenburgs Politische Korrespondenz*, iii. 1636.   [50] See Röhl, *Germany*, 168.
[51] 'Mitteilungen aus der Gesellschaft', *DKZ* no. 9, 29 Feb. 1896, 68.
[52] Ibid. 69.
[53] See Lieber's speech, Sten. Ber. IX/IV/60, 14 March 1896, 1473.

Wilhelm's Transvaal policy should not be viewed only as a calculated move to make gains in domestic policy.[54] True, Wilhelm, like many others in the government, was delighted to see the enthusiasm which his Transvaal policy had created, so that it was not surprising that he attempted to exploit this situation for his naval plans. However, his own ideas were perhaps as much influenced by the wave of public enthusiasm as his own policy was instrumental in fuelling nationalist feelings. It seems that there was a reciprocal mechanism of influence at work; otherwise Holstein's observation that the Kaiser was stimulated by the amount of public euphoria makes no sense. To emphasize Wilhelm's manipulative power also means obscuring the fact that naval expansion had been on the agenda of colonial and nationalist circles for some time. As in colonial matters, the government could not simply switch nationalist feelings on and off as it wished. In order to make capital from such enthusiasm, the ideological ground for it had to be there in the first place.

'AND BRUTUS IS AN HONOURABLE MAN': THE FALL

On 13 March 1896, just after one o'clock, the Reichstag assembled for its 59th session. The annual colonial budget was on the agenda, and most members will have expected just another day of parliamentary routine. The actual debate, however, took a quite surprising turn. No trade statistics or administrative budgets were discussed; instead, terrifying stories of colonial atrocities came to occupy the house. Prince Arenberg of the Centre Party, who was the first to speak, took up the case of the colonial official Wehlan in the Cameroons.

The issue was not a new one, and it had been discussed in the press for some time. Wehlan was accused of having maltreated and killed a number of Africans back in 1893. Arenberg complained bitterly that the colonial official had not been prosecuted under the terms of the German penal code. He criticized the government for having initiated only a disciplinary investigation. In his view, the outcome was entirely unacceptable; the disciplinary chamber had ruled that Wehlan must pay a fine of 500 marks and that he was to be transferred to a different position. But the list of serious charges against Wehlan had been long. He was alleged to have enforced confessions through torture, and to have been responsible for the brutal killing of three African captives.[55] Here, one of the darkest sides of colonial

[54] Such a tendency may be found in Deist, *Flottenpolitik*, 58; Röhl, *Germany*, 167.
[55] Sten. Ber. IX/IV/59, 13 March 1896, 1421.

conquest was brought to light: a representative of the colonial state who saw in his civilizing mission an opportunity for the unrestricted practice of sadistic pleasure. In a similar case, the disciplinary chamber had examined charges against Karl Leist, another colonial official stationed in the Cameroons.[56] Here reference to the appeal chamber was required before a ruling was given that Leist should be dismissed from the colonial service.[57] Among critics, there remained a bad aftertaste, since he had not been tried on the basis of penal law.

On a more general level, both cases pointed to a major deficiency of the young colonial empire: the lack of any legal framework for jurisdiction over the African population. Kayser sought to defend the application of exclusively disciplinary measures by pointing to the existing judicial constraints. Initially, he argued, the Foreign Office had examined the possibility of penal prosecution. But the Prussian Ministry of Justice, as well as the prosecutor, had concluded that this was impossible. The reason for this, Kayser explained in the Reichstag, was 'that hitherto the judicial process against natives has not been regulated by any law or order'.[58] In practice, this meant that officials were not bound by any rules in their treatment of Africans unless the Kaiser had issued specific orders. Legally, officials could not be punished, since they did not break any law which restricted them.

While Kayser's explanation was plausible from a purely legalistic point of view, it exposed the government to severe political criticism. How was it possible that such a legal gap had not yet been filled? Why had the government not yet taken action to lay down rules for the jurisdiction of whites over Africans?

To make things worse for the government, the Conservative Reichstag member Schall, who had close ties with Protestant missionary groups, came up with yet another case: Peters. He referred to rumours which 'had recently worried Christian circles'. Allegedly, Peters had killed an African woman, and had justified this by stating that he had married her according to Muslim law and therefore possessed complete power over her life.[59]

Schall did not offer any more details of this story, and for some time it looked as if the general debate would centre upon other issues. But then

[56] See Kayser Papers 51, newspaper clipping, reprinting the first ruling of the Imperial Disciplinary Chamber, Potsdam, against Leist on 16 Oct. 1894, N 2139, BAB.
[57] See Sten. Ber. IX/IV/60, 14 March 1896, 1459, speech by Minister of Justice Schönstedt. For further details on Leist and Wehlan see Adolf Rüger, 'Der Aufstand der Polizeisoldaten (Dezember 1893)', in H. Stoecker (ed.), *Kamerun unter deutscher Kolonialherrschaft*, i (Berlin, 1960), 97–147.
[58] Sten. Ber. IX/IV/59, 13 March 1896, 1425.   [59] Ibid. 1423.

August Bebel, the charismatic leader of the Social Democrats, stepped up to the speaker's rostrum, and his speech put Kayser in real trouble. Bebel's *j'accuse* was carefully structured and brilliantly presented, describing the history of colonial policy as one which had been 'written with blood and tears'.[60] Peters fitted well into this picture. Bebel started by quoting from Peters's account of his Emin Pasha expedition, in order to show the man's brutality and ruthlessness. Then he came to speak about the killings on Kilimanjaro. At the climax of his speech he surprised his audience with a spectacular revelation: the British Bishop Tucker, Bebel told his audience, had been informed of Peters's executions and had accused him of being a murderer. In return, Peters had written a letter to Bishop Tucker which contained the following statement: 'He [i.e. Peters] had been married to the hanged girl according to African customs, so that on the basis of African law he had had the right to punish the adultress with the death penalty.'[61] This disclosure caused a great commotion in the house.[62] Hitherto the public had only heard vague stories about the incident, such as had been presented by the Social Democrat Vollmar in the previous year. Bebel's story was more detailed. Most importantly, it seemed to prove that Peters's motive for the killings was pure jealousy. The letter to which Bebel referred contained a clear confession. However, it may be argued that the most provocative and scandalous element of Bebel's accusation was Peters's alleged adoption of African customs. Parliamentarians were not as excited about Peters hanging a black girl or a black boy, nor was the assumed motive of jealousy sufficient to cause such strong outcry. Otherwise it would have occurred long before Bebel came up with the letter. The worst and most incriminating factor was that Peters had acted as everybody expected a so-called savage to act. In other words, the scandalous aspect was Peters's alleged decline to the mental outlook of an African Chagga chief. Interestingly, the Social Democratic press maintained the strategy of turning Peters into an African native; they called him a Menelik who had defeated the German nation, or referred to him as the 'honourable chieftain' of the Leists and Wehlans.[63]

In his immediate response to Bebel, Kayser had to choose his words carefully if he wanted to limit the damage to himself and to the government. What strategy would he use in order to defend the government? In fact, Kayser's reaction provides interesting insights into the official handling of the affair. It is striking that with respect to Wehlan Kayser had

[60] Sten. Ber. IX/IV/59, 13 March 1896, 1431.
[61] Ibid. 1434; part of that speech is printed in Gustav Seeber (ed.), *August Bebel. Ausgewählte Reden und Schriften*, iv (Munich, 1995), 8–14.
[62] Ibid.   [63] *Vorwärts*, 14 March 1896, note in FP 21, BAK.

not been prepared to supply any further details. The less the Reichstag knew, the better. He simply pointed to the fact that the Foreign Office had appealed against the first judgment and noted that the house would have to await the outcome.[64] In the case of Peters, however, Kayser turned out to be surprisingly open and talkative. He could have said that the Foreign Office would examine Bebel's charges, and in particular, investigate whether the Tucker letter did in fact exist. But Kayser went a lot further than that, instead providing the Reichstag with a detailed account of the events on Kilimanjaro. In doing so he also disclosed embarrassing details and facts which were to strengthen the credibility of Bebel's story. Most importantly, he mentioned three girls who had sexual intercourse with *all* officers on the station. At the same time, he made it clear that the two executions did not occur simultaneously, but with an interval of several weeks. Kayser must have known that his explicit reference to the sexual relationships at the station would do much to discredit Peters, and it seems that this specific detail was carefully provided in order to enhance Peters's public destruction. 'We deplore these facts above all in the interests of humanity', Kayser stated at the end of his account.[65] He sought to distance himself and the government morally from the Peters debacle. At the same time he was anxious to explain why legal action had not been taken. According to the Colonial Director, it was impossible to disprove Peters's own claim that he had had to order the executions in order to maintain discipline, and thus to save his own life and the lives of his subordinates.[66] Thus Kayser had found a loophole which enabled him to defend the government without defending Peters himself.

Nevertheless, there remained one major problem for which Kayser had no solution to hand. How could he explain that the government wanted to give Peters a new leading post in the colony if they found his actions so deplorable? Kayser made only an evasive comment on this issue, maintaining that Peters would not have the opportunity to act freely again, being placed under the authority of Hermann von Wissmann, a man who in Kayser's eyes had a clean record. At the end of his speech he quoted at length a new order from the Chancellor, which required all officials to 'set a good example to their subordinates' by adopting a cautious and moderate line.[67]

This did little, however, to calm emotions in the Reichstag. The following speaker, Dr Lieber of the Centre Party, worked himself up into a

[64] Sten. Ber. IX/IV/59, 13 March 1896, 1439.   [65] Ibid. 1442.
[66] Ibid.   [67] Ibid. 1442–3.

passion. 'For me, the Kilimanjaro case outweighs everything else. If this case is indeed such as Reichstag member Bebel has reported, then it is my conviction that Mr Peters stands condemned in the eyes of the civilized world.'[68] With this comment, he received applause from several sides, indicating that the critics did not come only from those parties which were opposed in principle to colonial policy.

As far as the Centre Party was concerned, they still had an account to settle with Peters. A few weeks earlier he had triggered a quarrel in the Colonial Society and had intrigued against the president of the Berlin branch, Arenberg. The latter was a member of the budget committee and its spokesman in the Reichstag. He ardently opposed Peters's naval plans. Intrigue, as we have seen at various times, was one of Peters's special talents. Thus he succeeded in deposing Arenberg as president and having himself elected as head of the branch. As a result the Berlin branch split, and Arenberg set up his own group in Charlottenburg.

Secondly, it may be argued that Bebel's report provoked those who had always emphasized the civilizing task of colonialism. After all, the spreading of Christianity and the fight against the slave trade had been major arguments used to persuade the Centre Party to support colonial policy. Now they were confronted with a case in which one of the representatives of civilization made all these high-sounding goals seem ludicrous. Peters was said to have justified the executions on the basis of African law and customs. In other words, he had gone native, and this was something which people in Christian circles sharply condemned. Thus the anger about the Peters case was not only rooted in jealousy as the alleged motive for a murder; it was also fuelled by his supposed application of African customs. Whether the legal system of the Chagga would indeed have sanctioned such killings was not a question which interested anybody in Berlin. This mixture of cultural arrogance and ignorance of African realities was characteristic of the way in which discussions of that kind were conducted in the metropolis. The mere suspicion that Peters might have resorted to some supposed African law was as scandalous as the executions themselves, even if they were indeed ordered out of jealousy.

Interestingly, Muslim and African customs were referred to in the discussion as if they were identical. In any event, it was 'scandalous'[69] that a representative of European civilization should resort to such justifications. This clearly undermined the Christian mission, which parliamentarians such as Schall saw as the struggle against 'the gloomy powers in the

---

[68] Sten. Ber. IX/IV/59, 13 March 1896, 1443.   [69] Ibid. 1423.

dark continent, not under the sign of the crescent, but under the sign of the cross'. Schall had no doubt that Islam was 'in fact the most fanatical enemy of Christianity and the most dangerous opponent of colonial government'.[70]

Kayser could not have failed to notice that the protest against Peters was not confined to those notorious critics of colonial policy, the Social Democrats and the Left Liberals. Bebel's speech had also made an impression on other political groups in the Reichstag. This may have strengthened Kayser's conviction that Peters could not be protected any longer, if the reputation of the government and his own position were not to suffer further damage.

The press immediately picked up the news from the Reichstag. Important newspapers, such as the *Kölnische Zeitung*, printed the entire debate on their cover pages.[71] Peters was the topic of the day.[72] To Peters himself, the whole story came as a complete surprise. Still recovering from a weekend drinking bout,[73] he received Arnim after the Reichstag session to learn about Bebel's story. He immediately sat down to write a letter of defence, which Arnim was to read out on the next morning.

But the first speaker on 14 March was Kayser again. The evening before he had discussed the issue with Chancellor Hohenlohe and Foreign Secretary Marschall, who both offered to lend him personal support in the debate. Kayser declined, no doubt believing that a defence by several spokesmen risked becoming entangled in contradictions. If his superiors intervened he would lose control over the specific strategy he had chosen. He best knew the details of the case, and other official comments could turn out to be counter-productive.

Kayser continued to distance himself from Peters. If Bebel was right, he declared, and if the government had had known earlier of the Tucker letter, then they would immediately have ordered a criminal investigation. If Bebel was right, 'these actions would have to be considered as the most brutal and meanest acts of individual vengefulness.'[74] Simultaneously he emphasized that, according to their own official investigation, Bebel's accusations had not been proved. The alleged existence of a letter to Tucker had created a new situation and put the case 'in an entirely new light'. Therefore the Chancellor had ordered a new investigation.

[70] Ibid. 1424.
[71] Peters Papers Altena (PPA) 63b, *Kölnische Zeitung*, 15 March 1896 and 17 March 1896.
[72] See notes from a file of newspaper articles on the Peters scandal, FP 21, BAB.
[73] See *Elberfelder Zeitung* [1905], quoting from Otto Erich Hartleben's diary, PP 82, 50, BAB.   [74] Sten. Ber. IX/IV/60, 14 March 1896, 1447.

After Kayser, two Conservative members put forward their views. Massow emphasized that the saddest part of the whole affair was the alleged confession by Peters that he had applied Muslim law and had executed the girl for having committed adultery. Massow expressed his hope that Peters would be able to disprove the charge against him.

Then Arnim read out Peters's letter of defence, which explained that Jagodjo had been sentenced to six months' imprisonment in chains for having committed espionage. At that time Peters had publicly decreed that prisoners who escaped would suffer capital punishment. When the girl ran away he had had to punish her with the death penalty, but he claimed to have done it 'with much reluctance'. Three months earlier he had executed his servant because he had committed burglary. Arnim added that the female servant of Peters had been a different girl 'who had never had a hair on her head touched'.[75]

Kayser's response to Arnim's speech is particularly interesting. He was keen to direct attention again to Peters's sex life. Now he even quoted from the internal minutes of Peters's testimony of 9 April 1895. In this Peters had stated:

With the two girls lived a woman who had escaped from Marealle [i.e. the neighbouring Chagga chief]. This was the female negro sentenced to death at the end of January. I had intended to send her back to Marealle. He refused to take her up again, remarking that she was good for nothing. She stayed at the station as a kind of prostitute, and I admit that I used her once or twice at the beginning of her stay.[76]

The next speaker was Dr Hammacher, of the National Liberals, the party which had put Peters forward as their candidate in a by-election to the Reichstag in 1895. Hammacher demanded more details from Kayser, for instance the documents from the so-called court martial and the written sentences. This was a problem, since the Kilimanjaro station had been abandoned after Bülow's defeat by Meli, and many documents from that period had vanished. Hammacher asked why the facts that had been known to the government had not led to Peters's dismissal.[77]

In the further course of the debate, which was to last for three full days, the Peters scandal remained the central issue. The Conservatives appeared perplexed, while the National Liberals remained silent for the most part. The debate had become a feast for the left opposition, who enjoyed their triumph to the full. The Social Democrats spoke of colonialism as 'a costly national sport'.[78] They claimed that Peters, Leist, and Wehlan were not

[75] Sten. Ber. IX/IV/60, 14 March 1896, 1449–50.   [76] Ibid. 1452.
[77] Ibid. 1453, 1454.   [78] Sten. Ber. IX/IV/60, 14 March 1896, 1463.

isolated cases, but symptoms of a rotten system.[79] Eventually Bebel accused Kayser of being guilty of the affair as well; hence he was the wrong person for the post of Colonial Director.[80] Richter called Peters a scoundrel who set an example for people such as Leist and Wehlan. He asked why the government, knowing about the killings, had chosen such a person for a high administrative position in the colony.[81]

After three days the Reichstag debate concluded, but the political impact was still difficult to assess. 'Clearly, the storms of the last few days, the like of which have not occurred in the Reichstag for years, will not be without their consequences',[82] Kayser wrote to his uncle Baron on 19 March 1896. The Colonial Director observed that 'the Peters and the Bismarck press have again unleashed their pack and . . . in military officers' circles the mood starts to shift in favour of Peters'.[83] He suspected that the scandal might lead to his own replacement by Schele.[84] 'What the Kaiser himself thinks I don't know, but he seems to be influenced very much by his environment.' Apparently Wilhelm reacted angrily to the affair because it had given Bebel the opportunity to discredit the government and had made it look as if they wanted to hide something. 'This impression should have been avoided', he noted on Hohenlohe's report of 22 March 1896. On the other hand, he abstained from condemning Peters straight away. He favoured a wait-and-see attitude: if the charges were true then 'he is a scoundrel', if they were not 'he must be defended'.[85]

The public, as far as it found expression in the newspapers, was split over the Peters affair. In the *Kleine Journal* and the *Leipziger Neueste Nachrichten* Peters was given space to present his own version of the story.[86] Arendt's *Deutsches Wochenblatt* stood firmly behind him.[87] Other papers, such as the *Hamburger Nachrichten*, the *Hannoverscher Kurier*, the *Leipziger Neueste Nachrichten,* and *Die Post,* also sympathized with Peters rather than with his critics, or at least assumed a wait-and-see attitude.[88]

On the other hand, Peters could no longer count on support from

---

[79] Ibid. 1462.   [80] Ibid. 1472.   [81] Ibid. 1466, 1467.

[82] Kayser to Baron, 19 March 1896 (copy), Reichsinstitut für Geschichte des neuen Deutschland, R1/3, file 2, BAB.   [83] Ibid.

[84] Ibid.

[85] Wilhelm's marginal comment, Palermo, 2 April 1896, on Hohenlohe to Wilhelm, Berlin 22 March 1896, copy in FP 21, BAK.

[86] *Kleines Journal*, 17 March 1896, *Leipziger Neueste Nachrichten*, 15 March 1896, notes in FP 21, BAK.   [87] 19 March 1896, note in FP 21, BAK.

[88] See *Hamburger Nachrichten*, 15 and 16 March 1896; *Leipziger Neueste Nachrichten*, 15 March 1896; *Die Post*, 17 March 1896; reference to *Hannoverscher Kurier*, in *Germania*, 15 March 1896; all notes in FP 21, BAK.

important pro-colonial papers which stood close to National Liberal circles and to the Centre. Above all the *Kölnische Zeitung* distanced itself from Peters; the '*Übermensch* was now condemned', it summed up on 14 March 1896.[89] The paper also attempted to protect influential National Liberals such as Rudolf von Bennigsen, who were known as mentors of Peters.[90] However there seems to have been no unity within the National Liberal party over the issue. The Hanover branch, for example, expressed its sympathy for the colonizer.[91]

The Centre, on the other hand, appeared united over the matter. The *Kölner Volkszeitung* called Peters's 'moral condemnation' a 'sad satisfaction', pointing again to the controversy between Peters and Arenberg in the Colonial Society.[92] To them, the scandal was a welcome opportunity to strengthen their own position within the colonial movement.

Most evident was the harsh criticism of Left Liberal and Social Democratic papers. The *Vossische Zeitung* emphasized the fact that Peters had had influential mentors like Bennigsen who had helped him very much.[93] *Vorwärts* spoke of a black day for Germany's colonial policy. With a good deal of sarcasm, it portrayed Peters as 'a German Menelik', to whom the country had capitulated. Peters was a 'true German', a 'grim Aryan who wants to wipe out all Jews and, in the absence of any down in Africa, shoots negroes like sparrows and hangs negro girls for his pleasure, after they have served him for his lust'.[94] This comment is interesting in so far as Peters himself had *not* attracted public attention through any anti-Semitic comments. In 1895 he had lost the Reichstag by-election to the anti-Semitic candidate. A few years earlier he had argued against anti-Semitic pan-Germans that everybody, including Jewish applicants, should be allowed to become members of the Pan-German League. Peters believed that a large national movement could not be created otherwise.[95] It should also not be forgotten that one of his best friends, Otto Arendt, was a Jew. The *Vorwärts* article thus seems to refer to anti-Semitic press publications which defended Peters against his enemies and indicated that Jews such as Kayser were not the right people to be responsible for colonial policy.[96] The Social Democrats regarded this as proof of Peters's anti-Semitic attitude.

[89] 14 March, no. 240, note in FP 21, BAK.

[90] *Kölnische Zeitung*, 18 March 1896, note in FP 21, BAK.

[91] [18 March 1896?], Peters to Elli, PP 89, BAB.

[92] 14 March 1896, no. 177, note in FP 21, BAK.

[93] 17 March 1896, note in FP, BAK.   [94] 14 March 1896, note in FP 21, BAK.

[95] See declaration by the ADV executive committee, note in FP 23, BAK.

[96] See *Staatsbürgerzeitung*, [?] March 1896, note in FP 21, BAK. Kayser himself repeatedly spoke of attacks by the anti-Semitic and Bismarckian press.

The public scandal attracted the attention of foreign correspondents too. The *Pall Mall Gazette* called into question Germany's suitability for being a colonial power.[97] *The Times* expressed the hope that Germany would in the future implement 'the principles of Christianity, humanity and morals'.[98] The French correspondent of *Le Figaro* pursued a popular theme, employing racial theories to describe the case of Peters, a manifestation of 'the strong but primitive race of the Germans whose greatest man, Bismarck, had lived by the maxim: power comes before the law'.[99] International attention and criticism made life uncomfortable for the government and increased their desire to close the Peters chapter as soon as possible.

On 18 March 1896 the Imperial Chancellor notified Peters of a new investigation to shed further light on the killings on Kilimanjaro in 1891–2.[100] Schwarzkoppen, from the Foreign Office, was appointed to lead the investigation, and until its completion, Peters was to abstain from any public comments on the matter.

The Peters party soon gained new hope, as the Tucker letter could not be traced. Bebel's declaration that it had been printed in the CMS journal turned out to be wrong. Clemens Denhardt delivered a reply to the Foreign Office from the CMS in London; the society had not been able to find any letter from Peters to Tucker.[101] This was confirmed by ambassador Hatzfeld, who had made his own enquiries on behalf of the government. A few months later Tucker himself denied, as Peters had done previously, that they had corresponded on the issue.[102]

Indeed, there is good reason to suspect that the famous Tucker letter was never written. Correspondence in the Bernstein papers reveals that Bebel himself did not have a copy of such a letter, but had relied on information channelled to him by others. Soon after the scandal he admitted to Bernstein that the reference to Tucker had obviously been wrong.[103]

However, in the course of the investigation, other important documents surfaced.[104] Eugen Richter placed anonymous information in Kayser's

---

97   16 March 1896, note in FP 21, BAK.
98   Ibid.
99   20 March 1896, note in FP 21, BAK.
100   Hohenlohe to Peters, 18 March 1896, (copy) PP 42, 43, BAB.
101   16 May 1896, note in FP 21, BAK.
102   Zanzibar Consulate to AA, 24 Oct. 1896, enclosing a statement by Bishop Tucker of 9 Oct. 1896; AA to Bebel, 13 Feb. 1901, referring to a letter from Bishop Tucker of 9 Oct. 1896; notes in FP 21, BAK.
103   Bebel to Bernstein, 24 [?] March 1896, Bernstein papers, Moscow (IISH microfilm, Amsterdam), 204–5.
104   Some of these documents are also examined by Reuss, 'Disgrace', 134 ff.

hands that Peters had written the letter not to Tucker, but to Bishop Smithies from the Universities' Mission to Central Africa (UMCA).[105] This lead turned out to be more fruitful. In response to Hatzfeldt's enquiries, a certain Revd Travers, secretary of UMCA, supplied some correspondence between Peters and Smithies, who had died only recently. These were six letters which had been exchanged between Smithies and Peters and between Soden and Smithies.[106] Hatzfeldt discovered that the London correspondent of *Vorwärts*, Eduard Bernstein, acting on Bebel's instructions, had also attempted to get hold of copies of this correspondence.[107] However, Bebel was denied access to the material. In Berlin Bebel was summoned to the Foreign Office to provide further information. He noted at that time that officials in the Foreign Office would 'also like to sack him [i.e. Peters]'.[108]

Hatzfeldt was also able to trace a certain Major Kenrick, whom Peters had met in East Africa in April 1892. Kenrick stated that Peters had given him a letter for Bishop Tucker, but he had never delivered it. The German government was lucky that Kenrick had kept the original document and was willing to supply it as long as Peters had no objections. On 18 September 1896 the London embassy sent a copy of the letter to Berlin. Kenrick also said that the content contradicted some of what Peters had told him personally, but he stubbornly refused to provide further details of his encounter.[109] The letter ran as follows:

Magila, 3. April 1892.

Sir

I beg to acknowledge your to-day's letter. Although I should leave to the German Imperial Government to explain my conduct as an Imperial Commissioner I feel it right to explain privately to you as soon as possible a misunderstanding whose circulation could do harm as well to my reputation as to the circulator.

There have been two executions for death at the Kilimanjaro during my time, one in October last, one in January. Both as a matter of course after due examination and

---

[105] Marshall [to Hatzfeldt], 24 March 1896, and marginal comments, FP 21, BAB.

[106] Hatzfeld to Foreign Office, 9 April 1896, London 414, PA-AA, Bonn. The original letters could not be found; they are briefly paraphrased in FP 21, BAK.

[107] Bebel to Bernstein, 24 [?] March 1896, Bernstein papers, Moscow (IISH microfilm, Amsterdam), 204–5; Hatzfeld to Hohenlohe, 9 April 1896, London 414, PA-AA, Bonn.

[108] Bebel to Bernstein, 21 April 1896, Bernstein papers, Moscow (IISH microfilm, Amsterdam), 207.

[109] Hatzfeld to Hohenlohe, 17 Aug. 189[6]; Hatzfeld to Kenrick, 17 Aug. 1896; Hohenlohe to Hatzfeld, 25 Aug. 1896; Peters's testimony, 25 Aug. 1896 (copy); Marschall to Hatzfeld, 25 Aug. 1896; Hatzfeld to AA, 27 Aug. 1896; Hatzfeld to Kenrick, 28 Aug. 1896; Kenrick to Hatzfeld, 31 Aug. 1896; Hatzfeld to Hohenlohe, 1 Sept. 1896; AA to Botschaft London, 18 Sept. 1896; Botschaft London 415, PA-AA, Bonn.

by public sentence. The first case has been examined from end of August till end of October. The culprit was a Manyewa, who had broken into the house at night under aggravating circumstances and committed deception in the shrewdest way. He had also committed adultery with a female servant not of mine but of another gentleman. But into this latter case I have not even examined. I would have punished it with 25 lashes. The girl in question has not been punished at all. The sentence of death was pronounced in accordance with all gentlemen at the station who were of opinion that in the then critical position of affairs in East Africa and as the people at the Kilimanjaro had been watching the proceedings this crime for breaking boldly through the walls of the station's house and throwing the suspicion upon different other persons ought to be punished by capital law for the safety of our position.

The second case has been sentenced in January of a woman. It was a case for conspiracy against the German station with hostile tribes and in connexion with different fightings we had at the time. There was no adultery at all in this case, which was altogether clear and simple. I think your informers must have mixed up both cases. If you will ask again you will soon be able to dispel the rumours yourself.

Of course if there had not practically been a state of siege for our station then after the Uhehe catastrophe and mutiny threatening through my district I would have far preferred to follow clemency instead of severity. On my course I took last winter only the German Government has to judge.

I am much obliged to the goodness of forwarding my letter to Leva.

I am, Sir, sincerely yours.

sigd. Carl Peters[110]

This letter in fact presents Peters's first documented justification of the killings. It is not clear whether it was indeed meant for Bishop Tucker; Peters, at least, claimed that it was a draft letter to Smithies.[111] Since the letter refers to some previous correspondence, and Tucker denied having communicated with Peters at all, this may well have been right.

In any event, this letter did not confirm Bebel's story. It only stated that Peters's black servant had committed adultery in Peters's eyes. The document could be seen as backing the suspicion that Peters's sentence was to some degree motivated by the sexual relationship between his servant and one of the girls. On the other hand it could be interpreted another way as well; Peters clearly denied that sex had played a part in either of his decisions.

However, further testimonies strengthened the adultery thesis. Two railway engineers, Hermes and Mittelstaedt, whom Peters had met shortly after the killings in Ngomeni, remembered a conversation about the treatment of Africans. Peters had told them about the executions on

[110] Copy, London 415, PA-AA, Bonn; the English is as in the original.
[111] Peters's testimony, 20 Nov. 1896, FP 21, BAK.

Kilimanjaro and that the boy had committed adultery. They understood Peters to say that he had killed the black boy *because* the latter had slept with one of the girls.[112] The most serious charge resulted from the testimony of Oscar Baumann, the Austrian consul-general in Zanzibar. Baumann remembered Peters saying at a supper in the Hotel Bristol in winter 1893–4: 'I am a quiet, serious son of a pastor from Lauterbach on the Elbe, but I did not like *Lochbrüderschaft* [vaginal fraternity] with these swine.'[113] Baumann had obviously confused Lauterbach with Neuhaus, which was Peters's real home. Nevertheless, his statement could be read as further evidence that Peters had hanged the black boy (and possibly the girl as well) on the grounds of sexual jealousy.

In September the Chancellor ordered the initiation of formal disciplinary proceedings on the basis of the results of the preliminary investigation.[114] Hellwig was appointed to lead the prosecution. It should be noted that, apart from the engineers' and Oscar Baumann's statements, the Foreign Office did not have much new material against Peters. Most of it had been known to them *before* the story broke in March 1896.

The promise of proceedings against Peters did not bring much relief to the government. Increasingly, Kayser himself became a target of public debate and criticism. This was not surprising since Peters and his friends were now trying to discredit the colonial administration in order to turn the tables. If Kayser, and perhaps even Hohenlohe, fell, then things might be different. Such at least were Peters's hopes: 'The overthrow of this bunch would turn everything around for me. Therefore, I must ride out this crisis', he wrote to his sister.[115]

Kayser came under fire from two sides. On the one hand, there were those who blamed him for having deliberately sacrificed an alleged man of merit before all the evidence was presented. Arendt came up with Shakespeare's *Julius Caesar* to unmask the Colonial Director. He accused Kayser of having employed a truly 'Antonian defence', adding 'And Brutus is an honourable man'.[116] The *Staatsbürgerzeitung* wrote that it was Kayser who had given Peters 'the *coup de grâce*'.[117] Even papers which opposed Peters saw the role of Kayser in a similar way. The *Kölnische Volkszeitung*,

[112] Sentence of 24 April 1897, 18, Disziplinarkammer für die Schutzgebiete, PPA 1, KA.
[113] See Sentence of 15 Nov. 1897, 114, Disziplinarhof für die Schutzgebiete, PPA 2, KA.
[114] Hohenlohe's decree, 21 Sept. 1896, note in FP 21, BAK.
[115] [1896], Peters to Elli, PP 89, BAB.
[116] *Deutsches Wochenblatt*, 19 March 1896, note in FP 21, BAK.
[117] *Staatsbürgerzeitung*, March 1896, note in FP 21, BAK.

for example, remarked laconically:[118] 'There is hardly anyone who has been defended in a more unhappy way than Peters has been by the Director of the Colonial Department.' On the other hand a number of people asked why decisive measures against Peters had not been taken earlier if the government had been aware of the incidents. Increasingly, people questioned whether the Colonial Director was in fact suitable for his post.[119] Kayser did not fail to notice this development, and he felt 'a deep disgust'. From all sides he saw 'poisonous salamanders crawling near me, and bespattering me with their perfidies'.[120] True, Kayser felt that the Centre party stood firmly behind him, and he hoped that the National Liberals would not vacillate. However, he was most concerned 'that the agrarians, i.e. primarily the conservatives, being easily guided by Arnim and Arendt, will rise against me'.[121] In June he complained that 'the anti-Semites and the Peters people dig further and further.' Kayser, whose nerves had not been of the strongest for quite some time, increasingly suffered from the attacks which were launched against him in public. By autumn he noticed that he was shivering, and he could no longer sleep without taking pills.[122] While public discontent continued, he eventually concluded that it would be better to leave before he was thrown out. He asked for his discharge, which this time was granted. Kayser became president of the Imperial Court in Leipzig.

Thus the scandal of March 1896 had not only hit Peters; it had claimed a second victim, as *Kladderadatsch* fittingly illustrated in its cartoon of 25 October 1896.[123] Kayser was the price which the government had to pay to the right-wing parties if it wanted to regain their confidence.

The investigations against Peters continued until the end of 1896. Both prosecution and defence then had a few weeks to prepare their arguments for the public proceedings on 24 April 1897. Court room number 6 of the Royal Chamber Court at Potsdam was packed with people on that day. At ten o'clock, Senate President Groschuff, in his capacity as chairman of the Disciplinary Chamber for the Colonies, opened the Peters session.[124] The accused was present, accompanied by his lawyers Koffka and Gundlach. Among the audience, there were also Peters's close friends, Karl von der Heydt and Schroeder-Poggellow. Hellwig, from the

[118] 14 March 1896, note in FP 21, BAK.

[119] See *Deutsche Tageszeitung*, 15 March 1896; *Staatsbürgerzeitung*, March 1896, notes in FP 1896.   [120] Kayser to Baron, 19 March 1896, (copy) R1/3, file 8, BAB.

[121] Kayser to Baron, 3 May 1896, (copy) R1/3, file 8, BAB.

[122] Kayser to Baron, 25 Oct. 1896, (copy) R1/3, file 8, BAB.

[123] 'Spaßhaftes von der Rutschbahn', Beiblatt zum *Kladderadatsch*, no. 43, Cover Page, KPB 51, BAB.

[124] *Norddeutsche [Allgemeine] Zeitung*, 24 April 1897, no. 173, clipping in PP 51, BAB.

Foreign Office, represented the prosecution. The accused had to defend himself against a long list of charges: (1a) the arbitrary execution of a black boy in October 1891 and of a black girl in January 1892; (1b) the unjustified initiation of armed hostilities with chief Malamia; (1c) ordering arbitrarily inhumane corporal punishment against three black girls; (2) having sent various false reports to his superiors in November 1891, and April and June 1892; (3) having confessed to various people that he had killed a black boy for having sexual intercourse with one of his concubines. According to the prosecution, Peters had thereby abused his official authority.[125]

The prosecutor presented a detailed version of the Kilimanjaro story as it had been pieced together through the investigations since 1892. In the case of Mabruk, the major argument against Peters was that the sexual factor was the decisive motive for the execution. For a full day the public had the opportunity to follow the positions of prosecution and defence, and to witness the questioning of witnesses. At eight o'clock in the evening, the judges eventually retired for deliberation. Two hours later they pronounced their judgment: Peters was found guilty of malfeasance in office, and was therefore dismissed from the colonial service. This was the maximum punishment possible in a disciplinary proceeding, and it destroyed all hopes of the Peters party for a rapid rehabilitation of his damaged image.

Nevertheless, it should be noted that the judges had in fact found for the prosecution in respect of two charges only; these were the killing of Mabruk and the filing of wrong reports. The hanging of Jagodjo, the whipping of the girls, and the war against Malamia were not seen as illegitimate actions. The most severe abuse Peters had committed was the sending of false information to his superior, rather than any of his violent excesses.[126]

The irony of the judgment lay in the fact that the chamber had aquitted Peters of the one charge which had initially triggered the scandal: the hanging of Jagodjo. Four days later Peters appealed, and in the middle of May the prosecutor followed suit.[127] This was Peters's last chance to rescue his colonial career in Germany.

The appeal made things worse for the accused. Peters was found guilty of all charges, and he had to bear the full costs of the proceedings.[128]

[125] *Norddeutsche [Allgemeine] Zeitung*, 24 April 1897, no. 173, clipping in PP 51, BAB.
[126] *Norddeutsche [Allgemeine] Zeitung*, 25 April, no. 174, clipping in PP 51, BAB.
[127] FP 21, 101.
[128] Sentence of 15 Nov. 1897, Kaiserlicher Disziplinarhof für die Schutzgebiete, (copy), PP 2, Kreisarchiv Altena (hereafter KA); see newspaper clippings: *Die Post*, 14 Nov. 1897; *Vossische Zeitung* 15 Nov. 1897; *Berliner Börsen-Zeitung*, 16 Nov. 1897; *Die Post*, 16 Nov. 1897; *Vossische Zeitung* 16 Nov. 1897; *Frankfurter Zeitung*, 17 Nov. 1897; all cuttings in PP 51, BAB.

Hellwig convinced the judges with his argument that all punishments against the girls were illegitimate, since Peters had no formal disciplinary authority over them. The fact that they had been given to the Germans by African chiefs did not automatically place them under his official authority. Consequently, he had not been entitled to whip them, or to drag them back to the station from Malamia, or to sentence Jagodjo to death.

The ruling of the appeal chamber was mostly accepted 'in silence' by the newspapers sympathetic to Peters, as the *Frankfurter Zeitung* observed.[129] For the moment it marked the end of Germany's most spectacular colonial scandal. It was a victory for the Foreign Office which enabled them to distance themselves sufficiently from Peters and his actions.

Demands by the Social Democrats for criminal proceedings to be started against Peters were rejected by the government. They argued that prosecuting Peters under penal law would be 'hopeless', since his actions had occurred 'abroad'. At the time the killings took place Kilimanjaro had not yet been defined as part of the German Protected Territory, but only as part of the German sphere of interest.[130] The Secretary of State of the Interior, Bötticher, declared that Peters could not be prosecuted for murder unless it could be proved that the same action would be punishable under the law of the relevant country as well. Then the application of Article 4.3 of the Penal Code might be possible. But Hellwig from the Foreign Office pointed out that the necessary proof could not be produced from such a 'savage people'.[131] Interestingly, Hellwig had accepted the popular view that a local chief would have done the same as Peters. Hellwig stated this as though it were common knowledge, but it was no more than European prejudice. In fact, nobody in Germany had yet collected any detailed information about the Chagga legal system, nor had the government displayed any interest in such questions.

No efforts were made by the government to investigate the possibility of criminal prosecution any further. To employ Chagga law as a basis for criminal prosecution in Europe would have meant placing African legal systems on the same level as those of other so-called civilized countries, such as

---

[129] *Frankfurter Zeitung*, 17 Nov. 1897, no. 319, PP 51, BAB.

[130] Sentence of 24 April 1897, Disziplinarkammer für die Schutzgebiete, 35, PP 1, KA; 'Reichstags-Verhandlungen', *Norddeutsche [Allgemeine] Zeitung*, 27 April 1897, no. 176; Hohenlohe to Schönstedt, (draft by Hellwig), 27 April 1897, Schönstedt's reply, 23 June 1897, FP 21, BAB. Some legal aspects of the judgment are also discussed in: H. Schneppen, 'Der Fall Karl Peters: Ein Kolonialbeamter vor Gericht', *ZfG* 49 (2001), 869–85. However, the author has hardly explored the political significance of the Peters Scandal.

[131] 'Reichstags-Verhandlungen', *Norddeutsche [Allgemeine] Zeitung*, no. 176, 27 April 1897, PP 51, BAK.

France or Britain. This was not compatible with the belief in European superiority over African savage life, whose legal practices were believed to be primitive and unacceptable.

At first sight, the Peters debacle may appear as a paradox; at the very moment when the Reich was about to enter a new phase of *Weltpolitik*, a prominent agitator for German world power was destroyed politically. However, a character whose activities were explosive enough to discredit Germany's overseas policy to such an extent could no longer be backed by the government. The charge that he had gone native and allegedly acted like a savage was a stigma which was unacceptable for anybody who wanted to be part of the political establishment. Peters had obviously betrayed what was regarded as the civilizing mission of colonization. The Centre Party was the most outraged by the disclosure of the Kilimanjaro affair, and they still had a score to settle with Peters, who had managed to topple Arenberg as the president of the Colonial Society in Berlin. The Centre Party, the largest in the Reichstag, could not easily be ignored by the government. Their votes were needed for the passage of the legislative programme in the Reichstag, and they also had to be won for a future naval programme. Hence the government could no longer afford to be associated with a man whose reputation had been severely damaged among large sections of the Reichstag. Peters had to go not because his goals of *Weltpolitik* were seen as a great threat, but because he himself had become an obstacle to the pursuit of a world-political agenda.

8

Struggling for a Political Comeback
(1897–1918)

WILHELM'S FIRST ACT OF GRACE

The Peters story did not end with the decision of the appeal chamber. True, for the moment he seemed 'a dead man in political terms'.[1] In July 1896, Peters moved to London, and there he revived his interest in King Solomon's legendary gold mines at Ophir. From 1899 he undertook various expeditions to the Zambesi region to prove that Manicaland, Mashonaland, and Matabeleland, were indeed Solomon's Ophir as described in the Bible.[2] However Peters's theories failed to find general acceptance.[3] He also founded a mining company, called 'Dr. Carl Peters's Estates and Exploration Co.' (later renamed 'South East Africa Ltd.'), and established various mines in southern Africa. In 1910, however, he sold the enterprise to a British group of financiers. According to his own statement, he lost around 170,000 marks in the venture.[4] Peters private life also changed. At the age of 54 he decided to give up his life as a single man and married Thea Herbers from Iserlohn.

Although Peters did not return permanently to Germany until the outbreak of the First World War, he never gave up hope of achieving a political comeback, nor did his friends. The lever with which Peters hoped to restore his honour was still the missing Tucker letter. At the turn of the century the general political climate seemed to change in Peters's favour. The transitional Hohenlohe era had come to an end and his successor Bernhard von Bülow embarked on a vigorous course of *Weltpolitik*. Under the impact of the Boer War, nationalist agitation was revived, and in this

---

[1] *DKZ*, 27 Nov. 1897, 490.

[2] These activities cannot be treated here in any detail. For Peters's own account of this period see *Lebenserinnerungen*, GS i. 95 ff. For his Ophir theory and his expeditions see his book *Im Goldland des Altertums. Forschungen zwischen Zambesi und Sabi* (Munich, 1902). It was also published in English as *The Eldorado of the Ancients* (New York, 1902).

[3] See H. Schnee, 'Peters, Carl', in *Deutsches Biographisches Jahrbuch*, ii (Berlin, 1928), 295.

[4] Peters, *Lebenserinnerungen*, GS i. 106.

phase the question of Peters's rehabilitation again surfaced on the public agenda. On 29 March 1901 the *Tägliche Rundschau* published an article under the headline 'The Tucker Letter' which revived the debate about Peters's guilt in the Kilimanjaro affair. It complained that in 1896 Germany had 'sacrificed one of her greatest intelligences' to the British,[5] although Bebel had admitted that the Tucker letter did not exist. Hellwig, the prosecutor in the Peters case, was angry about the renewed debate: 'That is a bit thick in light of the reasons for the sentence! Surely the lack of the Tucker letter is not a proof of Dr Peters's innocence.'[6]

A year later the same paper surprised the public with the news that the writer of the Tucker letter had been found. Allegedly, this was the same man who had served as the main witness against Peters in 1896. The *Leipziger Neueste Nachrichten* concluded that this could be none other than Bronsart von Schellendorf, who had stayed with Peters on Kilimanjaro in 1891–2.[7] In fact, Peters had suspected for some time that Bronsart was the writer of the letter. He published his charges in the London-based *Finanz-Chronik*,[8] and these were then taken up in the German press.

By the summer of 1902 the whole issue had attracted the Kaiser's attention. In a conversation with Chancellor Bülow on colonial matters, Wilhelm bitterly complained 'about the way in which Peters had been sacrificed in those days'.[9] As Bülow wrote to the Foreign Office, the Kaiser believed that he had read that the charges arising from the Tucker letter had now been identified as defamation. He desired that this should be exploited in the press as proof of the unreliability of Peters's accusers, and as a welcome tool to undermine the political opposition's credibility. *Die Post* of 16 August 1902 followed suit, stating that public opinion had changed towards Peters since the Tucker letter had been proved to be a fake. It spoke of demands 'that a man of such colonial merits should be suitably rehabilitated and brought closer to his fatherland again'.[10] It also emphasized that the Colonial Society had again given Peters a place on the executive board.

Vorwärts immediately attacked *Die Post* and its sympathies for 'Hänge-Peters'.[11] Throughout the year the issue continued to occupy German newspapers. In January 1903 the debate was fuelled by the charge that

    [5] FP 21, BAK; SP 102, HStA-PK.
    [6] Marginal comment on *Tägliche Rundschau*, 29 March 1901, FP 21, BAK.
    [7] *Leipziger Neueste Nachrichten*, 21 June 1902, referring to an article of *Tägliche Rundschau*, note in FP 21, BAK.
    [8] Reported in *Leipziger Neueste Nachrichten*, 19 Sept. 1902, note in FP 21, BAK.
    [9] Bülow to AA, 10 Aug. 1902, FP 21, BAK.
    [10] Note on article in *Die Post*, 16 Aug. 1902, FP 21, BAK.
    [11] Note on *Vorwärts*, 17 Aug. 1902, FP 21, BAK.

Hellwig, an official in the Foreign Office, had triggered the entire scandal in 1895 in order to eliminate Peters as candidate for the East African governorship.[12] On 8 February Peters joined the debate with an article in *Der Tag*: he claimed that 'very important' people had long become convinced of the need to review his sentence,[13] although other papers speculated about the credibility of this bold statement.[14] The liberal *Berliner Tageblatt* observed at the time: 'The fuss about Peters has recently started again.'[15]

However, Peters could not sustain his charges against Bronsart and was soon forced to declare in public that he had erred.[16] Despite this setback, speculation about Peters's rehabilitation continued. In March the *Tägliche Rundschau* published the text of a petition on the subject which was said to be favoured by leading members of the National Liberals and the Centre.[17] Even the Left Liberals allegedly welcomed the step, although this appears unlikely. Nevertheless, the article gave the impression that the petition was about to be submitted. It was also suspected that the group around Peters wanted to install him as Colonial Director,[18] a possibility which Catholic and Social Democratic papers fervently opposed.[19]

In June 1903 Kardorff told Peters that Chancellor von Bülow, Foreign Secretary Richthofen, and the Kaiser were favourably disposed towards his rehabilitation. Kardorff only wanted to talk to Bülow again before submitting the petition, 'so that we can be sure'.[20] He had also worked through a mediator and confidant in order to win the Kaiser's support.[21] Surprisingly, however, the petition was not submitted in that year. The reasons are not entirely clear, and the sources do not shed much light on the issue. The *Leipziger Neueste Nachrichten*, a major promoter of Peters's rehabilitation, noted at the end of the year that Peters himself had asked for a postponement.[22] If this was so the government seems to have developed cold feet, given the mounting expectations that Peters would be employed again in the colonial service. Obviously, Peters had pushed too hard. This

[12] *Leipziger Neueste Nachrichten*, 31 Jan. 1903, notes in FP 21, BAK.
[13] *Der Tag*, 8 Feb. 1903, note in FP 21, BAK.
[14] See *Nationalzeitung*, 9 Feb. 1903; *Frankfurter Zeitung*, 10 Feb. 1903; *Staatsbürgerzeitung*, 10 Feb. 1903; *Vossische Zeitung*, 11 Feb. 1903; notes in FP 21, BAK.
[15] *Berliner Tageblatt*, 11 Feb. 1903, note in FP 21, BAK.
[16] *Hannoverscher Kurier*, 11 Feb. 1903, note in FP 21, BAK.
[17] 13 March 1903, note in FP 21, BAK.
[18] *Nationalzeitung*, 7 March 1903; *Freisinnige Zeitung*, 8 March 1903; notes in FP 21, BAK.
[19] *Vorwärts*, 8 March 1903; *Kölnische Volkszeitung*, 11 March 1903; notes in FP 21, BAK.
[20] Peters to brother Hermann, 16 June 1903, FP 5, BAK.
[21] See Kardoff to Peters, 1 May 1903, FP 8, BAK.
[22] See reference in *Berliner Tageblatt*, 29 Dec. 1903, note in FP 21, BAK.

was also true of his charges against Bronsart, which turned out to be unsustainable, so that his bold accusations backfired.[23]

A year later, colonial policy again became an acute issue in Wilhelmine politics, as South-West Africa became a flashpoint when the Hereros rose against German rule. It seems possible that the general anti-African climate also provided a new opportunity for the Peters party. After all, Peters had always advocated a hard-line policy in dealing with the African population. On 11 May 1905 fifty-one Reichstag members submitted a petition for his rehabilitation, and in an act of grace the Kaiser restored Peters's title on 4 July 1905.[24] Bülow endorsed the petition, and justified the act with 'the duty of thankfulness that the German people owed to this significant, energetic and patriotic man'.[25]

LITERARY SUCCESS: *ENGLAND UND DIE ENGLÄNDER*

It is one of the ironies of Peters's career that he produced his most popular literary work only after his political fall. *England und die Engländer* was first published in 1904 and ran through six editions, with more than 20,000 copies.[26] The British edition was also noted by prominent politicians such as Joseph Chamberlain. He referred to Peters's book when he warned that Britain should never sink into the rank of a Holland, 'rich indeed . . . but still an inconsiderable factor in the history of the world'.[27] Peters's work was a kind of national portrait, covering aspects of British social, economic, and political life. It presented a lot of statistical material which was fitted into a quite readable narrative. At the same time, it revealed a great many details of British daily life, as Peters had observed it over a number of years. In Germany the book was very well received and earned a good deal of praise in the press.[28]

It is beyond the scope of this study to examine all aspects of Peters's book in greater detail. Here it must suffice to take a closer look at one point, Peters's perception of British politics and his ideas about the British world empire, to which he dedicated a whole chapter. Peters repeatedly referred to the Chamberlain movement, which advocated a customs union of all

---

[23] See *Hamburgischer Korrespondent*, 22 July 1905, note in FP 21, BAK.
[24] Note on 'Begnadigung Peters', [1905?], PPA 10 (notes from Bülow Papers 16/29).
[25] Ibid.
[26] See 'Verzeichnis der Schriften von Carl Peters', GS i. 502.
[27] See copy of article 'Mr Chamberlain in the East-End', *The Standard*, 6 Dec. 1904, FP 12, BAK.   [28] See press clippings in PP 78, BAB.

parts of the empire.[29] 'It is an obvious advantage to proceed to future centuries as a national giant', Peters believed.[30] He saw this status as a means to establish a large territorial block which would be economically self-sufficient. 'As a result, a quarter of the world surface would quit international trade', he predicted.[31] He could not understand why this idea of a giant state produced such opposition in Britain itself. He failed to recognize the advantages of free trade, which had contributed to Britain's economic rise, and the political implications of protectionism, which ultimately convinced the British not to follow Chamberlain's plan.

If we relate Peters's book to his prior works the continuity is evident in various ways. In the 1880s he had also linked political power with close control over large stretches of territory. Then as now, he was impressed by the very size of the British Empire.[32] If Britain wanted to maintain its world power, it had to link Canada, South Africa, and Australia closely to the metropolis, with high tariff walls against the rest of the world. Peters believed that the foundation of a 'United States of Europe' might be a suitable counter-measure against an 'overseas world under English leadership'.[33] This idea was fairly unusual for Peters, who had always emphasized Germany's overseas expansion. Now he pointed to the necessities of continental politics. He envisaged a mid-European customs union, with which Russia and France would be associated. If the Anglo-Saxon world succeeded in uniting, then the salvation of all other white people would lie in a European Union. Once this stage was reached, the two blocks would have 'to clash in a struggle for life and death'.[34] This was Peters's vision of a future world war.

Peters thus agreed with those who believed that large-scale empires would increasingly monopolize power in the world, a thought which also seems to have guided Joseph Chamberlain or Tirpitz.[35] The latter propagated the enlargement of the fleet in order to make Germany one of the four great powers of the world, alongside Russia, Britain, and the United States.

Another aspect of continuity in Peters's book is the way in which he portrays the British as a specific race. In Peters's eyes, this British character was the ultimate reason for the growth of the British Empire and Anglo-Saxon 'genius of state building'. It was largely founded on a strong individualism which was exercised in a system of 'organized freedom' (the representative constitution). Not 'humanitarian cosmopolitanism' but

---

[29] *England*, GS iii. 84, 86, 189 ff.   [30] Ibid. 189.   [31] Ibid. 191.
[32] Ibid. 179.   [33] Ibid. 195.   [34] Ibid. 195–6.
[35] P. Kennedy, *Aufstieg und Fall der großen Mächte*, German edn. (Frankfurt, 1991), 303.

'national egotism' was the clue to British success. Therefore the British were ruthless, often brutal, towards their competitors. Their common sense would ensure that they were not bound by the limits of any theoretical stereotypes. Their 'natural flexibility' made them 'the born colonizers in the European world'.[36]

Peters's admiration for the British and their empire is striking throughout the book, and is more pronounced than in any of his previous essays. His book, however, did not only deal with Britain. In fact, various passages suggest that it was meant as much as a critique of German policy; Britain was used as the mirror which would enable Germany to recognize its own deficiencies. While this motive was already noticeable in Peters's early essays, it now became more pronounced, serving particularly as an explanation for his own political fall. Between the lines Peters wanted to indicate that a figure like him—having dedicated his whole life to the enlargement of the empire—would never have been sacked in a country like Britain. In Treitschke's words, the Germans were the most ungrateful people in the world.[37] The author thus portrayed himself as the victim of a country which failed to recognize his deeds on behalf of the nation.

Britain was a model, as far as it represented a world empire and a worldwide power. However, as far as domestic policy was concerned, Peters was not ready to accept the model. Parliamentary politics and democratic systems may have had their legitimacy in Britain; indeed Peters linked the British constitution to the same characteristics which he had identified as the basis for imperial expansion. Nevertheless, the British political system was not seen as a model to be transferred to Germany. Peters called his own state the 'moderate military dictatorship of the Hohenzollerns'.[38] This concept perhaps did not acccurately reflect the constitutional realities of the German system, but it indicated where Peters saw the ultimate strength of the German state—in its military power on land.

PETERS'S LIBEL SUITS AND A SECOND ACT OF GRACE

With *England und die Engländer* Peters had achieved a literary success which helped to revive his popularity. In June 1906, he completed another piece of written work. *Die Gründung von Deutsch-Ostafrika* was a kind of autobiography, covering the period from his childhood to the end of his Emin Pasha expedition. This book was to remind readers of Peters's great

---

[36] Peters, *England*, GS iii. 74–5.   [37] Ibid. 75.   [38] Ibid. 99

colonial efforts and to appeal to the nationalist feelings which were bound to the founding of Germany's empire overseas. The work was widely reviewed in the German press,[39] and *Der Tag* even devoted a cover story to the book. The author of the article was the prominent colonial propagandist Hübbe-Schleiden, who had advocated colonial acquisitions in the late 1870s and early 1880s. Hübbe-Schleiden sympathized with those who compared Peters with Sir Walter Raleigh and Lord Clive. Again the expansion of territory was seen as Peters's major achievement. His original acquisitions had almost reached the size of British India, he claimed, but the German government had chosen to give most of it away, so that only a quarter of the original territory was left. According to Hübbe-Schleiden, quite a few people would see Peters as the one who contributed most energy to German world power.[40]

In the summer of 1906 Peters received an invitation from the Neuer Verein in Munich. This society was intended as a platform for 'important people' who would speak on 'topics of general interest'.[41] Peters was asked to speak about the question: 'What can England and Germany learn from each other?' He also accepted another invitation for that same weekend. The Verein deutscher Studenten organized an assembly in the Bürgerbräukeller, with Peters as their guest. There he spoke on German colonial policy.

Perhaps Peters's visit to Munich would have passed quietly, had it not coincided with a crucial political event in Berlin. The day before Peters arrived, Chancellor von Bülow had dissolved the Reichstag after a heated debate over colonial matters. This caused great excitement among the political parties, which now hastily prepared their election campaigns. In this situation, the arrival of Peters was just what the Social Democrats in Bavaria had been waiting for. Their local organ, the *Münchner Post*, covered both his speeches on 14 and 15 December. The first assembly took place in the plush hotel Vier Jahreszeiten, where some 800 people came to listen. They were 'the intelligentsia of the Bavarian capital', 'the elite of the civil service and the military', 'great liberals', 'many women in full dress', prominent figures from the worlds of science, art, commerce, and industry; in short: 'the cream of society'.[42]

Peters kept his speech close to the ideas of his book *England und die*

[39] See review clippings in PP 79, BAB.
[40] 'Carl Peters. Ein geschichtliches Problem', *Der Tag*, 21 Oct. 1906, clipping in PP 82, BAB.
[41] Peters vs. Gruber, sentence of 2 July 1907, 14, PPA 3, Kreisarchiv Altena.
[42] Ibid. 18; *Augsburger Abendzeitung*, no. 346, 15 Dec. 1906, PP 80, BAB.

Engländer. By and large, he chose an unusually mild tone, but at some point, his speech became quite heated when he came to mention the imperial drive on the other side of the Channel: 'Like vultures, the British sit on their island and look over the oceans and continents to find areas for exploitation. Proudly, they look down upon other nations and don't even think of granting equal rights to others.'[43] The Germans, on the other hand, were a 'softer body', 'philistine', and always satisfied once they enjoyed equal rights among other peoples. But this attitude, Peters implied, was not good enough if Germany wanted to become a world power. As long as the Germans did not emulate the British, they could not claim to pursue *Weltpolitik.* In the end, however, he concluded that the political situation of the day would require both nations to stand together, so that perhaps a lasting entente could be achieved.

A day later Peters spoke in the Bürgerbräukeller, on Germany and her empire. Apart from the Verein deutscher Studenten, representatives of the pan-Germans, the Colonial Society, and the Eastern Marches Society filled the room.[44] With some 3,000 people, the hall was very overcrowded.[45] Peters demanded more liberal concessions for mining, railway, and land developments. For Africans he demanded 'a sort of military service, not with the rifle but with hoe and pick'. This would be better 'than collecting money so that the negroes could learn from the missionaries how to write and calculate'. He also fulminated against those who had put an end to his political career. In Germany 'philistines and old women search with a magnifying glass for all sorts of things' with which to discredit their fellow countrymen. 'This is the real colonial scandal', Peters claimed. He earned thunderous applause.[46]

Later the assembly threatened to sink into chaos when a certain Mr Sontheimer, 'a well-known free-thinker', attempted to join in the discussion. Angry students shouted him down and the organizers had difficulty in calming the crowd. They eventually closed the assembly with three cheers for the Kaiser, and expressed the hope that Peters would soon be fully rehabilitated and could return to the imperial service.[47]

The *Münchener Post* did not hold back with its headlines; it led with 'Hänge-Peters im Neuen Verein' and 'Hänge-Peters über National-

[43] See text of Peters's speech as printed in *Augsburger Abendzeitung*, no. 346, 15 Dec. 1906, and *Münchner Neueste Nachrichten*, no. 586, 15 Dec. 1906, PP 80, BAB.

[44] *Münchner Zeitung*, 17 Dec. 1906, PP 80, BAB.

[45] *Allgemeine Zeitung*, 17 Dec. 1906, PP 80, BAB.

[46] *Allgemeine Zeitung*, 18 Dec. 1906, PP80, BAB; *Münchner Neueste Nachrichten*, 19 Dec. 1906, note in FP 12, BAK.   [47] *Münchner Zeitung*, 17 Dec. 1906, PP 80, BAB.

politik'.[48] They called Peters 'a cowardly murderer' who had been worshipped by educated people. Peters fired back in the *Hamburger Nachrichten*; he called Bebel a social bandit and complained about the bold and impudent way in which 'these fellows try to bully political opponents'. 'Surely we do not want to tolerate the terrorism of a minority', he protested. 'How long do we want to watch a band of fanatical revolutionaries ... undermining the foundations of our social order?' This again provoked a polemical response by the *Münchener Post*, which spoke of Peters's 'mental illness' and 'mad stammering'. They noted that since the 'jolly hunting for negroes' was over Peters now called 'for the suppression of the true natives of Germany, the workers'. They also referred to the killings on Kilimanjaro as 'a ruthlessly ingenious sex murder'.[49]

Peters's performance in Munich was obviously impressive enough to convince colonial enthusiasts in Germany to engage his rhetorical skills for their election campaign. He was invited to the Reich Foundation Day rally of the nationalist societies in Dresden, along with General Liebert, ex-governor of East Africa. As the *Dresdner Nachrichten* reported, Peters spoke 'with almost unbridled passion', unfolding *Weltpolitik* in 'boundless perspectives', sometimes with bitter irony, sometimes with a great deal of humour.[50]

The three articles in the *Münchener Post* induced Peters to file a libel suit against the journalist responsible, Martin Gruber. The trial took place from 25 June to 2 July 1907, at the Royal High Court in Munich. The satirical journal *Simplicissimus* commented with its own version of the Kilimanjaro affair, illustrated by the cartoonist Olaf Gulbransson.[51] The court found Gruber guilty of 'repeated defamation' ('Hänge-Peters', 'cowardly murderer', and other phrases) and of 'making untrue claims in public'.[52] Above all, they rejected Gruber's presentation of Jagodjo's execution as 'a ruthlessly ingenious sex murder'.[53] The journalist was sentenced to pay a fine of 500 marks or to spend fifty days in prison, while Gruber's own charges against Peters's article in the *Hamburger Nachrichten* were rejected.[54] In the Court of Appeal, the fine was only slightly reduced, and Gruber's appeal was effectively rejected.[55]

[48] Nos. 285 and 286, 16 Dec. and 18 Dec. 1906, cf. sentence of 2 July 1907, Peters vs. Gruber, PPA 3, KA.
[49] All citations from: sentence of 2 July, Peters vs Gruber, PPA 3, Kreisarchiv Altena.
[50] Note on *Dresdner Nachrichten*, 19 Jan. 1906, FP 12, BAK.
[51] 'Der Prozeß Peters', *Simplicissimus* (1907), 265–6.
[52] Sentence of 2 July, Peters vs Gruber, PPA 3, 144–5, KA.   [53] Ibid. 125.
[54] Ibid. 151.   [55] Sentences in PPA 13 and 14, KA.

Peters was obsessed with filing libel suits at that time. In addition to the case mentioned, he became involved in at least seven other trials of a similar kind.[56] 'And I will institute legal proceedings until the others give up', he wrote defiantly to his sisters.[57] He even considered legal action against Ludwig Thoma, who had published nasty poems in *Simplicissimus* and *März*, as friends from Bavaria had written to tell him.[58] However this plan came to nothing.

Peters's aim behind all these trials was obvious. He sought to use them as a lever to achieve further rehabilitation and possibly a political comeback in Germany. In 1909, the twenty-fifth anniversary of the flag-hoisting in East Africa offered a new opportunity to bring the issue to the Kaiser's attention. Another petition was sent, signed by Peters's closest friends.[59] Peters's lawyer Rosenthal had prepared a paper which summarized the outcome of the libel suits, arguing that on the basis of these new verdicts the disciplinary judgments were no longer adequate.[60]

In any case, a lifting of the sentence through the ordinary legal processes was impossible in the circumstances. As Rosenthal himself pointed out, there was an unfortunate gap in the Reich civil servant law, which provided for two hearings only, both of which had already been exhausted. The existing law did not provide for a second appeal through which it would be possible to challenge the decision of the disciplinary tribunal.[61]

Hence all immediate hopes rested on another act of grace by the Kaiser. But Wilhelm could not simply remove the sentence itself. As Bülow had noted in 1907, any revision of the sentence had to be achieved through ordinary legal processes;[62] Wilhelm could only lift the legal effects of the sentence and thus mitigate the punishment, as he had done by restoring Peters's title. In theory he might have gone as far as to readmit Peters into

[56] Peters vs. Martin, July 1904, mentioned in PPA 18, 6; Peters vs. Donat, Oct. 1907, PPA 16; Peters vs. Weil, Nov. 1907, PPA 17; Peters vs. Müller, Sept. 1907, PPA 15; Peters vs. Wolf, March 1908, PPA 23; Peters vs. Bennigsen and Brüggemann, Jan. 1908, PPA 19, May 1908, PPA 20, May 1908, PPA 22; Kreisarchiv Altena.
[57] 31 Dec. 1907, PP 105, BAB.
[58] Ruederer to Peters, 17 July 1907, FP 8, BAK; Peters to his sisters, 31 Dec. 1907, PP 105, BAB.
[59] Petition to Wilhelm, 15 Oct. 1909, RKolA 946, 65 ff. BAB (signed by Vize-Admiral a.D. Livonius, Graf Baudissin, Kurt Hoffmann, Liebert, Oskar Wolff, Rudolf Hellgrewe, Prof. Robert Freidberg, Dr Schroeder Poggelow, Dr Arendt); a further copy of the text also in PPA 55, Kreisarchiv Altena.
[60] 'Zur Würdigung der Disziplinarurteile gegen Dr. Carl Peters, Reichskommissar a.D.', Sept. 1909, RKolA 946, 69 ff., BAB; further copies in PPA 60, Kreisarchiv Altena, and FP 8, BAK.   [61] See ibid.
[62] 'Prozeß Peters. Ungehörige Kritik der Disciplinarurtheile' [draft for RT speech 1907], copy in PPA 10, Kreisarchiv Altena.

the imperial service, but this would have meant not only questioning the entire disciplinary process, but also discrediting a number of high-ranking judges and Foreign Office officials. Two years earlier, following the Chancellor's intervention, Liebert had been forced to retract his criticism of the disciplinary sentences; if the Kaiser had now demonstrated similar doubts, this would have made a laughingstock of the entire government.

The Kaiser did not act upon the occasion of the anniversary as proposed. Interestingly, however, he decided at a later stage that another sign of Peters's rehabilitation should be given. In the spring of 1914, some time after Peters had suffered heavy financial losses with his mining venture, the Kaiser ordered the restoration of Peters's pension and the payment of a yearly amount of 3,900 marks from his disposition fund.[63] The *Leipziger Neueste Nachrichten* praised the decision with a major article on its cover page: 'Karl Peters as Educator'. It stated that nobody who accepted 'the right of the stronger as a dogma in the history of civilization' had any right to condemn Peters. On the contrary, the short period of Germany's colonial policy had been 'full of the most awkward *faux pas* of philanthropic over-enthusiasm'. In 1914 Peters still served as a model for the hardliners in colonial policy.[64]

As Arendt remembered later, Peters's friends also worked for a change in the Reich civil servant law so that another appeal could be brought against the disciplinary sentence of 1897.[65] Such demands had appeared in the press as early as 1907.[66] However, with the outbreak of the First World War other issues came to dominate the political debate, so that Peters's case was again pushed into the background. In the Weimar Republic, with its 'Social Democratic predominance',[67] a change of law was out of the question.[68]

From Peters's perspective, the course of his rehabilitation may have been disappointing as it did not result in a political comeback. Yet the Kaiser's decision to restore his title and pension was still a remarkable political sign. It demonstrated that the Reich could not refrain from some sort of recognition of a major colonial pioneer, and in this sense Peters's rehabilitation signalled that Germany was firmly committed to the goal of becoming a world power.

---

[63] Cabinet Order, 26 March 1914, copy in SP 24, GStA-PK.
[64] *Leipziger Neueste Nachrichten*, 5 April 1914, clipping in PP 82, BAB.
[65] See Arendt [to ?], 24 April 1935, copy in PPA 56, Kreisarchiv Altena; Thea Peters to Schnee, 27 July 1927, note in SP 47, GStA-PK.
[66] See *Hannoversches Tageblatt*, 4 July 1907, note in FP 12, BAK.
[67] Arendt [to ?], 24 April 1935, copy in PPA 56, KA.
[68] See Thea Peters to Schnee, 27 July 1927, note in SP 47, GStA-PK.

On the outbreak of the First World War Peters eventually returned to Germany. He continued to publish newspaper articles in *Der Tag* and other newspapers. A collection of his essays was published as a field edition for soldiers at the front.[69] On 9 September 1918 he wrote an article with the title 'England, unser eigentlicher Feind',[70] in which he claimed that Britain could only be defeated if it was invaded, starved out, or perhaps defeated at the Suez Canal. 'Otherwise Germany will perish.' These were his last written words. On the following day, Carl Peters died of a heart attack. He was buried at the Engesohder cemetery in Hanover, where the city provided a place of honour for its colonial hero.[71]

[69] *Zum Weltkrieg* (Hamburg, 1917); a series of earlier essays was published under the title *Zur Weltpolitik* (Berlin, 1912).

[70] Printed in GS iii. 506. According to Frank, this short article was published in the *Neue Gesellschaftliche Korrespondenz*, no. 65, 13 Sept. 1918.

[71] See Schnee, 'Peters', 297.

9

Towards New Glory
(1919–1945)

In a certain sense, Peters
is a precursor to Hitler.

Otto Arendt, 1935

WEIMAR AND COLONIAL REVISIONISM: THE ODYSSEY OF A MONUMENT

Carl Peters did not witness Germany's final defeat and the Treaty of Versailles, which sealed the loss of the colonies. However, an oversize replica of the colonizer survived the war. It lay hidden in a hangar in Dar es Salaam, 2.3 metres high and made of bronze. In 1913 a group of colonialists including Arendt, von der Heydt, and Bley, had collected money for a Peters monument to be put up at the harbour of Dar es Salaam.[1] The statue was made by the sculptor Kurt Möbius and was shipped in boxes to East Africa, where it arrived in the summer of 1914. However, fighting broke out before the monument was unpacked. When British ships shelled the harbour, a few workers rescued the statue and stored it in the warehouse of the German district office.[2] There it remained throughout the war, unnoticed by British forces.

After the war it did not take long for German colonial circles to trace the remains of the monument. They saw it as 'a patriotic duty' to keep alive the memory of Peters and his work.[3] The Colonial Society, which became the organizational centre of revisionist activities,[4] urged the Imperial Ministry for Reconstruction to negotiate with the British for the return of the statue. London eventually agreed, and Peters was shipped back home again.

[1] 'Aufruf für ein Carl Peters Denkmal in Dar es Salaam' [July 1913], DKG 1084, 287, BAB.
[2] Seitz to Imperial Ministry of Reconstruction, 10 Jan. 1921, RKolA 6915, 14, BAB.
[3] Ibid.
[4] See Pogge von Strandmann, 'Imperialism and Revisionism', 94 ff.

Another great *Afrikaner* was returned as well, in the form of a big statue of
Hermann von Wissmann which had been erected in Dar es Salaam in
1909.[5] In 1922, colonial circles formed a special 'committee for the re-erection
of colonial monuments', which was to look for a suitable location
where the statues could 'keep vivid the memory of colonial activity and the
colonial idea'.[6]

The colonial monuments were thus to function as sites of collective
remembrance.[7] As memorials fulfil a wide variety of functions in society,
historians have interpreted them in various ways. War memorials, for instance,
have been analysed 'as foci of the rituals, rhetoric and ceremonies of bereavement'.[8]
Other scholars have stressed their political significance, interpreting
'the cult of the fallen soldier' as a 'centrepiece of the religion of nationalism'.[9]

In the case of colonial monuments, there is good reason to emphasize
their political character, too. It may be argued that the pressure for re-erecting
colonial monuments primarily displayed political aspirations. In fact,
the statues reflected a twin dimension of historical memory.[10] Not only
were they a symbolic manifestation of the past as such, recalling Germany's
role as a colonizing power; they also contained a vision of the future, namely
the resurrection of the Reich as a world empire. In this sense the monuments
were to be instrumental to the wider revisionist agenda which called
for a return of the former colonies.

---

[5] For details of the Wissmann monument see M. Zeller, ' "Deutschlands größter
Afrikaner". Zur Geschichte der Denkmäler für Hermann von Wissmann', *ZfG* 44 (1996),
1089–111.

[6] [?] to Herzog Adolf Friedrich zu Mecklenburg, 26 Sept. 1921; Komitee zur Aufstellung
der Denkmäler aus den Kolonien to the Senate of Hamburg, 12 April 1922, RKolA 6915, 109,
196–7, BAB.

[7] The study of collective memory has been revived in recent years, building upon the
seminal works by Maurice Halbwachs in the 1930s. The most ambitious project in this respect
has been Pierre Nora's *Le Lieu de Memoire*; for a brief survey see K. Große-Kracht,
'Gedächtnis und Geschichte: Maurice Halbwachs—Pierre Nora', *GWU* 47, (1996), 21–31.

[8] J. Winter, *Sites of Memory, Sites of Mourning. The Great War in European Cultural
History* (Cambridge, 1995), 78.

[9] G. L. Mosse, *Fallen Soldiers. Reshaping the Memory of the World Wars* (New York and
Oxford, 1990), 7.

[10] This double dimension is also implicit in Nipperdey's interpretation of the Hermann
Monument in the Teutoburger Wald ('Nationalidee und Nationaldenkmal in Deutschland im
19. Jahrhundert', *HZ* 206 (1968), 529–85). The statue not only points to a victorious Teutonic
past. Hermann raises his sword after the battle, which gives the statue a challenging and
aggressive character, pointing to possible future conflict. The architect Ernst von Bandel saw
the statue as a symbol of 'our eternal youthful vigour, a signpost to the place of our glory and
to the recognition of our power' (cited in Nipperdey, 'Nationalidee', 569). Bandel himself
stated that a sword pointing to the ground would destroy 'the significance of the entire monument'.

Throughout the 1920s colonial interest groups widened their activities.[11] Thousands of posters and millions of leaflets were circulated seeking to win mass support for colonial demands. Local societies organized films, speeches, and slide-shows as part of the campaign. Nevertheless, leading revisionists remained dissatisfied with what was achieved as they failed to generate a true mass movement. In particular, the workers were little attracted by a colonial agenda.

It is worth noting in this context that the rising National Socialist Party initially did not play much part in these activities. They were, as Hildebrand put it, 'no pioneers of colonial revision'.[12] However, by the late 1920s colonial interest groups began to think about a possible collaboration with the Nazis to promote their own cause further. In 1928 Freiherr von Epp, an ex-general and a leading figure in the colonial movement, became a member of the Nazi Party, NSDAP. Some colonial enthusiasts started to believe that 'a German Mussolini' was needed to restore Germany's colonial glory. However, it was known that Hitler was not very enthusiastic about Africa and the return of colonies at that time. His ideas focused more on how he could establish hegemony over Europe as a first step on the envisaged road to world supremacy.

As far as the colonial monuments were concerned, the city of Hamburg was seen as a suitable location, being Germany's major port and door to the overseas world. Hamburg also was the home of the Colonial Institute, which had been established in 1908 as a training and research centre for the territories overseas. The local branch of the Colonial Society agreed to take on the project,[13] and the Hamburg senate expressed its readiness to put up the colonial monuments.[14] However, Peters caused far more problems than was initially expected. The Colonial Society was now reminded that he had been a person 'far more controversial in political terms' than Wissmann.[15] The initial agreement of the senate quickly waned, and further steps were delayed. When the DKG approached the mayor of Hamburg, Petersen, in 1928, they received only a vague answer. They were told that a decision about Peters could not be expected in the near future.[16] This obviously had to do with a strengthening of the left-orientated

---

[11] This paragraph is largely based on Hildebrand, *Reich*, and Pogge, 'Revisionism'; see also W. W. Schmokel, *Dream of Empire: German Colonialism, 1919–1945* (New Haven, 1964).
[12] Hildebrand, *Reich*, 40.
[13] Komitee zur Aufstellung der Denkmäler aus den Kolonien to the Senate of Hamburg, 12 April 1922, RKolA 6915, 109, 196–7, BAB.
[14] See AA note of 3 May 1929, referring to letters by the Senate of 5 May and 20 June 1922, DKG 1084, 92, BAB.   [15] DKG to AA, 14 Jan. 1928, RKolA 6916, 112, BAB.
[16] Klöckner to Seitz, 3 July 1929, DKG papers 1084, 56, BAB.

parties in the recent elections,[17] in which situation approval by the senate was doubtful. Obviously Social Democratic circles had not yet forgotten the former disputes about 'Hänge-Peters'. Wissmann, on the other hand, caused no difficulties, as he had not been involved in any political scandal. His statue was put up in front of the university in the summer of 1922. It is interesting that the university senate also voted unanimously for the erection of the Peters statue.[18] But colonial circles eventually decided to drop the plan, believing that the Hamburg senate would not give its *placet*. Hence the university put up only one further monument on 7 May 1935. It was that of Major Hans Dominik, who had been stationed in the Cameroons.[19]

For Peters an alternative solution was sought. Freiherr von Epp suggested that he should have a new home on the island of Heligoland,[20] a plan which was realized in 1931, on the occasion of a colonial agitation week.[21] Peters was placed on a large stone pedestal on the promenade, the plate of the monument reading as follows:

> To the vanguard of German colonial policy,
> the founder of German East Africa
>
> Dr Carl Peters
>
> Because of his deeds Heligoland became
> part of the German Empire in 1890

This was a fairly cavalier reading of German history, and not free of irony. If Germany owed the possession of the island to anybody, it was to Wilhelm II, who had insisted on the deal at all costs. Peters, on the other hand, had sought to reverse the agreement in favour of his Uganda treaties, and it is clear that Heligoland was returned not *because of* his support but rather *despite* his opposition. Certainly, if he had not laid claim to East Africa, there would have been nothing to swap, but this was a rather far-fetched justification for praising Peters as the saviour of Heligoland.

[17] See DKG to AA, 12 Jan. 1928, RKolA 6516, 112; DKG Hamburg to DKG Berlin, 13 Jan. 1928, DKG Papers 1084, 127; Klöckner to Seitz, 3 July 1929, DKG Papers 1084, 56, BAB.

[18] See 'Auszug aus dem Protokoll des Universitätssenats', 26 Oct. 1928; Sieveking to Hochschulbehörde, 29 Oct. 1928, Akte 91-50-22 (Die Denkmale Wissmann und Dominik), vol. i. 2, 3, University of Hamburg.

[19] See Reimer to Hinrichs, 3 Nov. 1959, Akte 91-50-22 (Die Denkmale Wissmann und Dominik), vol. i. University of Hamburg.

[20] Franz von Epp to AA, 23 April 1929, RKolA 6516, 127–8, BAB.

[21] 'Programm der Kolonial-Werbewoche', enclosed in LAS Abt. 309 no. 19445, Landesarchiv Schleswig-Holstein.

HITLER AND PETERS'S FINAL REHABILITATION

With Hitler's accession to power, the question of Peters's rehabilitation surfaced again. As early as 10 May 1933, the German Colonial Society demanded a reopening of the Peters case in order to revive the 'colonial will'.[22] They were supported by ex-governor Schnee, who channelled a personal request from Peters's widow to the Foreign Office.[23] There a rapid judgement on the issue was sought, since 'National Socialist circles also seem to be interested in the matter.'[24] Nevertheless, the officials reached a negative conclusion, arguing that with the acts of grace of 1905 and 1914 all legal possibilities had been exhausted. They stated that a complete lifting of the disciplinary ruling would be impossible.[25] The intervention by Epp, who later became Hitler's designated colonial minister, had no effect.[26]

But this was only a temporary setback. In 1935 colonial circles remembered the fiftieth anniversary of the East African imperial charter. This was a welcome opportunity to push the Peters case again. Now all hopes were focused on the Führer's new bill, which made it possible to revise previous disciplinary sentences. On 12 February 1935 Peters's Jewish friend Otto Arendt, now in his eighties, wrote a letter to the Foreign Minister demanding that the Führer himself should be acquainted with the matter: 'In a certain sense, Peters is a precursor to Hitler, and we are all convinced that if Hitler gets to know the facts he will be pleased to bring about an expiation of the injustice done to Peters.'[27] In Hanover a large Peters monument was inaugurated, with prominent speakers such as Epp and Schnee.

In the meantime, the Foreign Office had again looked at the question of rehabilitation, but to the annoyance of colonial enthusiasts, they continued to disapprove of the demand. They argued that if Hitler lifted the punishment of dismissal this would no longer have 'practical significance' since Peters was dead. On the other hand, such an act of grace would have constituted 'a quite extraordinary process'. In their eyes, even the new law for the lifting of disciplinary decisions provided no solution, since it was meant to

---

[22] Colonial Society to AA, 10 May 1933, note in FP 22, BAK.

[23] Schnee to AA, 6 July 1933, note in FP 22, BAK.

[24] AA note, 7 July 1933, ibid.

[25] Note of Foreign Office expertise, and AA to Mrs Peters, 19 Dec. 1933, ibid.

[26] Epp to AA, forwarding Thea Peters's correspondence of 11 Nov. 1933, note in ibid.

[27] Otto Arendt to Neurath, 12 Feb. 1935 (delivered to the AA by Schnee, 20 Feb. 1935), note in FP 22, BAK.

be applied in cases of 'unjust sentences' only. 'However, with regard to Peters . . . this does not apply.'[28]

The assessment by the Ministry of the Interior was entirely different. It bluntly refused to sign the draft of a letter which the Foreign Office intended to send to the Colonial Society in the name of both offices. Its officials regarded a potential act of grace by Hitler 'not only as an act of justice' but also as correct politically. In legal terms, they saw a potential lifting of the sentences as perfectly permissible and suggested that the petition should be forwarded to the Führer.[29]

How do we account for the conflicting views of the two ministries? A clue is provided by the correspondence between Foreign Minister Neurath and Frick, Minister of the Interior. Neurath was mainly concerned about the reaction that such a spectacular act would cause among the other powers. He emphasized that it could fuel damaging agitation against Germany's colonial aspirations, since Peters could easily be held up as an example of cruel treatment of the native population. He therefore doubted 'that the expected domestic propaganda effect . . . compares with the political damage which could be caused to the German struggle for our colonies'. Frick, on the other hand, argued that it was precisely Peters's case which had delivered 'the material for the colonial guilt lie to our enemies'. Therefore it was essential to demonstrate to the outside world that the sentence had been a judicial error.[30]

In the meantime the Ministry of the Interior had involved Prussian Prime Minister Goering in the issue. The latter felt obliged to take a careful look at the original case himself, and he concluded that the frequent attacks against the sentence were justified. He accepted Frick's assessment that the judgment had caused a great deal of damage in the past, and agreed that a removal was 'urgently imperative'.[31] He warned that if the Foreign Office did not prepare for an act of grace by Hitler, he would approach the Führer himself.

But Neurath was not convinced. He maintained his previous arguments and was only prepared to agree to a compromise. He suggested lifting the legal effects of the sentence further so that Peters's widow could receive a pension,[32] but without lifting the sentence itself. This was the solution to which all sides eventually gave the green light, although 'serious regret' was

[28] Note on judgment of the AA of 20 and 30 Sept. FP 22, BAK.
[29] Pfundtner an AA, 7 July 1936, note in FP 22, BAK.
[30] Frick to Neurath, 3 Oct. 1936, Neurath to Frick, 27 Nov. 1936, copies in FP 22, BAK.
[31] Goering to Neurath, 27 Nov. 1936, copy in FP 22, BAK.
[32] Neurath to Frick, 27 Nov. 1936, copy in FP 22, BAK.

expressed on behalf of the Ministry of the Interior.[33] After some further dispute about the amount of the widow's pension, Hitler signed the act of grace on 28 September 1937, as proposed by the Foreign Office. Mrs Peters was granted a monthly pension of 336.09 marks, plus an indemnity of either 50,000 or 80,000 marks.[34] The decision was made public in the *NS Rechtspiegel* on 6 December 1937.[35] Nevertheless, the Foreign Office sought to keep the act out of the public eye. When a journalist from *Angriff* came up with plans to write an article about Peters's rehabilitation, they made clear that such a publication was undesirable because it might be exploited by the British.[36]

The course of Peters's rehabilitation in the Nazi period shows that the initiative lay with the organized colonial movement and caused controversy in the ministries responsible. Hitler himself seems not to have been involved in the issue until he actually signed the act of grace which the Foreign Office had prepared. The Führer thus acted upon an initiative of his grandees, Goering and Frick.

'THE GREAT EDUCATOR OF THE GERMAN NATION'

During Nazi rule books about German colonizers appeared in great numbers. This was particularly true for Peters, who rose to new glory in a number of biographies and popular accounts. Extracts of his writings were published for German youth,[37] a theatre play was written,[38] and eventually a monumental film was made on the life of the colonial hero and founder of German East Africa.[39]

The 'wild conquistador' was rediscovered in the academic world as well. In 1943 the historian Walther Frank published the bulk of Peters's books and essays in an edition of three volumes,[40] and he praised Peters as 'the

[33] Pfundtner [to AA?], 23 March 1937, note in FP 22, BAK.
[34] See notes on correspondence between the ministries (12 May–28 Sept. 1937) in FP 22, BAK. It is not entirely clear from Frank's notes which of the two sums—both suggestions of the Foreign Office—was eventually granted.   [35] See ibid.
[36] See ibid.
[37] See *Karl Peters. Ein Kämpfer für Deutschlands Kolonien. Aus seinen Reiseberichten von Oskar Schele*, Schoedels Jugendbücher, Abt. Mein Volk, Heft 22 (Halle, 1939).
[38] J. Buchholz, *Weg in die Welt. Ein Schauspiel um den deutschen Mann Karl Peters* (Berlin, 1940).
[39] *Carl Peters. Ein deutsches Schicksal*, Bavaria Filmkunst GmbH, 1941.
[40] For Frank see Helmut Heiber, *Walter Frank und sein Reichsinstitut für Geschichte des neuen Deutschlands* (Stuttgart, 1966).

great educator of the German nation'.[41] Frank also planned a long biography, but the collapse of Nazi rule put an abrupt end to this plan, as the historian shot himself in May 1945.

By and large, the biographies of the Nazi period all display a similar pattern of glorification; the man from Neuhaus was reinvented as a 'genius' misunderstood by his contemporaries and forced into British exile. Peters had correctly recognized the importance of *Lebensraum* for the German people, and he had struggled for it throughout his life.[42] 'Petersland! Great was the colonial empire that the brave, unselfish and modest Peters won.'[43]

Apart from the concept of *Lebensraum*, there was one particular aspect of Peters's career which seemed to fit perfectly into Nazi propaganda. This was the Jewish origin of Paul Kayser, the director of the Colonial Department. Peters thus fell victim to a Jewish conspiracy. Frank, for instance, detected a plot in which 'a privy councillor of Jewish race' was pulling the strings,[44] turning Peters into a martyr who had fallen in Germany's struggle to develop into 'a people for the world'.[45]

In 1940 Peters was also made a film hero, when the Bavaria-Filmkunst GmbH produced their monumental piece *Carl Peters. Ein deutsches Schicksal*, directed by Herbert Selpin.[46] The part of Peters was taken by the popular actor Hans Albers, while a hundred or so black people, all prisoners of war, had to play the African counterparts. 'These poor devils are standing lined up and shivering with fear and cold', Goebbels noted after a visit to the Barrandow film studios in Prague. The propaganda minister was quite excited about the film. 'Something will come of this', he wrote. 'Selpin does a good job.'[47]

The film was advertised as 'history, German history, lively history'. The audience awaited a 'breathtaking' story 'with a rhythm of dramatic power'.[48] In fact, the film was history with a good deal of propagandistic distortion. For example, Peters's Kilimanjaro affair bore no resemblance to the facts at all; in Selpin's version Peters executes two blacks for the murder of his best friend Carl Jühlke. (In reality, Jühlke was killed in Somaliland six

---

[41] Frank's preface to GS i.

[42] R. Wichterich and F. T. Pabst, *Carl Peters erobert Ostafrika* (Stuttgart, 1934), 106.

[43] Ibid. 104. Other works of this kind include E. zu Klampen, *Carl Peters. Ein deutsches Schicksal im Kampf um Ost-Afrika* (Berlin, 1938); E. Banse, *Unsere großen Afrikaner. Das Leben deutscher Entdecker und Kolonialpioniere* (Berlin, 1940); J. Froembgen, *Wissman Peters Krüger* (Stuttgart, 1941).   [44] See Walter Frank, introduction of Peters, GS i.

[45] See Walter Frank, introduction of Peters, GS i. 12.

[46] A copy of the film is kept in the Film Archives of the Bundesarchiv, Berlin.

[47] See diary entry of 8 Nov. 1940, E. Fröhlich (ed.), *Die Tagebücher von Joseph Goebbels*, viii (Munich, 1998), 410.   [48] Film Materials, 2187 Carl Peters, BA-FA.

years before Peters went to Kilimanjaro.) Peters's executions succeed in deterring the population from a major uprising which the British seek to instigate. Not surprisingly, Paul Kayser is the perfidious Jew responsible for Peters's fall. The Reichstag scandal is nothing but a plot by Social Democrat and Jewish members of parliament. Peters has nothing but contempt for these parliamentarians. 'And these are the representatives of such a decent, hard-working people! Poor Germany; you are your own worst enemy', he states in his final speech before the Reichstag (although Peters never spoke there in his life).

On one of the advertising posters the hero stands behind a speaker's desk as if he were the Führer himself.[49] Other adverts show a martial Hans Albers with a grim look under his sun-helmet. The film had its premiere on 21 March 1941, and it was shown in almost all major German cities.[50] It was officially evaluated as 'politically valuable, artistically valuable, culturally valuable, and educational for the nation'. It was also judged as 'good for youth'.[51] In many cities the Peters film was shown for longer than planned.[52] In Hamburg 44,451 people came to see the film in the first eleven days,[53] and the Atrium cinema in Hanover achieved a visitor record of 20,000 in the first week.[54]

[49] Film Materials, 2187 Carl Peters, BA-FA.
[50] *Film-Kurier*, 9 April 1914, 1.
[51] Film-Prüfstelle, Zulassungskarte, Prüf-No. 55241, 20 March 1941, BA-FA.
[52] See, for instance, *Film-Kurier*, 8 April 1941, 2 (Hamburg); 22 April 1941, 2 (Kaiserslautern); 23 April 1941, 2 (Görlitz, Essen, Münster); 23 April 1941, 3 (München).
[53] *Film-Kurier*, 8 April 1941, 2.
[54] *Film-Kurier*, 28 April 1941, 2.

Peters's Disputed Legacy after 1945

With the collapse of Nazi rule, the Peters monument went on its final odyssey. It is not clear what exactly happened to the statue at the end of the war,[1] but it surfaced again at a Bremen scrapyard in the late 1940s.[2] It was then moved to the administrative district of Pinneberg (to which Heligoland then belonged) and its components were stored in various cellars. When one of the buildings was demolished, a few of the workers sold the torso to a local scrap dealer, who believed it to be part of a Hermann Goering monument. The illegal deal was exposed and the culprits were brought to court. The workers got away with a fine, but the scrap dealer was sentenced to a year in prison.[3]

In the early 1960s colonial enthusiasts in the Traditionsverband der Schutz- und Überseetruppen began to push for re-erection of the statue at Heligoland. The most prominent supporter of the idea became Kai Uwe von Hassel, a leading figure in the Christian Democratic Party (CDU).[4] Born in East Africa in 1913, he became Prime Minister of Schleswig-Holstein in 1954. In late 1962 he was appointed as Minister of Defence in the federal government under Adenauer. As complete restoration turned out to be too expensive, the original bronze head was turned into a bust and put on a stone pedestal. In 1966 this diminished version of the colonial hero was put up in front of the Heligoland Youth Hostel, but the new location did not remain uncontested either. In 1989, after Eckhard Groth's critical

---

[1] One version claims that the bronze monument was heavily damaged in an air raid on Heligoland in 1945. After the war, a fisherman is said to have sold it on the mainland. (I am grateful to Michael Peters, Director of the Heligoland Museum, for this information.) However, it may also be that the statue was earlier removed from the island in order to be melted down in the final phase of war (see *Mitteilungsblatt des Traditionsverbandes ehemaliger Kolonial- und Überseetruppen*, no. 28 (Hanover, Nov. 1963), 2). In this case it remains unclear how the statue survived the war. If not indicated otherwise in the footnotes, the following section on the monument is based on my telephone interview with Michael Peters, 8 March 1999.

[2] See *Mitteilungsblatt des Traditionsverbandes ehemaliger Kolonial- und Überseetruppen*, no. 28, (Hanover, Nov. 1963), 2.

[3] See *Kieler Nachrichten*, 24 May 1962, enclosed in Bestand 20/15, Kreisarchiv Pinneberg.

[4] Staatskanzlei Kiel to Rickmers, 13 Feb. 1965. I am indebted to Michael Peters for supplying me with a copy of the letter.

article on Peters's atrocities in *Die Zeit*,[5] Heligoland was showered with letters of criticism demanding a removal of the monument. Some raised the question of whether Peters's location in front of the youth hostel was intended to recommend him as a model for the younger generation. Moreover, the island awaited the visit of the Tanzanian ambassador on the occasion of the 100th anniversary of the Heligoland–Zanzibar Agreement. The Heligoland Cultural Committee therefore decided to remove the bust again,[6] and since 1996 it has been in the Heligoland Museum.

In various other places the memory of Peters also provoked public disputes, indicating that Germans are still divided in their views about how to handle this. City councils quarrelled about streets names, some of which were changed, while others were left untouched; of the larger German cities, twenty-two still have a Karl Peters Street today.[7] At the little village of Neuhaus, where Peters was born, the debate focused largely on a memorial stone, 1.7 metres high, that had been put up in front of the old pastor's house in 1931, on the occasion of Peters's 75th birthday. In the words of a colonial enthusiast it was 'a mighty stone, firm and defiant like a Germanic warrior'. It then carried a plate with the following words: 'To our Dr Carl Peters, the founder of German East Africa, born on 27.09.1856.'[8]

Ironically, it was the socialist youth organization FDJ in the early German Democratic Republic which became interested in the stone again after the Second World War. In 1951, on Peters's birthday, a group of local FDJ members celebrated the colonialist from Neuhaus by decorating the stone with flowers. The ruling communist party SED, however, was quick to intervene to make sure that its followers would not be misled by a wrong example. It was decided that the stone should be buried in the garden of the parsonage, and the local Carl Peters Street was turned into Stalin Street. (Today it is called Park Street.[9])

In 1994, the buried stone was rediscovered during restoration works on the house. After a municipal council debate it was decided by 10 votes to 9

[5] E. Groth, 'Galgen am Kilimanjaro', *Die Zeit*, 20 Jan. 1989, 41–2. The article gives no reference to the sources which were used. It seems that Groth has based his account on parts of the Frank documents in Koblenz. I am grateful to Gloria Mengual, Madrid, for allowing me to see some of his transcripts.

[6] Minutes of *Schul-Kultur- und Sozialausschuß*, session of 26 Sept. 1989.

[7] See Deutsche Bundespost, *Das Postleitzahlenbuch* [1993], register of streets of 209 larger German cities, *passim*.

[8] *Afrika-Nachrichten*, 15 Oct. 1930, *Übersee- und Kolonial-Zeitung*, 1 Oct. 1931, enclosed in RKolA 6916, 205, 206, BAB.

[9] *Hannoversche Allgemeine*, 28 March 1993; *Die Zeit*, 20 May 1994; *die tageszeitung*, 28 June 1994.

that the stone should be put up again. It was supplied with a new metal plate, carrying the following words:

Dr Carl Peters was born in this parsonage in Neuhaus on the Elbe on 27.09.1856. He pursued the idea of a large German colonial empire and is seen as the founder of the colony of German East Africa. This colonial policy turned out to be altogether mistaken. The personality of Dr Carl Peters, his activities, and the memorial stone are disputed.

The most intense debate about Peters developed in the city of Hanover, where a large square had been named after the colonizer as early as 1916,[10] soon to be nicknamed 'Kalle Pe'. As mentioned earlier, the Nazis had inaugurated a monument there in 1935. This was a huge rectangular sandstone with a front relief: next to Carl Peters's name, a German imperial eagle circled above the outline of the African continent. The bird was fashioned in some detail, contrasting sharply with the plain and empty space of Africa. The monument thus reflected German aspirations to rule vast tracks of African soil.

The major debate about Peters began in the mid-1980s, largely triggered by a local group of the peace movement, called 'Friedensforum Südstadt'.[11] On one occasion, demonstrators wrapped the Nazi monument in sheets and blankets, while a choir of members of the South West Africa People's Organization (Swapo) sang a few songs to attract public interest.[12] By then, the Peters monument had repeatedly become a target for grafitti sprayers (e.g. 'He was a murderer! & swine!').[13] In 1988, the city eventually decided to give the monument an additional plaque to convert it into a cautionary memorial.[14]

This monument was erected by the National Socialists in the year 1935. It stood for the glorification of colonialism and of the master race concept. To us it is a warning and a reminder to work for the equal rights of all human beings, peoples, and races, in accordance with the Charter of Human Rights.

For some people, the reinterpretation of the monument was not enough. In their opinion, the added text was rather playing down the colonial past. Moreover, they stated that the style of the new plaque did not contrast clearly with the old monument, but fitted into the Nazi aesthetics of the

---

[10] See *Hannoversche Allgemeine*, 11 April 1991.
[11] *Hannoversche Allgemeine*, Stadtteilzeitung Süd, 5 July 1984.
[12] *Hannoversche Allgemeine*, 28 Oct. 1985.
[13] *Hannoversche Allgemeine*, Stadtteilzeitung Süd, 5 July 1984.
[14] *Hannoversche Allgemeine*, 1 July 1988.

original. In 1991 two art students therefore built a temporary 'counter-monument', which was to draw attention to present-day forms of economic imperialism.[15]

Critics also urged a renaming of Karl Peters Square, suggesting that it should instead carry the name of the Austrian pacifist Bertha von Suttner, who won the Nobel Peace Prize in 1905. This demand, however, became an even more controversial issue than the monument itself. For more than a decade the quarrel filled the columns of the local newspapers. Apart from Expo 2000, noted a journalist from the *Hannoversche Allgemeine*, the issue of Carl Peters had become one of the 'most durable communal disputes' of the city of Hanover.[16]

The Social Democrats and sympathizers with the peace movement mostly argued that Peters was no longer acceptable as a figure to be associated with a public place. Many Christian Democrats and Liberals, on the other hand, saw no reason to take action. The chairman of the CDU councillors, Reinhard Apel, stressed that the name of the place had been firmly anchored in the consciousness of the people for years, and that the man was 'simply part of our history, even if he was a disputed figure'.[17]

Early in 1991, the *Hannoversche Allgemeine* invited the residents of the area to express their opinion on the issue. The result turned out as a surprise for the Social Democrats, who had not anticipated that 79 per cent of people would in fact want to keep the old name.[18] Academic experts became involved in the debate as well. The *Hannoversche Allgemeine* cited a letter which the colonial historian Helmut Bley, of Hanover University, had written to the city administration. Bley argued that the name of a discredited figure such as Peters could no longer be suitable for the square.[19]

In June 1991, Hanover council decided, by 32 votes against 23, to change the name of the square.[20] Legal interventions by some opponents delayed things further, but they turned out to be unsuccessful. In February 1994 Carl Peters's name was removed from the signs and replaced by that of Bertha von Suttner. Hanover also stopped paying for the maintenance of Peters's tomb at the Engeshohder graveyard out of public funds.[21]

[15] *Hannoversche Allgemeine*, Stadtteilzeitung Süd, 31 Jan. 1991.
[16] *Hannoversche Allgemeine*, 6 March 1993.
[17] Cited in *Hannoversche Allgemeine*, Stadtteilzeitung Süd, 16 March 1989.
[18] *Hannoversche Allgemeine*, Stadtteilzeitung Süd, 14 Feb. 1991.
[19] *Hannoversche Allgemeine*, Stadtteilzeitung Süd, 16 May 1991.
[20] *Hannoversche Allgemeine*, 28 June 1991.
[21] *Hannoversche Allgemeine*, 29 June 1993.

For the time being, a heated public debate had thus come to an end, although dissatisfaction about the new Bertha von Suttner name continued. In the words of Lothar Feicht, innkeeper of the local 'Karl-Peters-Klause', local people were 'still very cross'. Upon being asked when he would rename his pub, Feicht firmly answered: 'Never!'[22]

---

[22] *Hannoversche Allgemeine*, 16 June 1994.

Conclusion

This study has shown that many of Peters's contemporaries were fascinated by the man and his agitational skills, not least his ability to sway his audience in his public speeches. Peters had a sensitive appreciation of the appeal of colonial ideas in the 1880s, and he gave them a strong voice. Thus he came to ride the wave of public enthusiasm which formed a significant force behind Germany's colonial drive in 1884–5. As the historian Friedrich Meinecke recalled, 'we cheered our contemporaries Karl Peters, Jühlke, and Count Pfeil as they boldly seized a part of Africa.'[1] Essentially, Peters's ideology was a nationalist agenda in which the foundation of the Reich through war formed a central point of reference. Unification had laid the basis for colonial expansion, and pan-Germanism was portrayed as the primary political doctrine with which to achieve German world power. Peters's colonial ideology displayed pseudo-Darwinist ideas of international conflict, and the struggle between nations; Britain was the major rival in this conflict, which was dramatized as a matter of life and death. Moreover, Peters's ideas displayed a strong concern for German national identity. Colonies formed an important status symbol for the young Reich, and they were presented as an essential ingredient of Germany's self-image.

The course of Peters's career and his ideology shed some doubts on explanations which have presented German colonial expansion as a form of 'manipulated social imperialism'. Not only do these fail to recognize the importance of nationalist forces for colonial expansion; they also overlook the fact that in the 1880s and 1890s colonial policy often divided the nation rather than uniting it. Its integrative function is therefore doubtful. In fact, the colonial issue provided a focus for left-wing, but also for right-wing, opposition, and the colonial movement was by no means a convenient tool in the hands of the government.

Bismarck gave in to colonial demands as he depended on the support of the National Liberal and the Conservative camps. The relationship between the colonial movement and the government cannot properly be described as 'manipulation from above', as the movement was deeply rooted in society and was closely linked with the national movement as

---

[1] Friedrich Meinecke, *Die deutsche Erhebung von 1914* (Stuttgart and Berlin, 1914), 21.

such. Hence German overseas expansion is still best explained by tracing its nationalist roots. Only by promoting colonial expansion as a truly national cause did the colonial movement achieve its full dynamism, which moved even Bismarck, however sceptical he may have been about the usefulness of colonial acquisitions. Carl Peters emerged as a spearhead of this nationalist movement, and his rise would not have been possible without the backing of prominent figures in the National Liberal and Conservative camps. In the eyes of his patrons, Peters was a useful drummer.

Bismarck, though suspicious of the young activist, helped to pave the way for his rise. With the Imperial Charter in his pocket, Peters could present himself as fulfilling national aspirations under the auspices of the Reich. In this way he gained a prominent political status which he could hardly have achieved otherwise. In the 1880s Peters laid emphasis on pan-German ideas. Combining theory with concrete action, he managed to enhance and consolidate his position within the colonial movement. This was also true after 1890, which made the government eager to integrate him into their policies. They sought to prevent his agitational skills helping to strengthen a nationalist opposition to the government. However the attempt to accommodate Peters within the system failed, as he demanded more than the government was prepared to give. His tendency to ignore directives from above made him an unacceptable candidate for the governorship of East Africa.

In a remarkable political coup, Bebel managed to topple Peters as the spearhead of the radical nationalists. Consciously or not, Bebel's campaign against the Imperial Commissioner exploited a racial prejudice which seemed deeply rooted in all sections of society. In Bebel's accusations, Peters was turned into an African chief who had acted as a savage would do, that is without legal principles and without control over his emotions or his sexual behaviour. He thus became a demon unworthy of representing the civilizing mission to Africa. Peters had committed a major crime against the moral code of Wilhelmine Germany. It was not his pan-German ideas which sealed his fate, but his alleged relapse into a savage mode of life. This made it difficult for the government to protect their official any further.

While Peters himself disappeared from the political scene in 1896, his ideas did not. Above all, they found an outlet in pan-German circles, in the general enthusiasm for the navy, and in the call for further expansion of the colonial empire. They also trickled down into the conceptions of government officials, such as Kiderlen's Central Africa scheme, for instance.

Under Nazi rule Peters rose to new glory. Not only did they view him as a true German who had fallen victim to a Jewish conspiracy; they also praised him as a tireless fighter for German *Lebensraum*. Unlike Hitler, however, Peters had always agitated for overseas possessions, whereas the Führer was not very keen on Africa and colonial territories. His focus lay clearly in Europe.

BIBLIOGRAPHY

ARCHIVAL SOURCES

Bundesarchiv, Berlin

Reichskolonialamt

R1001: RKolA 249/3, 249/4, 249/5, 250, 251, 252, 253, 324, 359, 360, 374, 375, 382, 385, 386, 387, 388, 390, 391, 392, 393, 394, 395, 396, 397, 402, 406, 407, 409, 410, 421, 598, 644/3, 687, 688, 690, 691, 693, 730, 731, 732, 733, 751, 755, 776, 797, 834, 847, 848, 854, 861, 950, 978, 979, 980, 981, 982, 1019/2, 4694, 4812/1, 5739, 6410, 6516, 6915, 6916, 6925, 7010, 7154, 7155, 7156, 7157, 7158, 7159, 7160, 7161, 7249, 8891, 8892, 8893, 8895, 8902, 9325

Reichskanzlei

R 43: 913, 946

Reichsministerium des Innern

R1501: 102983, 103845

Reichsinstitut für Geschichte des neuen Deutschlands

R1/3: 2, 8, 9

Allgemeiner Deutscher Verband [ADV]

R 8048: 1, 2, 3

Deutsch-Ostafrikanische Gesellschaft [DOAG]

80 Ge 1/1, 80 Ge 1/2, 80 Ge 1/7

Deutsche Kolonialgesellschaft [DKG]

R 8023: 243, 253, 254, 255, 256a, 263, 265, 274, 509, 510, 828, 852, 854, 899, 928, 1084, 1111

Nachlaß Bennigsen

90 Be 5: 90, 198

Nachlaß Hammacher

N 2105: 10, 25, 31, 35, 57, 62

Nachlaß Paul Kayser [KPB]

N 2139: 5, 8, 18, 19, 32, 37, 39, 40, 41, 42, 43, 51, 52, 61, 83, 84

Nachlaß Carl Peters [PP]

90 Pe 1: 1, 2, 4, 10, 12, 14, 17, 18, 19, 20, 21, 22, 24, 25, 26, 27, 28, 29, 30, 32, 33, 34, 35, 36, 37, 38, 39, 40, 41, 42, 43, 44, 45, 47, 48, 51, 52, 53, 54, 55, 56, 57, 58, 59, 60, 61, 62, 64, 65, 66, 67, 68, 69, 70, 71, 78, 79, 80, 81, 82, 83, 84, 85, 86, 87, 88, 89, 90, 91, 92, 93, 94, 95, 96, 97, 98, 99, 100, 105

Bundesarchiv, Abteilung Koblenz

Nachlaß Frank [FP]

NL 1067: 1, 2, 3, 5, 7, 8, 10, 12, 13, 14, 15, 16, 18, 19, 20, 21, 22, 24, 25

Nachlaß Palezieux

NL 1047: 1, 2, 3, 4, 5, 6, 7

Kleine Erwerbungen 141

Bundesarchiv-Filmarchiv, Berlin

Film: *Carl Peters. Ein deutsches Schicksal*, Bavaria Filmkunst GmbH, directed by Herbert Selpin, 1941
Film Materials: 2187 Carl Peters
Film-Prüfstelle: Zulassungskarte, Prüf. No. 55241

Geheimes Staatsarchiv Preußischer Kulturbesitz, Berlin

I HA, Rep 84a, 10119; I HA, Rep 89, 32516; I HA, Rep. 109, 5360; I HA, Rep. 109, 5369

Nachlaß Schnee

I. HA, Rep 92

Staatsbibliothek zu Berlin, Preußischer Kulturbesitz

Nachlaß Treitschke
Nachlaß Mommsen
Sammlung Darmstaedter

Politisches Archiv des Auswärtigen Amtes, Berlin

London 372, 394, 395, 402, 403, 407, 409, 414, 415, 556, 557, 558, 561
R 5665 (England 78)
Nachlaß Michahelles

Niedersächsische Staats- und Universitätsbibliothek Göttingen

Nachlaß Wilhelm Hübbe-Schleiden 226, 908, 909, 922, 911, 1011, 1012

Kreisarchiv Altena, Märkischer Kreis

Nachlaß Peters [PPA]

NL Pe: 1, 2, 3, 4, 5, 6, 7, 8, 9, 10, 13, 14, 15, 16, 17, 18, 19, 20, 21, 22, 23, 24, 25, 26, 27, 28, 29, 30, 33, 35, 36, 37, 38, 39, 40, 42, 43, 44, 45, 46, 47, 48, 49, 50, 51, 52, 53, 54, 55, 56, 57, 58, 59, 62, 63, 64, 65, 66, 67, 70, 71, 72, 73, 74, 76, 77, 87, 94, 105

Bethel-Archiv Wuppertal

M 2, M 167, M 170, M 171

Landesarchiv Schleswig-Holstein

LAS Abt. 309 Nr. 19445

Kreisarchiv Pinneberg

Bestand 20/15

Universitätsarchiv Leipzig

PA 6053

Otto-von-Bismarck-Stiftung, Friedrichsruh

Bestand A: 20, 23, 35
Bestand B: 6, 48, 64, 73, 99, 102, 130, 132
Bestand D: 2, 4a, 17, 21, 22, 26, 27, 31, 46, 48
Bestand F: 2, 3
(microfiche)

Hauptstaatsarchiv Hamburg

622-1 Familie O'Swald; 621-1 Firma O'Swald & Co; 621-1 Firma Hansing & Co
622-1 Familie Hübbe M 6, M 10

Staats- und Universitätsbibliothek Hamburg

Nachlaß Paul Kayser [KPH]
2, 3, 10, 45, 48, 59, 68, 94, 113

Universität Hamburg

Akte 91-50-22 (Die Denkmale Wissmann und Dominik), vols. 1, 2

Public Record Office, London

FO 84/1679, FO 84/1680, FO 84/1714, FO 84/1715, FO 84/1793, FO 84/1794

International Institute for Social History, Amsterdam

Bernstein Papers, Moscow (microfilm)

Tanzanian National Archives, Dar es Salaam

G1/1, G1/2, G1/18

Zanzibar National Archives

German Consular Files, AL 1, 7, 12, Al 2, 1, 4, 5, 15, 23, 24, 25, 26, 27, 28, 31, 32,
    40, 41, 45, 50, 58, 61, 85, 87, 88, , 103, 107, 110, 111
British Consular Files, AA 1, 43, 52

Church Missionary Society, University Library, Birmingham

G3/A5/O 1892; G3/A5/O 1891

Rhodes House, Oxford

MSS Lugard 82/1; MSS BRIT. EMP. S 43

NEWSPAPERS AND PERIODICALS

Allgemeine Missions-Zeitschrift
Church Missionary Intelligencer
Deutsche Literaturzeitung
Deutsche Kolonialzeitung
Deutsche Rundschau für Geographie und Statistik
Deutsches Kolonialblatt
Die Gegenwart
Neue Preussische Zeitung
Norddeutsche Allgemeine Zeitung
Die Katholischen Missionen

Kladderadatsch
Kölnische Zeitung
Kolonial-Politische Korrespondenz
Leipziger Zeitung
Literarisches Zentralblatt für Deutschland
Der Missions- und Heidenbote
Petermanns Mittheilungen
Die Post
Preussische Jahrbücher
Simplicissimus
Der Tag
Tägliche Rundschau
The Times
Vossische Zeitung
Vorwärts

PRINTED SOURCES AND LITERATURE

ANDERSON, P. R., *The Background of Anti-English Feeling in Germany, 1890–1902* (Washington, 1939).

ARENDT, OTTO, *Ziele deutscher Kolonialpolitik* (Berlin, 1886).

ARNOLD, B., 'Die Schlacht bei Rugaro 1891 (Tansania, Iringa). Verlauf der Kämpfe und Ursachen der Niederlage des Expeditionskorps der kaiserlichen Schutztruppe für Ostafrika', in P. Heine and U. van der Heyden (eds.), *Studien zur Geschichte des deutschen Kolonialismus in Afrika* (Pfaffenweiler, 1995), 94–114.

August Bebel. Ausgewählte Reden und Schriften, ed. Gustav Seeber, iv (Munich, 1995).

BADE, KLAUS J., *Friedrich Fabri und der Imperialismus in der Bismarckzeit. Revolution—Depression—Expansion* (Freiburg im Breisgau, 1975).

—— 'Antisklavereibewegung in Deutschland und Kolonialkrieg in Deutsch-Ostafrika 1888–1890: Bismarck und Friedrich Fabri', *GG* 3 (1977), 31–58.

—— 'Die deutsche Kolonialexpansion in Afrika: Ausgangssituation und Ergebnis', in W. Fürnrohr (ed.), *Afrika im Geschichtsunterricht europäischer Lander. Von der Kolonialgeschichte zur Geschichte der Dritten Welt* (Munich, 1982), 13–47.

—— 'Das Kaiserreich als Kolonialmacht: Ideologische Projektionen und historische Erfahrungen', in J. Becker and A. Hillgruber (eds.), *Die deutsche Frage im 19. und 20 Jahrhundert* (Augsburg, 1983), 91–108.

—— 'Imperial Germany and West Africa: Colonial Movement, Business Interests, and Bismarck's "Colonial Policies" ', in S. Förster, W. J. Mommsen, and R. Robinson (eds.), *Bismarck, Europe and Africa*, 121–47.

—— 'Bismarcks "Verfehlte Hoffnungen" in Afrika: Schutzbriefkonzept, Kongokonferenz und koloniale Krise', in H. Christmann (ed.), *Kolonisation und Dekolonisation* (Schwäbisch Gmünd, 1989), 53–66.

—— 'Die "Zweite Reichsgründung" in Übersee: Imperiale Visionen, Kolonialbewegung und Kolonialpolitik in der Bismarckzeit', in A. M. Birke and G. Heydemann (eds.), *Die Herausforderung des europäischen Staatensystems: Nationale Ideologie und staatliches Interesse zwischen Restauration und Imperialismus* (Göttingen and Zurich, 1989), 183–215.

BARTH, B., *Die deutsche Hochfinanz und die Imperialismen. Banken und Außenpolitik vor 1914* (Stuttgart, 1995).

BAUMGART, W., *Imperialism. The Idea and Reality of British and French Colonial Expansion, 1880–1914* (Oxford, 1982)

—— 'Bismarcks Kolonialpolitik', in J. Kunisch (ed.), *Bismarck und seine Zeit* (Berlin, 1992)

BECKER, A., *Aus Deutsch-Ostafrikas Sturm- und Drangperiode* (Halle, 1911), 141–53.

BEIDELMAN, T. O., 'A History of Ukaguru: 1857–1916', *Tanganyika Notes and Records*, 58/59 (1962).

—— *The Matrilineal Peoples of Eastern Tanzania* (London, 1967).

BENDIKAT, E., *Organisierte Kolonialbewegung in der Bismarck-Ära* (Heidelberg, 1984).

—— *Wahlkämpfe in Europa 1884 bis 1889: Parteiensysteme und Politikstile in Deutschland, Frankreich und Großbritannien* (Wiesbaden, 1988).

BENNETT, N. R., 'The British on Kilimanjaro: 1884–1892', *Tanganyika Notes and Records*, 63 (1964), 43–52.

—— *Arab versus European. Diplomacy and War in Nineteenth-Century East-Central Africa* (New York, 1986).

BERGER, S., *The Search for Normality and Historical Consciousness in Germany since 1800* (Providence, 1997).

BERGHAHN, V., *Der Tirpitz-Plan: Genesis und Verfall einer innenpolitischen Krisenstrategie unter Wilhelm II* (Düsseldorf, 1971).

Bericht über die Verhandlungen des Allgemeinen Deutschen Kongresses zur Förderung überseeischer Interessen (Berlin, 1886).

BERNTSEN, J. L., *Maasai and Iloikop: Ritual Experts and their Followers*, Occasional Paper 9, (University of Wisconsin-Madison, 1977).

BEYME, K. VON, 'Deutsche Identität zwischen Nationalismus und Verfassungspatriotismus', in M. Hettling and P. Nolte (eds.), *Nation und Gesellschaft in Deutschland. Historische Essays* (Munich, 1996), 80–99.

Bismarck. Die Gesammelten Werke, 15 vols. (Berlin, 1924–35).

BLEY, F., *Die Weltstellung der Deutschen* (Munich,1897).

BLOOM, W., *Personal Identity, National Identity and International Relations* (Cambridge, 1990).

BÖHME, H., 'Thesen zur Beurteilung der gesellschaftlichen, wirtschaftlichen u. politischen Ursachen des deutschen Imperialismus', in W. J. Mommsen (ed.), *Der Moderne Imperialismus* (Stuttgart 1971), 31–59.

BRANDL, BERND, *Die Neukirchener Mission* (Cologne, 1998).

BREUILLY, J., *Nationalism and the State*, 2nd edn. (Manchester, 1993).

—— 'Approaches to Nationalism', in E. Schmidt-Hartmann (ed.), *Formen des nationalen Bewußtseins im Lichte zeitgenössischer Nationalismustheorien* (Munich, 1994), 15–38.

BRIERLEY, J. and SPEAR, T., 'Mutesa, the Missionaries, and Christian Conversion in Buganda', *IJAHS* 21/4 (1988).

BÜCKENDORF, J., *Schwarz-weiß-rot über Ostafrika. Deutsche Kolonialpläne und afrikanische Realität* (Münster, 1997).

BÜLOW, F. VON, *Reiseskizzen und Tagebuchblätter aus Deutsch-Ostafrika* (Berlin, 1889).

—— *Der Konsul. Vaterländischer Roman aus unseren Tagen* (Dresden, 1891).

BURKHARDT, J., 'Kriegsgrund Geschichte? 1870, 1813, 1756—Historische Argumente und Orientierungen bei Ausbruch des Ersten Weltkrieges', in idem and J. Becker, *Lange und Kurze Wege in den Ersten Weltkrieg* (Munich, 1996), 9–86

CAIN, P. J. and HOPKINS, A. G., *British Imperialism. Innovation and Expansion 1688–1914* (London, 1993).

CECIL, G., *Life of Robert, Marquis of Salisbury*, iv (London, 1932).

CHICKERING, R., *We Men Who Feel Most German. A Cultural Study of the Pan-German League, 1886–1914* (Boston, 1984).

CHRISTMANN, H. (ed.), *Kolonisation und Dekolonisation* (Schwäbisch Gmünd, 1989).

COETZEE, M. S., *The German Army League. Popular Nationalism in Wilhelmine Germany* (Oxford, 1990).

COUPLAND, R., *The Exploitation of East Africa 1856–1890: The Slave Trade and the Scramble*, 2nd edn. (London, 1968).

DARWIN, J., 'Imperialism and the Victorians: The Dynamics of Territorial Expansion', *EHR* 112 (1997), 614–42.

DEIST, W., *Flottenpolitik und Flottenpropaganda* (Stuttgart, 1976).

DESMOND, A. and MOORE, J. M., *Darwin* (London, 1991).

DEUTSCH, J.-G., 'Inventing an East African Empire: The Zanzibar Delimitation Commission of 1885/1886', in P. Heine and U. von der Heyden (eds.), *Studien zur Geschichte des deutschen Kolonialismus in Afrika* (Pfaffenweiler 1995), 210–19.

Dokumente der deutschen Verfassungsgeschichte, ed. Ernst R. Huber, ii (Stuttgart, 1964)

DÜLFFER, J. and HÜBNER, H. (eds.), *Otto von Bismarck. Person–Politik–Mythos* (Berlin, 1993).

ELEY, G., 'Sammlungspolitik, Social Imperialism, and the Navy Law of 1898', *MGM* 1 (1974), 29–63.

—— 'Some Thoughts on the Nationalist Pressure Groups in Imperial Germany', in A. Nicholls and P. Kennedy (eds.), *Nationalist and Racialist Movements in Britain and Germany before 1914* (London, 1981), 40–67.

—— *Reshaping the German Right. Radical Nationalism and Political Change after Bismarck* (London and New Haven, 1980, 2nd edn. 1991).

ESSNER, C., *Deutsche Afrikareisende im 19. Jahrhundert. Zur Soziologie des Reisens* (Wiesbaden, 1985).

EVANS, R. J., *Rereading German History. From Unification to Reunification 1800–1996* (London and New York, 1997).

FABRI, F., *Bedarf Deutschland der Colonien?* (Gotha, 1879).

—— *Deutsch-Ostafrika. Eine colonialpolitische Skizze* (Cologne, 1886).

FENSKE, H., 'Imperialistische Tendenzen in Deutschland vor 1866. Auswanderung, überseeische Bestrebungen, Weltmachtträume', *Historisches Jahrbuch*, 97/98 (1978), 337–83.

FIELDHOUSE, D. K., *Economics and Empire* (London, 1973).

FLINT, J., 'The Wider Background to Partition and Colonial Occupation', in R. Oliver (ed.), *History of East Africa*, i (Oxford, 1963).

FORBES, I. L. D., 'Social Imperialism and Wilhelmine Germany', *HJ* 22 (1979), 331–49.

FÖRSTER, S., MOMMSEN, W. J., and ROBINSON, R. (eds.), *Bismarck, Europe and Africa. The Berlin Africa Conference and the Onset of Partition* (Oxford, 1988).

FRANCOIS, E., SIGRIST, H., and VOGEL, J., 'Die Nation. Vorstellungen, Inszenierungen, Emotionen', in eidem, *Nation und Emotion. Deutschland und Frankreich im Vergleich; 19. und 20. Jahrhundert* (Göttingen, 1995), 13–35.

FRANK, W. (ed.), *Carl Peters. Gesammelte Schriften*, 3 vols. (Munich and Berlin, 1943–4).

—— 'Der geheime Rat Paul Kayser', *HZ* 168 (1943), 302–55, 541–63.

FRICKE, D. et al. (eds.), *Lexikon zur Parteiengeschichte. Die bürgerlichen und kleinbürgerlichen Parteien und Verbände in Deutschland (1789–1945)*, i–ii (Leipzig, 1983–4).

GALBRAITH, J. S., *Mackinnon and East Africa, 1878–1895* (Cambridge, 1972).

GALL, L., *Bismarck: Der weiße Revolutionär* (Frankfurt, 1980).

Die Geheimen Papiere Friedrich von Holsteins, ed. Norman Rich and M. H. Fischer, ii (Göttingen, 1957).

GIFFORD, P. and LOUIS, W. R., (eds.), *Britain and Germany in Africa* (London, 1967).

GILLARD, D. R., 'Salisbury's African Policy and the Heligoland Offer of 1890', *EHR* 75 (1960), 631–53.

—— 'Salisbury's Heligoland Offer: the Case against the "Witu Thesis" ', *EHR* 80 (1965), 538–52.

GLASSMAN, J., *Feasts and Riot. Revelry, Rebellion, and Popular Consciousness on the Swahili Coast, 1856–1888* (Portsmouth, NH, 1995).

GRAY, J. M., 'The Year of the Three Kings of Buganda, Mwanga—Kiwewa— Kalema, 1888–1889', *Uganda Journal*, 14 (1950).

Die Große Politik der europäischen Kabinette, 1871–1914. Sammlung der diplomatischen Akten des Auswärtigen Amtes, ed. J. Lepsius, A. M. Bartholdy, and F. Thimme, 40 vols. (Berlin, 1922–7).

268 *Bibliography*

GROBE-KRACHT, K., 'Gedächtnis und Geschichte: Maurice Halbwachs—Pierre Nora', *GWU* 47 (1996), 21–31.

GROTH, E., 'Galgen am Kilimanjaro', *Die Zeit*, 20 January 1989, 41–2.

GRÜNDER, H., *Geschichte der Deutschen Kolonien*, 3rd edn. (Paderborn, 1995).

GUENTHER, K., *Gerhard Rohlfs: Lebensbild eines Afrikaforschers* (Freiburg, 1912).

GUMPLOWICZ, L., *Der Rassenkampf: Soziologische Untersuchungen* (Innsbruck, 1883).

—— *Outlines of Sociology* (trans. of *Grundriss der Soziologie*, Vienna 1885), ed. I. L. Horowitz (New York, 1963).

GWASSA, G. C. K., 'The German Intervention and African Resistance in Tanzania', in I. N. Kimambo and A. J. Temu (eds.), *A History of Tanzania* (Nairobi, 1969), 85–122.

HAECKEL, E., *Natürliche Schöpfungsgeschichte*, 5th edn. (Berlin, 1874).

HAGEN, M. VON, *Bismarcks Kolonialpolitik* (Stuttgart, 1923).

HALE, O. J., *Publicity and Diplomacy. With Special Reference to England and Germany 1890–1914* (Gloucester, 1964).

HALLMANN, H., *Der Weg zum deutschen Schlachtflottenbau* (Stuttgart, 1933).

HAMPE, P., *Die ökonomische Imperialismustheorie. Kritische Untersuchungen* (Munich, 1976).

HARDTWIG, E., *Zur Politik und Entwicklung des Alldeutschen Verbandes von seiner Gründung bis zum Beginn des Ersten Weltkrieges 1891–1914* (Diss. Jena, 1966).

HARDTWIG, W., 'Bürgertum, Staatssymbolik und Staatsbewußtsein im Deutschen Kaiserreich 1871–1914', in idem, *Nationalismus und Bürgerkultur in Deutschland 1500–1914* (Göttingen, 1994), 191–218.

HAUSEN, K., *Deutsche Kolonialherrschaft in Afrika. Wirtschaftsinteressen und Kolonialverwaltung in Kamerun vor 1914* (Zurich, 1970).

HENNING, H., 'Bismarck's Kolonialpolitik—Export einer Krise?' in K. E. Born (ed.), *Gegenwartsprobleme der Wirtschaft und der Wirtschaftswissenschaft* (Tübingen, 1978), 53–83.

HERTSLET, E., *The Map of Africa by Treaty*, iii (London, 1908; repr. 1967).

HERTZ, F., *The German Public Mind in the Nineteenth Century. A Social History of German Political Sentiments, Aspirations and Ideas* (London, 1975).

HETTLING, M. and NOLTE, P. (eds.), *Nation und Gesellschaft in Deutschland. Historische Essays* (Munich, 1996).

HILDEBRAND, K., *Vom Reich zum Weltreich. Hitler, NSDAP und koloniale Frage 1919–1945* (Munich, 1969).

HÖHNEL, L. VON, *Zum Rudolph und Stephanie-See. Die Forschungsreise des Grafen Samuel Teleki in Ost-Aequatorial-Afrika 1887–1888* (Vienna, 1892).

HOLL, K. and LIST, G. (eds.), *Liberalismus und imperialistischer Staat. Der Imperialismus als Problem liberaler Parteien in Deutschland 1890–1914* (Göttingen, 1975).

HÜBBE-SCHLEIDEN, W., *Ethiopien. Studien über Westafrika* (Hamburg, 1879).

—— *Deutsche Colonisation. Eine Replik auf das Referat des Herrn Dr. Friedrich Kapp über Colonisation und Auswanderung* (Hamburg, 1881).

—— *Überseeische Politik. Eine Culturwissenschaftliche Studie mit Zahlenbildern* (Hamburg, 1881).

—— *Warum Weltmacht? Der Sinn unserer Kolonialpolitik* (Hamburg, 1906).

HUBER, E. R., *Dokumente zur deutschen Verfassungsgeschichte*, ii (Stuttgart, 1964).

ILIFFE, J., *A Modern History of Tanganyika* (Cambridge, 1979).

JAECK, H. P., 'Die deutsche Annexion', in H. Stoecker (ed.), *Kamerun unter deutscher Kolonialherrschaft. Studien*, i. (Berlin, 1960), 29–96.

JARAUSCH, K. H., 'Frequenz und Struktur. Zur Sozialgeschichte der Studenten im Kaiserreich', in P. Baumgart (ed.), *Bildungspolitik in Preußen zur Zeit des Kaiserreiches* (Stuttgart, 1980), 119–49.

KEHR, E., *Schlachtflottenbau und Parteipolitik 1894–1901* (Berlin, 1930).

KENNEDY, P., *The Rise of the Anglo-German Antagonism 1860–1914* (London, 1980).

—— *Aufstieg und Fall der großen Mächte*, German edn. (Frankfurt, 1991).

KIERAN, J. A. P., 'Abushiri and the Germans', *Hadith*, 2 (Nairobi, 1970), 157–201.

KLAUS, K., *Die deutsche Kolonialgesellschaft und die deutsche Kolonialpolitik von den Anfängen bis 1895* (Diss. Berlin, 1966).

KOCH, M., *Geschichte der deutschen Literatur*, 4th edn. (Leipzig, 1900).

KOPONEN, J., *Development for Exploitation. German Colonial Policies in Mainland Tanzania, 1884–1914* (Helsinki and Hamburg, 1994).

KRÄTSCHELL, H., *Karl Peters 1856–1918. Ein Beitrag zur Publizistik des imperialistischen Nationalismus in Deutschland* (Diss. Berlin, 1959).

KRUCK, A., *Geschichte des Alldeutschen Verbandes 1890–1939* (Wiesbaden, 1954).

KURTZE, B., *Die Deutsch-Ostafrikanische Gesellschaft* (Jena, 1913).

LAHME, R., *Deutsche Außenpolitik 1890–1894. Von der Gleichgewichtspolitik Bismarcks zur Allianzstrategie Caprivis* (Göttingen, 1990).

LANGE, F., *Reines Deutschtum. Grundzüge einer nationalen Weltanschauung*, 5th edn. (Berlin, 1904).

LANGER, W. H., *European Alliances and Alignments 1871–1890* (New York, 1954).

—— *The Diplomacy of Imperialism* (New York, 1956; 2nd edn. 1960).

LANGEWIESCHE, D., 'Nation, Nationalismus, Nationalstaat: Forschungsstand und Forschungsperspektiven', *NPL* 40 (1995), 190–236.

LENK, K., *Volk und Staat. Strukturwandel politischer Ideologien im 19. und 20 Jahrhundert* (Stuttgart, 1971).

LINK, J., and WÜLFING, W., (eds.), *Nationale Mythen und Symbole in der zweiten Hälfte des 19. Jahrhunderts* (Stuttgart, 1991)

LEWIS, H. S., 'The Origins of the Galla and Somalis', *JAH* 7 (1966), 27–46.

LOW, D. A., *Religion and Society in Buganda, 1875–1900* (Kampala, 1958).

McLYNN, F., *Stanley* (Oxford, 1991).

MEINECKE, F., *Die deutsche Erhebung von 1914* (Stuttgart and Berlin, 1914).

MERITT, H. P., 'Bismarck and the German Interest in East Africa, 1884–1885', *Historical Journal*, 21 (1978), 97–116.

MEYER, H., *East African Glaciers* (London, 1891).

MOORE, S. F. and PURITT, P., *The Chagga and Meru of Tanzania* (London, 1977).

MOSSE, G.L., *The Nationalization of the Masses. Political Symbolism and Mass Movements in Germany from the Napoleonic Wars through the Third Reich* (New York, 1975).

—— *Fallen Soldiers. Reshaping the Memory of the World Wars* (New York and Oxford, 1990).

MÜLLER, F. F., *Deutschland—Zanzibar—Ostafrika. Geschichte einer Kolonialeroberung* (Berlin, 1959).

MÜLLER, F. L., ' "Der Traum von der Weltmacht." Imperialistische Ziele in der deutschen Nationalbewegung von der Rheinkrise bis zum Ende der Paulskirche', *Jahrbuch der Hambach Gesellschaft*, 6 (1996/7), 99–183.

NICHOLLS, C. S., *The Swahili Coast. Politics, Diplomacy and Trade on the East African Littoral, 1798–1856* (London, 1971).

NIESEL, H.-J., *Kolonialverwaltung und Mission in Deutsch-Ostafrika 1890–1914* (Diss. FU Berlin, 1971).

NIPPERDEY, T., 'Nationalidee und Nationaldenkmal in Deutschland im 19. Jahrhundert', *HZ* 206 (1968), 529–85.

OLDEN, B., *Ich bin Ich* (Berlin, 1927).

PAULITSCHKE, P., *Ethnographie Nordost-Afrikas. Die materielle Cultur der Danakil, Gall und Somal* (Berlin, 1893).

PERST, O., 'Carl Peters Reichstagskandidat im Werraland 1895', *Das Werraland*, 19 (1967), 53–5.

PETERS, C., *Willenswelt und Weltwille. Studien und Ideen zu einer Weltanschauung* (Leipzig, 1883).

—— 'Deutschtum und Engländertum', *Die Gegenwart*, 12 May 1883 [also printed in Frank, GS iii].

—— 'Deutsche Kolonialpolitik aus englischer Perspektive', *Die Gegenwart*, 1 March 1884 [also printed in Frank, GS i].

—— 'Alltagspolemik und Kolonialpolitik', *Tägliche Rundschau*, 17 April 1884 [reprinted from the manuscript in Peters, *Deutsch-National*, and Frank, GS i].

—— 'Deutschtum in London', *Die Gegenwart*, 6 and 13 October 1884 [also printed in Peters, *Deutsch-National*].

—— 'Die Usagara-Expedition', *Tägliche Rundschau*, 7, 8, 15, 19, and 22 March 1885 [reprinted in Frank, GS i].

—— 'Die deutsche Kolonialbewegung, die Gesellschaft für deutsche Kolonisation und die Deutsch-Ostafrikanische Gesellschaft', *KPK*, 16 May 1885.

—— 'All-Deutschland', *KPK*, 16 May 1886 [also printed in Frank, GS iii].

—— 'Der Kosmopolitismus und die deutsche Kunst', *KPK*, 29 May 1886.

—— 'Nationalismus und Kosmopolitismus', *KPK*, 12 June 1886 [also printed in Frank, GS iii].

—— 'Die kulturhistorische Bedeutung des Deutschtums', in *Bericht über die Verhandlungen des Allgemeinen Deutschen Kongresses zur Förderung überseeischer Interessen* (Berlin, 1886).

—— 'Deutsch-nationaler Frauenbund', *KPK* , 29 January 1887 and 5 February 1887.

—— *Deutsch-National. Kolonialpolitische Aufsätze* (Berlin, 1887).

—— *Die deutsch-ostafrikanische Kolonie in ihrer Entstehungsgeschichte und wirtschaftlichen Eigenart* (Berlin, 1889).

—— *Die Deutsche Emin-Pascha Expedition* (Munich, 1891) [also printed in Frank, GS ii].

—— *Gefechtsweise und Expeditionsführung in Afrika* (Berlin, 1892) [also printed in Frank, GS ii].

—— *Das Deutsch-Ostafrikanische Schutzgebiet. Im amtlichen Auftrage* (Munich and Leipzig, 1895).

—— *Im Goldland des Altertums. Forschungen zwischen Zambesi und Sabi* (Munich, 1902) [English translation: *The Eldorado of the Ancients* (New York, 1902)].

—— *England und die Engländer* (Berlin, 1904)[GS iii].

—— 'Das Deutschtum als Rasse', in *Deutsche Monatsschrift für das gesamte Leben der Gegenwart*, 7 (April 1905) [also reprinted in Frank, GS iii].

—— *Die Gründung von Deutsch-Ostafrika. Kolonialpolitische Erinnerungen und Betrachtungen* (Berlin, 1906) [also printed in Frank, GS i].

—— *Zur Weltpolitik* (Berlin, 1912).

—— *Zum Weltkrieg* (Berlin, 1917).

—— *Lebenserinnerungen* (Hamburg, 1918) [GS i].

PETERS, M., 'Der "Alldeutsche Verband" ' in U. Puschner, W. Schmitz, and J. Ulbricht (eds.), *Handbuch zur 'Völkischen Bewegung' 1871–1918* (Munich, 1996), 302–15.

PFEIL, J., *Zur Erwerbung von Deutsch-Ostafrika* (Berlin, 1907).

Phillip Eulenburgs Politische Korrespondenz, iii, ed. John Röhl (Boppard am Rhein, 1983).

POGGE VON STRANDMANN, H., 'Domestic Origins of Germany's Colonial Expansion under Bismarck', *Past and Present* 42 (1969), 140–59.

—— 'Imperialism and Revisionism in Interwar Germany', in W. J. Mommsen and J. Osterhammel (eds.), *Imperialism and After* (London, 1986), 90–119.

—— 'Consequences of the Foundation of the German Empire: Colonial Expansion and the Process of Political-Economic Rationalization', in S. Förster, W. J. Mommsen, and R. Robinson (eds.), *Bismarck, Europe and Africa. The Berlin Africa Conference and the Onset of Partition* (Oxford, 1988), 105–20.

—— and SMITH, A., 'The German Empire in Africa and British Perspectives: A Historiographical Essay', in P. Gifford and W. R. Louis (eds.), *Britain and Germany in Africa* (London, 1967).

Die politischen Reden des Fürsten Bismarck, ed. H. Kohl, 14 vols. (Stuttgart, 1892–1905).

PUSCHNER, U., SCHMITZ, W., and ULBRICHT, J. H. (eds.), *Handbuch zur 'Völkischen Bewegung' 1871–1918* (Munich, 1996).

RANGER, T. O., 'The Invention of Tradition Revisited: The Case of Colonial

Africa', in idem and O. Vaughan (eds.), *Legitimacy and the State in Twentieth Century Africa: Essays in Honour of A. M. H. Kirk-Greene* (London, 1993), 62–116.

RATZEL, F., *Wider die Reichsnörgler. Ein Wort zur Kolonialfrage aus Wählerkreisen* (Munich, 1884).

REICHSAMT DES INNERN (ed.), *Handbuch für das Deutsche Reich* (Berlin, 1883–1897).

REUSS, M., 'The Disgrace and Fall of Carl Peters: Morality, Politics and Staatsräson in the Time of Wilhelm II', *CEH* 14 (1981), 110–41.

—— and HARTWIG, G. R., 'Bismarck's Imperialism and the Rohlfs Mission', *The South Atlantic Quarterly*, 74 (1975), 74–85.

RIEHL, A. T. G., *Der 'Tanz um den Äquator'. Bismarck's antienglische Kolonialpolitik und die Erwartung des Thronwechsels in Deutschland 1883 bis 1885* (Berlin, 1993).

RITTER, G. A., *Wahlgeschichtliches Arbeitsbuch. Materialien zur Statistik des Kaiserreichs, 1871–1918* (Munich, 1980).

ROBINSON, D. and SMITH, D., *Sources of the African Past* (London, 1979).

ROBINSON, R. and GALLAGHER, J., *Africa and the Victorians*, 2nd edn. (London, 1981), (1st edn., 1961).

RÖHL, J. C. G., 'The Disintegration of the Kartell and the Politics of Bismarck's Fall from Power, 1887–1890', *HJ* 9 (1966), 60–89.

—— *Germany without Bismarck* (London 1967).

ROSENBACH, H., *Das Deutsche Reich, Großbritannien und der Transvaal 1896–1902* (Göttingen, 1993).

RUETE, E, *Memoirs of an Arabian Princess from Zanzibar* (Princeton, 1989) [original German edn., Berlin 1886].

RÜGER, A., 'Der Aufstand der Polizeisoldaten (Dezember 1893)', in H. Stoecker (ed.), *Kamerun unter deutscher Kolonialherrschaft*, i (Berlin, 1960), 97–147.

SANDERSON, G. N., 'The Anglo-German Agreement of 1890 and the Upper Nile', *EHR* 78 (1963), 49–72.

—— *England, Europe and the Upper Nile, 1882–1899* (Edinburgh, 1965).

SCHELLACK, F., *Nationalfeiertage in Deutschland von 1871 bis 1945* (Frankfurt, 1990).

SCHILLING, K., *Beiträge zu einer Geschichte des radikalen Nationlismus in der Wilhelminischen Ära 1890–1909* (Diss. Cologne, 1968).

SCHINZINGER, F., 'Die Rolle der Zölle in den Beziehungen zwischen dem Deutschen Reich und seinen Kolonien', in M. Feldsieper and R. Groß (eds.), *Wirtschaftspolitik in weltoffener Wirtschaft* (Berlin, 1983), 125–142.

SCHMOKEL, W. W., *Dream of Empire: German Colonialism, 1919–1945* (New Haven, 1964).

SCHNEE, H., 'Peters, Carl', in *Deutsches Biographisches Jahrbuch*, ii (Berlin, 1928), 285–98.

SCHNEE, H. (ed.), *Deutsches Kolonial-Lexikon*, 3 vols. (Leipzig, 1920).

SCHNEPPEN, H., *Why Kilimanjaro is in Tanzania* (Dar es Salaam, 1996).

—— 'Der Fall Karl Peters; Ein Kolonialbeamter vor Gericht', *Zeitschrift für Geschichtwissenschaft* 49 (2001), 869–85.

—— *Sansibar und die Deutschen* (Münster, 2003).

SCHÖN, M., *Die Geschichte der Berliner Bewegung* (Leipzig, 1889).

SCHRAMM, P. E., *Deutschland und Übersee* (Brunswick, 1950).

SCHUNGEL, W., *Alexander Tille (1866–1912). Leben und Ideen eines Sozialdarwinisten* (Husum, 1980).

SCHWARZ, M. (ed.), *MdR. Biographisches Handbuch der deutschen Reichstage* (Hanover, 1965).

SELL, M., *Die deutsche öffentliche Meinung und das Helgolandabkommen im Jahre 1890* (Diss. Bonn, 1926).

SHERIFF, A. M. H., 'Tanzanian Societies at the Time of the Partition', in N. H. Y. Kaniki (ed.), *Tanzania under Colonial Rule* (London, 1980).

—— *Slaves, Spices and Ivory in Zanzibar* (London 1987).

SMITH, A. D., *National Identity* (London, 1991).

SMITH, A. D., 'The Nation: Invented, Imagined, Reconstructed?' in M. Ringrose and A. J. Lerner (eds.), *Reimagining the Nation* (Buckingham, 1993), 9–28.

SMITH, A. D., *Nationalism* (Oxford, 2001).

SMITH, IAN R., *The Emin Pasha Relief Expedition* (Oxford, 1972).

SMITH, W. D. 'The Ideology of German Colonialism, 1840–1906', *JMH* 46 (1974), 641–62.

—— *The German Colonial Empire* (Chapel Hill, 1978).

—— 'German Imperialism after Wehler', *CEH* 12 (1979), 387–91.

—— *The Ideological Origins of Nazi Imperialism* (New York, 1986).

—— *Politics and the Sciences of Culture in Germany, 1840–1920* (Oxford, 1991).

Staatssekretär Graf Herbert von Bismarck. Aus seiner politischen Privatkorrespondenz, ed. W. Bussmann (Göttingen, 1964).

STAHL, K., 'Outline of Chagga History', *TNR* 64 (1965).

—— *History of the Chagga People* (The Hague, 1964).

Stenographische Berichte über die Verhandlungen des Reichstages (Berlin).

STOECKER, H. 'The Annexations of 1884–1885', in idem (ed.), *German Imperialism in Africa* (London, 1986), 21–38.

STURSBERG, J., *Ferdinand Würtz, Missionar und Missionspionier im Pokomoland in Brit.-Ostafrika* (Neukirchen, 1910), 50.

Die Tagebücher von Joseph Goebbels, ed. E. Fröhlich (Munich, 1998).

TAYLOR, A. J. P., *Germany's First Bid for Colonies 1884–85* (London, 1938).

THOMSON, J., *Through Masai Land* (London, 1885).

TIEDEMANN, A. VON, *Tana—Baringo—Nil*, 3rd edn. (Berlin 1907).

TREITSCHKE, H. VON, 'Die ersten Versuche deutscher Kolonialpolitik', *PJ* 54 (1884).

—— *Politik. Vorlesungen gehalten an der Universität zu Berlin*, ed. Max Cornicelius, i, 4th edn. (Berlin, 1918).

TURNER, H. A., 'Bismarck's Imperialist Venture: Anti-British in Origin?', in P. Gifford and W. R. Louis (eds.), *Britain and Germany in Africa* (London, 1967), 47–83.

VOLKENS, G., *Der Kilimanjaro* (Berlin, 1897).

VOM BRUCH, R., 'Wilhelminismus—Zum Wandel von Milieu und politischer Kultur', in U. Puschner, W. Schmitz, and J. H. Ulbricht (eds.), *Handbuch zur 'Völkischen Bewegung' 1871–1918* (Munich, 1996), 3–21.

WAGNER, J., *Deutsch-Ostafrika. Geschichte der Gesellschaft für deutsche Kolonisation, der Deutsch-Ostafrikanischen Gesellschaft und der Deutsch-Ostafrikanischen Plantagengesellschaft nach den maßgeblichen Quellen* (Berlin, 1888).

WAKEFIELD, E. S., *Thomas Wakefield. Missionary and Geographical Pioneer in East Equatorial Africa* (London, 1904).

WARMBOLD, J., *Germania in Africa. Germany's Colonial Literature* (New York, 1989).

WASHAUSEN, H., *Hamburg und die Kolonialpolitik des Deutschen Reiches, 1880 bis 1890* (Hamburg, 1968).

WEBER, E. VON, *Die Erweiterung des deutschen Wirtschaftsgebietes und die Grundlegung zu überseeischen deutschen Staaten* (Leipzig, 1879).

WEDI-PASCHA, B., *Die deutsche Mittelafrika-Politik 1871–1914* (Pfaffenweiler, 1992).

WEHLER, H. U., *Bismarck und der Imperialismus* (Frankfurt, 1984, 1st edn. 1969).

WEIDENFELD, W., 'Die Identität der Deutschen—Fragen, Positionen, Perspektiven', in idem, *Die Identität der Deutschen* (Munich, 1983), 13–49.

WEIKART, R., 'The Origins of Social Darwinism in Germany, 1859–1895', *Journal of the History of Ideas*, 54 (1993), 469–89.

WERTHEIMER, M, *The Pan-German League, 1890–1914* (New York, 1924).

WILDENTHAL, L. J., *German Women for Empire, 1884–1945* (Durham, 2001).

WINTER, J., *Sites of Memory, Sites of Mourning. The Great War in Central European Cultural History* (Cambridge, 1995).

WINZEN, P., 'Treitschke's Influence on the Rise of Imperialist and Anti-British Nationalism in Germany', in A. Nicholls and P. Kennedy (eds.), *Nationalist and Racialist Movements in Britain and Germany before 1914* (London, 1981), 154–70.

WRIGHT, M., 'Local Roots of Policy in German East Africa', *JAH* 9 (1968).

ZELLER, J., ' "Deutschlands größter Afrikaner". Zur Geschichte der Denkmäler für Hermann von Wissmann', *ZfG* 44 (1996), 1089–111.

—— *Kolonialdenkmäler und Geschichtsbewußtsein* (Frankfurt, 2000).

ZIEGLER, T., *Die geistigen und sozialen Strömungen des neunzehnten Jahrhunderts* (Berlin, 1899).

ZIMMERMANN, A. *Geschichte der Deutschen Kolonialpolitik* (Berlin, 1914).

UNPUBLISHED THESES

BAGLIONE, F. M., 'Mysticism and Domination. Theories of Self-Preservation, Expansion and Racial Superiority in German Imperialist Ideology' (Tufts University Ph.D. thesis, 1981).

BAIR, H. M., 'Carl Peters and German Colonialism: A Study in the Ideas and Actions of Imperialism' (Stanford University Ph.D. thesis, 1968).

BENNETT, N. R., 'The Arab Power of Tanganyika in the Nineteenth Century' (University of Boston, Ph.D. thesis, 1961).

BERNTSEN, J. L., 'Pastoralism, Raiding and Prophets: Maasailand in the Nineteenth Century' (University of Wisconsin-Madison, Ph.D. thesis, 1979).

DE KIEWIET, M. J., 'History of the Imperial British East Africa Company, 1876–1895' (London Ph.D. thesis, 1955).

DUKES, J. R., 'Heligoland, Zanzibar, East Africa: Colonialism in German Politics, 1884–1890' (University of Illinois, Ph.D. thesis, 1970).

ELEY, G., 'The German Navy League in German Politics, 1898–1909' (University of Sussex, Ph.D. thesis, 1974).

GIBLIN, J. L., 'Famine, Authority and the Impact of Foreign Capital in Handeni District, Tanzania, 1840–1940' (University Wisconsin-Madison, Ph.D. thesis, 1986).

GLASSMAN, J., 'Social Rebellion and Swahili Culture: The Response to German Conquest of the Northern Mrima' (University of Wisconsin-Madison, Ph.D. thesis, 1983).

JACOBS, A. H., 'The Tradition Political Organization of the Pastoral Masai' (University of Oxford, D.Phil. thesis, 1965).

LOW, D. A, 'The British and Uganda, 1862–1900' (University of Oxford D.Phil. thesis, 1957).

PERRAS, A., 'Carl Peters and German Imperialism 1856 to 1918. A Political Biography' (University of Oxford, D.Phil. thesis, 1999).

PIERARD, R. V., 'The German Colonial Society, 1882–1914' (University of Iowa, Ph.D. thesis, 1964).

WILDENTHAL, L. J., 'Colonizers and Citizens: Bourgeois Women and the Woman Question in the German Colonial Movement, 1886–1914' (University of Michigan, Ph.D. thesis, 1994).

WINFIELD, J. A., 'Carl Peters and Cecil Rhodes. A Comparative Study of Imperialist Theory and Practice' (University of Connecticut, Ph.D. thesis, 1972).

INDEX

Printed in the United Kingdom
by Lightning Source UK Ltd.
109409UKS00001B/14